Rachmaninoff's Complete Songs

Russian Music Studies
Malcolm Hamrick Brown, founding editor

Rachmaninoff's Complete Songs

A Companion with Texts and Translations

Richard D. Sylvester

INDIANA UNIVERSITY PRESS
Bloomington & Indianapolis

This book is a publication of

Indiana University Press
Office of Scholarly Publishing
Herman B Wells Library 350
1320 East 10th Street
Bloomington, Indiana 47405 USA

iupress.indiana.edu

Telephone 800-842-6796
Fax 812-855-7931

♾ The paper used in this publication meets the minimum requirements of the American National Standard for Information Sciences—Permanence of Paper for Printed Library Materials, ANSI Z39.48–1992.

Manufactured in the United States of America

Library of Congress Cataloging-in-Publication Data

Sylvester, Richard D., author, translator.
Rachmaninoff's complete songs : a companion with texts
and translations / Richard D. Sylvester.
pages ; cm
Includes bibliographical references and index.
ISBN 978-0-253-35339-9 (cloth : alkaline paper) — ISBN 978-0-253-01259-3 (ebook) 1. Rachmaninoff, Sergei, 1873–1943. Songs. 2. Rachmaninoff, Sergei, 1873–1943. Songs—Texts. I. Title.
ML54.6.R18S95 2014
782.42168092—dc23
2013040934

1 2 3 4 5 19 18 17 16 15 14

for
Nancy Ries

Contents

Preface

The Moscow public first learned of a young composer named Sergei Rachmaninoff in the spring of 1893, when the Bolshoi Theater announced production of his one-act opera *Aleko*. He was known before that to insiders at the Moscow Conservatory, where he performed some of his early piano works. An opera, however, based on Alexander Pushkin's brilliant narrative poem *Tsygany* (*The Gypsies*, 1824), was an important musical event. By the time the young composer reached his twentieth birthday, on 2 April 1893, rehearsals were already under way.

Aleko was never imagined as a career-launching move, but that is what it turned out to be. It was composed in 1892 as a final diploma project at the Conservatory. The libretto, patchily contrived for pedagogical purposes by the Moscow critic and dramaturge Vladimir Nemirovich-Danchenko, invited comparison, in its *verismo* plot of jealousy and murderous revenge, with Mascagni's *Cavalleria rusticana*, a recent hit at the Bolshoi (for details, see Richard Taruskin: "Aleko," *The New Grove Dictionary of Opera*, 1992). Given a deadline of one month to write the opera, Rachmaninoff (the only one of the three seniors in the class to finish the job on time) submitted the score in less than three weeks (for exact dates, see *T/N*, 178-80). The result was quite astonishing: not only did it make good use of specifically "Russian" and "oriental" musical strategies worked out by Glinka, Borodin, Tchaikovsky, and others, but it contained choral and solo numbers with original, well-crafted melodies. The performance at the Bolshoi Theater was given on 27 April 1893, with lead singers and the Bolshoi's principal conductor, Ippolit Altani. Some of the arias were sung and later recorded by famous singers, with Feodor Chaliapin first and foremost (Chaliapin recorded Aleko's cavatina in 1923 in Hayes and 1930 in London). In our own day, baritone Mariusz Kwiecien included it on his compact disc "Slavic Heroes" (2011). The opera brought Rachmaninoff early fame: Tchaikovsky found him a publisher, and mentored him during rehearsals; the Kiev Opera invited the composer to conduct it there, which he did in October 1893; and in St. Petersburg, Rimsky-Korsakov himself conducted the "Dance of the Gypsy Girls" at a Russian Symphony concert in December 1894. In a special performance in St. Petersburg on the centenary of Pushkin's birth in May 1899, Chaliapin sang the lead part, with "true suffering in his sobs at the end," according to the composer (*LN 1*, 290).

Beyond Russia, audiences first heard music by Rachmaninoff in December 1893, when his cousin, the celebrated pianist Alexander Siloti, performed the First Piano Concerto in Wiesbaden and Frankfurt. The German reviewers heard echoes of Chopin, Liszt, and Grieg in the piano writing but failed to grasp the "Russian" character of the music (*Keldysh*, 79). In 1895, Rachmaninoff was discovered in the West in a major and lasting way. That is when Siloti first played the "Prelude in C-sharp Minor" in London. Once heard, the public demanded Siloti play it without fail in every recital in England and Scotland, and later in 1898 in New York, Boston, and Chicago (*Barber*, 55-70). Rachmaninoff himself played it in England on his first tour abroad in 1899. Eventually he came to regret its popularity, as he was expected to play "it" (as the piece was called in the newspapers) after every piano recital. For decades in the twentieth century, this short work of 1892 was widely considered to be the best known piano composition ever written.

Today Rachmaninoff is universally known as a composer of major works for piano and orchestra which have a permanent place in the concert repertoire, especially his Second Concerto (1900-01), his Third Concerto (1909), and his "Rhapsody on a Theme of Paganini" (1934). He is admired for many other works too, among them his Second Symphony with its sweeping Adagio (1906-08), and his singularly moving "All-Night Vigil" (sometimes called "Vespers," for four-part unaccompanied mixed chorus, 1915). In his solo piano works he stands with Chopin and Liszt. Only his songs remain less well known, especially outside Russia, although this is changing today as younger singers discover them and learn to sing them in Russian.

Rachmaninoff's eighty-three songs, or "*románsy*" as they are called in Russian, include some of his finest and most memorable music. The "romances" come out of the Russian current of the great nineteenth-century stream of Romantic song that goes back to Beethoven and Schubert. Like German *Lieder* and French *mélodies*, they are songs written to be sung by one singer, with a piano accompaniment especially composed for the song. Instead of writing the words, the composer customarily chooses a lyric poem or other text and sets it to music by writing a voice part and a piano part. The success of *Aleko* owed something to Rachmaninoff the youthful songwriter—to his love of drama, skill in crafting melodies, originality in writing declamatory parts for voice, and supreme pianistic gifts. His best early compositions are piano pieces and songs.

The purpose of this book is to collect and translate the lyrics of all the songs written by Sergei Rachmaninoff, and to comment on their musical realization. The texts are presented in their entirety, as they appear in each song, in the original Russian (there is one early song in French). These are followed by a transcription of the Russian words in the Latin alphabet, and, printed line by line alongside it, a translation into plain, unrhymed English. My translations are not "singing" versions, but they will allow a reader who does not know Russian to listen to a song and follow the words from start to finish as they are sung.

The order of the songs and the consecutive numbering of them used here follow the 1957 Moscow edition of Rachmaninoff's songs *Romansy: Polnoe sobranie* ("Romances: Complete Collection," abbreviated *PSR*). A new academic edition of Rachmaninoff's complete works in some fifty volumes is being undertaken jointly by the Central State Glinka Museum in Moscow and Russian Music Publishers (with Bärenreiter-Verlag in Germany), but as of this writing only two volumes of piano works have been issued. Valentin Antipov, the editor of these volumes, told me in Moscow in 2007 that preparation of the songs had not begun, because a "textologist" had not yet been found. The present volume is an attempt to establish the lyrics of Rachmaninoff's songs as accurately as possible. The research was carried out over a dozen years, including visits to many libraries in Moscow and elsewhere to track down the various publications of the texts Rachmaninoff used in his songs. In my research I found a number of errors which are corrected here, including a bowdlerized lyric (Song 53), which was censored in the Soviet period and rewritten to remove religious language.

I claim no originality in matters of musical interpretation. Historical and descriptive information—poets or other authors of the text, dates, other settings of the text, key signatures, voice range, and so on—is provided at the end of each song. Recordings of the song are also listed there, by the singer's last name (or the full names of each instrumentalist, in cases of transcriptions, which are abundant in several of Rachmaninoff's songs). At the back of the book, further information about the singers and a list of the songs recorded by each of them are placed together in an Index of Singers. Throughout the book, in lieu of footnotes, the names of works cited are given in *italics*, with page numbers as necessary. Information about sources will be found in the Bibliography; major sources are also described in the "List of Abbreviations" on pages xxi-xxii.

Rachmaninoff's song texts have been collected and translated into English once before, in *The Singer's Rachmaninoff*, compiled by Natalia Challis (New York, 1989). That was a useful volume, but it is now out of print; it repeats some stubborn errors, and uses an inaccurate system of phonetic transcriptions. Singers who want to see a correct phonetic transcription of the songs should consult the excellent manual by Professor Laurence R. Richter, *Rachmaninov's Complete Song Texts* (Leyerle Publications, Geneseo, New York, 2000). His book also contains literal and idiomatic English translations, making it a new and up-to-date singer's manual for Rachmaninoff's songs.

My book may be used as a reference to find information about a particular song, but it can also be read as a continuous narrative. Each group of songs is preceded by a short section about Rachmaninoff's life, ideas, and contacts in the artistic world during his twenty-six years as a composer of *romansy*. He had connections, sometimes very close ones, with leading figures of the

"Silver Age" of Russian art at the turn of the twentieth century. He knew the writers Anton Chekhov, Maxim Gorky, and Ivan Bunin. He knew theater people, including Savva Mamontov at the "Private Opera" and Vladimir Teliakovsky, director of the Imperial Theaters, both of whom hired him as a conductor. He knew Konstantin Stanislavsky at the Moscow Art Theater, and Sergei Diaghilev, who brought him to Paris to take part in his first "Saison Russe" in 1907. He worked with Feodor Chaliapin and other singers of his generation (to whom he dedicated some of his songs), and concert organizers like Alexander Siloti and Serge Koussevitzky. I hope some glimpses into these relationships will humanize Rachmaninoff, too often thought of as a dour and humorless man, "a six-and-a-half-foot-tall scowl" in the words of Igor Stravinsky.

As in my book about Tchaikovsky's songs (*TCS*), the aim of the commentary is to illuminate the composer's professional life, his life as an *artist*. Both men were born into loving, extended families, but, unlike Tchaikovsky, Rachmaninoff had a successful marriage and was at peace in his private life. As professionals the two men were exceptionally disciplined and stood out in their insistence on the highest artistic standards. As a composer, Tchaikovsky was inexhaustibly gifted, and he accomplished more. As a musician, however, Rachmaninoff was gifted in more ways, and was torn between three callings. He wanted first and foremost to compose. When he had to learn to conduct early in his life in order to find a job, he became (like Gustav Mahler, a contemporary he greatly admired) an outstanding conductor. When he left Russia in 1917, already famous as a pianist, he honed his skills, learned new repertoire, and practiced every day to be able to give recitals to support his family. A recent assessment of his place as a pianist in his lifetime is one by Alex Ross, who wrote, in a *New Yorker* review of recordings of the "hundred greatest" pianists of the 20th century, "The most immediately impressive volumes are those in which a player's personality swamps every piece on the program. The lord of them all is probably Rachmaninoff. Of the Slavic pianists who fill the twentieth-century pantheon, Horowitz may have produced more electricity and Paderewski more tears, but Rachmaninoff is the one who pins you in your chair with the force of his mind" (*Ross 1999*).

Rachmaninoff always thought of his songs as performances coming out of and written for a specifically Russian milieu. After he left Russia, for good, at the end of 1917, he wrote no more songs.

Acknowledgments

First, I wish to thank Malcolm Hamrick Brown, founding editor of Russian Music Studies, who encouraged my work on this project from the first time we met in New York to discuss it. For his sage advice and unfailing support I am deeply grateful. My thanks extend to the wise and steady Director of Indiana University Press, Janet Rabinowitch, and to her editorial staff, whose bright and ready responses have eased my way and made the production of the book a pleasant task.

Part of my research for this book was supported by travel grants from the Colgate University Faculty Research Council in October 1996 and January 2000, and a summer grant in May 1998 from the International Research & Exchanges Board, with funds provided by the U. S. Department of State (Title VIII program) and the National Endowment for the Humanities. I thank them all for their generosity and trust, and I assume sole responsibility for the views expressed in this book.

My colleagues at Colgate University helped and encouraged me in many important ways, especially Alice Nakhimovsky, Nancy Ries, Matt and Denise Leone, Albert and Rebecca Ammerman, Jane Pinchin, Anthony Aveni, Chris Vecsey, and Tim Byrnes. I am also grateful to the staff of the Colgate Library, especially to the resourceful Ann Ackerson, head of Interlibrary Loan.

It was an inspiration to work in the hallowed reading rooms of the Slavic and Baltic Division of the New York Public Library, the Library of Congress, and the State Lenin Library in Moscow. Libraries at Stanford and Cornell, and Bird Library and the Belfer Audio Archive at Syracuse University, made me welcome and offered ready assistance. I owe a special thanks to Robert Hodge, who played rare vocal recordings for me at the Belfer Archive.

In Moscow, Vyacheslav Nechayev, Director of the Library of the Union of Theatrical Workers, and his staff welcomed me during various projects for more than twenty-five years in their historic reading room on Strastnoi Boulevard located a block away from Rachmaninoff's Moscow apartment (the room was originally the university typography, where *Crime and Punishment* was first printed). At the Moscow Conservatory Library, Lyudmila Dedyukina cheerfully supplied books and cuttings from journals and newspapers of the pre-1917 period. Eleonora Mamedova-Sokolova and the late Nikolai Sokolov of the Chaliapin Museum have been resourceful and valued friends in all matters pertaining to the Russian vocal scene. Irina Medvedeva of the Glinka Museum welcomed this project and allowed me access to their Rachmaninoff archive. To Alexander Abramovich Makarov, a friend of many years and son of the renowned accompanist Abram Makarov, I am grateful for personal introductions to Konstantin Lisovsky, Tatyana and Olga Reizen, and Zara Dolukhanova: to each of them I owe thanks for their warm hospitality and readiness to answer my questions about performing Rachmaninoff's songs.

For information about recordings not in my own collection, I am greatly indebted to Donald Seibert, Greg Audette, Victor Han, and Richard Kummins, who have been generous in sharing their records and knowledge with me. Ian Harvey, in addition to sharing recordings over many years, has faithfully kept me up to date on new recordings and performances of Rachmaninoff's songs.

Nancy Ries inspired me throughout my work, sharing her ideas and insights with me in Moscow and in Hamilton. Laurel Fay and David Cannata gave me invaluable advice at the beginning stage of my work. Donald Seibert, Ronald Rebholz, Joseph Miller, and Nancy Ries read portions of the manuscript and brought their wisdom to fundamental issues of interpretation and presentation. I was inspired by friends of many years who expressed interest and support: Edward Lobb, Charlotte Douglas, Joseph and Susan Higgins, Stuart Anthony, Will Rogers, Anne Gregory, and many of my former students. I owe very much to friends in Moscow and Novgorod who listened to the songs and shared their ideas with me: Svetlana Golybina, Nina Drozdetskaya, Olga Kazakova, Galina Krasnova, Natalia Kulakova, and my dear friend and partner Vasily Petyarkin.

I am indebted to Rimgaila Salys, author of the catalogue of Leonid Pasternak's Russian years (see *Salys* in the Bibliography), who put me in touch with the Pasternak family in Oxford and Moscow. Dr. Ann Slater-Pasternak, on behalf of The Pasternak Trust in Oxford, graciously permitted me to use Leonid Pasternak's portrait of the composer as an illustration for the book.

This book would not have been written had it not been for the collaboration of Joseph Miller, wisest of friends. He originally showed me the need for such a book of texts of Russian songs with parallel translations. Since then he has given selflessly of his time and companionship while reading and editing the manuscript, making each page better: *il miglior fabbro*.

R. D. S.

Hamilton, New York
April 2013

A Note on Dates and Spelling

Before 1918, the Julian Calendar ("Old Style") was used in Russia and is still used by the Russian Orthodox Church. The Gregorian Calendar ("New Style") was adopted in February 1918: this moved the calendar ahead by thirteen days, or twelve in the 19th century. Dates in this book are given in Old Style if the event took place in Russia before 1918, and in New Style if outside Russia or after 1918.

Except in the Bibliography, where authors and titles are transliterated according to the simplified Library of Congress system, Russian names are spelled in this book as we are used to seeing them, even if that entails some inconsistencies. For example, Tchaikovsky and Chekhov begin with the same Cyrillic letter, but I have retained the older spelling for Tchaikovsky's name because it is more familiar than "Chaikovsky." In cases of individual artists who adopted a non-standard spelling, I use that: Rachmaninoff (not Rakhmaninov), Chaliapin (not Shaliapin). Names of artists are spelled as they would be in a concert program or recording: Hvorostovsky (not Khvorostovski). In the narrative, first names common to both English and Russian are spelled as in English: Alexander, not Aleksandr; at the bottom of each song, however, where the author's name is given, the full name is spelled in a more exact transliteration with stress marks: Aleksándr Sergéyevich Púshkin.

To follow the words of a song as sung on recordings or in performance, a reader who does not already know Russian needs a phonetic transcription of the words rather than a transliteration. With each song, there is a phonetic transcription of the lyric in Latin letters, side by side with a translation into English. The purpose of these parallel texts is to enable readers who do not know Russian to follow the words, and what they mean, as they are being sung.

My transcriptions are an attempt to show better than the LC system what the words actually sound like. In my transcription, the composer's name would be spelled "Chajkófskij," and the writer would be "Chékhaf." Unlike transliteration, these spellings show the automatic changes that take place in voicing and devoicing of consonants, and in reduction of the vowel "o" to "a" when it is not stressed. They also show which syllable in the word is stressed, a feature that stands out very strongly in spoken Russian, less so when it is sung.

First, and most important, is the sound "j" (called "yot" from Greek "iota"). It is exceedingly common in Russian. This is not "j" as in English or Spanish, but the sound "y" in "you," "bayou," or "boy." When it begins a word, the reader should interpret the letter "j" in transcriptions of songs in this book as sounding like the German "Johann," never like French Jean, Spanish Juan, or English John.

I retain the LC convention of an apostrophe for the "soft sign" used in Russian spelling. Its use has nothing to do with the meaning of an apostrophe in English, but indicates that the letter it follows is "softened" or made with the palate ("palatalized"). When following words being sung, it may be ignored.

In words where spelling and speaking are at variance, the transcription shows the sound rather than the spelling for obvious reasons. There are few such cases in Russian, but they occur in some very common words and endings.

I have kept the LC convention of using "y" to stand for the tense Russian vowel that is a variant of "i" as in "Bill" or "wit," only deeper. To master this sound, one needs to work with a Russian speaker. For an amusing illustration of the facial contortions required to pronounce this vowel in a loud voice from the rostrum of the Hall of Columns in Moscow, see the photograph of Nicolas Slonimsky in his autobiography *Perfect Pitch* (*Slonimsky 1988*, plate 29).

The vowel system is very easy. The vowels are a, e, i, o, u, plus the deeper variant of "i" just mentioned. Every vowel is a syllable, and every syllable has one vowel in it. Russian words are stressed on one of the syllables only; unlike English, Russian does not have secondary stress. When a, e, and o are not in the stressed syllable, they are "reduced" in spoken Russian, but "o" to "a" is generally the only reduction heard in singing, and then not uniformly.

a	as in "Mahler"
e	as in "bet"
i	as in "beet"
y	as in "Bill" (tense "i" explained above)
o	as in "coat" but deepened toward "call" (as in "kot," tomcat)
u	as in "flute"

Consonants are transcribed as in the LC system except for "j." My transcriptions do not show the difference between plain and palatalized consonants, but it is not necessary to understand the distinction in order to follow a song.

b	as in "boy"
d	as in "dish"
f	as in "father"
g	as in "Gogol"
j	as in "Johann"
k	as in "kaftan" (but without any puff of air)
l	as in "bull"
m	as in "Moscow"
n	as in "noble"
p	as in "Paul" (no puff of air)

r	trilled once, as in Italian "Roma"
s	as in "soul"
t	as in "Tomsk" (no puff of air)
v	as in "Volga"
z	as in "Zachary"

Some Russian consonants require two or more letters in transcription:

ch	as in "China"
kh	as in "Bach" or Scottish "loch"
sh	as in "shoot"
shch	as in "fresh chips"
ts	as in "bats" or "pizza"
zh	as in "azure" or French "Jean"

Some examples of Russian names follow in the table below:

1) The "LC" column shows Library of Congress transliteration, used in the Bibliography of this book.

2) The "Translation" column shows the spelling used in the narrative and commentary throughout the book.

3) The "Song Text" column shows the transcription used in this book for each song, devised to approximate the way the words actually sound.

Cyrillic	LC	Translation	Song Text
Петербург	Peterburg	Petersburg	Peterbúrk
Киев	Kiev	Kiev	Kíjef
Новгород	Novgorod	Novgorod	Nóvgarat
Толстой	Tolstoi	Tolstoy	Talstój
Достоевский	Dostoevskii	Dostoyevsky	Dastajéfskij
Невский	Nevskii	Nevsky	Njéfskij
Елизавета	Elizaveta	Yelizaveta	Jelizavéta
Федор (Фёдор)	Fedor	Feodor	Fjódar

Readers who want to sing these songs will, I hope, understand that these transcriptions do not teach the pronunciation; but a course in Russian, even a short one, will. Singers without Russian who want to perform these songs should have the excellent *Richter 2000* in hand while working with a Russian coach.

List of Abbreviations

Baker's. *Baker's Biographical Dictionary of Musicians*, ed. Nicolas Slonimsky and Laura Kuhn. Six vols. New York: Schirmer, 2001.

B/L. Bertensson, Sergei and Jay Leyda with the assistance of Sophia Satina. *Sergei Rachmaninoff. A Lifetime in Music*. Bloomington and Indianapolis: Indiana University Press, 2001. The best biography in English.

Harrison. Harrison, Max. *Rachmaninoff. Life, Works, Recordings*. London and New York: Continuum, 2005. An insightful musical study, marred by erroneous transcription of Russian names ("Prokovief," "Tioutchef," etc.).

Ianin. Ianin, V. A. and Griunberg, P. N. *Katalog vokal'nykh zapisei Rossiiskogo otdeleniia kompanii "Grammofon"* (A Catalogue of Vocal Recordings of the Russian Division of the "Gramophone" Company). Moscow: Iazyki slavianskoi kul'tury, 2002. Lists recordings prior to 1915.

Ivanov. Ivanov, Georgii K. *Russkaia poeziia v otechestvennoi muzyke (do 1917 goda)* [Russian poetry in music of the fatherland (to 1917)]. Two vols. Moscow: Muzyka, 1966, and Sovetskii kompozitor, 1969.

LN. S. Rakhmaninov. *Literaturnoe nasledie* [Literary Heritage], ed. Z. A. Apetian, Three vols. Moscow: Sovetskii kompozitor, 1978–1980.

Martyn. Martyn, Barrie. *Rachmaninoff. Composer, Pianist, Conductor*. Aldershot: Scolar Press, 1990. The most useful and thorough study in English.

ME. *Muzykal'naia èntsiklopediia* [Musical encyclopedia], ed. Iu. V. Keldysh. Six volumes. Moscow: "Sovetskaia èntskiklopediia," 1973–1982.

OP. *Otechestvennye pevtsy* [Singers of the fatherland] 1750–1917, two vols., ed. A. M. Pruzhanskii. Moscow: Sovetskii kompozitor, 1991 (vol. 1); Kompozitor, 2000 (vol. 2). A unique encyclopedia of Russian singers to 1917, with extensive professional biographies and a photograph of each singer.

PRP. *Pesni russkikh poètov v dvukh tomakh* [Songs of Russian poets in two volumes], ed. V. E. Gusev. Biblioteka poèta, Bol'shaia seriia. Leningrad: Sovietskii pisatel', 1988.

PRZ. *Pisateli russkogo zarubezh'ia* [Writers of the Russian emigration], ed. A. N. Nikoliukin. Moscow: ROSSPEN, 1997.

PSR. Rakhmaninov, S. V. *Romansy: polnoe sobranie* [Romances: complete collection], ed. P. Lamm. Moscow: Gosudarstvennoe muzykal'noe izdatel'stvo, 1957; reprinted 1963.

RGALI. Russian State Archive of Literature and Art (Moscow).

RP. *Russkie pisateli 1800–1917: biograficheskii slovar'* [Russian writers 1800–1917: a biographical dictionary], ed. P. A. Nikolaev et al. Five volumes to date. Moscow: Sovetskaia èntsiklopediia, 1989 (vol. 1); Bolshaia rossiiskaia èntsiklopediia, 1992–2007 (vols. 2-5).

RS. *Record of Singing.* Recordings of vocal artists in four volumes from the earliest sound recordings to the end of the 78 rpm era, published by EMI (formerly HMV) in the 1970s. A fifth volume, from the LP to 2007, was issued in 2009. Vols. 1 and 2 are on LP sets; vols. 3, 4, and 5 are on multiple CDs.

TCS. Sylvester, Richard D. *Tchaikovsky's Complete Songs: A Companion with Texts and Translations.* Bloomington and Indianapolis: Indiana University Press, 2002; 2004 (paperback).

T/N. Threlfall, Robert and Geoffrey Norris. *A Catalogue of the Compositions of S. Rachmaninoff.* London: Scolar Press, 1982. Indispensable catalog of the music with dates.

VOR. *Vospominaniia o Rakhmaninove* [Reminiscences about Rachmaninoff], ed. Z. A. Apetian. Two vols. Moscow: Gosudarstvennoe Muzykal'noe Izdatel'stvo. First edition: 1957. Fifth, enlarged edition: 1988.

Rachmaninoff's Complete Songs

Early Years (1873–1892)

1.

Sergei Vasilievich Rachmaninoff was born into a gentry family of modest means in the spring of 1873, on a family estate near Novgorod. He spent his early boyhood in that flat river and lake country in the far north with its long winter nights and its white nights in summer, near the Volkhov River and Lake Ilmen, the scene of Rimsky-Korsakov's opera *Sadko*. Novgorod is the oldest city in Great Russia, a city rich in medieval churches and monasteries on both sides of the river; on the right bank stands a large walled and towered Kremlin built around the eleventh-century Cathedral of St. Sophia, with its silver domes and sonorous bells. In Novgorod, as in Moscow, where the composer later lived, the sound of church bells was a constant accompaniment to daily life. In both cities, Rachmaninoff went to hear bells and came to know master bell ringers (*VOR 1*, 116, and *LN 3*, 427). Bells are a motif in such compositions as the Easter movement of the First Suite for two pianos, Op. 5 (1893), the Second Symphony, Op. 27 (1906–7), and the choral symphony *The Bells*, Op. 35 (1913), which Rachmaninoff considered one of his best works.

In its extended lines of grandparents, aunts, uncles, and cousins, Rachmaninoff's family situated him within a circle of kinship and acquaintance that was decisive in shaping all the important events of his formative years—the development of his musical gifts, his education, his early friendships, and even his marriage. The Rachmaninoff clan was typical of 19th-century noble families of moderate means: they lived in the country at least part of the year, were welcome in society in town, and had a network of connections that could gain them access to just about anyone they might need or wish to meet. A century earlier, Gerasim, Rachmaninoff's great-great-grandfather, was a soldier in the Preobrazhensky Guards of Peter the Great's daughter Elizabeth, who in 1741 seized the throne with the help of her Guards. She rewarded Gerasim with officer's rank and a "diploma of nobility, which had not heretofore been given to the Rakhmaninovs," allowing him to buy land in Tambov province, where he and his descendants lived on their family estate called Znamenskoye (*Keldysh*, 18). Of his children, Nadezhda married Yury Alekseyevich Pushkin, whose sister was Maria Gannibal, the grandmother of Alexander Pushkin; his son Ivan translated Voltaire and opened a publishing house in St. Petersburg; and his other son, Alexander, Rachmaninoff's great-grandfather, was an officer who played the violin well, but who died in 1812 at the age of thirty trying to save a man who was freezing to death in the steppe. Military service remained the traditional form of service for most of Gerasim's sons and grandsons all the way down to Rachmaninoff's father Vasily, who was a Guards officer.

Amateur music-making was another tradition that ran in the family. Rachmaninoff's grandfather Arkady was a systematic and ambitious musician who had studied piano with John Field (1782–1837), the Irish pianist and composer. He played at musical soirées, composed romances and piano pieces, and is said to have sat down at the piano every morning of his life. Arkady's mother, Maria, was of the Bakhmetyev family, who were landed gentry too, and very active musically; she played the piano; her cousin Nikolai was a solo violinist with the serf orchestra and choir he kept on his estate; he wrote church music and romances, and for more than twenty years was director of the Imperial Court Chapel Choir. In the Rachmaninoff family lore it was said that a good singing voice and the perfect pitch that many of them possessed were inherited from Maria Bakhmetyeva (*VOR 1*, 14).

Rachmaninoff's father Vasily was technically a good pianist and could play with a beautiful, soft tone. He was an inventive and whimsical improviser: his sister recalled that "he would play the piano for hours, not well-known pieces, heaven only knows what they were, but you could listen to him for hours" (*VOR 1*, 15). He liked a certain impish polka (written by Franz Behr, though Rachmaninoff thought his father had written it); in 1911 Rachmaninoff arranged it and published it as "Polka de W. R.", spelling Vasily with a "W" (see *T/N*, 152 and 190). Rachmaninoff recorded this polka in 1919, 1921, and 1928 (this latter recording is on the Sergei Rachmaninoff volume, no. 81, of the "Great Pianists of the 20th Century" series of Philips CDs). Vladimir Horowitz also liked this polka and played it in his Moscow recital in 1986.

Rachmaninoff was born on 20 March 1873 Old Style (1 April New Style) on a family estate in Novgorod province. There is disagreement about whether this estate was Oneg, near Novgorod, or Semyonovo, near Staraya Russa. The evidence for the latter is an official document, the church registry of births, marriages, and deaths, which records his baptism at Starye Degtyari, four kilometers from Semyonovo. Semyonovo was his father's house. It is so far from Novgorod that to take an infant born in Oneg to Semyonovo for baptism would have been not just unlikely but impossible, given the season and the duration of a trip of nearly two hundred kilometers over snowy or muddy roads. The director of the Rachmaninoff Museum in Novgorod believes the family was at Semyonovo when Sergei was born. Rachmaninoff, however, always gave Oneg as his place of birth, and for that reason the matter remains undecided: in the new *New Grove*, Geoffrey Norris gives Oneg, while Richard Taruskin (in the *Opera* volume) gives Semyonovo. At any rate, it was at Oneg, near Novgorod, that Rachmaninoff had his first memories of his childhood, and that is where he lived until the family left Novgorod when he was nine.

He was lucky to be born into a musical family that recognized the boy's talent early and took steps to give him regular piano lessons, first with his mother, who started teaching him to play and read music at the age of four.

When his grandfather Arkady came for a visit, they played duets. When he was seven, he suggested to his sisters' French governess that if she would sing Schubert's "The Maiden's Lament" (Des Mädchens Klage, D 191), he would accompany her. The piano part of this song gives the right and left hands two different repeating figures, simple but expressive; he had heard his mother play it many times. She at first didn't take him seriously, but he pleaded, and when they had finished, he asked her to sing it again twice more; she was astonished that he played it so well, from memory, his hands not big enough to play all the chords, but without a single wrong note (*B/L*, 3). This performance sprang from the boy's own imagination, and once they had gone through it, he wanted it to be repeated: the idea of the drama and even thrill inherent in a good song performance remained with him when he grew up and shaped his conception of the songs he wrote. The next morning news of this performance was dispatched to grandfather Arkady, who came by train from Znamenskoye and sent Vasily to St. Petersburg to bring back a teacher from the Conservatory. Anna Ornatskaya, a Conservatory graduate and friend of Rachmaninoff's mother, was brought to Oneg to live in the household and teach Sergei. She taught the boy there from 1880 to 1882, when the family moved to St. Petersburg. Many years later, in 1896, Rachmaninoff dedicated "Spring Waters," Song 32, to Anna Ornatskaya; one of his best songs, it has an especially thrilling and dramatic piano part.

Rachmaninoff's mother, Lyubov Petrovna, was the daughter of General Piotr Butakov, who taught history at the Novgorod military college. He died when Rachmaninoff was only four, but his widow, Rachmaninoff's grandmother Sophia Aleksandrovna Butakova, was important in Rachmaninoff's childhood. He was the third of six children—Vasily and Lyubov had three sons and three daughters—but of the six Sergei was Sophia's favorite. She spoiled him, but did not indulge him; she let him play and encouraged his time at the piano, but she expected him to behave himself, which he did, without rebellion; he was happy being with her and came to have the highest respect and affection for her. She was a connoisseur of church choirs, and she took him to services to hear the best liturgical singing; she knew the bell ringer "Yegorka," whom Sergei first saw in her house. When Lyubov and the children moved to St. Petersburg, she bought an estate near Novgorod, Borisovo, just so Sergei could come to live with her on his summer vacations. His time spent there was the happiest in his childhood. Her maiden name was Litvinova, and she was related by marriage to the famous soprano Félia Litvinne. Rachmaninoff and Litvinne both performed in Diaghilev's "Saison Russe" in Paris in 1907, and Rachmaninoff dedicated one of his romances to her, Song 75, "Dissonance" (1912).

Vasily Rachmaninoff planned to send his two older sons, Vladimir and Sergei, to the Corps of Pages to train as officers, but he squandered away the five estates in Lyubov's dowry, and when the family left Oneg in 1882 the marriage was breaking apart. Volodya, as eldest, did go to military school, but, for Sergei, Anna Ornatskaya arranged a scholarship to the Conservatory school, and he undertook a three-year course of study there.

The move from the comfortable estate at Oneg to a crowded apartment in St. Petersburg near the Haymarket—the neighborhood of Dostoyevsky's *Crime and Punishment*—was a further strain on the family. Vasily and Lyubov separated, and Lyubov was left with the care of the children. For Sergei, this period went badly, because his mother had no time to supervise him; she sent him to live with the Trubnikovs, a lenient aunt and uncle and their children, but he was fiercely independent and they could not control him. He refused any kind of help and insisted on doing everything himself: "ya sam" he would say, "I can do it myself," and this became his nickname at the Trubnikovs (*B/L*, 3). Instead of doing his homework, he played hooky on the streets. He liked the city and its opportunities for jumping on and off the trams and spending his carfare at the ice rink, but he was unhappy living away from Oneg, and he missed his grandmother especially. His father's departure was a blow, because, despite his immaturity, or perhaps owing to it, the children were happier being around him than with their mother. The only thing Sergei looked forward to was summer at Borisovo. His piano playing improved, but he failed his other subjects in 1885. His mother did not punish him and allowed him to go to grandmother's for the summer, but now something would have to be done to save him.

She turned to the family for help. One of Vasily's sisters was married to Ilya Siloti, and among their children was Alexander (Sasha) Siloti (1863–1945). Ten years older than his cousin, Siloti was embarking on a brilliant career as a pianist himself. His teachers were Nikolai Rubinstein, Tchaikovsky, and Franz Liszt. Lyubov Petrovna asked him to hear Sergei play and to test his ear, which he did. He said there was only one place to send him: to Moscow to study with Nikolai Zverev, a renowned piano teacher (who had taught Siloti) and strict housemaster who tolerated no nonsense from any of his pupils, especially the boys who lived under his roof. At the end of the summer of 1885 in Novgorod his grandmother put him on the Moscow train after taking him to a convent for a special service. She had sewn a hundred rubles into an amulet she put around his neck, and gave him her blessing. When the train pulled out, he burst into tears (*VOR 1*, 18-19).

2.

When Sergei appeared before Nikolai Sergeyevich Zverev (1832–1893) on the recommendation of his cousin Sasha Siloti, Zverev asked him to play something and agreed to take him as a pupil. He taught both boys and girls, but every year two or three of the boys lived on full room and board in his house near the crowded bazaar called the Smolensk Market, a twenty-minute walk from the Conservatory. Rachmaninoff had aunts he could have lived with in Moscow, but Siloti wanted Sergei to live in Zverev's house, as he had done in 1871 and for ten more years until he graduated (with a gold medal) from the Conservatory.

Zverev, a bachelor, and his sister, a spinster, ran the house with some strict rules: no fighting and no horseplay; no ice-skating or riding or rowing or other dangerous activity that could result in injury to a hand; and obligatory piano practice three hours a day, six days a week. Zverev made good money from the many pupils he had, so he did not charge his "cubs" for room and board (*zver'* means "wild animal" in Russian, so the boys were called *zveryáta*, "cubs"). To develop their understanding of the performing arts he took them to concerts, the opera, and the theater, always buying good seats. The first practice period was at 6 a.m., and each of the three boys had to take that period twice a week; if they had come home late from the theater the night before, that was not an excuse to miss early practice if it was their turn. But the strict regime was relaxed on Sundays, when Zverev held open house from noon till evening. Those afternoons were, in Rachmaninoff's words, a "musical paradise," with distinguished guests from the musical world dropping in. Guests at the Sunday soirées were not invited to play, but to listen to the boys play. Zverev was hugely pleased by these performances, as Rachmaninoff later recalled: "No matter what we played, his verdict was always 'Fine! Well done! Excellent!' He let us play anything we felt like playing... I cannot adequately describe what a spur to our ambition was this opportunity to play for the greatest musicians in Moscow, and to listen to their kindly criticism—nor what a stimulant it was to our enthusiasm" (*B/L*, 11). Among the guests at the soirées were Muscovites like Tchaikovsky and Sergei Taneyev, or visitors, like Anton Rubinstein, who came to Moscow early in 1886 to give a series of brilliant recitals that covered the history of piano music. Each of Rubinstein's recitals was performed in the evening for ticket holders, and the next day for students at a free matinee. Zverev's "cubs" heard every recital twice.

When Rachmaninoff arrived at Zverev's, fellow cub Matvei Presman wrote of him, "he was not well prepared technically, but what he was already playing was incomparable" (*VOR 1*, 152). Presman also said that the only thing Zverev taught them was to keep their hands and arms relaxed and not to saw their elbows back and forth. But there was more to it than that. It was Zverev's task to prepare his pupils in two or three years to be turned over to the piano faculty at the Conservatory who would complete their training—Taneyev, Vasily Safonov, Paul Pabst, Siloti, and others; and they had to be so well prepared that they did not have to be retrained. Zverev's pupils included eminent pianists like Siloti and Konstantin Igumnov; and pianists who were composers, too, like Feodor

Keneman and Arseny Koreshchenko, who were two of Chaliapin's favorite accompanists; and Rachmaninoff's contemporary of genius Alexander Scriabin (1872–1915), who was in Rachmaninoff's same class but as a day student.

The "Russian pianistic method" Zverev taught was known for its "songful melody and freedom of hand movement" (*Baker's*, 4046). Igumnov was admired as an artist of impeccable taste "who worked out every detail of the music to the utmost perfection" (ibid., 1659).This approach to playing the piano can be traced back to John Field, who lived in Russia most of his adult life and was an enormously influential teacher there. Of those who studied with him, two were especially important in passing on his legacy: Alexander Villoing (1804–1878), who gave lessons to the Rubinstein brothers, and Alexander Dubuque (1812–1898), who taught Mily Balakirev in St. Petersburg and Nikolai Zverev in Moscow. Field's playing had "unmatched beauty of tone," "sweetness and shading," "speed, evenness and purity of embellishment"; Mikhail Glinka, who took lessons from Field, admired "his forceful, gentle, and distinct playing. It seemed that he did not strike the keys but his fingers fell on them as large raindrops and scattered like pearls on velvet." To Liszt's charge that Field's playing was "sleepy" Glinka answered that "Field's music was often full of energy, capricious and diverse, but he did not make the art of music ugly by charlatanism, and did not chop cutlets with his fingers like the majority of modern fashionable pianists." He emphasized "effortless command and equality of all fingers, slow practice, and tonal control through hand techniques far in advance of his time, the whole subordinate to musical ends" (*Langley*). "Feeling" is not a part of this description, and Zverev never asked his pupils to play with "feeling." He insisted on perfect knowledge of the musical text, including the "punctuation marks"; he expected clean technique, clarity in the phrasing and precision in the execution; and the player had to pay attention to the quality and tone of the sound being produced, and to learn to control it. He passed on what Dubuque had shown him was a method to master the soft, singing line, the technical ease and elegance which characterized the strong but poetic style of John Field (*Keldysh*, 29). These were core attributes of the "Russian piano school" as it was understood and being taught in Moscow when Rachmaninoff began his training at Zverev's in the fall of 1885.

To widen the knowledge of music of his pupils and to cultivate their taste, Zverev employed a woman to come twice a week for two hours to play eight-hand arrangements of orchestral works with them at two pianos. They played symphonies by Haydn, Mozart, and, their favorite, Beethoven. At the end of the spring exams, Zverev invited Taneyev, who was Director of the Conservatory, to hear Rachmaninoff, Presman, and two of the other boys play an eight-hand arrangement of Beethoven's Fifth Symphony. Taneyev was amazed that they played it all the way through from memory (*VOR 1*, 158).

In 1888 Rachmaninoff finished Zverev's piano course and was assigned to study with his cousin Sasha Siloti. He had matured during those three years, and he and Siloti became friends, playing music together not only during lessons, going to concerts, and visiting the relatives and friends they had in common. Siloti was newly married to Vera Tretyakova, a daughter of the Moscow textile magnate and art collector Pavel Tretyakov.

3.

Rachmaninoff began composing in his second year at Zverev's. It is striking that his early efforts range over several genres, not only piano pieces but also orchestral, chamber, and vocal works. He was ambitious, and in this he emulated Tchaikovsky, who was his hero at the Moscow Conservatory. In February 1887 he wrote a Scherzo for orchestra, his earliest extant composition, based on Mendelssohn's Scherzo from *A Midsummer Night's Dream* (*T/N*, 162). Over the next year he wrote his early piano pieces (ibid., 147-8). He made sketches for an opera, "Esmeralda," a subject he took from Victor Hugo's *Hunchback of Notre Dame* (ibid., 182). He impressed his theory teacher Anton Arensky, who took him into his course in harmony for composers. By the fall of 1889 he had set his sights on composition; that spur to "ambition" he felt playing Sunday afternoons in the presence of Tchaikovsky was turning toward composing music. As we shall see, some of his early unpublished songs show him taking Tchaikovsky as a model.

The living arrangements at Zverev's house now posed a problem. He wanted his own room with his own piano to compose. He asked Zverev to do this for him, but it led to a quarrel. Whether as "ya sam" he insisted too strongly to be allowed to have his way without any interference from others, or whether Zverev was offended at what seemed a lack of gratitude for the home and schooling he had given Rachmaninoff for three years, tempers flared. Zverev could not forgive him, and broke with him as a result. Rachmaninoff tried repeatedly to ask forgiveness, but Zverev ceased speaking to him. After a month, Zverev led him on foot to his cousins the Satín family, who lived on Prechistenka Street, not far from Zverev's house. A family council called by his two aunts, Siloti's mother and Aunt Varvara Satiná, also a sister of his father's, considered the matter but could not agree that Sergei was their responsibility. The next day he moved in with Mikhail Slonov, a friend at the Conservatory who was five years older, and had his own rooms (*B/L*, 20).

Varvara Satina and her husband had four children, two girls and two boys. Of the boys one was Sergei's age and one eight years younger. The girls, Natalia (Natasha) and Sophia (Sonya), were younger than Sergei by four and six years. Natasha played the piano and would, in 1902, become Rachmaninoff's wife.

Sophia loved music and science (she eventually was a geneticist on the faculty of Smith College); she became Rachmaninoff's faithful friend and chronicler. Their mother took Sergei's side and, in the fall of 1889, offered him a home and family. They immediately made him feel welcome, and he showed the winning way he had with younger children, a quality he inherited from his father. He was happier with them than he had been since he moved to Moscow. In the following spring he wrote his first two songs (Songs 1 and 2, 1890).

The girls' father, Alexander Satin, managed the large Naryshkin estate southeast of Moscow and had his own estate "Ivánovka" a few hours' ride from there, in Tambov province (*VOR 1*, 253). Rachmaninoff spent the summer at Ivanovka with the Satins in 1890 and again in 1891. It was in a beautiful natural setting, wooded steppe country with rivers and forest paths; he came to love it and found there the peace and quiet he needed to compose. These were exceptionally happy times in a household crowded with young people who all loved music; the Silotis were there, too. Satin's sister was married to a man named Dmitri Skalon, a cavalry general who played the cello and lived in St. Petersburg. His three daughters Natalia, Lyudmila, and Vera, also came down to Ivanovka. Natalia Skalon, five years his elder, became Rachmaninoff's first regular correspondent the following winter. He wrote music for them, and he and Vera, two years younger, were romantically fond of each other. He was not allowed to write her, but to Vera he dedicated his fine early song, later revised for Op. 4, "In the silence of the secret night" (Song 12). He was devoted to the Skalon sisters and corresponded with Natalia Skalon until his marriage to Natalia Satina in 1902. He finished his First Piano Concerto at Ivanovka in July 1891; the dedication read "À Monsieur A. Ziloti."

At the end of the 1890–91 academic year Siloti left the Conservatory. To avoid having to work with a different teacher, Rachmaninoff asked to take his final exams in piano that spring, a year early; he passed with a gold medal. The next year, when he asked to be examined in theory and composition a year early, his request was also granted. One of the requirements was to write an opera on the subject of Pushkin's narrative poem *The Gypsies*. This was *Aleko*. When he played it for the examiners on May 7, he received a grade of "5" with a plus. Then Zverev came up to him, took out his gold watch, and presented to it to him, ending their two years of estrangement. Upon graduation, he was awarded the highest honor, the Great Gold Medal. It was an astonishingly brilliant finish to his schooling, showing how well he had learned to work and to work hard. He was nineteen, on his own, with the official title of "Free Artist."

1 *У врат обители святой* *At the gates of the holy abode*

Like several other Russian composers, Rachmaninoff was drawn to this lyric of Mikhail Lermontov (1814–1841) by the powerful and original way it expresses rejection, "best feelings" spurned, in the image of the beggar by the monastery gates who asks for a piece of bread and is handed a stone. It is a scene easily imagined by a Russian reader; in fact, as we know from the memoirs of Yekaterina Sushkova, a scene like this actually took place outside St. Sergius Lavra near Moscow. In August 1830 a party of young people, including the 18-year-old Sushkova and the sixteen-year-old Lermontov, made an excursion to the monastery, with Sushkova's grandmother riding in the lead as chaperone. At the gates they gave some coins to a beggar, who thanked them and told them the story of some other young people who had dropped stones into his cup. Later, at the inn, Lermontov, instead of joining them all at dinner, found a pencil and a scrap of paper, and, kneeling at a chair, wrote out this poem, handing it to Sushkova as he sat down to his bowl of chilled fish soup with kvass (*Sushkova*, 114-7). This intense Romantic gesture just before the soup course is almost a parody of what Lermontov would do so well later in mature work like his novella "Princess Mary," but this early poem already shows his authentic voice.

Rachmaninoff saw the emotional power in this lyric, and his response to it is impressive. His music pays attention to the words. His own authentic voice is heard unmistakably in the piano part, which establishes the emotional terms at the outset, and supports the voice part eloquently throughout. A third of the song's 45 bars are for piano alone. The beginning of the voice part, with its six repeated B-flats, contrasts with the emotionally strong introduction, and it can be ponderous if taken too slowly and allowed to drag. The baritone Sergei Leiferkus, who sings it in the original key, manages the right tempo, moving ahead as he rises to the high point of the song, marked *con moto* (with animated movement), "thus did I beg for your love, with bitter tears, with longing." At this point the piano again has a moment all to itself, to pause for lyrical reflection and let the words sink in. The song can work with other voices, too, as the fine recording by the Swedish soprano Elisabeth Söderström shows. She brings an underlying sense of animation to the whole song, while her accompanist, Vladimir Ashkenazy, plays the notes in the piano part with a chaste lyricism, not adding false emotional emphasis or arpeggios that are not in the score.

У врат обители святой
Стоял просящий подаянья,
Бессильный, бледный и худой
От глада, жажды и страданья.

Куска лишь хлеба он просил,
И взор являл живую муку.
И кто-то камень положил
В его протянутую руку.

Так я молил твоей любви,
С слезами горькими, с тоскою;
Так чувства лучшие мои
Навек обмануты тобою.

U vrát abíteli svjatój Stajál prasjáshchij padaján'ja, Bessíl'nyj, blédnyj i khudój Ad gláda, zházhdy i stradán'ja.	At the gate of the holy cloister A man stood begging for alms, Weak, pale, and thin From hunger, thirst, and suffering.
Kuská lish khléba on prasíl, I vzór javljál zhyvúju múku. I któ-ta kámen' palazhýl V jevó pratjánutuju rúku.	A piece of bread was all he asked, His look revealed keen torment. And someone put a stone Into his outstretched hand.
Tak já malíl tvajéj ljubví, S slezámi gór'kimi, s taskóju; Tak chústva lúchshyje mají Navék abmánuty tabóju.	Thus did I beg for your love, With bitter tears, with longing; Thus were my best feelings Forever betrayed by you.

Text. **Mikhaíl Yúrievich Lérmontov**, 1830. Title: Нищий (A Beggar); first published in 1844. Lermontov revised line 3 to read "A withered wretch, barely alive," but this reading was not published until 1910.

Set by many Russian composers, including Donaurov (1871), Shashina (1879), Nápravník (Op. 31/3, 1879), Cui (Op. 27/3, 1884), Medtner (Op. 3/1, 1904), and Alfred Schnittke (Two Songs for Voice and Piano, Early Works, 1954–5).

Meter. Binary. Iambic tetrameter:

A piece of bread was all he asked...

Music. Dated 29 April 1890 on the manuscript. Without opus number. G Minor. 4/4, Andante. For Low Voice: A–e[1] flat. Dedicated to **Mikhaíl Akímovich Slónov** (1868-1930), a singer (baritone), a fellow student at the Moscow Conservatory and one of Rachmaninoff's closest friends. First published posthumously in 1947 in *Lamm* (see *Lamm* in the Bibliography).

Recordings. Amaize, Burchuladze, Kharitonov, Koptchak, Leiferkus, Pirogov, Reizen, Söderström, Stepanovich, Suchkova, Verbitskaya, Vladimirov.

Donaurov: Andrei Labinsky, Klavdiia Tugarinova.

Medtner: Vassily Savenko.

2 *Я тебе ничего не скажу*
I shall tell you nothing

Like Tchaikovsky before him, Rachmaninoff wrote five songs to lyrics by Afanasy Fet (1820–1892). Tchaikovsky had admired Fet as a poet who could move him *musically*: as he wrote in a letter to Grand Duke Konstantin, "he has the power to touch strings of the soul that no artist, however great, can touch with words alone… he even avoids subject matter that can easily be expressed in words" (*Romanov* 1999, 52). This unusual lyric by Fet entitled "Romance" is such a poem.Tchaikovsky noticed it as soon as it was published in 1886, and chose it for one of his Opus 60 songs, which he wrote in May of that year.

The subject is first awareness of being in love, when it is still an unspoken secret. The metaphor of the *heart in flower* is highly unusual in Russian poetry; here the feeling of love, opening like a flower, is *felt*, as a physical sensation. Fet used "flowers" as a metaphor for something inexpressibly beautiful and tender. That this heart is a "night flower" makes it more romantic, more mysterious.

Rachmaninoff tried his hand at this text as a variation on Tchaikovsky's song, which he admired. Tchaikovsky set his song (for high voice) in E Major, 6/8 *Allegretto con moto*, in an ABA form where the B section (the second stanza and first two lines of the third) slows down to *più tranquillo*; the rapt lead-in to the word "heart" is further held back and preceded by a series of 16 repeated notes. The A sections are a light dance, almost playful, but the B section is reflective, expressing a quiet awe. Rachmaninoff modeled his 3/4 *Allegro* song in C Major on this pattern, including some repeated notes, but he wrote it for low voice, with no gradations in tempo indicated. It is a youthful exercise never intended for publication, but the result is an ardent song with a strong, *con moto* ending. The excellent recording by the Russian baritone Sergei Shaposhnikov makes a convincing case for it by moderating and varying the tempos to give it shape.

Я тебе ничего не скажу,
И тебя не встревожу ничуть,
И о том, что я молча твержу,
Не решусь ни за что намекнуть.

Целый день спят ночные цветы,
Но, лишь солнце за тучи зайдёт,
Раскрываются тихо листы,
И я слышу, как сердце цветёт.

И в больную, усталую грудь
Веет влагой ночной… я дрожу,
Я тебя не встревожу ничуть,
Я тебе ничего не скажу.

Я тебе ничего не скажу,
Я тебя не встревожу ничуть,
Я тебе ничего не скажу.

Ja tebé nichevó ne skazhú,
Ja tebjá ne fstrevózhu nichút',
I a tóm, shto ja mólcha tverzhú,
Ne reshús' ni za shtó nameknút'.

I'm not going to say a word to you,
I'm not going to alarm you in any way,
And what I'm silently repeating to myself,
I wouldn't mention even with a hint.

Tsélyj dén' spját nachnýje tsvetý,
No, lish sóntse za túchi zajdjót,
Raskryvájutsa tíkha listý,
I ja slýshu, kak sérttse tsvetjót.

Night flowers sleep all day,
But when the sun sets behind the clouds,
Their petals softly open up,
And I feel my heart flowering.

I v bal'núju, ustáluju grút'
Véjet vlágaj nachnój... ja drazhú,
Ja tebjá ne fstrevózhu nichút',
Ja tebé nichevó ne skazhú.

And into my aching, tired breast
Flows moist night air... I'm trembling,
I won't alarm you in any way,
I won't say anything to you.

Ja tebé nichevó ne skazhú.
Ja tebjá ne fstrevózhu nichút',
Ja tebé nichevó ne skazhú.

I won't say anything to you.
I won't alarm you in any way,
I won't say anything to you at all.

Text. **Afanásy Afanásievich Fet**, 1885. First published in *Vestnik Evropy* (Herald of Europe) in 1886, no. 1. Title: Романс (Romance). First set by Tchaikovsky in 1886, Op. 60/2. Rachmaninoff changed one word in line 6 of the poem (for woods, рощи, he substituted clouds, тучи); he repeated three lines at the end.

Georgi K. Ivanov, who catalogued all the songs by Russian composers with lyrics in Russian in his *Russian Poetry in Music of the Fatherland (to 1917)*, names 16 composers who wrote songs to this text after Tchaikovsky (*Ivanov*, vol. 1, 372). Only two are well known today: Tchaikovsky's song and the "popular" version by Tatiana Konstantinova Tolstaya (for a list of recordings of these, see below). Information is hard to find on Tolstaya, but see *Korabelnikova 2004*, 781.

Meter. Ternary. Anapest, 3-foot, with masculine endings:

After sundown a breath of fresh air
And my flowering heart is revived...

Music. Dated 1 May 1890. Without opus number. C Major. 3/4, Allegro. For Bass Voice: c–f^1. First published posthumously in *Lamm* in 1947. No dedication.

Recordings. Del Grande, Kharitonov, Leiferkus, Shaposhnikov, Söderström, Suchkova.

Tchaikovsky: Ivan Kozlovsky, Sergei Larin, Sergei Lemeshev, Jennie Tourel, Georgi Vinogradov, Sherri Weiler.

Tolstaya: Boris Gmyria, Nadezhda Obukhova, Nikita Storozhev, Tatiana Tolstaya, Lyudmila Zykina.

3 *Опять встрепенулось ты, сердце* *Again you leapt, my heart*

Nikolai Grekov (1807–1866) is nearly forgotten today, but in 1860 he was as well known as Fet and Polonsky, and many 19th-century Russian composers found attractive lyrics in his poetry: Mussorgsky's fine early song "Where are you, little star?" (late 1850s) uses a shortened Grekov lyric, and Tchaikovsky wrote three of his most charming songs to lyrics by him (Songs 12, 26, and 28 in *TCS*).

Grekov was of the landed gentry like Fet and the Tolstoys, but his small estates in Tula and Kaluga were modest and did not bring in much income. He graduated from Moscow University in 1827, served a few years in a government job, then retired to the country, supporting his family by writing and translating Shakespeare, Goethe, Heine, Calderón, and others. His wife died young; this loss, and his memory of first love, inspired his best song lyrics, including "little star" and the present poem. His verse was musical; he wrote about love in outdoor settings that evoke the Russian countryside—subjects very close to Rachmaninoff's heart. In one of his poems, he defines poetry this way: "In life, poetry is the *rose* in a garland of *thorns.*" Both those images appear in the present text, as does the word *music*; the lyric is about the poet's heart reawakening to love and accepting life anew in both its beauty and its pain.

In Rachmaninoff's song, for the first time in his early songs, the voice part takes the lead, with the piano playing a strong but supporting role. The verb in the first line means the sudden rising up in flight of a bird, or sudden beating of the heart. As the voice part rises and falls, Rachmaninoff finds trembling figures in the piano to suggest flight. The song bears his own signature. It is a slight but beautiful song, recognizably by Rachmaninoff and promising original songs to come.

Опять встрепенулось ты, сердце, и снова
  В душе моей вспыхнули грёзы,
И рвётся из груди кипучее слово,
  И льются горячие слёзы...

И снятся опять ей всё звуки да звуки,
  Всё музыки полные речи,
Да чёрные очи, да белые руки,
  Да кудри, да белые плечи.

И снова душа отозваться готова
  На всё, в чём есть терньяи розы,
И рвётся из груди кипучее слово,
  И льются горячие слёзы...

Apját' fstrepenúlas' ty, sérttse, i snóva V dushé majéj fspýkhnuli grjózy, I rvjótsa iz grúdi kipúcheje slóva, I l'jútsa garjáchije sljózy...	Again you beat faster, my heart, and again Bright dreams live in my soul, And a passionate word flies from my breast, And hot tears pour out...
I snjátsa apját' jej fsjo zvúki da zvúki, Vsjo múzyki pólnyje réchi, Da chórnyje óchi, da bélyje rúki, Da kúdri, da bélyje pléchi.	And my soul dreams of sounds, those sounds, Words you spoke full of music, And black eyes, and white hands, And curls, and white shoulders.
I snóva dushá atazvátsa gatóva Na vsjó, f chom jest' térn'ja i rózy, I rvjótsa iz grúdi kipúcheje slóva, I l'jútsa garjáchije sljózy...	And again my soul is ready to respond To everything that has thorns and roses, And a passionate word flies from my breast, And hot tears pour out...

TEXT. **Nikolái Porfírievich Grékov**, 1850s; published 1860 (*Grekov*, p. 30). Untitled. Not set by any other composers.

METER. Ternary. Amphibrachs, alternating 4-foot and 3-foot lines, with feminine rhymes:

Again you beat faster, my heart, and as always
The passionate words are the music...

MUSIC. Date uncertain. Pavel Lamm, the song's editor, assumes 1890; *Bortnikova*, 30, and *LN* 2, 413, date it 1893, an opinion based on ink, paper, and handwriting. Without opus number. G Minor. 6/4, [Andante sostenuto] (editor's brackets). For High Voice: d^1–a^2 flat. First published posthumously in Lamm's *Unpublished Vocal Works*, 1947. No dedication.

RECORDINGS. Korshunov, Piavko, Rodgers, Söderström, Suchkova, Timokhin.

4 *C'était en avril* *It was in April*

Rachmaninoff found this French lyric in *Amours et haines* (Loves and Hates, 1889) by Édouard Pailleron (1834–99), author of comedies and editor of *Revue des Deux Mondes*. He was not well known in Russia, and I have not found any other Russian songs that use lyrics by him.

The song is dated 1 April 1891, soon after Rachmaninoff's eighteenth birthday. Spring—the coming of spring, sudden joy, and first love—was one of his favorite themes. He went on to write a cantata for baritone, chorus, and orchestra to a famous Nekrasov poem about the "verdant noise" of spring's coming ("Spring," Op. 20, 1902); and several of his best songs are celebrations of spring (Song 32 "Spring waters," Song 38 "Lilacs," and Song 56 "Before my window"). In the case of this early song, the French lyric is pretty in a conventional way but pale and precious compared to Aleksey Tolstoy's exuberant celebration of spring which Tchaikovsky made into one of his most well-known songs ("In early spring," Song 40 in *TCS*). The theme, however, is exactly the same: looking back and remembering the happiness of a spring morning which was also the morning of love.

Rachmaninoff wrote a love song with a soaring, passionate vocal line, and then tenderness in the last words "do you remember?". These words work better in the Russian version of the song, and indeed the whole song works better in Russian. There is a good recording of the song in French (but only one) by the tenor Sergej Larin. Everyone else sings the song in Russian. The tempo is not indicated in the manuscript and the editor has marked it "Moderato," which gives performers some room for interpretation. The recordings vary, with a fleet performance by Elisabeth Söderström in just over two minutes, and a much slower, beautifully articulated reading of the song as an anthem of love by the baritone Pavel Lisitsian that is just under three minutes.

Rachmaninoff added two words to the French original and repeated a few phrases, which I have enclosed in brackets below.

C'était en avril, un dimanche,	It was in April, a Sunday
Oui, le dimanche!	Yes, on Sunday!
J'étais heureux...	I was happy...
Vous aviez une [jolie] robe blanche	You wore a [pretty] white dress
Et deux gentils brins de pervenche,	And two nice sprigs of periwinkle,
Oui, de pervenche,	Yes, periwinkle,
Dans les cheveux	In your hair
[brins de pervenche].	[sprigs of periwinkle].

Nous étions assis sur la mousse,
Oui, sur la mousse,
Et sans parler,
Nous regardions l'herbe, [l'herbe]
qui pousse,
[Et] la feuille verte, et l'ombre douce,
Oui, l'ombre douce,
Et l'eau couler.

Un oiseau chantait sur la branche,
Oui, sur la branche,
Puis il s'est tu,
J'ai pris dans ma main ta main blanche...
C'était en avril, un dimanche,
Oui, le dimanche...
T'en souviens-tu?

We were sitting on the moss,
Yes, on the moss,
And without speaking,
We looked at the grass, [the grass]
that grows,
[And] the green leaf, and the soft shade,
Yes, the soft shade,
And the rippling water.

A bird was singing on a branch,
Yes, on a branch,
Then it was silent,
In my hand I took your white hand...
It was in April, a Sunday
Yes, on Sunday...
Do you remember it?

The Russian translation was made by the Soviet poet Veronika Tushnova (1915–65) when the song was first published in 1947.

Апрель! Вешний праздничный день,
да, вешний день!.. Луга в росе.
Ты пришла в белом платье своём
и два подснежника в косе,
да, два цветка, два цветка в тёмной косе.

И без слов мы сели на мох, бархатный мох;
в блеске лучей весь мир зеленел,
каждый листок влагой блестел,
в лёгкой тени, где-то у ног,
журчал ручей...

А в кустах звенел голосок
птички лесной. Руки твои
в своих я так бережно сжал
в то ясное утро, весной,
светлой весной... Помнишь, помнишь?

Aprél'! Véshnij práznichnyj dén',
Da, véshnij dén'!..
Lugá v rasé.
Ty prishlá v bélam plát'je svajóm
i dva patsnézhnika f kasé,
da, dva tsvetká, dva tsvetká
f tjómnaj kasé.

April! a festive spring day,
Yes, a spring day!..
Dew lay on the meadows.
You came in your white dress
with two snowdrops in your braid,
yes, two flowers, two flowers
in your dark braid.

I bes slóf my séli na mókh,	And without words we sat down
bárkhatnyj mókh;	on the moss, the velvety moss;
V bléske luchéj	In the bright sunlight
ves' mir zelenél,	the whole world was green,
kázhdyj listók vlágaj blestél,	every leaf was shiny with moisture,
v ljókhkaj tení,	and in the light shade,
gdé-ta u nók,	somewhere at our feet,
zhurchál ruchéj…	a brook was babbling…
A f kustákh zvenél galasók	And in the bushes rang out the
ptíchki lesnój.	sweet voice of a little forest bird.
Rúki tvají f svajíkh ja tak	I held your hands
bérezhna zzhál	so tenderly and lovingly
f to jásnaje útra, vesnój,	that clear morning, in the spring,
svétlaj vesnój… Pómnish,	in radiant spring... Do you remember,
pómnish?	do you remember?

Text. **Edouard Pailleron**, published 1889 (*Pailleron*, pp. 27-8). Title: "Chanson." Russian translation by **Veroníka Tushnóva**. Not set by any other composers.

Meter. Mixed ternary and binary lines, but the first line, an amphibrach, sets up the dominant ternary pattern of the lines. This underlying ternary rhythm is heard in the triplets of the voice part and in the piano part throughout the song.

On Sunday, an April spring day,
April spring day!

Music. Dated 1 April 1891. Without opus number. E-flat Major. 3/4, Moderato. For High Voice: d^1–a^2 flat. First published posthumously in *Lamm*, 1947. No dedication.

Recordings. Gedda, Kharitonov, Larin (in French), Lisitsian, Naoumenko, Söderström, Suchkova.

5 *Смеркалось* *Twilight was falling*

Aleksei Tolstoy (1817–1875), cousin of the novelist Lev Tolstoy, is very well known in Russia as a writer of dramas in blank verse and excellent lyrics, in a variety of styles, often set to music. Tchaikovsky chose thirteen of them, with an unerring eye, for eleven of his songs and two of his duets. This is the first of six songs by Rachmaninoff to lyrics of Tolstoy's.

The theme is twilight, the passage from day to evening, in this case a hot day, which carries oppressive implications in the Russian context. So twilight brings relief, and another passage, too, from the present to a memory of the face of the woman the poet loves. Rachmaninoff made a good choice here of a lyric for a song, but he did a poor job of finding music for these words. The restless, rising phrases are at odds with the passage to stillness, to the contemplation of a bond, in this case a tender romantic bond. The long iambic hexameter phrases of the lyric do come across clearly in Rachmaninoff's use of eighth notes for each syllable in the line until the last one, which is a quarter note, or a dotted quarter note, or a dotted half note; this design culminates in the last word of the second stanza, a whole note high B. But the song searches too strenuously for a convincing melody, and the closing phrase comes as a relief. Singers have not taken the song up: except for the four complete sets of Rachmaninoff's songs, there are no recordings of it, making it (together with Song 77, a setting of two lines in Church Slavonic from the Gospel of St. John written for the war effort) the composer's least recorded song.

Жаркий день бледнел неуловимо,
Над озером туман тянулся полосой,
И кроткий образ твой, знакомый и любимый,
В вечерний тихий час носился предо мной.

Улыбка та же была, которую люблю я,
И мягкая коса, как прежде расплелась,
И очи грустные, по прежнему тоскуя,
Глядели на меня в вечерний тихий час.

Жаркий день бледнел неуловимо,
Над озером туман тянулся полосой,
И кроткий образ твой, знакомый и любимый,
В вечерний тихий час носился предо мной,
В вечерний тихий час.

Zhárkij dén' blednél neulavíma,	The hot day grew paler imperceptibly,
Nad ózeram tumán tjanúlsa palasój,	A band of mist stretched out over the lake,
I krótkij óbras tvój, znakómyj i ljubímyj,	And your gentle image, so familiar and beloved,
V vechérnij tíkhij chás nasílsa preda mnój.	Floated before me in the quiet evening hour.
Ulýpka tá zhe bylá, katóruju ljubljú ja,	Your smile was the smile I love so much,
I mjákhkaja kasá, kak prézhde rasplelás',	And your soft braid, as before, came undone,
I óchi grúsnyje, pa prézhnemu taskúja,	And your sad eyes, with a look of longing,
Gljadéli na menjá v vechérnij tíkhij chás.	Were gazing at me in the quiet evening hour.
Zhárkij dén' blednél neulavíma,	The light of a hot day faded imperceptibly,
Nad ózeram tumán tjanúlsa palasój,	A band of mist stretched out over the lake,
I krótkij óbras tvój, znakómyj i ljubímyj,	And your gentle image, so familiar and beloved,
V vechérnij tíkhij chás nasílsa preda mnój,	Floated before me in the quiet evening hour,
V vechérnij tíkhij chás.	In the quiet evening hour.

Text. **Alekséy Konstantínovich Tolstóy**, 1856. Untitled. Rachmaninoff removed the first word of the poem, "Смеркалось," and used it as the title of the song; he repeated the first stanza at the end to make it a three-part song. Set by César Cui (Op. 10/3, 1876), the cellist Karl Davydov (Op. 28/5, 1878), and many minor composers.

Meter. Binary. Iambic hexameter (except for the truncated first line), with a caesura after the third foot:

You smiled your lovely smile, your soft braid came undone…

Music. Dated 22 April 1891. Without opus number. G Major. 4/4, [Moderato]. For High Voice: d^1–b^2. First published posthumously in *Lamm*, 1947. No dedication.

Recordings. Mazurkevich, Naoumenko, Söderström, Suchkova.

Cui: Valentina Sharonova.

6 *Песня разочарованного* *Song of the disillusioned*

Daniil Ratgauz (1868–1937) was first noticed in 1893 when Tchaikovsky wrote his last six songs to lyrics by this young unknown poet of German descent. There was a boom in the next two decades in sentimental urban romances, and Ratgauz's melancholy poems were the perfect expression of what Russian composers were looking for in this vein. By 1917, Ratgauz had 144 poems set to music by contemporaries like Arensky, Ippolitov-Ivanov, Grechaninov, Koreshchenko, and Glière. In the list of Russian poets whose poems were made into songs before 1917, Ratgauz is fifth, ahead of poets like Aleksei Tolstoy, Yakov Polonsky, Aleksei Pleshcheyev, and Feodor Tyutchev, and behind only the top four—Konstantin Balmont, in first place, followed by Alexander Pushkin, Afanasy Fet, and Mikhail Lermontov. As a poet he is not even close to being in the same league as any of these other poets, but Tchaikovsky chose his texts well and wrote powerful music for them. Indeed, some consider Op. 73 to be Tchaikovsky's finest set of songs.

Rachmaninoff chose less well. He found this poem in 1893, when it first appeared in print. By that time, he had written Op. 4 and Op. 8, which contain several very good songs. They include sad songs, but nothing to match the extremes of despair and impossible hopes in this text. It is hard to imagine Rachmaninoff sharing these sentiments, except maybe the penultimate line, a wish to bring back the happy summers spent at Ivanovka with the Satins and the Skalon sisters. The song is well shaped, with "portentous repeated quaver octaves" in the bass accompaniment (*Martyn*, 84) to the midpoint of the song, line 7, where there is a shift to a major key, then back to the minor for the last stanza; there is a strong piano postlude of seven bars. It is a big, ambitious song, but he rightly decided not to publish it.

«Умри!» – твердит мне день, томительный и скучный,
«Умри!» – мне шепчет ночь таинственною мглой.
И в жизни тягостной, с тоскою неразлучный,
Без цели я брожу усталою стопой.

«Умри!» – твердил мне ум, когда в душе унылой
Почуял я намёк на светлый сон любви...
Но ты, мой нежный друг, мой ангел светлокрылый,
Ты взором ласковым мне всё твердишь: «Живи!»

О, как я жить хочу! Как страстно жажду света,
Возврата пылких грёз, несбыточной мечты!..
Скажи, как возвратить умчавшееся лето?
Скажи, как оживить увядшие цветы? Скажи!

"Umrí!" – tverdít mne dén',
  tamítel'nyj i skúshnyj.
"Umrí!" – mne shépchet nóch
  taínstvennaju mglój.
I v zhýzni tjágasnaj, s taskóju
  nerazlúchnyj,
Bes tséli ja brazhú ustálaju stapój.

"Umrí!" – tverdíl mne úm,
  kagdá v dushé unýlaj
Pachújal ja namjók na svétlyj són ljubví…
No tý, moj nézhnyj drúk,
  moj ángel svetlakrýlyj,
Ty vzóram láskavym mne fsjo tverdísh:
  "Zhyví!"

O, kák ja zhýt' khachú!
  Kak strásna zházhdu svéta,
Vazvráta pýlkikh grjós,
  nezbýtachnaj mechtý!..
Skazhý, kák vazvratít'
  umcháfshejesa léta?
Skazhý, kák azhyvít'
  uvjátshyje tsvetý? Skazhý!

"Die!" the day keeps saying,
  wearisome and tedious,
"Die!" whispers night
  in its mysterious gloom.
And in a life of hardship, melancholy
  my inseparable companion,
I wander aimlessly with weary steps.

"Die!" – my mind kept telling me,
  when in my downcast soul
I sensed a hint of love's bright dream...
But you, my gentle friend,
  my bright-winged angel,
With loving gaze keep saying to me:
  "Live!"

Oh, how I want to live!
  How passionately I long for light,
For the return of ardent wishes,
  the unattainable dream!..
Tell me, how can you bring back
  the summer that has flown away?
Tell me, how do you bring to life
  the flowers that have faded? Tell me!

Text. **Daniíl Maksímovich Ratgáuz**, 1893. Title: Песня разочарованного (Song of the disillusioned). First published in *Ratgauz 1893*, p. 104. This book was passed by the censor in Kiev on 9 July 1893, so presumably Rachmaninoff saw the poem after that date. He changed the word order in the first phrase of line 9 to make it more natural, and repeated the first word of line 12 at the end of the song. Not set by any other composers.

Meter. Binary. Iambic hexameter, with a caesura (word boundary) after the third foot:

But you, my gentle friend, || *my loving guardian angel...*

Music. 1893. Without opus number. F Minor – A-flat Major. 4/4, [Andante]. For Low Voice: c–f[1]. First published posthumously in *Lamm*, 1947. No dedication.

Recordings. Del Grande, Koptchak, Leiferkus, Pirogov, Söderström, Suchkova.

7 *Увял цветок*
The flower has faded

In Song 7, to another lyric by Ratgauz, Rachmaninoff takes a different musical approach. The theme is the fragility of the happiness love brings, requiring the beloved's early demise. The piano part is carefully crafted, with a laconic, but expressive accompaniment to the first stanza and the last 7 lines of the poem; this frames the impassioned music for lines 5 and 6, with *forte* arpeggio chords; then there is a reflective postlude to close the song. Like the preceding song, it has a conscious design, but except for the two passionate lines that speak of love, the voice part lacks really strong, defining phrases.

In Russian, the verb "died" cannot be used with "flower," but "faded" means "died" in this context, and that is how I have translated it below. The masculine pronoun "он" in the first line of the second stanza is sometimes translated as "it," meaning the flower, but that makes no sense. This can only mean "he" who loved her, the lover named in the third person as "your poor friend" (there is no first person pronoun in this poem).

Увял цветок! Лазурным утром мая
Нашла гроза, сломился стебелёк...
И, словно слёзы, лепестки роняя,
    Увял цветок!

Тебя любил он с неземною силой, –
Как только жрец любить богиню мог, –
Но ты взята безжалостной могилой...
    Увял цветок!

Чужой мечтам, чужой желаньям ясным,
Твой бедный друг душою изнемог.
Возврата нет к угасшим дням прекрасным...
    Увял цветок! Увял цветок!

Uvjál tsvetók! Lazúrnym útram
  mája
Nashlá grazá, slamílsa
  stebeljók...
I, slóvna sljózy, lepestkí ranjája,
    Uvjál tsvetók!
	The flower died! On an azure morning
	  in May
	A thunderstorm came, breaking its
	  stalk...
	And shedding its petals like tears
	    The flower died!

Tebjá ljubíl on s nezemnóju sílaj, –
Kak tól'ka zhréts ljubít' bagínju mók, –
No ty vzjatá bezzhálasnaj magílaj...
    Uvjál tsvetók!
	He loved you with an unearthly power,
	As only a priest could love a goddess,
	But you were taken by the pitiless grave...
	    The flower died!

Chuzhój mechtám, chuzhój zhelán'jam jásnym,	Alien to dreams, alien to clear desires,
Tvoj bédnyj drúk dushóju iznemók.	Your poor friend is stricken in his soul.
Vazvráta nét k ugásshym dnjám prekrásnym…	The lovely burned-out days are gone beyond return…
Uvjál tsvetók! Uvjál tsvetók!	The flower died! The flower died!

TEXT. **Daniíl Ratgáuz**, 1893. Untitled. First published in *Ratgauz 1893*, p. 49. This book was passed by the censor in Kiev on 9 July 1893, so presumably Rachmaninoff saw the poem after that date. Not set by any other composers.

METER. Binary. Iambic pentameter, except for the truncated final lines:

The lovely days are gone beyond return.
The flower died.

MUSIC. 1893. Without opus number. A Minor. 4/4, [Andante]. For Middle Voice: c^1–g^2. First published posthumously in *Lamm*, 1947. No dedication.

RECORDINGS. Borisenko, Del Grande, Popescu, Semenchuk, Söderström, Suchkova, Sumatchova.

8 *Ты помнишь ли вечер*
Do you remember the evening?

In May and June of 1856, Aleksei Tolstoy and Sophia Miller, Tolstoy's wife and the addressee of his best love lyrics, traveled to the Crimea. There Tolstoy began a group of fourteen lyrics he called "Crimean Sketches." Rachmaninoff found the text of this song in that cycle. Like Song 5, this lyric describes an intimate memory, this time on an evening when the poet and his lover were riding horses together by the Black Sea. Rachmaninoff shortened the poem by leaving out two stanzas not needed for the song (they are printed below).

This is a straightforward song to a good text that works in performance. The ternary rhythm of the poem is brought out clearly in the placement of word stresses in the voice part and in the triple note figures in the piano part; it has a good melodic phrase that is flexible enough for variation, first with tenderness in the memory of a happy time together, then building to the repeated lines at the end of the second stanza, and finally ending in the quiet close. It has not been widely sung, but singers have noticed it, including Daniil Shtoda, a tenor from St. Petersburg, who included it on his first recording of Russian romances. There is also a fine recording of the song by Konstantin Lisovsky.

Ты помнишь ли вечер, как море шумело,
В шиповнике пел соловей...
Душистые ветки акации белой
Качались на шляпе твоей?

Меж камней, обросших густым виноградом,
Дорога была так узка;
В молчании над морем мы ехали рядом,
К руке прилегала рука!
В молчаньи над морем ехали мы рядом,
К руке прилегала рука.

Ты помнишь ли рёв дождевого потока
И пену, и брызги кругом?
И нам наше горе казалось далёко,
И как мы забыли о нём!

Ty pómnish li vécher,
  kak móre shuméla,
F shypóvnike pél salavéj...
Dushýstyje vétki akátsii bélaj
Kachális' na shljápe tvajéj?
	Do you remember that evening,
	  how the sea roared,
	How a nightingale sang in the sweetbrier?
	How fragrant sprigs of white acacia
	Swayed on your hat?

Mesh kámnej, obrósshykh	Between the rocks, overgrown
gustým vinagrádam,	with thick grapevines,
Daróga bylá tak uská;	The road was so narrow;
V malchánii nad mórem my jékhali rjádam,	We rode in silence together above the sea,
K ruké prilegála ruká!	Hand in hand!
V malchán'ji nad mórem jékhali my rjádam,	In silence above the sea we rode together
K ruké prilegála ruká.	Hand in hand.
Ty pómnish li rjóf	Do you remember the roar
dazhdevóva patóka	of the pouring rain,
I pénu, i brýzgi krugóm?	And the foam and spray all around?
I nam náshe góre kazálas' daljóka,	And how our grief seemed so far away,
I kak my zabýli a njóm!	And how we forgot all about it!

Text. **Alekséi Tolstóy**, 1856. Untitled; No. 4 in "Крымские очерки" (Crimean Sketches). First set by Rachmaninoff, who removed two stanzas, repeated lines 7 and 8, and made two minor changes in wording. He was not satisfied with it but decided not to revise it (*LN 1*, 178-9). Cui set this same text in his late opus of 18 songs to Tolstoy's poems (Op. 67/14, 1904).

A setting was made in 1894 by G. E. Konyús (Georgi Conus, 1862–1933), composer and piano teacher of Scriabin and Medtner. Rachmaninoff knew the Conus family well; he played his trio with Julius, the violinist (see p. 46); in 1932 Julius's son Boris married Tatiana, Rachmaninoff's younger daughter.

Meter. Ternary. Amphibrachs, alternating lines of 4 and 3 feet:

Remember the evening we rode by the sea,
A nightingale sang in the brier...

Music. Dated 16–17 July 1891, Ivanovka. Without opus number. E Major. 12/8, [Moderato]. For Middle Voice: e^1–a^2. First published posthumously in *Lamm*, 1947. No dedication.

Recordings. Korshunov, Leiferkus, Lisovsky, Popescu, Shtoda, Söderström, Suchkova, Zimmermann.

Stanzas 4 and 5, omitted from the song

Ты так на седле нагибалась красиво,	You sat forward so handsomely on the saddle,
Ты алый шиповник рвала,	You plucked a wild rose off the brier,
Буланой лошадки косматую гриву	And lovingly you placed a corsage
С любовью ты им убрала;	In the shaggy mane of your dun horse;
Одежды твоей непослушные складки	The unruly folds of your clothing
Цеплялись за ветви, а ты	Caught in the branches, while you
Беспечно смеялась, цветы на лошадке,	Laughed gaily, flowers on your horse,
В руках и на шляпе цветы.	Flowers in your hands and on your hat.

9 *Икалось ли тебе*
Were you hiccuping?

Because it was never published, this song follows the other eight unpublished songs in the Moscow edition of the Complete Romances (*PSR*) and is thus out of chronological order. It was written in June 1899 at the Krasnenkoye estate of the Kreutzer family, where Rachmaninoff was spending the summer (*VOR 1*, 292-5). Yelena Kreutzer took piano lessons from Rachmaninoff for many years and was a friend of Natalia Satina, Rachmaninoff's future wife, by that time a student at the Moscow Conservatory. They invited Natasha to visit them in June. In this period of his life Rachmaninoff was performing and conducting, but was still recovering from the botched premiere of his First Symphony and finding it difficult to undertake any large compositions. Hence the jocular words at the top of the manuscript of the song: "No! My muse has not died, dear Natasha. I dedicate my new romance to you."

Yelena and Natasha used the large library at Krasnenkoye to look for good poems to give Rachmaninoff as texts for songs. He dropped in on them one day and started reading himself, whereupon he found this lyric in the poems of Pushkin's contemporary Prince Vyazemsky (1792–1878). The idea behind this comic song is the notion that if you get the hiccups it means someone must be thinking about you. When Vyazemsky visited Épernay in the champagne district of France he thought of his friend Denis Davydov and wrote this poem to him while drinking champagne in the Moët cellars. Davydov, who was a cavalry officer (and a poet), had once told him the story of how he happened to be in that very place in 1812 with partisans in pursuit of Napoleon's retreating army. Rachmaninoff used only the first three stanzas, changing the addressee to Natasha, and situating the champagne-drinking in a cellar in Voronezh, a mundane town near Krasnenkoye. He thought it was a huge joke and promised to write a song to those words, and on the next day he performed it with gusto. The song goes from romping gaiety to tender romanticism (there are musical quotes fromTchaikovsky's opera *Eugene Onegin*), and the last four words are to be sung "à la hiccup." Barrie Martyn finds these antics "heavy-handed" and "forced" (*Martyn*, 121) but Max Harrison defends it as being in the vein of Stravinsky's nonsense songs (*Harrison*, 88). In his spirited recording, Sergei Leiferkus reads the words of the dedication before singing the song.

Нет! Не умерла моя муза, милая Наташа. Посвящаю тебе мой новый романс.

Икалось ли тебе, Наташа,
Когда шампанское я пил
Различных вкусов, свойств и видов,
Различных возрастов и сил?

Когда в воронежских подвалах
Я жадно поминал тебя,
Любя Наташу, поэтессу,
Да и шампанское любя?

Здесь бьёт кастальский ключ, питая
Небаснословною струёй;
Поэзия, – здесь вещь ручная:
Пять франков дай и пей, и пой!

No! My muse has not died, dear Natasha. I dedicate my new romance to you.

Ikálas' li tebé, Natásha, Kagdá shampánskaje ja píl Razlíchnykh fkúsaf, svójstf i vídaf, Razlíchnykh vózrastaf i síl?	Were you hiccuping, Natasha, While I was drinking champagne Of various tastes, characteristics, and kinds, Of varied vintages and strengths?
Kagda v varóneshskikh padválakh Ja zhádna paminál tebjá, Ljubjá Natáshu, poetéssu, Da i shampánskaje ljubjá?	When in the cellars of Voronezh I was thinking about you so ardently, Loving Natasha, my poetess, And loving the champagne too?
Zdéz' b'jót kastál'skij kljúch, Pitája nebasnaslóvnaju strujój; Poézija, - zdés' véshch ruchnája: Pját' fránkav dáj i péj, i pój!	Here flows a Castalian spring, that inspires Not like the fabled stream [of the Muses]; Here poetry comes in wine by the glass: Pay your five francs, then drink and sing!

Text. **Prince Piotr Andréyevich Vyázemsky**, 1838. Title: Эперне (Épernay, a town in the Champagne district of France). Only Rachmaninoff has set this text. He used only the first 3 of 18 stanzas, changing the references to Davydov to fit Natasha and replacing the cellars of Moët with Voronezh. He added a note to the title which reads "Please read the verses carefully first!"

Meter. Binary. Iambic tetrameter:

While drinking glasses of champagne
Of varied vintages and strengths.

Music. Dated 17 May 1899, but this date was written in later, and is probably erroneous; the actual date of June 1899 is given by Kreutzer in her memoir (*VOR 1*, 292-5). Without opus number. F Major. 4/4, Быстро [Fast]. For Low Voice: c–f[1]. First published posthumously in *Lamm*, 1947. Dedicated to the composer's wife.

Recordings. Burchuladze, Crona, Del Grande, Kharitonov, Leiferkus, Nesterenko, Söderström, Suchkova.

First Published Songs, Opus 4 (1893)

1.

Word of a new talent named Rachmaninoff spread quickly. The music publisher Karl Gutheil approached him with an offer to publish *Aleko* and pay him a fee of 500 rubles for it. He also bought two pieces for cello and piano, Op. 2, and the first set of songs, Op. 4. It was a large sum, but there were delays in getting the money to him, so he took a job giving piano lessons in the summer of 1892 after graduation. He received good fees and became friends with some of his pupils, like Yelena Kreutzer, but he did not like having to teach in order to support himself (*VOR 1*, 28).

Among the works Rachmaninoff composed in 1892–3 were five pieces for piano, called "Morceaux de Fantaisie," Op. 3, written in the autumn of 1892. The second of these, a Prelude in C-sharp Minor, made an immediate impression when he first played it in Moscow on 26 September 1892, and later that year in Kharkov. His cousin Alexander Siloti played it for the first time outside Russia in London in 1895 (*Barber*, 61), and first brought it to the U.S. in 1898, where it became a sensation. Rachmaninoff himself played it in England on his first tour there in 1899. It has an arresting beginning, dignified but menacing, with its three-note descending octave unison chords; there is drama in the middle section, and then a chordal climax, a "mournful tolling of bells," and a final sequence of chords "each held in suspense as the music gradually vanishes into the distance" (*Martyn*, 69). In an interview published in *The Delineator* in February 1910, Rachmaninoff cautioned against playing it too loudly or yielding to the temptation to play the final chords as arpeggios.

This three-and-a-half to four-minute Prelude in C-sharp Minor became one of the most famous piano works ever written. He sold Op. 3 to Gutheil for 200 rubles, or 40 rubles a piece (about 20 dollars, as he said in his interview for *The Delineator* during his North American debut in 1909–10); he regretted not publishing the work in Germany to protect his rights, as he did later with other sets of piano works. But since Russia was not a signatory to international copyright agreements, the twenty dollars he received for the Prelude was all he ever got for it. It has been estimated that, had it been protected by copyright, the composer might have made $100,000 on this work alone (*Harrison*, 50). At any rate, it passed into the public domain, and was played by everyone for free. Rachmaninoff's recording of it on the Philips "Great Pianists of the 20th Century" set is played exactly as he calls for in the interview above, the melodic lines clearly articulated and the chords not pounded out showily but played with a stately restraint. The prelude became well known beyond the world of classical music. In 1918 George L. Cobb published a Tin Pan Alley instrumental version called "Russian Rag." It was played by jazz musicians who arranged it, including Duke Ellington ("Cotton Club Nights," 1938), Jack Teagarden ("It's Time for T," 1941), and Nat Cole in his early King Cole Trio period (1944); for many more curious offshoots of the prelude, see *Harrison*, 227-9. The piece hardly survives Teagarden's band, but Nat Cole's version for piano, guitar, and bass conveys a certain respect for the original. Whether Rachmaninoff would have liked it is hard to say, but it is known that he admired Art Tatum's piano improvisations and Paul Whiteman's orchestra, and was at Aeolian Hall in 1924 when Whiteman introduced *Rhapsody in Blue* with George Gershwin as soloist.

2.

During Rachmaninoff's last year at the Conservatory, in late 1891 or early 1892, his friend Yury Sakhnovsky (see Song 11) introduced him to a married woman named Anna Lodyzhenskaya; she was in her mid-twenties, and of Gypsy blood. Her husband Piotr was a dilettante composer and carouser and a friend of Chaliapin's. He wrote a song which he dedicated to Rachmaninoff, "Those fleeting dreams" (Пронеслись мимолетные грезы, 1896), which Lamm in 1947 mistakenly included in Rachmaninoff's unpublished songs because a score of the song in Rachmaninoff's hand was found among his papers (*PSR*, 326); there are several recordings of this song, including a good one by Nadezhda Obukhova. Anna's sister Nadezhda Aleksandrova was a well-known singer of "Gypsy" songs whom Rachmaninoff certainly admired; she made recordings of two such songs (*Ianin*, 418), including "White and Pale (Night Flowers)," a song later in Obukhova's repertoire and recorded by her.

Rachmaninoff found this "Gypsy" company irresistible, and particularly Anna, with her deep-set, dark eyes, her kind manners, her engaged interest in the younger men. After graduation, the evenings he spent at Anna's were frequent. He called her "Rodnaya," a term of the closest endearment in Russian, and referred to her by that name with his friends Slonov and Sakhnovsky. In the words of Lyudmila Skalon, she was his "passionate platonic love" (*VOR 1*, 239). He was living with his cousins the Satins during most of these years. It is not surprising that they disapproved of Anna Lodyzhenskaya; they did not like her and found her "unattractive." Since so much of what we know about Rachmaninoff comes to us through the Satin sisters, or through Soviet keepers of archives not curious enough to tell us anything about this woman of whom they also disapprove, we have to imagine this relationship rather than construct it out of known facts. But Anna's hold on Rachmaninoff and his lasting devotion to her cannot be doubted: he would ask Sakhnovsky or Slonov to spend the evening with Rodnaya ("dearest heart") when he could not go himself; he sent money to her "regularly" and, years later, sent money to Piotr after she had died (Irina Chaliapin in *VOR* 2, 177-8). Rachmaninoff dedicated his "Capriccio on Gypsy Themes" (1892–4) to Piotr, his song "Oh, do not grieve" (Song 29, 1896) to Nadezhda, and to Anna he dedicated the first song in Op. 4 (Song 10, 1892) and his First Symphony. In January 1893, when Rachmaninoff and Mikhail Slonov went to Kharkov to give a recital, Anna advised them to "be happy and have fun" (*LN 1*, 207). During this recital, Slonov, a baritone, performed two songs from Opus 4, including the song dedicated to Anna.

3.

When Rachmaninoff and Slonov were in Kharkov, they stayed in the town house of a rich merchant and his wife whom Rachmaninoff had met when he gave his first recital there in December 1892. This couple, the Lysikovs, had a summer estate called "Lebedin" outside town, and they invited the two young men to visit them there in the summer of 1893. For Rachmaninoff it was a productive summer. There he wrote the last two songs of Opus 4, (he dedicated number 5 to Mrs. Lysikova); he also wrote a Suite for Two Pianos (Fantaisie-Tableaux), Op. 5, which he dedicated to Tchaikovsky; two Morceaux de Salon for Violin and Piano, Op. 6; and a Fantasy for Orchestra "The Crag," Op. 7, which Tchaikovsky promised to include in a concert he was to conduct in January 1894. It was the last work Rachmaninoff showed to Tchaikovsky before Tchaikovsky's untimely death in October 1893.

The songs of Opus 4 are a remarkable achievement for a young composer making his debut as a song writer. All six of them are good songs, and two of them, Songs 12 and 13, are classics, ranking second and third of all his songs in performance frequency. Rachmaninoff's gifts for lyrical melody and imaginative support from the piano are everywhere apparent. The first in the set, Song 10, "Oh no, I beg you, do not leave!", dedicated to Anna Lodyzhenskaya, is an urban romance in the popular "Gypsy" style. Song 11, "Morning," has an amorous text and casts a musical spell. Song 12, "In the silence of the secret night," is a song on the scale of Tchaikovsky's "None but the lonely heart," to an excellent text by Fet, realized musically in a powerful and original way. Song 13, "Sing not to me, beautiful maiden," is an "oriental" song to a famous Pushkin lyric, set by many others before and after him, including Glinka and Balakirev, but Rachmaninoff outdoes them all. Song 14, "Harvest of sorrow," is a moving lament in Russian folk style. Song 15, "How long, my friend," is a dramatic song of lovers' separation, transformed by the end into an ecstatic song of reunion, with a change of key from minor to major. Although the composer himself did not transcribe any of them for piano, all six of the songs have been transcribed by others for various instruments, an indication of the compelling melodic material in this first published set of songs.

10 *О, нет, молю, не уходи!* *Oh no, I beg you, do not leave!*

Op. 4, No. 1

Sophia Satina tells us that Rachmaninoff wrote this song at one sitting, as an improvisation on the piano. The musical phrases are a perfect match for the words. The first line of text is like a title to what follows, an introductory phrase "centered on a pivotal note (F), a prominent feature of much of Rachmaninoff's music" (*Norris*, 140); then, with agitated triplets in the piano, the voice rushes ahead with pleading intensity. The sentiments are very like an urban romance made famous by the Gypsy singer Varya Panina "Не уходи, побудь со мною" (Don't leave, stay with me). This shows Rachmaninoff's affinity for the popular "Gypsy" style of the day (his song was actually written before the Panina song), but the text and music of his song are much more interesting and expressive.

The Symbolist Dmitri Merezhkovsky (1865–1941) was a serious poet who rarely wrote this kind of "cruel romance" text; he published it in a literary magazine in 1890, but he did not include it in his collected works of 1914. Rachmaninoff found it in the magazine, or perhaps Anna Lodyzhenskaya found it and showed it to him. He referred to it in a letter to Natalia Skalon describing the pain he felt while he was writing the elegiac trio after Tchaikovsky's death: "As it says in one of my romances, I was in torment the whole time and sick in my soul" (*LN 1*, 229). Though Slonov and Rachmaninoff first performed it in public in Kharkov, its first performance in Moscow was in March 1893, when Leonid Yakovlev, a baritone, sang it at a concert of the Russian Musical Society; it was so well received he had to sing it twice (*LN 1*, 520).

О, нет, молю, не уходи!
Вся боль ничто перед разлукой,
Я слишком счастлив этой мукой,
Сильней прижми меня к груди,

Скажи: « люблю». Пришёл я вновь, —
Больной, измученный и бледный.
Смотри, какой я слабый, бедный,
Как мне нужна твоя любовь...

Мучений новых впереди
Я жду, как ласк, как поцелуя,
И об одном молю, тоскуя:
О, будь со мной, не уходи!
О, будь со мной, не уходи!

O, nét, maljú, ne ukhadí!	Oh no, I beg you, don't leave!
Fsjá ból' – nishtó pered razlúkaj,	This pain is slight compared to separation,
Ja slíshkam shcháslif ètaj múkaj,	I'm too happy in this state of torment,
Sil'néj prizhmí menjá ggrudí,	Press me hard against your breast,
Skazhý "ljubljú." Prishól ja vnóf'	Say "I love you." I've come to you again,
Bal'nój, izmúchennyj i blédnyj.	Sick, tormented, and pale.
Smatrí, kakój ja slábyj, bédnyj,	See how weak and pitiful I am,
Kak mné nuzhná tvajá ljubóf'...	How much I need your love...
Muchénij nóvykh fperedí	New torments lie ahead,
Ja zhdú, kak lásk, kak patselúja,	I greet them like caresses, like kisses,
I ab adnóm maljú, taskúja:	And beg for one thing only in my agony,
O, but' samnój, neukhadí!	Oh, stay with me, don't leave!
O, but' samnój, neukhadí!	Oh, stay with me, don't leave!

TEXT. **Dmítri Sergéyevich Merezhkóvsky**, 1890. First published in *Russkaia mysl'* (Russian Thought), 1890, no. XI, p. 111. First set by Rachmaninoff.

Varya Panina's song, written ca. 1900, is by N. Zubov with words by M. P. Poigin (*Petrovsky 2005*, 343, note 197). A variant song (ibid., 183) is a "reply" to the Poigin text, which uses phrases from the Rachmaninoff-Merezhkovsky song. Alexander Blok quotes the opening words of the Panina song as epigraph to his 1909 lyric "Smoke from the fire—a blue-gray ribbon," and Mayakovsky alludes to the song in his 1929 play "The Bedbug." Panina recorded the song in 1905.

METER. Binary. Iambic tetrameter:

I know new torments lie ahead,
I greet them like caresses, kisses...

MUSIC. Op. 4, no. 1. D Minor. 3/4, Con Allegro. For Middle Voice: b–f². The autograph is dated 26 February 1892, but dates a year or two earlier were given (perhaps mistakenly) by both Rachmaninoff and Sophia Satina. First published with Opus 4 by A. Gutheil in Moscow in 1893.

Dedicated to **Ánna Aleksándrovna Lodýzhenskaya**. The RGALI catalogue lists a transcription for piano of this song by the popular composer of romances A. N. Shefer (born 1866). It is also dedicated to A. A. Lodyzhenskaya.

RECORDINGS. Amaize, Arkhipova, Atlantov, A. Bolshakov, Borisenko, Christoff, Del Grande, Furlanetto, Gmyria, Guleghina, Hvorostovsky, An. Ivanov, Koptchak, Kozlovsky, Larin, Leiferkus, Levko, Pavel Lisitsian, Magomayev, Mishura, Mkrtchyan, Ognivtsev, Oja, Olli, Orda, Pogossov, Preobrazhenskaya, Rautio, Reizen, Rosing (in English), Rozum, Seleznev, Serkebayev, Souzay, Söderström, Suchkova, Talvela, Tikhonov, Westman.

TRANSCRIPTIONS. *Flugelhorn:* Sergei Nakariakov.

11 *Утро* *Morning*

Op. 4, No. 2

No one has established where Rachmaninoff found this poem or exactly who its author is. The poem could be a translation of a French poem, perhaps, or an imitation by a lesser poet of Balmont's hyper-Romantic Symbolist imagery.

The song begins with the feminine image of dawn (*zarja*) and a four-note phrase "I love you," a rise and then a fall, "as if descending from above," as Russian friends perceived it when we listened to this song in 2006. These four notes become a reference point around which the song develops and expands harmonically; the piano repeats it many times. The second half of the song is the masculine image of day (*den'*), perceived as rising phrases in the music. The harmony, F major to E major and back to F, expresses "the gradual opening out of the morning light" (*Vasina-Grossman*, 322). The song was written for contralto or bass: of the many good recordings, those by Zara Dolukhanova and Ewa Podleś are especially fine.

«Люблю тебя!» – шепнула дню заря
И, небо охватив, зарделась от признанья,
И солнца луч, природу озаря,
С улыбкой посылал ей жгучие лобзанья.

А день, как бы ещё не доверяя
Осуществлению своих заветных грёз,
Спускался на землю, с улыбкой утирая
Блестевшие вокруг ряды алмазных слёз…

"Ljubljú tebjá!" – shepnúla dnjú zarjá I, néba akhvatíf, zardélas' at priznán'ja, I sóntsa lúch, priródu azarjá, S ulýpkaj pasylál jej zhgúchije labzán'ja.	"I love you!" whispered dawn to the day And, embracing the sky, blushed from the confession, And a ray of sunlight, smiling, lit up nature, Sending burning kisses to the dawn.
A dén' kag by jeshchó ne daverjája Asushchestvléniju svaíkh zavétnykh grjós Spuskálsa ná zemlju, s ulýpkaj utirája Blestéfshyje vakrúk rjadý almáznykh sljós…	But day, not yet believing That his cherished dreams had come true, Descended to the earth with a smile That wiped away the rows of diamond tears shining all around…

Text. **M. Yánov** (?), date unknown. Set only by Rachmaninoff. The poet's name is given as M. Yanov or M. L. Yanov in later engravings. In concert programs which include the song, the poet is identified as M. Yanov, which is what the Moscow edition, *PSR*, also gives. Geoffrey Norris in the *New Grove* and in *Norris 2001* retains M. Yanov, but see *Threlfall and Norris* (*T/N*) below. No one I queried in Moscow or St. Petersburg could find any information about a man with this name who was a poet.

The list in *Ivanov* of Russian poems set to music before 1917 cites the poet as a woman, **M. N. Yánova**, with no dates or other information. She has only two poems in his list: one is this poem, published as Rachmaninoff's song, with a censor date of 1892. The other is a song published in Kiev in 1915 (*Ivanov 1*, 398). Ivanov searched regularly in the leading journals to identify the place and year a poem was first published, but her two poems are identified as being published only with the music.

In *Threlfall and Norris*, the poet is identified as **Mariya Yanova** (1840–1875), although no source is given for this information (*T/N*, 41). In an obituary in the RGALI archive in Moscow, I found an obituary of one Mar'ya Nikolaevna Yanova (1840–1875). She was an actress in St. Petersburg who performed at the German Club and the Hall of the Nobility and was "a favorite of the public." She was known for her skill as a poetry recitalist, but there is no mention of her as a poet, nor is it likely a song by her would have published in Kiev in 1915.

The question remains, where did Rachmaninoff find this text, and who wrote it?

Meter. Binary. Mixed iambic pentameters and hexameters:

A ray of sunlight, smiling, lit the earth,
And sent its burning kisses to the dawn.

Music. Op. 4, no. 2. F Major. 4/4, Moderato. For Low Voice: a–c^{2}sharp. Composed in 1891 or 1892. First published with Opus 4 by Gutheil in 1893.

Dedicated to **Yúry Sergéyevich Sakhnóvsky** (1866–1930). Conductor, composer, music critic, close friend of Rachmaninoff's and Slonov's from the Conservatory years. He was the only one of them who was moderately well-off; his family gave Rachmaninoff a room in their large house for six weeks in the autumn of 1891 when he was ill (*B/L*, 37-9). He had a good music library at his house, including the scores of all Wagner's operas (*VOR 1*, 399). Rachmaninoff also dedicated Song 25 (Op. 14/4) to him.

Recordings. Arkhipova, Borisenko, Burchuladze, Christoff, Crona, Del Grande, Dolukhanova, Hvorostovsky, Koptchak, Leiferkus, Maynor, Milashkina, Mkrtchyan, Mróz, Oja, Olli, Orda, Pirogov, Podleś, Popescu, Reshetin, Siniavskaya, Söderström, Suchkova, Verbitskaya.

Transcriptions. *Cello:* Anthony Elliott, David Geringas. *Piano:* Arcady Volodos.

12 *В молчаньи ночи тайной*
In the silence of the secret night

Op. 4, No. 3

This 1844 poem of reverie "in the silence of the mysterious night" is an early poem that brought Afanasy Fet (1820–1892) to the attention of other writers as a poet: what they marvelled at was the way it expressed "in concentrated, clear, definite, and at the same time subtle language one of the most complex and elusive feelings of the heart" (*Fet*, 635). Rachmaninoff wrote the song at seventeen and revised it when he was nineteen, and the text does seem to fit what a young man might feel recalling a lost love, perhaps a first love. He remembers her smile, her silky hair in his fingers, but he also remembers things that were hurtful—her words had "cunning" in them; her gaze sometimes fell on him by chance, not by her choice; she made him confused and shy. He drives the painful memories out of his mind, but, against his will, he calls them back, and cannot, will not, forget her. These memories bring sadness, but this love nevertheless envelops him in something bright and elevated: her name is "sacred."

A sadness (*grust'*) is felt at the outset in the opening piano figure, falling sixths; these anticipate the falling sixths in the beginning of the vocal part, an improvement Rachmaninoff made when he revised the song in 1892 (*Martyn*, 71-4). This is not unlike the beginning of Tchaikovsky's "None but the lonely heart," though that interval is a falling minor seventh. Also like the famous Tchaikovsky song (which Rachmaninoff knew well as a boy, accompanying his sister Yelena, *B/L*, 6), when we think we have come to the end of the song, there is a continuation. This *forte* culmination (lines 8-9 of the text) is followed by a reprise sung *piano* at the end (the last two lines of the text); the falling sixths are heard again in the piano chords of the culmination. But despite the "sadness" they convey, Rachmaninoff put the song into a major key (D), and ended it in a beautiful, delicate coda with rising intonation.

As can be seen from the long list of recordings of the song, it has been a favorite of singers. The German soprano Lotte Lehmann (1888–1976) devoted an essay to it in her book about how to sing well-known lieder, recommending that it not be sung too slowly (*Lehmann*, 191-2). Fritz Kreisler, who befriended Rachmaninoff in the United States, arranged it for violin obbligato and recorded it with John McCormack; this arrangement seems to have had Rachmaninoff's approval (*T/N*, 42). Marian Anderson recorded it with a viola obbligato of William Primrose, and it was a standard recital number for her, as it was for Jussi Björling. These are all fine recordings of the song in English (McCormack did his own translation), but today singers like Placido Domingo and Renée Fleming perform it in Russian.

Rachmaninoff shortened Fet's poem by removing four lines from the middle of the poem. This is an improvement for his purposes: the song is less self-absorbed, more concentrated on the memories that conjure up a vision of his beloved in the mysterious night. He repeated some words and lines shown in bold below; the four omitted lines are shown at the end of the song.

О, долго буду я, в молчаньи ночи тайной,
Коварный лепет твой, улыбку, взор, **взор** случайный,
Перстам послушную волос, **волос твоих** густую прядь
Из мыслей изгонять, и снова призывать;
Шептать и поправлять былые выраженья
Речей моих с тобой, исполненных смущенья,
И в опьяненьи, наперекор уму,
Заветным именем будить ночную тьму,
Заветным именем будить ночную тьму.
О, долго буду я, в молчаньи ночи тайной,
Заветным именем будить ночную тьму.

O, dólga búdu já, v malchán'ji nóchi tájnaj,	Oh, long will I, in the silence of the mysterious night,
Kavárnyj lépet tvój, ulýpku, vzór, vzór sluchájnyj,	Your sly chatter, smile, glance, casual glance,
Perstám paslúshnuju valós, valós tvaíkh gustúju prját'	Hair pliant to my fingers, your thick shock of hair,
Iz mýslej izganját' i snóva prizyvát';	Banish from my thoughts and summon back again;
Sheptát' i papravlját' bylýje vyrazhén'ja	Whisper and improve past words
Rechéj maíkh s tabój, ispólnennykh smushchén'ja,	I spoke to you, so full of shy confusion,
I v ap'janén'ji, naperekór umú,	And in rapture, against all reason,
Zavétnym ímenem budít' nachnúju t'mú,	With your cherished name, awake night's darkness,
Zavétnym ímenem budít' nachnúju t'mu.	Awake night's darkness with your cherished name.
O, dólga búdu já, v malchán'ji nóchi tájnaj,	Oh, long will I, in the silence of the mysterious night,
Zavétnym ímenem budít' nachnúju t'mú.	Awake night's darkness with your cherished name.

Text. **Afanásy Fet**, 1844. First published with the title Элегия (Elegy) in *Otechestvennye zapiski* (Notes of the Fatherland) in 1844, but in subsequent editions untitled. The poem is found in songbooks from the 1860s on. Set in 1878 by B. A. Vietinghoff-Scheel; after Rachmaninoff, by Georgi Conus (Op. 9/2, 1895) and Leonid Nikolayev (1905).

Meter. Binary. Iambic hexameter:

Oh, long will I, in silence of the secret night,
Awake nocturnal darkness with your cherished name.

Music. Op. 4, no. 3. D Major. 4/4, Lento. For Middle Voice: b–f² sharp. First draft dated 17 October 1890, but revised in the autumn of 1892.

Dedicated to **Véra Dmítriyevna Skalón** (1875–1909). Youngest of the three Skalon sisters, Vera "fell in love" with Rachmaninoff, who also had tender feelings for her, in the summer of 1890 when they were all visiting the Satin family at Ivanovka. A part of her diary for that summer is in volume 2 of *VOR*. Even though Vera was only fifteen at the time, her diary contains revealing vignettes of Rachmaninoff at play and at work ("does he really think we don't know he's writing a piano concerto?"), his expert handling of horses, the summer rituals of swimming, boating, picnics, picking cherries in the orchard and berries in the garden; everyone going out to the fields to watch the mowing; the daily lessons in piano and English and French, even in the summer, for the girls; and the relationships between the three families—Satins, Skalons, and Silotis, and their many children, all cousins to each other.

Recordings. Anderson (in English), Arkhipova, Asawa, Atlantov, Battle, Björling (in English), Borodina, Burchuladze, Cehanovsky, Chaiter, Danto, Del Grande, Dimitrieff, Dolukhanova, Domingo, Fleming, Furdui, Furlanetto, Gedda, Gigli (in English), Gorin, Hendricks, Hvorostovsky, Kharitonov, Kisselburgh (in English), Kolomyec, Korshunov, Koshetz, Kullman (in English), Kurenko, Kushpler, Kuuzik, Labinsky, Larin, Lee, Leiferkus, Lemeshev, Levko, Lisitsian, Lloyd (in English), Magomayev, Makarina, McCormack (in English), Melton (in English), Merrill (in English), Milcheva, Mishura, Mkrtchyan, Mormon Tabernacle Choir (in English), Morozov, Nortsov, Ognivtsev, Oja, Olli, Orda, Petrenko, Pirogov, Podleś, Pogossov, Preobrazhenskaya, Rautio, Reizen, Rosing, Serkebayev, Shaposhnikov, Shumskaya, Silja, Simonova, Siniavskaya, Söderström, Stevens (in English), Storozhev, Suchkova, Tourel, Troyanos, Urmana, Valletti (in English), Weiler, Yeend.

Transcriptions. *Cello:* Anthony Elliott, Dmitri Ferschtman, David Geringas, Mischa Maisky, Felix Salmond, Brian Stucki. *Piano:* John McArthur, Earl Wild.

Lines 5–8, omitted from the song

Дыша порывисто, один,	Breathing fitfully, alone,
никем не зримый,	unseen by anyone,
Досады и стыда румянами	Burned by the blush of frustration
палимый,	and shame,
Искать хотя одной загадочной черты	Seeking the smallest hint of mystery
В словах, которые произносила ты…	In the words you spoke…

13 *Не пой, красавица* *Sing not to me, beautiful maiden*

Op. 4, No. 4

More than forty composers have written songs to this lyric by Alexander Pushkin (1799-1837), but Rachmaninoff's is the best known.

The earliest of them, called "a Georgian song," was written in 1828 by Mikhail Glinka (1804–1857). It is an unusual case of a lyric's being written for a melody Glinka already had. Glinka was twenty-four at the time and would study and travel for several more years before writing the operas for which he is known as the "father" of Russian music, but he was active in the cultural life of St. Petersburg and meeting Pushkin and other poets regularly. The Moscow playwright Alexander Griboyedov (1795–1829) was in the city the spring of 1828 between diplomatic missions to Persia. Griboyedov had spent time in Georgia and had a Georgian wife. In his memoirs, Glinka described meeting him, probably in late May (*Hodge*, 178): "I spent nearly a whole day with Griboyedov (author of the comedy *Woe from Wit*). He was a very good musician and gave me the theme (*tema*) of a Georgian song for which A. S. Pushkin shortly thereafter wrote the romance "Do not sing, sorceress, for me" (*Glinka 1955*, 334). Glinka must have played this melody for Pushkin, who knew Griboyedov and held him in the highest esteem, and Pushkin wrote the poem as a lyric for the song. Glinka's song (sung very well by Georgi Vinogradov in just over one minute) is a graceful, simple harmonization of the Georgian melody, but the music has no "oriental" qualities at all.

Mily Balakirev (1837–1910) did try to achieve an "oriental" sound in the song he wrote to this same lyric in 1865, called "Georgian Song"; it is four times longer than Glinka's song, partly because he uses Pushkin's final version of the poem which has four stanzas instead of two, but also because it has piano passages laden with exotic color from the very first notes. In Russian songs, "oriental" coloring is suggested by commonly used devices like decorative melismas and augmented seconds. These and other devices can be heard in Rimsky-Korsakov's "Oriental Romance" (Op. 2/2, 1865), or in Anton Rubinstein's "Persian Songs" (Op. 34, 1854); it is rare in Tchaikovsky, but he did write one "oriental" romance, "Canary" (Op. 25/4, 1875). Balakirev actually went to the Caucasus several times, looking for real Eastern folk music. His song is, from its very first notes, an extreme example of the usual techniques, plus others—highly colored, with four very elaborate melismas on the words "shore" and "distant." Richard Taruskin has shown that Balakirev's song has nothing in common with Georgian folk music, but is closer to Armenian, Turkish, and Persian influences (*Taruskin 1997*, 156). There are two beautiful recordings of Balakirev's song, by the Russian soprano Nadezhda Kazantseva, and by the French soprano Ninon Vallin, who sings it in French with an orchestra, which makes it sound rather like an aria from Borodin's opera *Prince Igor*.

The "oriental" coloring Rachmaninoff gives his song has features Taruskin traces back to Borodin's opera (and ultimately to Glinka): "sweeping" melismas, "syncopated undulation" together with a "drone bass" and "a chromatic accompanying line that in this case steadily descends along with the sequences of undulating melismas." In the climax of the song (the last two lines of the text) this descending chromatic line is given to the singer (ibid., 165-6). *Prince Igor* was not performed until two years before this song, but that was time enough for Rachmaninoff to understand how Borodin's music worked.

The song is well made, shaped into its different sections in a design that varies the material and provides continual interest. The piano and postlude are eight bars, each with a final arpeggio; the melody here does sound like it might be Georgian, though it is not. The first two lines are sung as recitative. The third word of the third line is sung as a long melisma that lasts one whole bar; when this line is repeated at the end of the song, the melisma is given to the piano instead of the voice. After the first stanza there is a "meno mosso" passage (slowed down a bit), and again after the second stanza. These are short piano interludes, pauses, which reflect on that element of the erotic which Taruskin points to as a feature of this music that conjures up the seductive East. In the third stanza, power and control are needed to sing first the crescendo rise to *fortissimo*, then diminuendo on the last line of the stanza. In the final two lines of the song, the singer has to negotiate a *pianissimo* descent from high A down the "descending chromatic line" through the concluding bars of the voice part.

This is a difficult song to perform well, not only for the singer, but for the pianist too. There are many outstanding performances among the more than eighty recordings I have found, and some unusual ones. Jennie Tourel's live Carnegie Hall recital with Leonard Bernstein is extraordinarily fine ensemble work: her long melisma is shapely and lovely, and she brings out beautifully the held middle syllable on "daljókij" in line 8; Bernstein commands the piano part from the first note—his arpeggio at the end of the introduction is arresting—no apologies here, only superb shaping everywhere; singer and pianist are entirely together on this recording. Among the unusual recordings are transcriptions of the song for trumpet and tuba, and, in an astonishing performance that conveys everything in the song beautifully except the words, Clara Rockmore on the theremin, accompanied by the Russian-American pianist Nadia Reisenberg, her sister.

Не пой, красавица, при мне
Ты песен Грузии печальной:
Напоминают мне оне
Другую жизнь и берег дальной.

Увы, напоминают мне
Твои жестокие напевы
И степь, и ночь, и при луне
Черты далёкой бедной девы!..

Я призрак милый, роковой,
Тебя увидев, забываю;
Но ты поёшь, и предо мной
Его я вновь воображаю.

Не пой, красавица, при мне
Ты песен Грузии печальной:
Напоминают мне оне
Другую жизнь и берег дальной.

Ne pój, krasávitsa, pri mné Ty pésen Grúzii pechál'naj: Napaminájut mné ané Drugúju zhýzn' i béreg dál'naj.	Do not sing for me, fair beauty, Your songs of sad Georgia: They remind me Of another life and distant shore.
Uvý, napamnájut mné Tvají zhestókije napévy I stép', i nóch, i pri luné Chertý daljókaj bédnaj dévy!..	Alas, they bring back memories, Your cruel melodies, Of the steppe at night, and, in the moonlight, The features of a poor maiden far away!..
Ja prízrak mílyj, rakavój Tebjá uvídev, zabyváju; No tý pajósh i preda mnój Jevó ja vnóf' vaabrazháju.	Seeing you, I forget That dear, fateful vision; But when you sing, again I imagine it before me.
Ne pój, krasávitsa pri mné Ty pésen Grúzii pechál'naj: Napaminájut mné ané Drugúju zhýzn' i béreg dál'naj.	Do not sing for me, fair beauty, Your songs of sad Georgia: They remind me Of another life and distant shore.

TEXT. **Aleksándr Sergéyevich Púshkin**, written 12 June 1828. Untitled. First published in 1828 in *Severnye Tsvety na 1829 god* (Northern Flowers for 1829). Glinka used Pushkin's early draft, which had only the first two stanzas; instead of *krasavitsa*, a beautiful girl or woman, this draft read *volshebnitsa*, sorceress (*Glinka 1955*, 334). Rachmaninoff's song uses Pushkin's final version of the poem, the one published in *Northern Flowers* and later with Pushkin's works.

More than forty composers have set this poem (a list of them is in *Vinokur and Kagan*, 221), including Pauline Viardot (1865), Ippolitov-Ivanov (Op. 4/7, 1884), and Rimsky-Korsakov (Op. 51/2, 1898). But the two earlier settings by Glinka (1828) and Balakirev (1865) discussed here are the most important.

Meter. Binary. Iambic tetrameter:

Your cruel refrains recall to me
Another life and distant shore.

Music. 1892 or summer of 1893. Op. 4, no. 4. A Minor. 4/4, Allegretto. For High Voice: e^1–a^2. Dedicated to **Natália Aleksándrovna Satiná** (1877–1951), who, after 1902, was Rachmaninoff's wife.

Recordings. Amaize, Arkhipova, Battle, Borisenko, Bryleva, Cebotari (in German), Celine, Chaiter, Christoff, Christova, Danto, Davrath, Davtian, Del Grande, Dilbèr, Dionne, Dnishev, Dodoka, Domingo, Eizen, Fagan, Fiset, Fleming, Galante, Gedda, Gmyria, Gorin, Gruberova, Guleghina, Guliayev, Hendricks, Hvorostovsky, Izotova, Kazarnovskaya, Kelessidi, Kennedy, Kharitonov, Kipnis, Korshunov, Koshetz, Kozlovsky, Kurenko, Kuuzik, Lapina, Larin, H. Lawrence, Lear, Lee, Leiferkus, Lemeshev, Ludwig, Magomayev, Makarina, Makarova, Mattila, McCormack (in English, with Fritz Kreisler's violin obbligato), Melton (in English, with violin obbligato), Milcheva, Mkrtchyan, Mok, Naoumenko, Nesterenko, Netrebko, Nezhdanova, Obraztsova, Ognivtsev, Olli, Petrov, Piavko, Pishchayev, Pons (in French, with cello and orchestra), Pusar, Raitscheff, Rautio, Rodgers, Rosing, Rouzaud (in French), Savenko, Shtoda, Shumskaya, Silja, Smirnov, Söderström, Sotkilava, Suchkova, Sumatchova, Talvela, Tear, Tourel, Vayne, Vishnevskaya, Weiler, Woytowicz (in Polish), Zelenina, Zhadan, Zhurina, Zimmermann.

Glinka: Irina Arkhipova, Nicolai Gedda, Boris Gmyria, Ivan Kozlovsky, Joan Rodgers, Alexander Vedernikov, Georgi Vinogradov, Galina Vishnevskaya.

Balakirev: Nicolai Gedda, Nadezhda Kazantseva, Ninon Vallin (in French), Georgi Vinogradov.

Rimsky-Korsakov: Alexei Martynov, Joan Rodgers.

Transcriptions. *Cello:* Dmitri Ferschtman, David Geringas, Tim Hugh, Nina Kotova, Mischa Maisky. *Oboe:* Eugene Izotov. *Piano:* Earl Wild. *Theremin:* Clara Rockmore. *Trumpet:* Rick Bogard. *Tuba:* Gene Pokorny.

14 *Уж ты, нива моя*
Harvest of sorrow

Op. 4, No. 5

In Russian folk songs, the singer often directly addresses the natural world, summoning it, speaking to it, using it as a metaphor for a state of the soul or a fateful outcome. In one common old folk song, the singer addresses the "wide open field" (*Sobolevskii 1*, 470):

Уж ты, поле мое, поле чистое,	Oh you, my field, virgin field,
Ты, раздолье мое, степь широкая!	You, my open space, wide steppe!
Ничего ты, поле, не породило!	You brought nothing, field, to life!

The poem by Aleksei Tolstoy that Rachmaninoff chose for this song starts out with the same *zachin*—the language, imagery, and rhythm of the opening line—but Tolstoy personalizes it, changing the image of the open field to a man's own field, a field planted and harvested, or buffeted by the wind and ruined. The crop sowed is "thoughts," the intentions and hopes of a life, the soul's dreams, the heart's loves, which have come to naught. The poem is not "a typical literary gloss on a folk subject" (*Harrison*, 45), but a potent reimagining of old formulas and poetic folk language. A failed crop was real and common in Tolstoy's (and Rachmaninoff's) day; that it is paralleled, in folk style, with the sorrow of a ruined life makes it a completely convincing vehicle for lament. The image still has its potency: W. G. Sebald recast a line from Chidiock Tichborne's 16th-century "Tower Verse," "My crop of corn is but a field of tares," into an epigraph to a chapter of his remarkable book *The Emigrants* (1992), given in English in the German original: "My field of corn is but a crop of tears."

Rachmaninoff's song is a skillfully worked out lament in folk style. Laments are "drawn-out" songs, sung in melismatic style. The song contains more than two dozen melismas, in groups of two or three notes. The pivotal notes are D (the tonic), A, and F, the latter interval being a minor sixth, which is heard in more than half the lines. These devices, plus tempo shifts, make the music sound like a drawn-out folk song, yet it is a continally interesting composed song. The second section, lines 4-6, is a dramatic crescendo; the next section (the field ruined) has arpeggios and dark rumblings in the piano. The voice part ends in a vocalise melisma (Ah!) beginning on the tonic and going up a minor sixth to a B flat fermata before the long, elaborate descent to the tonic. Christa Ludwig sings the song and vocalise beautifully; her pianist, Geoffrey Parsons, unlike some, plays only the arpeggios that are written in the score.

Уж ты, нива моя, нивушка,
Не скосить тебя с маху единого,

Не связать тебя всю во единый сноп!
Уж вы, думы мои, думушки,
Не стряхнуть вас разом с плеч долой,
Одной речью-то вас не высказать!
По тебе ль, нива, ветер разгуливал,
Гнул колосья твои до земли,
Зрелы зёрна все размётывал!
Широко вы, думы, порассыпались,
Куда пала какая думушка,
Там всходила люта печаль-трава,
Вырастало горе горючее. А! А!

Úsh tý, níva majá, nívushka,
Ne skasít' tebjá s mákhu jedínava,
Ne svjazát' tebjá fsjú va jedínyj snóp!
Úsh vý dúmy maí, dúmushki,
Ne strjakhnút' vás rázam s pléch dalój,
Adnój réchju-ta vás ne výskazat'!
Pa tebé l', níva, véter razgúlival,
Gnúl kalós'ja tvaí dó zemlí,
Zrély zjórna fsé razmjótyval!
Shyrakó vy dúmy parassýpalis',
Kudá pála kakája dúmushka,
Tam fskhadíla ljúta pechál'-travá,
Vyrastála góre garjúcheje. A! A!

Oh you, my field, dear field of mine,
You can't be mowed down at one stroke,
You can't be bound up in one sheaf!
Oh you, my thoughts, dear thoughts of mine,
You can't be shaken off with a single shrug,
You can't be told in a single tale!
Have you not been battered by the wind, field,
Your ears of grain bent down to the ground,
Your ripe grain scattered here and yonder!
You've been scattered, thoughts, far and wide,
And wherever a thought fell,
The bitter grass of sorrow sprouted up,
And grew into burning misery. Ah! Ah!

Text. **Alekséi Tolstóy**, 1854. Untitled. Earlier set by Viktor N. Paskhalov (1873) and Boris A. Vietinghoff-Scheel (1879); later by Cui (Op. 67/4, 1904). In line 2, *PSR* prints с маха (at a stroke) but I have kept the old genitive с маху used by Tolstoy and by Rachmaninoff in the *Gutheil* edition.

Meter. Imitation unrhymed folk line of nine, ten, or eleven syllables, with strong downbeats on the third syllable after the beginning of the line and the third syllable before the end of the line:

Who could mów you down in a síngle stroke,
Who could bínd you up in a síngle sheaf!

As *sung*, however, many more syllables are stressed.

Music. 1893. Op. 4, no. 5. D Minor. 4/4, with shifts to 7/4 and 6/4. Lento. For High Voice: g^1–b^2 flat. Dedicated to **E. N. Lýsikova**, hostess to Rachmaninoff and Slonov in Lebedin in 1893 (see *B/L*, 57).

Recordings. Anderson, Bolotin, Boons (in French), Christoff, Davrath, DeGaetani, Del Grande, Dodoka, Gedda, Hvorostovsky, Kipnis, Korshunov, Lapina, Lemeshev, Lisovsky, Ludwig, Milcheva, Mok, Naoumenko, Obukhova, Olli, Orda, Plishka, Pusar, Söderström, Suchkova, Talvela, Tkachenko, Tourel, Verrett, Yeend, Zimmermann.

Transcriptions. *Tuba*: Gene Pokorny.

15 *Давно ль, мой друг*
How long, my friend

Op. 4, No. 6

Poems by Count Arseny Golenishchev-Kutuzov (1848–1913) were set to music by Arensky, Balakirev, Cui, and others, but Mussorgsky's settings are the best known: the poet and the composer were close friends who collaborated on Mussorgsky's two song cycles, "Sunless" (1874) and "Songs and Dances of Death" (1875–7). Rachmaninoff used poems by Kutuzov for this song and two others, Songs 43 and 51.

This lyric tells a story about the separation and reunion of two lovers, an inherently dramatic theme which appealed to Rachmaninoff's dramatic side. The song begins as an elegy, "Andante tranquillo," rather in the style of Glinka or Dargomyzhsky (*Martyn*, 74). Then passion mounts. In the second stanza, the emotion is intensified in a crescendo and *fortissimo* in line 7. The third stanza begins *pianissimo*, but again the dynamics intensify to *fortissimo* to express the impatient passion in line 11; line 12 is sung *accelerando*. Those two lines are the turning point in the song. In the final stanza, separation is transformed into reunion, with a change of key from G Minor to G Major, and a change of tempo to "Agitato"; the voice part ends on a loud high B, but there is an optional D if the singer prefers the lower note.

The song is fresh and very attractive, but not easy to sing well. It calls for an engaged, nuanced performance that conveys the mounting passion, the ebb and flow of emotion leading to the culmination, where the music "takes flight" (ibid.). Rachmaninoff characteristically marks the score in detail to show gradations in tone and tempo, duration and emphasis. This song calls for fine musical judgment, not too slow, not too fast, always dynamic and alive. If sung too slowly, it loses its excitement and winning charm. Aleksei Ivanov is the only singer I have heard who takes the optional D instead of the high B at the end; but he is a baritone, and this is a song written for high voice. The performances by Elisabeth Söderström and Joan Rodgers are both very fine.

Давно ль, мой друг, твой взор печальный
Я в расставанья смутный миг
Ловил, чтоб луч его прощальный
Надолго в душу мне проник.

Давно ль, блуждая одиноко,
В толпе теснящей и чужой
К тебе желанной и далёкой
Я мчался грустною мечтой.

Желанья гасли... Сердце ныло...
Стояло время... Ум молчал...
Давно ль затишье это было?
Но вихрь свиданья набежал...

Мы вместе вновь, и дни несутся,
Как в море волн летучих строй,
И мысль кипит, и песни льются
Из сердца, полного тобой!
Из сердца, полного тобой!

Davnó l', mój drúk, tvój vzór pechál'nyj
Já v rasstaván'ja smútnyj mík
Lavíl, shtob lúch jevó prashchál'nyj
Nadólga v dúshu mné praník.

Davnó l', bluzhdája adinóka,
F talpé tesnjáshchej i chuzhój
K tebé zhelánnaj i daljókaj
Ja mchálsa grúsnaju mechtój?

Zhelán'ja gásli... Sérttse nýla...
Stajála vrémja... Úm malchál...
Davnó l' zatíshje éta býla?
No víkhr' svidán'ja nabezhál....

My vméste vnóf', i dní nesútsa.
Kak v móre vóln letúchikh strój,
I mýsl' kipít, i pésni l'jútsa
Is sérttse pólnava tabój!
Is sérttse pólnava tabój!

How long has it been, my friend, since I studied
Your sad gaze in the bleak moment of our parting,
So the farewell ray of light in your eyes
Would fill my soul for a long time.

How long has it been, wandering alone
In the pressing, alien crowd,
I've hastened to join you, my distant love,
As if in a sad dream?

Desires faded... My heart ached...
Time stood still... My mind was mute...
How long did this lull last?
But the whirlwind of reunion has come...

We're together again, and the days flow.
Like sea waves flying tall,
My mind seethes, and songs pour
From my heart, filled with thoughts of you!
From my heart, filled with thoughts of you!

Text. **Arsénii Arkádiyevich Goleníshchev-Kutúzov**, 1891. Untitled. First published in *Russkii vestnik* (Russian Herald) in April 1891. Set only by Rachmaninoff.

Meter. Binary. Iambic tetrameter:

How long I wandered in the crowd
And dreamt of you, my distant love...

Music. 1893. Op. 4, no. 6. G Minor, G Major. 3/4, 4/4. Andante tranquillo, Agitato. For High Voice: d^1–b^2.

Dedicated to **Ólga Andréyevna Goleníshcheva-Kutúzova** (1859–1924), whom the poet married in 1876. I have seen no evidence of Rachmaninoff's acquaintanceship with her, but his other song dedications are all to people he knew.

Recordings. Arkhipova, Borisenko, Del Grande, Dionne, Guleghina, Guryakova, Isakova, Al. Ivanov, Korshunov, Mirakian, Olli, Pusar, Rautio, Rodgers, Söderström, Suchkova.

Transcriptions. *Cello*: Petja Svensson. *Clarinet*: Wagner Campos. *Trumpet*: Sergei Nakariakov.

Six Romances, Opus 8 (1893)

At the end of September 1893, Rachmaninoff's teacher Nikolai Zverev died suddenly in Moscow: "We buried him yesterday. We're awfully sorry," he wrote the Skalon sisters on 3 October (*LN 1*, 227). At about the same time in Paris the poet Aleksei Pleshcheyev (1825–1893) died and was brought back to Moscow for burial on 7 October. Pleshcheyev's death was a public event, with poets and intellectuals paying tribute to a man who had stood for free expression of ideas under the police state of Nicholas I, who had been sent into exile for ten years in 1849, like his friend Dostoyevsky (for a fuller sketch of his life, see *TCS*, 152–3). Whether he attended that funeral or not, Rachmaninoff would have known about it, and may have been reminded that Pleshcheyev had been a source of texts for many composers, not only well-known composers like Tchaikovsky, Borodin, and Mussorgsky, but his very own grandfather Arkady (*Briantseva*, 179). In mid-October Rachmaninoff went to Kiev to conduct *Aleko*. While there, he visited the Lysikovs at Lebedin, where he wrote the six songs of Opus 8. All of them are settings of translations by Pleshcheyev from the German of Heine and Goethe and the Ukrainian of Shevchenko. If indeed he chose the texts after Pleshcheyev's death and wrote the songs before returning to Moscow, they were written in a matter of a few days.

Rachmaninoff was back in Moscow on October 25 when he learned the shocking news that Tchaikovsky had died of cholera in St. Petersburg. He sat down that day to write an "elegiac trio" for piano, violin, and cello, "to the memory of a great artist," taking as his model Tchaikovsky's own elegiac trio, Op. 50 (1882), written after Nikolai Rubinstein's sudden death in Paris. He finished the trio, Op. 9, on December 15. At the first all-Rachmaninoff concert on 31 January 1894, he performed the trio with two outstanding musicians, the violinist Julius Conus (1869–1942), just back after two years as concertmaster of the New York Philharmonic, and the cellist Anatol Brandukov (1856–1930), to whom Tchaikovsky had dedicated his *Pezzo capriccioso* for cello and orchestra (Op. 62, 1888) and to whom Rachmaninoff dedicated his Prelude and Oriental Dance for Cello and Piano (Op. 2, 1892) and, later, his Cello Sonata (Op. 19, 1901). The program of that concert included two of Rachmaninoff's songs, Song 14, Op. 4/6, and Song 19 from the new Opus 8 songs, a lament in folk style to a poem by Shevchenko (*LN 1*, 523). The songs were performed by a famous singer and professor at the Conservatory, the contralto Yelizaveta Lavrovskaya (1845–1919)—the woman who, in 1877, when Tchaikovsky was paying her a visit, suggested to him that *Eugene Onegin* might make a good subject for an opera (see *TCS*, 108).

Karl Gutheil bought the new set of songs, and his publishing house (named after its founder, his father Alexander) published them later that year.

16 *Речная лилея* *Water lily*

Op. 8, No. 1

For the first song in the set, Rachmaninoff chose Heine's lyric "Die schlanke Wasserlilie" (The slender water lily). A shy maiden and her lovesick swain are figured in images of a water lily looking up at the silvery moon, and then looking down at his pale reflection mirrored in the water. The nouns for lily and moon are feminine and masculine in both the German and Russian texts.

The song is a miniature that works very well. As frame there is a piano introduction and conclusion which are nearly identical. In these two brief sections, marked *Vivo* and *leggiero e grazioso*, drops of water are suggested with expressive little rising, then falling, ornamental appoggiaturas. An arpeggio in the second line of text announces the entrance of moonlight onto the scene.

In the voice part, the song slows down to Moderato. The vocal line has been criticized for lacking simplicity (*Norris*, 140), but the lyric describes a scene that is itself restive, looking up, looking down, with changing points of view, a sense of things coming into focus unexpectedly: reflections in water by moonlight. The declamatory voice part conveys this very well in its moves up and down the scale, embodying the lily at the high end up to G, and the moon at the low end down to B; the sudden coming into focus of the moonlight is rendered by the chromatic passage from A to dotted A sharp to B in the last word of the first stanza. A "mirror" effect (with variations) is at work in the voice part too, as points of view go back and forth every two lines.

Max Harrison rather crossly finds the piano frame "irritatingly skittish," but he is right in saying that the song needs "good understanding between singer and accompanist" (*Harrison*, 56). The recording by Zara Dolukhanova and Nina Svetlanova is an outstanding example of this.

Речная лилея, головку
Поднявши, на небо глядит.
А месяц влюблённый лучами
Уныло её серебрит.

И вот она снова поникла
Стыдливо к лазурным водам.
Но месяц всё бледный и томный,
Как призрак, сияет и там…

Rechnája liléja, galófku	The water lily, her head
Padnjáfshy, na néba gljadít.	Raised, looks up at the sky.
A mésjats vljubljónnyj luchámi	And melancholy, the amorous moon
Unýla jejó serebrít.	Illumines her with his silver beams.

I vót aná snóva paníkla	And now her head droops down again
Stydlíva k lazúrnym vadám.	Shyly toward the azure waters.
No mésjats fsjo blédnyj i tómnyj,	But the moon, all pale and lovelorn,
Kak prízrak, sijájet i tám...	Like a phantom, glimmers there too...

TEXT. **Alekséi Nikoláyevich Pleshchéyev**, 1845. First published in the almanac *Vchera i segodnia* (Yesterday and Today), 1846, no. 2. Translation of a poem by **Heinrich Heine** "Die schlanke Wasserlilie" (The slender water lily), 1831.

First set in Russian in 1882 by Eduard Goldstein (1851–1887), a cousin of the Rubinstein brothers, pianist and conductor, who premiered Mussorgsky's opera *Khovanshchina* in 1886. In German set by Carl Loewe (1847) and Robert Franz (1879).

METER. Ternary. Amphibrach, 3-foot:

The lily looks down at the water,
Reflecting the amorous moon.

MUSIC. October 1893. Op. 8, no. 1. G Major. 3/4, Vivo (piano introduction and conclusion), 9/8, Moderato (vocal part). For Middle Voice: b–g^2. First published with Opus 8 by A. Gutheil in Moscow in 1894.

Dedicated to **Adolph Yaroshévsky** (1863–1910), pianist and professor at the Moscow Conservatory. Rachmaninoff also dedicated to "kind, good Adolph AdolphovichYaroshevsky" his arrangement for voice and piano of the Russian Boatmen's song (1891, *LN* 2, 413).

RECORDINGS. Arkhipova, Del Grande, Dodoka, Dolukhanova, Fleming, Furdui, Keenlyside, Lee, Levko, Olli, Popescu, Rautio, Söderström, Suchkova.

TRANSCRIPTIONS. *Clarinet:* Wagner Campos.

17 *Дитя! как цветок, ты прекрасна*
Child! you are as fair as a flower

Op. 8, No. 2

The song begins with 35 eighth-note piano chords in 9/8 time, to be played *mezzo forte harmonioso*, that step up and then skip down, gradually descending like falling water. This 4-bar introduction and the 4-bar piano coda take up a third of the song's 25 bars, framing and supporting the very warm and expressive voice part with its tender lyric. It is a short, effective, lovely song, completely sincere, that conveys its sentiments directly, without ambiguity or irony. Rachmaninoff's cousin Alexander Siloti liked it so much that he transcribed it for solo piano and presumably played it in public.

Heinrich Heine (1797–1856) is the author of the original lyric (his German text will be found at the end of the song). One of Heine's best known lyrics, it has been set to music more times than any other German poem (*Draper*, 852). It has been called "classic in its simplicity" (*Russell*, 55), and yet it is a striking example of the different ways a lyric so "simple" can be read, depending on the reader.

The original poem is said to have been inspired by a "poor Jewish girl" Heine found "destitute" on a Berlin street (*Draper*, 852). If so, there is irony in it, implicit pity and pain, even a "j'accuse" addressed to society (or to God?), in this context of an innocent girl not likely to remain innocent for long.

For composers, Heine's lyric has been seen as a love poem, a statement of high Romantic love, adoring and chaste. Robert Schumann's exalted setting of the poem breathes serenity and purity; he included it in the cycle *Myrthen* (Myrtles, 1840) which he presented to his bride Clara on their wedding day. For a completely different take on this Romantic reading of the poem, D. H. Lawrence saw "Du bist wie eine Blume" as the worst kind of "sentimentality" and therefore "pornography," wondering "why should sadness strike through the heart because the maid was pure and beautiful?" In "praying God to keep her forever so pure," her sexuality is denied and she is condemned to be "an unhappy old maid, and not pure nor beautiful at all, only stale and pathetic" (*Lawrence*, 81).

A glance at Heine's original poem shows that it is not addressed to a child. Pleshcheyev's use of the word "child" introduces an ambiguity in Russian: it could mean a small child, or it could mean a young woman, especially a beloved, still innocent girl. In that meaning it is "poetic" but not uncommon in songs: an example is Tchaikovsky's serenade to Konstantin Romanov's lyric "Oh child! Beneath your window," Op. 63/6. In addition to this ambiguity, Pleshcheyev replaced Heine's image "sadness steals into my heart" with "I admire you and my soul comes alive." This pulls the ambiguity toward the "small child" interpretation, whether Pleshcheyev intended that or not. (Fet had earlier translated the poem without the word "child" and keeping Heine's "sadness"—it is, by the way, in exactly the same meter as Pleshcheyev's translation and could be sung to Rachmaninoff's music). It is no surprise, then, that Rachmaninoff's song is seen as a "simple blessing on a young child," "quietly attractive, matching the somewhat cloying sentimentality of the words" (*Martyn*, 83).

Certainly, as a lyric it lost in Pleshcheyev's translation what complexity of feeling it had. Musically, however, it is not "cloying," but moving and lovely, a song that engages the listener immediately. Rachmaninoff highlighted the two words that fall on the tonic ("soul" in line 4 and "God" in line 7), and marked for emphasis the piano chords accompanying the phrase "I admire you," as well as the last line and a half of the voice part. Even the shortest pause in performance is carefully marked, with a fermata sixteenth-note rest just before the last word. Like many of his songs, it is conceived as a performance, and is a challenge to perform well. Söderström and Ashkenazy bring it out warmly in an Andante on the brisk side; the baritone Andrei Ivanov sings it at a more leisurely walk, bringing beautiful tone and perfect diction to every word.

Дитя! Как цветок, ты прекрасна,
Светла, и чиста, и мила,
Смотрю на тебя и любуюсь,
И снова душа ожила...

Охотно б тебе на головку
Я руки свои возложил,
Прося, чтобы Бог тебя вечно
Прекрасной и чистой хранил.

Ditjá! kak tsvetók, ty prekrásna, Svetlá, i chistá, i milá, Smatrjú na tebjá i ljubújus', I snóva dushá azhylá...	Child! You are fair as a flower, Bright, and pure, and dear, I look at you and admire you, And again my soul is alive...
Akhótna-p-tebé na galófku Ja rúki svají vazlazhýl, Prasjá, shtoby Bókh tebjá véchna Prekrásnaj i chístaj khraníl.	Gladly would I lay My hands on your small head, Asking that God keep you Fair and pure forever.

Text. **Alekséi Pleshchéyev**, 1845. First published in the almanac *Vchera i segodnia* (Yesterday and Today), 1846, no. 2. Translation of a poem by **Heinrich Heine** "Du bist wie eine Blume" (You are like a flower), 1823 or 1824. First set in Russian by Otto Dütsch (1858); later by Pavel Chesnokov (Op. 1/3, 1902). A different translation of the poem by Afanasy Fet, "Kak tsvet ty chista i prekrasna," 1843, was set by Alexander Varlamov between 1843 and 1848.

There are innumerable settings in German—one count is "222 times: the record for German poems" (*Draper*, 852). These include Robert Schumann (Op. 25/24, 1840), Liszt (1844/1860), Anton Rubinstein (Op. 32/5, 1856), Hugo Wolf (1876), and Charles Ives (1891?).

Meter. Ternary. Amphibrach, 3-foot:

I ask that God keep you forever
As fair and as pure as a flower.

Music. October 1893. Op. 8, no. 2. E Flat Major. 9/8, Andante. For Middle Voice: d^1–f^2. First published with Opus 8 by A. Gutheil in Moscow in 1894. Transcribed for solo piano by Siloti (*T/N*, 50).

Dedicated to **Mikhaíl Slónov** (1868–1930), a singer (baritone), fellow student at the Conservatory, and close friend of Rachmaninoff's. He was in Lavrovskaya's singing class at the Conservatory. He sang Songs 10 and 12 in a recital in Kharkov with the composer in 1893 (*LN 1*, 207). Rachmaninoff also dedicated Song 1 to Slonov.

Recordings. Arkhipova, Borodina, Chaiter, Del Grande, Furdui, Gerzmava, Gorokhovskaya, Hvorostovsky, An. Ivanov, Lear, Leiferkus, Milcheva, Nortsov, Olli, Otdelenov, Rautio, Rozum, Semenchuk, Söderström, Suchkova.

Transcriptions. *Piano:* Leslie Howard.

Heine's original poem, from "Die Heimkehr", The Homecoming, 1823–24

Du bist wie eine Blume,
So hold und schön und rein;
Ich schau dich an, und Wehmut
Schleicht mir ins Herz hinein.

Mir ist, als ob ich die Hände
Aufs Haupt dir legen sollt,
Betend, daß Gott dich erhalte
So rein und schön und hold.

You are like a flower, so dear and lovely and pure; I look at you, and sadness steals into my heart. It seems to me I should lay my hands on your head, with a prayer that God keep you so pure and lovely and dear.

18 *Дума* *Brooding*

Op. 8, No. 3

The Ukrainian national poet Taras Shevchenko (1814–1861) was born a serf. He had artistic talent and could draw well; while still serving as a footman, he received some training in Vilnius and Warsaw, then in St. Petersburg, where he came to the attention of artists at the Academy. In 1838 the Russian artist Karl Bryullov sold a portrait of the poet Zhukovsky at auction for 2,500 rubles (it was bought by the Empress), and gave the sum to Shevchenko to buy his freedom (*Shevchenko 1964*, xiii). Though he stayed on in St. Petersburg working with Bryullov, he was also writing poetry and making visits to Ukraine; there he met members of the "Brotherhood of Sts. Cyril and Methodius," a Ukrainian organization which aimed at abolishing serfdom and establishing a liberal constitution. Under Nicholas I, even discussing such questions was grounds for imprisonment. He was arrested in Kiev in April 1847 and brought to St. Petersburg for interrogation, then banished to a remote fort on the Kazakhstan frontier to do military service for an indefinite period. Nicholas I added his own particularly cruel note to the sentence, ordering that he be forbidden to write and paint (Shevchenko nevertheless did paint and write poetry during his exile). Two years later, Aleksei Pleshcheyev was arrested for possessing a document considered seditious, and was banished, like Shevchenko, to the frontier. The two men met in the Cossack fortress town of Uralsk in 1850, where they were serving in the army, and became fast friends. After the death of Nicholas in 1855, exiles were gradually allowed to return home, Shevchenko in 1857 and Pleshcheyev in 1859. Pleshcheyev translated eight of Shevchenko's poems and his narrative poem "Naimichka" (The Hired Girl). Shevchenko thought of him as a "brother" (*Pleshcheev 1964*, 396).

Shevchenko's original Ukrainian poem of 1845, which is the text to this song, has no title. When Pleshcheyev translated it into Russian from a manuscript in 1858 he left the poem untitled; but for his collected poems three years later, Pleshcheyev called it "Duma." Rachmaninoff kept that title for his song. In Russian, poems called "Duma" were written by Lermontov, Khomiakov, Maikov, Tyutchev, and Pleshcheyev himself, to name but a few. The word means thought, reflection, a serious meditation, taking stock; what triggers it is a disturbing awareness of the absence of purpose and meaning in life—the life of his whole generation, as in Lermontov's poem, or one's own life, as in this poem of Shevchenko's. For Khomiakov and Pleshcheyev, it is a call to stop dreaming, to wake up, to stop blaming fate, and to take responsibility for one's life.

The song is declamatory, pensive through the phrase "all's asleep," with the piano singing more than the voice; then the meter changes to 4/4, and the first fortissimo appears in the voice part. The song is an outcry of the spirit for life, for meaning, for anything, good or bad, but not "coldness of heart" (marked Agitato). Rachmaninoff ends his song on a somber note that "bondage is fearful, heavy to bear." This is a foretaste of the stark ending of Song 39, "Excerpt from Musset" (Op. 21/6), "Oh, loneliness! Oh, poverty!" Barrie Martyn sees the theme of the present song as "the perpetual and losing struggle in life against fate," a theme which had already become a "keynote" in Rachmaninoff's songs (*Martyn*, 84). But the culmination of the song is the cry for life at the beginning of the last stanza; there is struggle and suffering here, but not defeat.

Проходят дни… проходят ночи;
Прошло и лето; шелестит
Лист пожелтевший; гаснут очи;
Заснули думы; сердце спит.
Заснуло всё… Не знаю я,
Живёшь ли ты, душа моя?
Бесстрастно я гляжу на свет,
И нету слёз, и смеха нет!

И доля где моя? Судьбою,
Знать, не дано мне никакой…
Но если я благой не стою,
Зачем не выпало хоть злой?
Не дай, о Боже, как во сне
Блуждать… остынуть сердцем мне.
Гнилой колодой на пути
Лежать меня не попусти,

Но дай мне жить, Творец,
О, дай мне сердцем, сердцем жить!
Чтоб я хвалил твой мир чудесный,
Чтоб мог я ближнего любить!
Страшна неволя! Тяжко в ней…

Prakhódit dní… prakhódit nóchi;	Days pass… nights pass;
Prashló i léta; shelestít	Summer's gone; the yellowed leaf
Líst pazheltéfshyj; gásnut óchi;	Rustles; my eyes grow dim;
Zasnúli dúmy; sérttse spít.	My thoughts are idle; the heart sleeps.
Zasnúla fsjó… Ne znáju já,	All's asleep… I wonder,
Zhyvjósh li tý, dushá majá?	Are you alive, my soul?
Besstrásna já gljazhú na svét,	I survey the world without passion,
I nétu sljós, i smékha nét!	Without tears, without laughter!

I dólja gde majá? Sud'bóju,	And where's my destiny? Fate,
Znat', ne danó mne nikakój...	I guess, hasn't given me one...
No jésli já blagój ne stóju,	But if I don't deserve a good one,
Zachém ne výpala khat' zlój?	Why didn't a bad one befall me?
Ne dáj, o Bózhe, kak va sné	Don't let me, God, as in a dream,
Bluzhdát'... astýnut' sérttsem mne.	Wander... grow cold in my heart.
Gnilój kalódaj na putí	Don't let me be a rotten log
Lezhát' menjá ne papustí.	That lies across the path.
No zhýt' mne dáj, Tvaréts,	But let me live, Creator,
Daj mne sérttsem, sérttsem zhýt'!	Let me live by my heart, by my heart!
Stob já khvalíl tvój mír chudésnyj.	So I can praise your wondrous world,
Shtob mók ja blízhneva ljubít'!	So I can love my neighbor!
Strashná nevólja! Tjáshka v néj...	Bondage is fearful! Heavy it is to bear...

Text. **Alekséi Pleshchéyev**, 1858. First published in *Sovremennik* (The Contemporary), 1858, no. 10. Untitled initially; later "Duma" (Thoughts). Translation of a poem by **Taras Shevchenko** "Минають дні, минають ночі" (The days pass by, the nights pass by, 1845). Set (in Russian) only by Rachmaninoff. He omitted the last three lines of the poem: "To live and sleep in freedom is more fearful! Terrible it is to live without leaving a mark—then life and death are one." Shevchenko's original poem was set by the well-known Ukrainian composer Nikolai Lysenko (1842–1912), who wrote music for a great many of the poems in Shevchenko's book of poems *Kobzar'* (The Bard, 1860).

Meter. Binary. Iambic tetrameter:

The days pass by, the nights pass by,
The summer's gone, the leaves turn pale,
My eyes grow dim, my thoughts are idle...

Music. October 1893. Op. 8, no. 3. D Minor. 3/4, 4/4, Moderato. For Middle Voice: c^1 sharp–g^2. First published with Opus 8 by A. Gutheil in Moscow in 1894.

Dedicated to the baritone **Leoníd Yákovlev** (1858–1919), who sang at the Mariinsky Theatre in St. Petersburg from 1887 to 1906. Rachmaninoff met him in March 1893 when Yakovlev gave the first performance in Moscow of Song 10 at a concert of the Russian Musical Society; it was such a success it had to be repeated. But Rachmaninoff had reservations about his singing and did not like the way he performed the song, singing it as if it were a salon piece, taking liberties and making changes in the score (*LN 1*, 215).

Recordings. Bock (in German), Del Grande, Koptchak, Leiferkus, Levko, Murzayev, Ognivtsev, Oja, Olli, Pirogov, Shaposhnikov, Söderström, Suchkova.

Lysenko: K. Sukhomlinova (*Ianin*, 533).

19 *Полюбила я на печаль свою* *The soldier's wife*

Op. 8, No. 4

The lament of the soldier's wife, like Song 14, "Harvest of Sorrow," is a "Russian" song in folk style. The pathos here is not that the woman is "left alone in a foreign country" (*Jackson*, 173), but that in marrying an orphan drafted into the army for twenty-five years, she is left without family and home, a menial outsider in the village living in "a stranger's hut."

Such long recruitments were lamented by Russian peasant women just as if a death had occurred, and in the same way. The song is simple, effective, and shows great economy of means. There are many good recordings of it, including two rare ones by men, Boris Christoff and Kalevi Olli. Especially fine are two different recordings by Jennie Tourel. In the later one, for Decca, she sings the second vocalise at the end with closed lips to good effect. "Her gentle approach, blaming nobody, is exactly right for this song" (ibid.)

Полюбила я,
На печаль свою
Сиротинушку
Бесталанного.
Уж такая доля
Мне выпала.
Разлучили нас
Люди сильные;
Увезли его,
Сдали в рекруты...
И солдаткой я,
Одинокой я,
Знать, в чужой избе
И состарeюсь.
Уж такая доля
Мне выпала.
А! А!

Paljubíla já	I fell in love
Na pechál' svajú	To my sorrow
Siratínushku	With a poor orphan
Bestalánnava.	An unlucky lad.
Ush takája dólja	Such is the fate
Mne výpala.	That has befallen me.
Razluchíli nas	Powerful folks
Ljúdi síl'nyje;	Separated us;
Uvezlí jevó,	They took him away
Zdáli v rékruty...	Made him an army recruit...
I saldátkaj ja	And I'm a soldier's wife,
Adinókaj ja,	All alone,
Znat', f chuzhój izbé	In a stranger's hut
I sastárejus'.	I'll grow old, it seems.
Ush takája dólja	Oh what a fate
Mne výpala.	Has befallen me.
A! A!	Ah! Ah!

Text. **Alekséi Pleshchéyev**, 1858. First published in *Narodnoe chtenie* (Popular Reading), 1860, no. 1. Untitled. Translation of a poem by **Taras Shevchenko** "Полюбилася я..." (I fell in love..., 1848). Earlier set by Dmitri Usatov, 1891. Usatov, a tenor admired by Tchaikovsky, was Chaliapin's teacher in Tiflis (*TCS*, 202, 298).

Meter. Imitation folk line of five syllables, downbeat on the third:

I'm a soldier's wife,
All alone I am,
I'll grow old, it seems,
In a stranger's hut.

Pleshcheyev keeps this arrangement throughout, with lines 5 and 6 and their repetition in the last two lines reading Уж такая мне/Доля выпала. Rachmaninoff reversed the word order of мне and доля in the song, a very minor change but one which allows a melisma on the first syllable of доля.

Music. October 1893. Op. 8, no. 4. G Minor. 4/4, Adagio sostenuto. For Middle Voice: f^1 sharp–g^2. First published with Opus 8 by A. Gutheil in Moscow in 1894. First performed by Yelizaveta Lavrovskaya on 31 January 1894 (*LN 1*, 523).

Dedicated to **Maríya Olfér'eva**, common-law wife of Rachmaninoff's father Vasily. They had a son, Nikolai, who was Rachmaninoff's half brother. He was still in high school in 1914, but left before graduation, and died young (in 1915?). Through his St. Petersburg cousins, Zoya and Arkady Pribytkov, Rachmaninoff regularly sent money to his father; he also apparently paid for Nikolai's school tuition (*LN 1*, 472, and *LN 2*, 74-9).

Recordings. Andreyeva-Delmas, Arkhipova, Bolotin, Borisenko, Borodina, Braslau, Christoff, El-Tour, Fiset, Furdui, Gorchakova, Guleghina, Kabaivanska, Karnobatlova-Dobreva, Kelessidi, Kurenko, M. Kuznetsova, Lapina, Lear, Lee, Levko, Makarina, Makarova, Maksakova, Mikhailova, Milcheva, Milina, Mkrtchyan, Obraztsova, Obukhova, Olli, Popescu, Price, Pusar, Radina-Figner, Rautio, Sari, Sharubina, Slobodskaya, Söderström, Suchkova, Sumachova, Tourel, Weiler, Zbruyeva, Zimmermann.

Transcriptions. *Cello:* Dmitri Ferschtman, Brian Stucki.

20 *Сон* *A dream*

Op. 8, No. 5

Of the six songs in Opus 8, this song to Heine's expressive lyric is the simplest and most beautiful. It is in two parts, with an eloquent brief piano interlude and coda. Each of the two parts is itself divided in two: an Allegretto phrase rising to the tonic E Flat on the last syllable of the third line of each short stanza; then Lento, with tender feeling, "But it was a dream."

Rachmaninoff scholars have all praised it. Here the composer "combines simplicity of vocal line with perfect musical balance" (*Norris*, 140). It has "a directness and economy that match the previous song; note the simple yet telling melodic line and the impulsive modulation for the brief piano interlude echoed in the coda" (*Harrison*, 57). Barrie Martyn judges it the best song in the opus: "The lyrical beauty of the vocal line and the restraint of the accompaniment make this the best song of the set, as Rachmaninoff himself saw" (*Martyn*, 84). Rachmaninoff told Lyudmila Skalon that he considered the song "especially successful," (*VOR 1*, 240).

Despite the symmetry and economy of the writing, it is a nuanced score with moving small details at telling moments: a C Flat on the second word of line 4; differently distributed dotted notes in the second stanza; a legato rising from E Flat to G on the last syllable of line 7. Despite repeated hearings, one never tires of this song. There are many good performances, but none better than that of the Armenian baritone Pavel Lisitsian.

И у меня был край родной;
Прекрасен он!
Там ель качалась надо мной...
Но то был сон!

Семья друзей жива была.
Со всех сторон
Звучали мне любви слова...
Но то был сон!

I u menjá býl kráj radnój; Prekrásen ón! Tam jél' kachálas' nada mnój... No tó býl són!	I too had a native land; So beautiful! A fir tree swayed above me there... But it was a dream!
Sem'já druzéj zhyvá bylá. Sa fsékh starón Zvucháli mné ljubví slavá... No tó býl són!	My family were living friends. And all around me Words of love were spoken... But it was a dream!

TEXT. **Alekséi Pleshchéyev**, 1845. First published in *Repertuar i Panteon* (Repertoire and Pantheon), 1846, no. 2. Untitled. Translation of a poem by **Heinrich Heine** "Ich hatte einst ein schönes Vaterland," (I once had a beautiful fatherland) from "In der Fremde" (In Exile), 1834.

There were a few earlier settings in Russian by minor composers. Grigori Demidov (1838–71) set Heine's poem to a different Russian translation by Mikhail Mikhailov (1858), called "То был лишь сон" (It was just a dream); there is a fine recording of it by the Soviet tenor Georgi Vinogradov.

In German, the poem has been set twice, by Leopold Damrosch and Eduard Lassen. The Lassen setting, translated into Russian by an unknown hand, was well known in Russia before the Revolution: it was recorded by several singers, including the tenor Andrei Labinsky in 1908, and the tenor Sergei Yudin in 1912, who also recorded the Rachmaninoff song (see below).

METER. Binary. Iambic, alternating 4-foot and 2-foot lines:

I also had a native land
So beautiful!
Above me there a fir tree swayed...
It was a dream!

MUSIC. October 1893. Op. 8, no. 5. E Flat Major. 3/4, Allegretto (first three lines of each stanza), Lento (last line of each stanza). For High Voice: e^1 flat–g^2. First published with Opus 8 by A. Gutheil in Moscow in 1894.

Dedicated to **Natália Dmítriyevna Skalón** (1868–1943), eldest of the three Skalon sisters, whom Rachmaninoff first met in 1890 when they all spent the summer as guests of the Satin family at Ivanovka. They were first cousins of the Satin children: Alexander Satin's sister Elizaveta was their mother. The Skalons lived in St. Petersburg. Natalia Skalon was Rachmaninoff's constant correspondent from 1890 to the spring of 1902, when he married Natalia Satina.

RECORDINGS. Arkhipova, Borele, Borodina, Chaiter, Christoff, Del Grande, Dionne, Dnishev, Dodoka, Fiset, Furdui, Furlanetto, Gedda, Gerzmava, Ghiaurov, Gorchakova, Hvorostovsky, Kabaivanska, Karnobatlova-Dobreva, Koptchak, Korshunov, Larin, Lear, Lee, Lemeshev, Lisitsian, Magomayev, Makarina, Makarova, Morozov, Naoumenko, Nesterenko, Nortsov, Obukhova, Ognivtsev, Oja, Olli, Piavko, Pusar, Rautio, Semenchuk, Serkebayev, Silja, Söderström, Sotkilava, Storozhev, Suchkova, Talvela, Yudin, Zimmermann.

Demidov: Georgi Vinogradov.

Lassen: Andrei Labinsky, Sergei Yudin.

TRANSCRIPTIONS. *Cello*: Petja Svensson. *Clarinet*: Wagner Campos.

21 *Молитва* *Prayer*

Op. 8, No. 6

Opus 8 ends with a song to a long melodramatic text by Goethe. A woman has coldly ignored a young man's innocent but passionate love, not even granting him a smile, with the result that he has pined away to his death; tormented by guilt, she asks God's forgiveness for her sin. It is an ambitious song, for which Rachmaninoff wrote some moving sections like the second stanza and the first three lines of the last stanza, marked *con moto*, with animated movement, where the singer describes the man's love and his death after long suffering. It is operatic in its use of recitative and aria-like material. Rachmaninoff clearly was aiming at a performance that would evoke compassion for the distraught woman's suffering, and he dedicated the song to a singer he admired very much for her performance in his opera *Aleko*. But despite the challenging material the song contains, it has not often been performed. Nevertheless, there are good recordings by Zara Dolukhanova, Galina Gorchakova, and others.

О, Боже мой!
Взгляни на грешную меня;
Я мучусь, я больна душой,
Изрыта скорбью грудь моя.
О, мой Творец, велик мой грех,
Я на земле преступней всех.

Кипела в нём младая кровь,
Была чиста его любовь,
Но он её в груди своей
Таил так свято от людей.
Я знала всё... О, Боже мой!
Прости мне, грешной и больной.

Его я муки поняла;
Улыбкой, взором лишь одним
Я б исцелить его могла,
Но я не сжалилась над ним.

Томился долго, долго он,
Печалью тяжкой удручён;
И умер, бедный, наконец.
О, Боже мой, о, мой Творец!
Тронься грешною мольбой...
Взгляни, как я больна душой.

O, Bózhe mój!
Vzgljaní na gréshnuju menjá;
Ja múchus', ja bal'ná dushój,
Izrýta skórb'ju grút' majá.
O, mój Tvaréts, velík moj grékh,
Já na zemlé prestúpnej fsékh.

Kipéla v njóm mladája króf',
Bylá chistá jevó ljubóf',
No ón jejó v grudí svajéj
Taíl tak svjáta at ljudéj.
Já znála fsjó… O, Bózhe mój!
Prastí mne, gréshnaj i bal'nój.

Oh my God!
Look down on me, a sinner;
I'm miserable, sick in spirit,
My heart is torn with remorse.
Heavenly Father, my sin is great,
There is no greater crime on earth.

His youthful blood was ardent,
His love was pure,
But he kept it secret, telling no one
For it was sacred to him.
I knew all this… Oh, Lord!
Forgive me, a sinner in pain.

Jevó ja múki panjalá;	I understood his torments;
Ulýpkaj, vzóram lish adním	With just a smile, a single glance,
Já b ystselít' jevó maglá,	I could have made him well,
No já ne zzhálilas' nad ním.	And yet I took no pity on him.
Tamílsa dólga, dólga ón,	He suffered for a long, long time,
Pechál'ju tjáshkaj udruchón;	In pain and deep sorrow;
I úmer, bédnyj, nakanéts.	And finally he died, poor soul.
O, Bózhe mój, o, mój Tvaréts!	Oh, Lord, oh, heavenly Father!
Trón'sa gréshnaju mal'bój...	Hear my sinful prayer...
Vzgljaní, kak já bal'ná dushój.	Behold, how my soul is in pain.

Text. **Alekséi Pleshchéyev**, 1845. First published in *Sovremennik* (The Contemporary), 1846, no. 4. Title: Молитва (Prayer). Translation of a poem by **Johann Wolfgang von Goethe** "Sieh mich, Heil'ger, wie ich bin, eine arme Sünderin" (Behold me, Lord, wretched sinner that I am) from Goethe's 1775 Singspiel "Erwin und Elmire," based on Oliver Goldsmith's ballad "The Hermit, or Edwin and Angelina," 1764. Set in Russian only by Rachmaninoff; in German, by Nicolai Medtner (Op. 6/7, 1904-5).

Meter. Binary. Iambic tetrameter:

With just a smile, a single glance,
I could have made him well again...

Music. October 1893. Op. 8, no. 6. C Minor. 4/4, changing to 3/4 in the *con moto* sections. Moderato. For High Voice: c^1–a^2. First published with Opus 8 by A. Gutheil in Moscow in 1894.

Dedicated to **Maríya Adriánovna Deisha-Sionítskaya** (1859–1932), a dramatic soprano, who sang the role of Zemfira in the first performances of Rachmaninoff's opera *Aleko*.

Recordings. Borele, Dodoka, Dolukhanova, Gorchakova, Guleghina, Levko, Olli, Pusar, Rautio, Rodgers, Söderström, Suchkova.

Medtner: Susan Gritton.

Twelve Romances, Opus 14 (1896)

With the death of Tchaikovsky in October 1893, "my career, which had begun so promisingly with Tchaikovsky's support, came to a halt" (Rachmaninoff's "Dictated Reminiscences," *LN I*, 54). Tchaikovsky had encouraged him, attending rehearsals of his opera at the Bolshoi Theater and showing his enthusiastic approval after the performance. Tchaikovsky persuaded the Bolshoi to produce his own short opera *Iolanta* on a double bill with *Aleko*, and he promised to conduct Rachmaninoff's first orchestral score "The Crag," a fantasy for orchestra, in a concert in St. Petersburg in January 1894. But those plans fell through with Tchaikovsky's death. His last helping hand came in the form of his publisher Peter Jurgenson, who bought "The Crag" and published it as Op. 7 in 1894. Rachmaninoff now had two publishers. Gutheil bought everything the composer offered him, his two sets of songs and his early piano pieces, Opuses 5, 10, and 11, this latter set frankly written for the money and without a dedication. But from 1894 to 1897 he found it "harder and harder to live" (ibid.) because the independence he needed to compose anything on a large scale was constantly being interrupted by his need to give lessons in order to support himself. Nevertheless, it was during this difficult period that he began sending money to his mother to help her make ends meet.

In the first half of the summer of 1895 Rachmaninoff again took a summer job in the country, giving a boy his daily piano lesson. In August he went to Ivanovka, where he read the proofs of "The Crag" and orchestrated the "Capriccio on Gypsy Themes," Op. 12, which Gutheil later published. He had been living the previous year alone in furnished rooms in a rooming house called "America," not far from the Conservatory. He had many good friends on the faculty of the Conservatory, but the director, Safonov, had feuded with his cousin Siloti, and his hostility extended to Siloti's relatives (*B/L*, 76). Rachmaninoff was cheerless at the thought of returning to Moscow in the fall, living alone and on little money. He lined up a salaried teaching post at a girls' school, where he could teach classes instead of private lessons; the directress was understanding, doing what she could to shorten his hours. That winter, the Satins moved to a larger house and invited him to live there in a bedroom studio of his own, which occupied the whole third floor. This excellent arrangement lasted until Rachmaninoff's marriage in 1902: being with the Satins, especially the younger generation, was one thing he could almost always count on to cheer his spirits.

Despite Safonov's boycott of him as a soloist in concerts of the Russian Musical Society, he was not forgotten as a pianist, and occasional engagements in Moscow, Kiev, and other cities did turn up. But when he returned to Moscow from Ivanovka in the fall of 1895 (with his finished First Symphony in hand), he needed a good paying engagement. He signed a contract to do a three-month musical tour of Poland and Russia as an accompanist to a then famous Italian violinist, Teresina Tua. He would perform some solo pieces, but mostly he was present to accompany her violin numbers. These failed to inspire him, nor was there anything rewarding artistically for him in what he was doing. Moreover, the long distances travelled from town to town in November, sometimes in unheated horse-drawn carriages, made the conditions of the tour intolerable. When the tour manager violated his contract by not paying him when his fee was due, Rachmaninoff quit the job and returned to Moscow with relief, giving as his excuse the broken contract.

A dry spell followed in 1896. In April he wrote Natalia Skalon that he felt "old, sick, and unhappy," and was disheartened by "people, circumstances, my own music, and alcohol." He was so poor the eight kopecks for a stamp had to be found. He complained that he was "unrecognized as a musician," even though he had written "a pretty good song" for her (Song 20), a song "that has something worthwhile to say" (*LN 1*, 249). This self-deprecation was tossed off in a joking style, but he wanted to be taken seriously and felt frustrated that he was not.

He did meet regularly with other younger musicians at the house of Sergei Taneyev. He brought his symphony to show them, but Taneyev's first impression was that the musical themes (based on traditional Russian Orthodox chants) seemed "pale" (*Sabaneev*, 95-6). One of their topics that spring was Wagner: Taneyev, Scriabin, Goldenweiser, Igumnov, and others were going through Wagner's operas together, everyone in turn playing parts at the piano. At one point during the first of two sessions devoted to *Tristan und Isolde*, Rachmaninoff, sitting in a corner in a rocking chair, was heard to mutter "only 1,500 pages to go" (ibid., 134).

A crisis forced him into action later that year: a substantial sum of money that did not belong to him was stolen from him on a train, and this debt had to be repaid (*LN 1*, 375). Rachmaninoff sat down in the fall of 1896 to write some songs and piano pieces he could sell to Gutheil to pay off this debt. He wrote eleven new songs in October for the new Opus 14, adding to them one song already written two years earlier; these were published by Gutheil before the end of the year. Then he composed his six "Moments musicaux" for piano, Op. 16, which he sold to Jurgenson, who also published his Six Choruses for women's or children's voices with piano, Op. 15. He dedicated the piano pieces to his new friend, the composer and musical ethnographer Alexander Zatayevich (1869–1936), whom he had met in Łódź on his tour with the Italian violinist.

The texts Rachmaninoff chose for the new songs are of varied quality, which he realized, confessing to Zatayevich "I work systematically [to finish the songs quickly], but on the other hand it means my taste is not always especially discriminating" (*LN 1*, 253). Nevertheless, at least half the songs in Opus 14 are among Rachmaninoff's best.

22 *Я жду тебя* *I'll wait for you*

Op. 14, No. 1

Any Russian speaker who has ever heard Rachmaninoff's songs recognizes this song immediately because the basic musical phrase of the song is made out of the first three words, and these words are a common phrase everyone uses on a daily basis in Russian. In English, we might say "I'll wait for you" or "I'll be waiting for you" or "I'll expect you" or "I'll see you then," depending on the situation. The musical phrase Rachmaninoff found for these three words—four syllables—is very striking, up a sixth on the black keys for the first two syllables, then down a sixth on the adjacent white keys for the third word "you" (tebjá). This opening phrase is repeated at the beginning of the second stanza and at the end of the song, but each time higher than before.

As a lyric, the images of dark veils and perfumed shadows are effective in suggesting the erotic implications of this rendezvous: a woman (the adjective in the penultimate line is feminine) is waiting to meet her lover, with passion, longing, and eagerness to surrender. The music for the last stanza, to be sung "con moto" (with energetic movement), conveys this mounting passion well, although the piano coda has been criticized as a "gratuitous purple patch" (*Martyn*, 109). The song is very effective in performance, and singers, men as well as women, have found it attractive.

Я жду тебя! Закат угас,
И ночи тёмные покровы
Спуститься на землю готовы
И спрятать нас!

Я жду тебя! Душистой мглой
Ночь напоила мир уснувший
И разлучился день минувший
На век с землёй!

Я жду! Терзаясь и любя,
Считаю каждыя мгновенья,
Полна тоски и нетерпенья.
Я жду тебя!

Ja zhdú tebjá! Zakát ugás,	I'm waiting for you! Dusk has fallen,
I nóchi tjómnyje pakróvy	And night's dark veils
Spustítsa ná zemlju gatóvy	Are ready to descend to earth
I sprjátat' nás!	And make us hidden.

Ja zhdú tebjá! Dushýstaj mglój	I'm waiting for you! Night has suffused
Nóch napaíla mír usnúfshy,	The sleeping world with fragrant shadows
I razluchílsa dén' minúfshy	And the passing day has said farewell
Na vék z zemljój!	Forever to the earth!
Ja zhdú! Terzájas' i ljubjá,	I'm waiting! In torment and in love,
Shchitáju kázhdyje mgnavén'ja,	I count each moment,
Palná taskí i neterpén'ja.	In longing and impatience.
Ja zhdú tebjá!	I'm waiting for you!

Text. **Maríya Ávgustovna Davídova**, 1893. Untitled. Signed M. (A.) Davidova. First published in the theatrical and musical journal *Artist* (Artiste), 1893, no. 11, p. 133. (This issue of the St. Petersburg journal contains an interesting, deeply felt tribute to Tchaikovsky, who had just died.) Set by several minor composers before Rachmaninoff, including Erik Meyer-Gelmund (1893): the recording of Meyer-Gelmund's song below by Konstantin Isachenko uses gender-neutral endings.

The poet's dates are unknown. She was also a biographer and musicologist. Her surname, a common one, can be spelled Davydova, and that is how she spelled it in two books she published on Meyerbeer (1892) and Schumann (1893). Her father was a professor of mathematics at Moscow University. Her uncle was Carl Davidov (Karl Davydov, 1838–89), Russian cello virtuoso; his cello, the "Davidoff Stradivari" made in 1712, was owned by Jacqueline du Pré and is now owned by Yo-Yo Ma.

Meter. Binary. Iambic tetrameter, with the last line shortened to two feet:

I'll wait for you! When darkness falls
To cover us and keep us hidden,
In fragrant shadows of the night,
I'll wait for you!

Music. 1894 (date on the manuscript). Op. 14, no. 1. F Major. 4/4, Largo. For High Voice: c–b^2 flat. First published with Opus 14 by A. Gutheil in Moscow in 1896.

Dedicated to **Lyudmíla Dmítriyevna Skalón** (1874–1962), second of the three Skalon sisters, who knew Rachmaninoff from 1890 to 1917. Like her sisters, she corresponded with the composer, and, under her married name (Rostovtsova), she wrote an interesting memoir of him (*VOR 1*, 232-50).

Recordings. Arkhipova, Asawa, Borele, Borodina, Diciute-Treciokiene, Dionne, Dodoka, Furdui, Gmyria, Gorokhovskaya, Guleghina, Hvorostovsky, Izotova, Kazarnovskaya, Kelessidi, Kushpler, Labinsky, Lee, Makarina, Makarova, L. Maslennikova, Milcheva, Mkrtchyan, Oja, Olli, Podleś, Preobrazhenskaya, Pusar, Rautio, Rodgers, Rudenko, Serkebayev, Shpiller, Silja, Simonova, Siniavskaya, Söderström, Suchkova, Sumatchova, Vishnevskaya, Zimmermann.

Meyer-Gel'mund: Konstantin Isachenko (1908).

23 *Островок* *The isle*

Op. 14, No. 2

In contrast to the preceding song, "The isle," with a text by Shelley, is distinguished by its great economy of means. Laconic, restrained, delicate, it is a musical *paysage* that evokes a sense of stillness appropriate to Shelley's lyric. The well-executed translation is by Konstantin Balmont (1867–1942), who translated Shelley's poetry in the 1890s. He described this poem, one of Shelley's last, as "a tender cameo"; to Shelley's purely pictorial description he adds the image of dreamlike tranquillity in the last line. Rachmaninoff later wrote two very good songs to Balmont's own original lyrics (Songs 66 and 83).

The first two stanzas are declamatory, built around the note D, which the singer returns to and repeats again and again. With the third stanza there is a three-bar stirring of melody that reaches down lower in the scale, but only for the first two lines of the stanza; then the song returns to the declamatory line centered on the repeated D. The piano part is "two statements of a descending scale, separated by an inspired, voluptuous three-bar juxtaposition of G Major and E-flat Major harmonies" (*Norris*, 142).

Из моря смотрит островок,
Его зелёные уклоны
Украсил трав густых венок,
Фиалки, анемоны.

Над ним сплетаются листы,
Вокруг него чуть плещут волны,
Деревья грустны, как мечты,
Как статуи, безмолвны.

Здесь еле дышит ветерок,
Сюда гроза не долетает,
И безмятежный островок
Всё дремлет, засыпает.

Iz mórja smótrit astravók,
Jevó zeljónyje uklóny
Ukrásil tráv gustýkh venók,
Fiálki, anemóny.

At sea there lies a little isle,
Its slopes of green a carpet thick
With grasses dense and lush,
Violets and anemones.

Nad ním spletájutsa listý,
Vakruk nevó chut' pléshchut vólny,
Derév'ja grúsny, kak mechtý,
Kak státui, bezmólvny.

Leafy canopies spread above,
Waves lap lightly all around;
Tall stand the trees, sad as dreams,
Silent as statues.

Zdés' éle dýshyt veterók,	A light breeze barely stirs the air,
Sjudá grazá ne daletájet,	No storm can venture there,
I bezmjatézhnyj astravók	And in tranquility the little isle
Vsjó drémlet, zasypájet.	Dreams gently on, falling into sleep.

Text. **Konstantín Dmítriyevich Balmónt**, 1892. Translation of a poem by **Percy Bysshe Shelley** (1792–1822), shown below. First set by Rachmaninoff; later settings by Leonid Nikolayev (1902), Sergei Taneyev (Op. 17/1, 1905) and Reinhold Glière (Op. 55/2 for women's chorus, 1911). The Shelley poem has been set in English by Percy Fletcher, Eric Fogg, John Gerrard Williams, and Charles Wood; in Swedish by John Fernström (*Pollin*).

Meter. Binary. Iambic, 4-foot, with a 3-foot line at the end of each stanza:

At sea there lies a little isle,
Its slopes of green a carpet thick
With lovely grasses dense and lush,
Anemones and violets.

Shelley's poem (below) is trochaic, with first and last two lines iambic.

Music. 1896. Op. 14, no. 2. G Major. 4/4, Lento. For High Voice: e[1] flat–g[2]. First published with Opus 14 by A. Gutheil in Moscow in 1896.

Dedicated to **Sófya (Sophia) Aleksándrovna Satiná** (1879–1975), Rachmaninoff's cousin and younger sister of his wife Natalia. She was in close touch with the composer for most of his life and wrote the key memoir of him (*VOR 1*, 12-115); she assisted Sergei Bertensson and Jay Leyda when they were writing their biography of Rachmaninoff in the late 1940s (*B/L*).

Recordings. Arkhipova, Borele, Borg, Dionne, Dodoka, Gedda, Guleghina, Kharitonov, Koshetz, Kozlovsky, Lapina, Larin, Lee, Lemeshev, Levko, Makarina, Olli, Pusar, Rodgers, Rosing, Savenko, Shumskaya, Slobodskaya, Söderström, Suchkova, Sumatchova, Tear, Troyanos, Valletti (in English).

Taneyev: Vassily Savenko, Evgeny Vladimirov, Nina Zaznobina.

Transcriptions. *Cello:* Anthony Elliott. *Piano:* John McArthur, Earl Wild.

Shelley's original poem, "The Isle", 1822

There was a little lawny islet
By anemone and violet,
Like mosaic, paven:
And its roof was flowers and leaves
Which the summer's breath enweaves,
Where nor sun nor showers nor breeze
Pierce the pines and tallest trees,
Each a gem engraven;—
Girt by many an azure wave
With which the clouds and mountains pave
A lake's blue chasm.

24 *Давно в любви*
So long our love has known so little joy

Op. 14, No. 3

A common theme in the Russian romance is the notion "gone are the days," to which is often added "and they will not return." One well-known turn-of-the-century popular romance on this theme has the refrain "the chrysanthemums in the garden have long since faded," and goes on to say "but love still lives in my ailing heart" (*Petrovskii 1997*, 92). The poet Osip Mandelstam, incidentally, once tried to perform that classic Russian sentimental romance at the "Stray Dog" cabaret in Petrograd in 1915 (*Ivanov 1994*, 342).

The present Rachmaninoff song uses a late lyric by Afanasy Fet that takes as its starting point this same theme: "the joy in our love has long since faded." However, this being a love lyric by Fet, it is not sentimental, but rather has emotional depth and psychological realism. Fet's lyric implies a relationship with its own particular story; the story remains untold, but the emotional impasse is felt as something clear and authentic. In this case, the man knows the joy will not return, but the woman is still "afflicted" and cannot let go; the two lovers are left with their own, different, feelings of vulnerability and pain.

Musically, Rachmaninoff's song is as original a departure from the cliches of the sentimental romance as Fet's lyric. It is a challenging text to set to music. The summing up in the first stanza of the lyric is in a kind of shorthand, a fast succession of images one after the other, ending in the scattering of rose petals and lovers' dreams. So too the logjam of conflicted feelings in the second stanza of the poem. The rhythm is a very unusual alternating binary and ternary verse line, which impels the forward drive of accumulated emotions.

The voice part of the song conveys this emotional turbulence in restless, chromatic declamatory lines with falling intonation. The ends of lines 2, 4, and 8 are "sinking" cadences, falling sixths, with the first note doubled to a quarter note for emphasis; they seem to fall into sadness and resignation until the voice picks itself up again. The score itself is restless, with frequent changes in meter to reflect the changing rhythms of Fet's lines, and there are numerous changes in the notations for loudness, speed, style, and emphasis. It is sung "Allegro," not as a slow lament; it has a kinetic drive which is quite original. The engaging piano part gives harmonic support to the voice, but the eloquence of the song comes out of the rather austere, brave, emotionally honest voice part, with its longing for resolution. The song calls for a supple, elastic performance that expresses all this, such as the outstanding recording by the Russian contralto Valentina Levko.

Давно в любви отрады мало.
Без отзыва вздохи, без радости слёзы;
Что было сладко, горько стало,
Осыпались розы, рассеялись грёзы.

Оставь меня, смешай с толпою!
Но ты отвернулась, а сетуешь, видно,
И всё ещё больна ты мною.
О, как же мне тяжко, и как мне обидно!

Davnó v ljubví atrády mála.	So long our love has known so little joy.
Bez ódzyva vzdókhi, bez rádosti sljózy;	Unanswered sighs, unhappy tears;
Shtó býla slátka, gór'ka stála,	What was sweet has turned bitter,
Asýpalis' rózy, rasséjalis' grjózy.	The roses have lost their petals, the dreams have scattered.
Astáf' menjá, smesháj s talpóju!	Let me go, lose me in the crowd!
No tý atvernúlas', a sétujesh, vídna,	But you turned away, yet still feel regret,
I fsjó jeshchó bal'ná ty mnóju.	Still love me, still cling to this affliction.
O, kág zhe mne tjáshka, i kák mne abídna!	Oh, how hard this is for me, how it hurts me!

Text. **Afanásy Afanásiyevich Fet**, 24 June 1891. Untitled. First published in *Russkoe obozrenie* (Russian Review) in 1891, no. 12, p. 516. Set only by Rachmaninoff.

Meter. Alternating Binary and Ternary. Odd lines of 4-foot Iambs and even lines of 4-foot Amphibrachs:

So long our love has known no joy.
Our sighs go unanswered, our tears are unhappy,
What once was sweet is bitter now,
Our dreams are all scattered like petals of roses.

Music. October 1896. Op. 14, no. 3. F-sharp Minor. 4/4, 2/4, 9/8, 12/8, 6/8, Allegro. For Low Voice: g sharp–f^2 sharp. First published with Opus 14 by A. Gutheil in Moscow in 1896.

Dedicated to **Zóya Arkádievna Pribýtkova** (1892–1962). Her grandmother was a sister of Rachmaninoff's father. Zoya was a favorite cousin of Rachmaninoff's, a pianist and theater director, who wrote an interesting memoir about the composer's visits to St. Petersburg, where she lived (*VOR* 2, 52-89).

Recordings. Borisenko, Chaiter, DeGaetani, Del Grande, Gorokhovskaya, Isakova, Lemeshev, Levko, Murzayev, Ognivtsev, Olli, Podleś, Popescu, Semenchuk, Söderström, Suchkova.

25 *Я был у ней* *I came to her*

Op. 14, No. 4

Aleksei Koltsov (1809–1842) was the son of a cattle merchant in the town of Voronezh. His father took him out of school after one year to put him to work; he spent his boyhood and youth in the Don steppe, herding cattle and driving them to market. He lacked education but he was literate and had a passion for poetry even in his young years out on the steppe. Before 1830, he wrote romantic and sentimental verse in the style of the school of Zhukovsky, strongly influenced by German sources. His real contribution was made after that, in his "Russian songs" written in a "folk" style, not copies of folk songs, but original songs on themes close to the folk spirit, like "Грусть девушки," a girl's sadness, the complaint of a girl whose lover has gone away, one of Alexander Gurilyov's best songs. Many of Koltsov's lyrics are put into the voice of a woman; others express "a typically Russian longing for freedom, adventure, and elbow room" (*Mirsky*, 131). Koltsov's "Russian" songs written after 1830 were immediately admired by his contemporaries, including Pushkin and Turgenev, and have become "classics."

Although Rachmaninoff later used two of Koltsov's "Russian" texts in Songs 50 and 60, the text of this song belongs to the poet's earlier period. It is an innocent, naive love song, put into the mouth of a young man. In the third stanza of Koltsov's lyric, the two lovers kiss, but Rachmaninoff omitted that from the song, so that it remains a song of declarations of "true love" and vows of fidelity. The song "deftly catches the exhilaration of a love that is mutual, with its eager vocal line and arpeggiate accompaniment" (*Martyn*, 109). There is a suspicion that the girl's words may be too good to be true. Nevertheless, it is an ardent love song, which some very good singers have found attractive.

Я был у ней, она сказала:
«Люблю тебя, мой милый друг!»
Но эту тайну от подруг
Хранить мне строго завещала.

Я был у ней, на прелесть злата
Клялась меня не променять;
Ко мне лишь страстию пылать,
Меня любить, любить, как брата.

Я был у ней, я вечно буду
С её душой душою жить.
Пускай она мне изменит,
Но я изменником не буду.

Ja býl u néj, oná skazála:	I came to her, and she told me:
"Ljubljú tebjá, mój mílyj drúk!"	"I love you, my dear friend!"
No étu tájnu at padrúk	But made me take a solemn vow
Khranít' mne stróga zaveshchála.	To keep this secret from her girlfriends.
Ja býl u néj, na prélest' zláta	I came to her, and she swore
Kljalás' menjá ne pramenját';	Not to forsake me for the lure of gold;
Ka mné lish strástiju pylát',	To burn with passion for me alone,
Menjá ljubít', ljubít' kak bráta.	To love me, to love me, like a brother.
Ja býl u néj, já véchna búdu	I came to her, and will forever
S jejó dushój dushóju zhýt'.	Live with her in my heart.
Puskáj aná mne izmenít,	Let her betray me if she will,
No ja izménnikam ne búdu.	I will never be a traitor.

TEXT. **Alekséi Vasíliyevich Kol'tsóv**, 1829. Untitled. First published in 1846 in the posthumous edition of Koltsov's poems; this edition had an introduction by Vissarion Belinsky, who befriended the poet and encouraged him, helping him get his poems published and introducing him to other writers. First set in 1860 by a minor composer, Nikolai Trubetskoy; in 1863 by Nikolai Derviz; in 1868 by Alexander Dubuque. Rachmaninoff omitted the third stanza, shown below.

METER. Iambic tetrameter:

She made me take a solemn vow
To keep this secret from her friends.

MUSIC. October 1896. Op. 14, no. 4. E-flat Major. 4/4, Vivente. For Middle Voice: b flat–g^2. First published with Opus 14 by A. Gutheil in Moscow in 1896.

Dedicated to **Yúri Sergéyevich Sakhnóvsky** (1866–1930), Rachmaninoff's friend and fellow student at the Moscow Conservatory. He made his career as a composer, music critic, and organizer and director of concerts. Rachmaninoff also dedicated Song 11 to him (Op. 4/2).

RECORDINGS. Atlantov, Baturkin, Del Grande, Furdui, Furlanetto, Hvorostovsky, Kharitonov, Koptchak, Larin, Leiferkus, Lemeshev, Lisitsian, Milcheva, Murzayev, Nesterenko, Ognivtsev, Olli, Pogossov, Serkebayev, Söderström, Storozhev, Suchkova, Vassilieff.

Third stanza, omitted from the song

Я был у ней; я с уст прелестной	I came to her; from my sweetheart's lips
Счастливое забвенье пил,	I drank blissful oblivion,
И все земное позабыл	And forgot everything mundane
У девичьей груди прелестной.	At my sweetheart's girlish breast.

26 *Эти летние ночи*
These summer nights

Op. 14, No. 5

This song about the happiness of two lovers on a summer night is the third of Rachmaninoff's five songs to lyrics by Daniil Ratgauz (Songs 6, 7, 26, 46, 61). Ratgauz was one of the most popular sources for romance texts at the turn of the century (see p. 20 above). The story of how Tchaikovsky first discovered this poet, a completely unknown young man of German-Russian heritage living in Kiev, can be found in the introduction to Tchaikovsky's great last set of songs, Op. 73, in my book *Tchaikovsky's Complete Songs* (*TCS*, 268-70, and 271-82 passim). The poet took his credo from Edgar Allan Poe: "Melancholy is the most legitimate of all the poetical tones."

In this rhapsodic lyric, sublime summer nights bring out "surges of love" but also "vague feelings of alarm." Such happiness contrasts with the "boundless melancholy bestowed by sorrowful life." A subtle awareness of love and alarm together was noticed by Lev Tolstoy in the poetry of Afanasy Fet (see *TCS*, 52), and Fet was a principal model for the young Ratgauz in the early 1890s. Rachmaninoff set out to capture that ambiguity of feeling—love and alarm—in this restless, chromatic, Wagnerian song. It begins with a strong, forward drive that builds to an ecstatic culmination on a long, *fortissimo* high B. The voice part, with its minimal intervals and differing time values, hews to a flat line at the lower end of the scale, then leaps up to the next higher octave. After the first stanza, there is a piano interlude of seven bars, with alternating tonalities that express "ecstasy and restless desire" (*Martyn*, 109). The piano part is a great outpouring of notes with incessant chords: the song is five pages long, making it, with "Spring Waters," the longest song in the opus.

Эти летние ночи прекрасные,
Ярким светом луны озарённые,
Порождают тревоги неясные,
Пробуждают порывы влюблённые.

Забывается скорбь необъятная,
Что даруется жизнью унылою,
И блаженства края благодатные
Раскрываются тайною силою.

И открыли друг другу, не властные
Над собою сердца мы влюблённые.
В эти летние ночи прекрасные,
Светом ярким луны озарённые.

Éti létnyje nóchi prekrásnyje,
Járkim svétam luný azarjónnyje,
Parazhdájut trevógi nejásnyje,
Prabuzhdájut parývy vljubljónnyje.

These beautiful summer nights,
Resplendent in the moon's bright light,
Give birth to vague feelings of alarm,
Give rise to surges of love.

Zabyvájetsa skórp' neobjátnaja,
Shto darújetsa zhýzn'ju unýlaju,
I blazhénstva krajá blagadátnyje
Raskryvájutsa tájnaju sílaju.

Forgotten is the boundless melancholy
That is bestowed by sorrowful life,
And a promised land of happiness
Is revealed by a mysterious power.

I atkrýli drug drúgu, ne vlásnyje
Nat sabóju serttsá my vljubljónnyje.
V éti létnije nóchi prekrásnyje,
Svétam járkim luný azarjónnyje.

And we open up to one another
Our hearts so helplessly in love.
On these beautiful summer nights,
Resplendent in the moon's bright light.

Text. **Daniíl Maksímovich Ratgáuz**, 1893. First published in *Ratgauz 1893*, page 32. Rachmaninoff set the text exactly as written, but reversed the order of the first two words of the last line to be able to have the open "ja" sound on the long fortissimo high B at the culmination of the voice part.

Rachmaninoff was the first composer to set this text. There is a later setting by Leonid V. Nikolayev (Op. 12/1, 1904), remembered as an influential piano teacher (among his pupils were Maria Yudina, Vladimir Sofronitzky, and Dmitri Shostakovich).

In a lapse in their otherwise meticulous descriptions of Rachmaninoff's compositions, Robert Threlfall and Geoffrey Norris indicate that this text was set by Tchaikovsky as his Op. 73/3 (*T/N*, 62), but Tchaikovsky's song, "On this moonlit night," uses a different Ratgauz text. Max Harrison compounds this erroneous lead in his comment "it has to be said that Tchaikovsky's setting of this poem as his Op. 73/5 (*sic*) is less memorable" (*Harrison*, 69).

Meter. Ternary. Anapest, lines of three feet, with dactylic endings:

And a promise of beautiful happiness
Is revealed by a power mysterious.

Music. October 1896. Op. 14, no. 5. E Major. 6/4, 9/4, Allegro. For High Voice: d^1 sharp–b^2. First published with Opus 14 by A. Gutheil in Moscow in 1896.

Dedicated to **Maríya Ivánovna Guthéil**, the wife of Karl Gutheil, Rachmaninoff's principal publisher until 1914.

Recordings. Arkhipova, Del Grande, Dolukhanova, Fagan, Fleming, Furdui, Korshunov, Kurenko, Lee, L. Maslennikova, Milcheva, Naoumenko, Olli, Siniavskaya, Söderström, Suchkova.

Transcriptions. *Cello:* Brian Stucki. *Piano:* Earl Wild.

27 *Тебя так любят все* *You are so loved by all*

Op. 14, No. 6

"You are so loved by all" is a "gentle elegy" (*Challis*, 78) to one of Aleksei Tolstoy's intimate occasional lyrics addressed to his wife. These lyrics inspired some of Tchaikovsky's best songs. Their subject is the well of sadness within the woman the poet loves, some "hidden torment" to which she is "condemned," his grief that she should have to bear it, and his pain that he cannot alleviate it. It is a mournful poem in long iambic hexameter lines. It has to be understood, however, that its sadness not only does not detract from it as a Russian lyric, but seals its very "truth and beauty" for the Russian audience. To describe this "grief in the heart" as one which "destroys all pleasure in life" and the song as "unrelievedly lugubrious" (*Martyn*, 109) is to misjudge the nature of the material Rachmaninoff was working with here—material that is heartbreaking, yes, but inescapably so.

The song succeeds very well in conveying this loving sadness. It has been compared to Tchaikovsky (*Keldysh*, 126, *Harrison*, 69), but Rachmaninoff's musical language here is his own. The vocal line is declamatory and tender, with falling phrases, but unexpected intervals and accidentals that make it difficult to be sure where the song is going or where resolution will be found; line 7 brings rising phrases that culminate in the image "whispering in the oaks" with its hint of lovely, but unattainable resolution. The voice part is peppered with tenuto marks that highlight particular words: "your quiet look," "your secret torment," "a verdict of some kind," "the air you breathe," "seems to you a blessing undeserved." The piano gives spare, muted support until the arpeggio and crescendos of the last four lines; the coda is a muted reflection on the sad conclusion. The song is heard at its best in the beautifully articulated reading by the Russian baritone Sergei Shaposhnikov. Not many have noticed the song, but there is an eloquent cello transcription by Mischa Maisky.

Тебя так любят все; один твой тихий вид
Всех делает добрей и с жизнию мирит.
Но ты грустна, в тебе есть скрытое мученье,
В душе твоей звучит какой-то приговор.
Зачем твой ласковый всегда так робок взор,
И очи грустные так молят о прощенье,
Как будто солнца свет и вешние цветы,
И тень в полдневный зной, и шёпот по дубравам,
И даже воздух тот, которым дышишь ты, —
Всё кажется тебе стяжанием неправым?

Tebjá tak ljúbjat fsé; adín tvój tíkhij vít
Fsékh délajet dabréj
i z zhýzniju mirít.
No ty grusná, f tebé est' skrýtaja
muchén'je,
V dushé tvajéj zvuchít kakój-ta
prigavór.
Zachém tvoj láskavyj fsegdá
tak róbak vzór,
I óchi grúsnyje tak
móljat a proshchén'je,
Kak bútta sóntsa svét y véshnije tsvetý,
I tén' f paldnévnyj znój,
i shópat pa dubrávam,
I dázhe vózdukh tót, katórym dýshesh tý,-
Vsjo kázhetsa tebé stjazhánijem neprávym?

You are so loved by all; just your quiet look
Makes everyone better and life
worth living.
But you are sad, you have a secret
torment,
Within your soul a verdict of some
kind has been read.
Why is your tender gaze
so diffident,
And why do your sad eyes
beg forgiveness,
As if the sun's light and the spring flowers,
The shade in the noontime heat,
the whispering in the oaks,
And even the air you breathe,
Always seem to you a blessing undeserved?

Text. **Alekséi Konstantínovich Tolstóy**, 1858. Untitled. First published in *Russkaya beseda* (Russian Colloquy), 1858, no. 11, p. 3. Set earlier by Georgi Catoire (1888); later by A. S. Taneyev (Op. 35/2, 1907)—not to be confused with Rachmaninoff's teacher, Sergei Taneyev, to whom he was distantly related.

Meter. Binary. Iambic hexameter, with a caesura between the sixth and seventh syllables:

You are so loved by all; || your quiet look alone
Gives everyone a lift, || we're reconciled with life...

Music. 1896. Op. 14, no. 6. G Minor. 4/4, Moderato. For Middle Voice: d^1–e^2 flat/g^2. First published with Opus 14 by A. Gutheil in Moscow in 1896.

Dedicated to **A. N. Ivanóvsky**, the only unidentified name among Rachmaninoff's dedications. Challis says he was "a friend" of Rachmaninoff's; this is almost certainly true, but she gives no evidence and lists him as A. I. Ivanovsky (*Challis*, 78, 87). Ivanov gives an interesting lead, but without name and patronymic or dates, in the form of a song to words by Kruglov composed by one "A. Ivanovsky" and published in 1909 by Karl Gutheil, Rachmaninoff's publisher (*Ivanov 1*, 166). If this is the dedicatee, he was a friend of Rachmaninoff's, probably a fellow student from the Moscow Conservatory.

Recordings. Christoff, Del Grande, Furdui, Khromchenko, Leiferkus, Milcheva, Olli, Shaposhnikov, Söderström, Suchkova.

Transcriptions. *Cello:* Mischa Maisky.

28 *Не верь мне, друг!* *Don't believe me, friend!*

Op. 14, No. 7

In 1869 Tchaikovsky chose this text by Aleksei Tolstoy as the very first song in his first published set of songs, Opus 6. When he did so, he found that he could not work with the text as it was, but had to make some small phonetic and stylistic emendations and to use repetition on a rather extensive scale. He repeated the entire first stanza at the end of the song, changing the two-part lyric into a three-part song; and the phrase "don't believe," which occurs once in Tolstoy's poem, occurs ten times in Tchaikovsky's song, transforming Tolstoy's reasoned, self-possessed poem into the tender, pleading love song Tchaikovsky wanted to write (see *TCS*, 11-13).

After Tchaikovsky, more than a dozen composers had written songs to this text by the time Rachmaninoff wrote his. He preferred using texts no other composer had set to music (about two-thirds of his songs), but, for poets he especially admired, he was willing to try his hand, and was usually able to write a good song or an even better one than anyone else, as we have seen in Songs 12, 13, 14, 19, and 20. Tolstoy was such a poet, and even though Tchaikovsky had set the text very well, Rachmaninoff clearly felt he had something of his own to say.

The approach he took is completely different from Tchaikovsky's: he did not tamper with the text at all, but set it exactly as he found it. The song has a headlong forward movement with an excellent melody for the voice in C Major, with a few piquant accidentals, C sharp and A and B flat. The piano is an eager and involved participant from the outset with throbbing triplets that suggest the ebb and flow of water in the text, and then a rush of notes in the brilliant coda that celebrates the incoming tide. This coda "runs gloriously amok at the end" (*Martyn*, 109) and is "a real pianistic outburst that may leave the singer feeling thrust aside" (*Harrison*, 69), but the song does work well in performance, and often appears in recital programs.

Не верь мне, друг, когда, в избытке горя,
Я говорю, что разлюбил тебя.
В отлива час не верь измене моря:
Оно к земле воротится, любя.

Уж я тоскую, прежней страсти полный,
Мою свободу вновь тебе отдам.
И уж бегут с обратным шумом волны
Издалека к любимым берегам.

Ne vér' mne, druk, kagdá v yzbýtke górja,	Don't believe me, friend, when, overwhelmed by troubles,
Já gavarjú, shto razljubíl tebjá.	I say I do not love you anymore.
V atlíva chas ne vér' izméne mórja:	Do not believe the ebbing sea's inconstancy:
Anó g zemlé varótitsa, ljubjá.	It will return to land, loving as before.
Ush já taskúju, prézhnej strásti polnyj,	Full of passion I long for you again,
Majú svabódu vnóf' tebé addám.	Again I'm ready to surrender to you.
I ush begút s abrátnym shúmam vólny	And rushing back the loud waves run
Izdaleká k ljubímym beregám.	From far away to their beloved shore.

Text. **Alekséi Konstantínovich Tolstóy**, Summer 1856. Untitled. First published in *Sovremennik* (The Contemporary), 1857, no. 1, p. 9. First set by Tchaikovsky (Op. 6/1, 1869); later by many other composers, including an unremarkable setting by Rimsky-Korsakov (Op. 46/4, 1897).

Tolstoy's lyric had a life of its own in the popular urban romance tradition, where it was well known at the turn of the century as a song called "Море и сердце" (The sea and my heart, *Petrovskii 1997*, no. 49). More than one composer wrote an urban romance to this poem, sometimes with changes in wording or word order, but the best-known version was revived in the Soviet period by Georgi Vinogradov and Ivan Kozlovsky, both of whom recorded it with guitar accompaniment. The music for this popular version is attributed to Vladimir Timofeyevich Sokolov (1830–90), one of the Sokolov family, who were prominent Gypsy musicians in the 19th and 20th centuries.

Meter. Binary. Iambic pentameter:

And rushing back the waves come crashing loudly
From far away to their beloved shore.

Music. 1896. Op. 14, no. 7. C Major. 4/4, Allegro moderato. For High Voice: e^1– b^2 flat. First published with Opus 14 by A. Gutheil in Moscow in 1896.

Dedicated to **Ánna Geórgievna Klokachóva**, née **Pribýtkova**, Rachmaninoff's first cousin on his father's side (her mother was a sister of Rachmaninoff's father). Rachmaninoff was close to the Pribytkov family in St. Petersburg, and dedicated Song 24 to Zoya Pribytkova. Anna's dates are not given in the Russian sources, but her brother, Arkady Georgievich, lived from 1865–1918.

Recordings. Atlantov, Chaiter, Gorchakova, Guleghina, Guliayev, Hvorostovsky, Isakova, Kennedy, Korolev, Korshunov, Larin, Lear, Levko, Mirakian, Ognivtsev, Olli, Price, Pusar, Rautio, Reshetin, Rodgers, Rozum, Söderström, Suchkova, Tear, Verbitskaya, Viktorova.

Tchaikovsky: Olga Borodina, Elisabeth Söderström, Christianne Stotijn, Galina Vishnevskaya, Sherri Weiler.

Rimsky-Korsakov: Aleksei Martynov.

Sokolov: Ivan Kozlovsky, Georgi Vinogradov.

29 *О, не грусти!* *Oh, do not grieve!*

Op. 14, No. 8

This is the first of three Rachmaninoff songs (the others are Songs 34 and 39) to words by Aleksei Apukhtin (1840–1893), an exact contemporary and lifelong friend of Tchaikovsky's. They met at age 13 at the Law Academy in St. Petersburg where they were both enrolled. Later, Tchaikovsky wrote four of his best songs to original poems by Apukhtin (see *TCS*, 31-2 and passim).

Apukhtin's gay circle put him in touch with some of the young dukes in the house of Romanov who were gay, or gay-friendly, first and foremost Grand Duke Konstantin Romanov, a poet and musician; Apukhtin was present when Tchaikovsky was introduced to him in 1880, a meeting which resulted in a lasting friendship and correspondence between the composer and "K. R." as he signed his poetry (*TCS*, 237-8). The following year, when Tchaikovsky was in Rome, Konstantin was on a naval cruise with Alexander II's younger sons Sergei and Pavel (like Konstantin, they were also in their early twenties), and they all came up from Naples to Rome, where Tchaikovsky dined with Konstantin and met the young dukes (*Poznansky 1991*, 387). Apukhtin's friendship extended to Sergei and Pavel and Pavel's young wife, the Greek Princess Alexandra, who died in 1891. It was in her memory that Apukhtin wrote the present lyric and dedicated it to her.

Rachmaninoff removed Apukhtin's dedication to Alexandra and dedicated his song to the Gypsy singer Nadezhda Aleksandrova. He also discarded Apukhtin's title "Voice from Afar" and changed the opening words "ne toskui" (don't long) to "ne grusti" (don't be sad). Written for middle voice, its range extends down to the chest notes admired in classic Gypsy singing, a style carried into the mid-twentieth century by singers like Nadezhda Obukhova. In Obukhova's recording she expresses all the shades and nuances of the carefully marked score, with beautifully shaped phrases like line 6 of the text; in the last two lines, where loudness and speed diminish, sometimes on a single note, the words "your wounded soul" are sung with tender legato.

О, не грусти по мне! Я там, где нет страданий.
Забудь былых скорбей мучительные сны.
Пусть будут обо мне твои воспоминанья
    Светлей, чем первый день весны.

О, не тоскуй по мне! Меж нами нет разлуки,
Я так же, как и встарь, душе твоей близка.
Меня по-прежнему твои волнуют муки,
    Меня гнетёт твоя тоска.

Живи! Ты должен жить! И если силой чуда
Ты здесь найдешь отраду и покой,
То знай, что это я откликнулась оттуда
На зов души твоей больной.

O, ne grustí pa mné! Ja tám, gde nét stradánij,
Zabúd' bylýkh skarbéj muchítel'nyje sný.
Puzd' búdut aba mné tvají vaspaminán'ja
Svetléj, chem pérvyj dén' vesný.

Oh, do not grieve for me! There is no suffering where I am.
Forget the painful dreams of past sorrows.
May all your memories of me be
Brighter than the first day of spring.

O, ne taskúj pa mné! Mezh námi nét razlúki,
Ja tág zhe, kak i fstár', dushé tvajéj bliská.
Menjá pa-prézhnemu tvají valnújut múki,
Menjá gnetjót tvajá taská.

Oh, do not pine for me! We are not separated from each other.
I am as near to you in soul as in the past.
As before, your anguish troubles me,
And your longing brings me pain.

Zhyví! Ty dólzhen zhýt'! I jesli sílaj chúda
Ty zdés' najdjósh atrádu i pakój,
To znáj, shto éta já atklíknulas' attúda
Na zóv dushý tvajéj bal'nój.

Live! You must live! And if by some miracle
You should find happiness and peace here,
Know that it was I who answered from afar
The call of your wounded soul.

Text. **Alekséi Nikoláyevich Apúkhtin**, October 1891. Title: Голос издалека (Voice from Afar), with a dedication to Grand Duchess Alexandra Georgievna. Published after the poet's death in the fourth and fifth editions of Apukhtin's works in 1895 and 1896, with an introductory essay by Modest Tchaikovsky; Rachmaninoff found the poem in one of these two editions. First set by Rachmaninoff. Later set by several composers, including Georgi Conus (Op. 12/5, 1897), Vladimir Rebikov (Op. 20/6, 1901), and Leonid Sabaneyev (1911).

Meter. Binary. Iambic; three hexameters followed by a tetrameter:

Oh, do not pine for me! No distance now divides us,
I am as near to you in soul as in the past.
And as before, your every anguish makes me sad,
Your every longing brings me pain.

Music. 1896. Op. 14, no. 8. F Minor. 4/4, Andante. For Middle Voice: b^1 flat–a^2 flat. First published with Opus 14 by A. Gutheil in Moscow in 1896.

Dedicated to **Nadézhda Aleksándrovna Aleksándrova**, dates unknown. Well known as a singer of Gypsy songs, of which she recorded two in 1911 (*Ianin*, 418). Rachmaninoff knew her through her sister Anna Lodyzhenskaya, (see Song 10).

Recordings. Arkhipova, Bolotin, Borisenko, Borodina, DeGaetani, Diciute-Treciokiene, Dolukhanova, Furdui, Gedda, Gorokhovskaya, Guleghina, Kharitonov, Levko, Mkrtchyan, Obraztsova, Obukhova, Oja, Olli, Podleś, Popescu, Rautio, Simonova, Siniavskaya, Söderström, Suchkova, Verbitskaya, Viktorova.

Transcriptions. *Piano:* Earl Wild. *Trumpet:* Sergei Nakariakov.

30 *Она, как полдень, хороша* *She is as beautiful as midday*

Op. 14, No. 9

This song has a pronounced "oriental coloring" heard in the music, with its frequent melismas, its unexpected flatted notes that spell out augmented intervals, and the slowly pulsing, arpeggiated pedal point in E-flat Major in the left hand of the piano part, while the right hand plays "violin-like thirds in the keyboard treble" (*Harrison*, 70). The exotic mood reaches its climax in the beautiful vocalise of bars 20-22, on the "o" vowel at the end of line 6. Some who have mentioned the "orientalism" of the song have faulted the composer for employing it with a text that has "nothing oriental" about it (*Vasina-Grossman*, 324), as if it were "more a mannerism than a necessity" (*Martyn*, 110). However, Rachmaninoff's source text was the last poem in a cycle of eight poems called "From the Oriental." In any case the poem depicts a fatal attraction to a mysterious, impassive beauty, and the song is hypnotic and very beautiful.

Rachmaninoff found the poem in an 1887 edition of the poems of Nikolai Minsky, born in 1856 in the Vilensk Province of Belarus. His surname was Vilenkin; he took his pseudonym from Minsk, where he finished the *gymnasium* with a gold medal in Greek and modern languages before going on to St. Petersburg University to read law (*RP 4*, 79). He was "the first full-blooded Jew to win a reputation in Russian letters" (*Mirsky*, 360). He used to say his poems were "conceived on black days, and born on white nights" (*Aikhenval'd*, 365). His poetry is rather cold and philosophical; he liked working with antitheses, as the present poem shows. Minsky went on to ally himself with Merezhkovsky and the early Symbolists. In the year Rachmaninoff wrote this song, he published his translation of *The Iliad*; he also translated Judah Halevi, Byron, Verlaine, and Shelley. He travelled to Europe frequently and after 1905 lived there primarily; in the 1920s he worked for a time at the Soviet Embassy in London. He died in Paris in 1937.

Она, как полдень, хороша,
Она загадочней полночи.
У ней не плакавшие очи
И не страдавшая душа.

А мне, чья жизнь борьба и горе,
По ней томиться суждено.
Так вечно плачущее море
В безмолвный берег влюблено.

Aná, kak pólden', kharashá,	She is as beautiful as midday,
Aná zagádachnej palnóchi.	More enigmatic than midnight.
U néj ne plákafshyje óchi	Her eyes have not known weeping
I ne stradáfshaja dushá.	Nor her soul suffering.
A mné, ch'ja zhýzn' bar'bá i góre,	And I, who know but strife and grief,
Pa néj tamítsa suzhdenó.	Am destined to long for her.
Tak véchna pláchushcheje móre	Thus eternally the weeping sea
V bezmólvnyj bérek vljublenó.	Is drawn by love to the silent shore.

TEXT. **Nikolái Maksímovich Mínsky (Vilénkin)**, 1880s. Untitled. No. 8 in a cycle of eight poems called "С Восточного" (From the Oriental). First published in *Minskii 1887*, p. 144. First set by Rachmaninoff; later by two minor composers.

METER. Binary. Iambic tetrameter:

She is as beautiful as noon,
Mysterious as the midnight hour.

MUSIC. 1896. Op. 14, no. 9. E-flat Major. 4/4, Lento. For Middle Voice: b flat–g^2 flat. First published with Opus 14 by A. Gutheil in Moscow in 1896.

Dedicated to **Yelizavéta Andréyevna Lavróvskaya** (1845–1919), Russian contralto. Rachmaninov knew her at the Moscow Conservatory, where she was on the faculty from 1888 until her death. She sang the premiere of Song 19 in a recital of the composer's works in 1894. Lavrovskaya was a famous singer in her day. She studied with Henriette Nissen-Saloman at the St. Petersburg Conservatory when Tchaikovsky was a student there, and she knew Tchaikovsky all his life. It was Lavrovskaya who suggested to Tchaikovsky that he use Pushkin's novel in verse *Eugene Onegin* as the subject of an opera (*TCS*, 108).

RECORDINGS. Amaize, Asawa, Chaiter, Furdui, Gmyria, Hvorostovsky, Keenlyside, Leiferkus, Levko, Lisitsian, Murzayev, Obraztsova, Obukhova, Olli, Podleś, Savenko, Seleznev, Söderström, Suchkova.

31 *В моей душе* *Within my soul*

Op. 14, No. 10

Like the preceding song, this lyric is from Minsky's cycle of poems "From the Oriental." The music has an oriental coloring of its own, with moments that recall Borodin's *Prince Igor*. Indeed, by the end of the song, a sensuous atmosphere of *nega* (erotic longing) has been conjured up by the music (on *nega*, see *Taruskin 1997*, 165-182).

Like Song 30, it has a sinuous vocalise passage at the beginning of line 7. Unlike Song 30, the music is in 3/4 meter, and since the lyric is iambic tetrameter, the melismas here are motivated by the need to give a binary verse line a ternary musical line. This is first heard in the opening line in the phrase "ljubóf' vaskhódit," which consists of the noun "love" and the verb "is rising," a verb associated with the sun making its ascent at dawn: the first syllable of the verb (vas) becomes a triplet melisma (va–a–as) on the notes E–F Sharp–G. Analogous triplet melismas occur at the end of every line of the poem, marking the line ends clearly throughout the song; in the second half of the song, additional melismas are employed earlier in the line, compounding the melismatic density of the voice part (these are indicated in my transcription below).

The piano provides a pulsing, muted pedal with delicate grace notes as the song builds, making "a beautiful and indeed hypnotic duet between the voice and the accompanist's right hand, entwining two quasi-oriental melodies" (*Harrison*, 70). Of the recordings of the song, an outstanding one is by the Russian bass Mark Reshetin on the "Complete Songs of Rachmaninoff" issued by Melodiya Records.

В моей душе любовь восходит,
Как солнце в блеске красоты,
И песни стройные рождает,
Как ароматные цветы.

В моей душе твой взор холодный
То солнце знойное зажёг.
Ах, если б я тем знойным солнцем
Зажечь твой взор холодный мог!

V majéj dushé ljubóf' va-a-askhódit,
Kak sóntse v bléske kra-a-satý,
I pésni strójnyje ra-a-azhdájet,
Kak aramátnyje tsve-e-etý.

Within my soul love makes its ascent
Like the sun in a blaze of beauty,
And creates harmonious songs
Like aromatic flowers.

V majéj dushé tvoj vzór kha-a-aló-o-odnyj
To sóntse znójnaje-e zazhók.
Ákh (vocalise with melismas),
je-esli b j-a-á te-e-m znójnym s-o-óntsem
Za-a-azhéch tvoj vzór khalódny-yj mók!

In my soul your cold gaze
Sets the burning sun ablaze.
Ah, (vocalise)
if only I could make the burning sun
Set your cold gaze on fire!

Text. **Nikolái Maksímovich Mínsky (Vilénkin)**, 1880s. Untitled. No. 2 in a cycle of eight poems called "С Восточного" (From the Oriental). First published in *Minskii 1887*, p. 138. Set by four minor composers before and after Rachmaninoff.

Meter. Binary. Iambic tetrameter:

Within my soul love makes ascent
Like sunrise in a blaze of beauty...

Music. 1896. Op. 14, no. 10. D Major. 3/4, Lento. For Low Voice: a–d^2. First published with Opus 14 by A. Gutheil in Moscow in 1896.

Dedicated to **Yelizavéta Andréyevna Lavróvskaya** (see preceding song). These two songs dedicated to Lavrovskaya were written for the range of her voice.

Recordings. Burchuladze, Crona, Del Grande, Hvorostovsky, Levko, Lisitsian, Oja, Olli, Popescu, Pusar, Reshetin, Shaposhnikov, Söderström, Suchkova, Zimmermann.

Transcriptions. *Cello:* Brian Stucki.

32 *Весенние воды* *Spring waters*

Op. 14, No. 11

After the long, cold Russian winter, the coming of spring is not just a relief but a liberation, in which dancing for joy, ideally in bare feet, would be a natural response. It almost seems to arrive with a boom, which is the metaphor the poet Nikolai Nekrasov uses for spring's arrival in his poem "Zeljony shum", ("The verdant noise," used by Rachmaninoff in his Spring Cantata). A vivid description of what this moment is like in the city—indeed, in the neighborhood of the Moscow Conservatory where Rachmaninoff lived—was written down by Jacqueline du Pré when she was studying with Rostropovich in Moscow in 1966: "... it means months of snow and ice are being unwillingly melted into big brown streams and puddles. Water overflows from the gutter down one's neck... and everyone waits, longs for the first glimpse of fresh green and from then on there will be no looking back ..." (*Wilson 1999*, 191-2).

The rush of overflowing water and sense of "no looking back" are captured in the marvelous text Rachmaninoff chose for this song, the first of his five songs to poems by Feodor Tyutchev (1803–1873). The scene is the countryside, where the fields still have patches of snow, but the spring runoff has begun. These flowing waters are noticed not by the eye, but the ear (the verb *shumját* at the end of line 2 means in the literal sense "to make a noise," but also, used with the word "spring" in the instrumental case, it means "to proclaim"). This noise proclaims spring's arrival. The word is singled out in the score because the singer can drop the G of the first syllable down to B-flat, an option that is more expressive. (Note values here are in the original key of the song as written; singers do, of course, transpose to different keys in performance). Ewa Podleś, being a true contralto, does this easily and to fine effect; the Dutch soprano Elly Ameling also takes this low note in her excellent recording of the song.

There is another variant note in performances of the song, in this case one which is *not* written in the score, but which some singers take the liberty of singing. It is in the last word of the song (a three-note phrase *za-a néj*, "behind" in my translation). As written, the sequence is D above middle C, down to B Flat, and up to E Flat. But some singers sing the second, penultimate note up by an octave to high B Flat. This is a dramatic way to end the song, but it thwarts the steadier ending the composer wrote. Artists who end the song as written include Elisabeth Söderström, Shirley Verrett, Joan Rodgers, and Jennie Tourel; those who interpolate the high note include Barbara Hendricks (whose album is called "Hommage à Jennie Tourel"), and Dmitry Hvorostovsky, who, on his 1994 recording, sings the last *two* notes high. In his second (2009) recording he sings the song as written. Nicolai Gedda ends the song as written in his 1965 recording with Gerald Moore, but in his 1973 recording with Alexis Weissenberg he sings the high note.

There are many other details to be considered in a performance of this challenging song. Both singer and pianist have to negotiate continual changes in tempo and dynamics. The voice part starts out *Allegro vivace* and *forte*, but in line 2 there is a slowing down for emphasis on the word "spring." The tempo resumes, but now the dynamics grow from *piano* in line 3 to triple *forte* in line 6 on the words "spring is coming." This leads to a loud, sustained high B-flat at the end of line 8 which has to be sung without shouting. Here begins the most difficult section of the song, which slows down to *Andante*, then accelerates and grows louder. The challenge to the singer in this final stanza of the song is to be noticeably slower at first, but not so slow as to drift before accelerating gradually to the end.

The piano part is "uncommonly difficult," with a "recurring sextolet figure" that "conveys a strong impression of pent-up waters that have at last broken loose in the spring thaw; and the concentrated yet thunderous postlude is essential to bring this motion to an end" (*Harrison*, 70). All these notes have to be played without drowning out the singer.

Instrumental transcriptions of the song have been made for piano, piano duo, cello, and, interestingly, for brass, to bring out the "fanfare" quality of parts of the music (*Blagoi*, 573), such as the transcription by the trumpet virtuoso Timofei Dokshitser. A ballet "Spring Waters," choreographed by Asaf Messerer, was performed at Indiana University in 2005. Dmitri Shostakovich made a witty allusion to the song in the piano part of his satire "Spring's Awakening," to words by Sasha Chorny (Op. 109/2, 1960). The song makes an ecstatic impression and is often placed at the end of a recital or recorded program.

Ещё в полях белеет снег,
А воды уж весной шумят,
Бегут и будят сонный брег,
Бегут и блещут, и гласят.

Они гласят во все концы:
«Весна идёт! Весна идёт!
Мы молодой весны гонцы,
Она нас выслала вперёд.

Весна идёт! Весна идёт!»
И тихих, тёплых майских дней
Румяный, светлый хоровод
Толпится весело за ней.

Jeshchó f palják h beléjet snék,	The fields are still white with snow,
A vódy ush vesnój shumját,	But already the waters are proclaiming spring,
Begút y búdjat sónnyj brék,	Running along and waking sleepy riverbanks,
Begút y bléshchut y glasját.	Running and glittering and declaring.
Aní glasját va fsé kantsý:	They declare in all directions:
"Vesná idjót! Vesná idjót!	"Spring is coming! Spring is coming!
My maladój vesný gantsý,	We are the heralds of young spring,
Aná nas výslala fperjót.	She sent us in advance.
Vesná idjót! Vesná idjót!"	Spring is coming! Spring is coming!"
I tíkhikh, tjóplykh májskikh dnéj	And the still, warm days of May
Rumjányj, svétlyj kharavót	In a rosy, bright circle-dance,
Talpítsa vésela za néj.	Crowd together and gaily follow behind.

TEXT. **Fyódor Ivánovich Tyútchev**, 1829 or 1830. Title: Весенние воды (Spring waters). First published in the journal *Teleskop* (Telescope), 1832. Editors disagree about where the poet's quotation marks are meant to end: after line 8 (*Tiutchev 1965* and *Tiutchev 2002*), or at the end of the poem (*Liberman* and *Tiutchev 1987*). The placement in Rachmaninoff's text, after line 9, works just as well for the purposes of his song.

Set by over thirty composers since 1861, including Grechaninov (for women's chorus, Op. 10/2, 1896) and Nicolas Tcherepnin (Duet, Op. 3/1, 1898).

METER. Binary. Iambic tetrameter, masculine rhymes (from *Liberman*, 59):

Declare the great and joyful thing:
"The spring is born! The spring is born!
We've come as heralds of the spring,
We've come to wake, we've come to warn.

MUSIC. 1896. Op. 14, no. 11. E-flat Major. 4/4, Allegro vivace, Andante, Allegro vivace. For High Voice: e^1 flat (or b flat)–b^2 flat. First published with Opus 14 by A. Gutheil in Moscow in 1896.

Dedicated to **Ánna Dmítrievna Ornátskaya**, Rachmaninoff's first piano teacher and his mother's friend at the St. Petersburg Conservatory.

RECORDINGS. Ameling, Atlantov, Celine, Davrath, Davtian, Del Grande, Delunsch, Dickson (in English), Dionne, Dnishev, Dodoka, Fiset, Furlanetto, Galante, Gedda, Gruberova, Gruszczynski, Guleghina, Guryakova, Hendricks, Hvorostovsky, Kabaivanska, Kazarnovskaya, Kennedy, Kolomyjec, Korshunov, Kozlovsky, Lapina, Larin, M. Lawrence (in English), Lear, Leiferkus, Lemeshev, Lyon, Magomayev, Makarova, Milashkina, Mishura, Mkrtchyan, Olli, Orda, Plishka, Podleś, Rautio, Rodgers, Rosing, Sari, Shevelev, Shumskaya, Slivinsky, Söderström, Sotkilava, Storozhev, Suchkova, Tourel, Troyanos, Urmana, Vayne, Verrett, Vishnevskaya, Weiler, Zvetkova.

TRANSCRIPTIONS. *Cello:* Dmitri Ferschtman, David Geringas, Moray Welsh. *Piano:* Babin-Vronsky (piano duo), John McArthur, Yevgeny Sudbin, Earl Wild. *Trumpet:* Sergei Nakariakov, Timofei Dokshitser. *Tuba:* Morton Feldman.

33 *Пора!* *It's time!*

Op. 14, No. 12

Semyon Nadson (1862–1887) was the son of a baptized Jew and a Russian Orthodox mother. He died very young of tuberculosis. His civic-minded poetry appealed to the radical intelligentsia of the 1880s, a decade that saw the assassination of Alexander II, rising discrimination against Jews under Alexander III, and rapid industrialization that led to the rise of workers' awareness and the spread of Marxist ideas. Nadson was strongly opposed to the aestheticism of Fet and Golenishchev-Kutuzov, whom he thought capable of "Herculean nonsense." He took the "revolutionary Populist" idea of the 1870s, that the peasants were ready to rise up if thousands of students "went to the people" as propagandists, and turned it into a posture of "suffering with the people." The predominant note in his verse is one of gloom in the midst of struggle. Pleshcheyev helped him get published (and even brought his own doctor to see Nadson when he was ill). Merezhkovsky and Chekhov admired his poetry, but Briusov, a Symbolist of systematic aestheticism, called it "whining." In any case, Nadson's poetry was immensely popular: editions of his poems before 1917 sold more than 200,000 copies (*RP 4*, 213-16). He was the "best-seller among the poets well into the 20th century," as D. S. Mirsky wrote in his notes to the *Oxford Book of Russian Verse*. In Mirsky's own judgment, Nadson's poetry "marks the low-water mark of Russian poetical technique; and his great popularity the low-water mark of Russian poetical taste" (*Mirsky 1958*, 360). Russian composers set 101 of his poems between 1885 and 1917.

The present text is from a set of fragments that cry out for a "prophet" who will come and show the way—feverish outbursts written two or three years before the poet's death. Rachmaninoff found them in one of the posthumous edition of Nadson's poems. This impassioned appeal for a leader with a new vision and the strength to prevail in Russia's "struggle" is sincere, though ironic in the light of history. The song seems to have been avoided in Soviet Russia.

It has been described as an expression of "Rachmaninoff's hopes for the new twentieth century" (*Challis*, 79, an opinion based on Soviet commentators, not on anything the composer said). Musically, it is "a throbbing *allegro appassionato* in E-flat minor ... of great power" (*Harrison*, 70). With its "massive piano accompaniment... the song brings the set to a powerful conclusion" (*Martyn*, 111). As a song, it has power and sincerity of feeling: baritones and basses especially have sung it well.

Пора! Явись, пророк! Всей силою печали,
Всей силою любви взываю я к тебе!
Взгляни, как дряхлы мы, взгляни, как мы устали,
Как мы беспомощны в мучительной борьбе!
Теперь, иль никогда! Сознанье умирает,
Стыд гаснет, совесть спит. Ни проблеска кругом,
Одно ничтожество свой голос возвышает.

Pará! Javís', prarók! Fsej sílaju
  pecháli,
Fsej sílaju ljubví vzyváju já k tebé!
Vzgljaní, kak drjákhly mý,
  vzgljaní, kak mý ustáli,
Kak mý bespómashchny
  v muchítel'naj bar'bé!
Tepér', il' nikagdá! Saznán'je umirájet,
Stýd gásnet, sóvest' spít.
  Ni próbleska krugóm,
Adnó nichtózhestva svoj gólas vazvyshájet.

It's time! Prophet, appear!
  With all the power of grief,
With all the power of love, I summon you!
Look, how infirm we are, look,
  how tired we've become,
How helpless we are
  in the agonizing struggle!
It's now, or never! Consciousness expires,
Shame dies out, conscience sleeps.
  There's not a ray of light anywhere,
Only petty nothingness raises its voice.

Text. **Semyón Yákovlevich Nádson**, 1883–1885. Untitled. First published in the sixth (posthumous) edition of Nadson's Стихотворения (Poems), Moscow, 1887, page 444. The poem is Fragment 4 in a series of four fragments. Set first by Rachmaninoff, later by two minor composers.

Meter. Binary. Iambic hexameter:

Look how decrepit we've become, how we're exhausted,
It's now or never! shame dies out and conscience sleeps ...

Music. 1896. Op. 14, no. 12. E-flat Minor. 4/4, Allegro appassionato. For Low Voice: b flat–f^2. First published with Opus 14 by A. Gutheil in Moscow in 1896.

No dedication.

Recordings. Amaize, Del Grande, Furlanetto, Guleghina, Hvorostovsky, Kharitonov, Koptchak, Leiferkus, Milcheva, Nikitina, Ognivtsev, Olli, Savenko, Seleznev, Söderström, Storozhev, Suchkova, Sutey.

Twelve Romances, Opus 21 (1902)

1.

A period of nearly six years fell between the Opus 14 romances and Rachmaninoff's next set of songs. The interval itself was not unusual, and in future there would be a space of four to six years between sets of songs: Op. 26 (1906), Op. 34 (1912), and Op. 38 (1916). But during this 1896–1902 period a serious crisis in Rachmaninoff's life as a composer, a crisis brought on by the failure of his First Symphony, Op. 13. When the symphony was given its premiere in St. Petersburg on 15 March 1897, the performance was a disaster. After that, Rachmaninoff did not return to it, the score was left in Moscow in 1917 and then lost, and not until the orchestral parts were found in an archive in Leningrad in 1945 was it reconstructed and performed. From 1897 to 1900 Rachmaninoff found himself unable to compose (but see Song 9).

The First Symphony was an ambitious work in which Rachmaninoff consciously set out to say something new. When the difficult work of composition was completed in 1895, he was convinced he had "discovered and opened up entirely new paths in music" (*Riesemann*, 98). He later felt that some of it was "childish" (*LN* 2, 101), though today, hearing a good performance of it shows its interest, originality, and appeal. The young composer reveled in the possibilities of varying and elaborating formal elements, like the *Dies irae* theme, through brass fanfares or string fugato passages; giving shades of light and dark to the orchestral colors and trying out different kinds of forward motion, from soaring melody to triumphal procession to Gypsy-like figures in the strings to eddies of stillness and repose. A century later, the symphony is admired for "the grandeur of its conception, its controlled emotional intensity, and its thematic integration," and it is seen to be "a step forward for Russian music" (*Martyn*, 102-3).

The symphony was a challenging new work which needed serious preparation, but Alexander Glazunov, who was a poor conductor, gave it only two perfunctory rehearsals, ignoring Rachmaninoff's suggestions and making cuts in the score. Taneyev did not like the symphony, but did everything he could to have his former student's symphony performed; Rimsky-Korsakov said primly "Forgive me, but I do not find this music at all agreeable"; and Cesar Cui wrote in his review: "If there's a Conservatory in Hell, and one of its gifted pupils should be given the problem of writing a programmatic symphony on the Seven Plagues of Egypt, and if he should write a symphony resembling Mr. Rachmaninoff's symphony—his problem would have been carried out brilliantly and he would enchant all the inmates of Hell" (*B/L*, 71-2).

Hearing his symphony mutilated was an excruciating experience for Rachmaninoff and caused him to doubt his music and himself. He fled after the performance, first to the Skalons, where he was given sympathy and train fare, and then to Novgorod to stay with his grandmother. His older brother Vladimir, newly married, happened to be staying there too with his young wife; their company touchingly cheered him (*LN 1*, 260). Two vulnerabilities we have already noticed played a part in all this. First, there was his understandable impatience to see his work performed: he was ambitious, and he strove for the recognition he felt he deserved as a composer. Second, he hastened to have his symphony performed because "fiscal matters were uppermost in his mind" (*Cannata 1999*, 18). A lack of money with no certain prospect of solvency made Rachmaninoff anxious in a way that displaced every other priority. All his life this was basic to his character: it explains why he did not hesitate to make a career as a full-time concert pianist when he left Russia nearly penniless at the end of 1917.

Karl Gutheil generously gave him five hundred rubles for the symphony, with no questions asked. But this did not help for long, and although he told himself he would be able to resume composing as soon as he could get away to Ivanovka, his attempts to compose (he wanted to write a new piano concerto) led to something like writer's block. He felt, in his own words, "like a man who has been hit, and for a long time lost the use of his head and hands" (*LN* 2, 101).

2.

Nevertheless, Rachmaninoff found head and hands in working order in the fall of 1897 when "suddenly and quite unexpectedly" he had an offer from the Moscow "Private Opera" to work as the second of their two conductors (*LN 1*, 54). He immediately accepted the offer. He had little experience conducting and his first rehearsal was a failure because he did not realize he had to cue the singers (the first conductor, an Italian named Eugenio Esposito, saw him as a rival and did not coach him). But after his debut on 12 October 1897, a performance of Saint-Saëns' *Samson et Dalila*, the critic of the *Moscow News* wrote that "in his hands the orchestra has an utterly special sound: soft, not overpowering the singing, but exact in every detail, with the result that it sounded like symphonic music rather than operatic accompaniment" (*LN 1*, 539). One week later, he conducted a performance of Dargomyzhsky's *Rusalka*, in which the role of the miller was sung by a young bass who that very season was beginning to create the roles that would make him a great star—Feodor Chaliapin (1873–1938). He was Rachmaninoff's same age (older by a few weeks), and the two of them soon began a close friendship that would last all their lives.

The "Private Opera" was doing for Russian opera what Stanislavsky's Art Theater was doing for Russian drama. It was started in 1885 by the railroad magnate Savva Mamontov (1841–1918), a famously creative and seminal figure in the flowering of modern Russian art at the turn of the century. Mamontov was a graduate of both the Mining Institute in St. Petersburg and Moscow University Law School, and chairman of the board of the Trans-Siberian and other railroad lines; but his real passion was for the performing arts, especially opera, which, like Wagner, he understood as a synthesis of music, drama, and the visual arts. A decade earlier, at his estate in Abramtsevo outside Moscow, he had formed an artists' colony, where leading artists—Ilya Repin, Valentin Serov, Konstantin Korovin, Alexander Golovin, Isaak Levitan, Viktor Vasnetsov, Mikhail Vrubel—could live and work together on artistic and even architectural projects. There was a special emphasis on Russian folk art. He had "house theaters" on the estate and in his Moscow house, where plays were produced, with the artists providing the set and costume designs. Many landmark productions in modern Russian theater were brought into being by Mamontov, who was, in Rachmaninoff's words, "a sincere friend and patron of all that was talented in literature, music, and art, and who put his artist friends to work in his enterprise designing sets and costumes" (*LN 1*, 55). Konstantin Stanislavsky, the actor and director who co-founded the Moscow Art Theater in 1898, came out of the same enlightened Moscow merchant class as the Mamontovs and the Tretyakovs, and he attended Mamontov's domestic theater productions written in-house: "Mamontov was in charge of the entire production, writing the script, jesting with the young people, and dictating business letters and telegrams in his complex railroad-building affairs" (*Stanislavsky 1952*, 142-3). Many of his artists were associated with the "World of Art" group (partly sponsored by Mamontov), out of which came Sergei Diaghilev and, eventually, his "Russian Seasons" in Paris a decade later in which Rachmaninoff and Chaliapin would take part.

Mamontov, who had studied singing in Italy, brought Italian singers to Moscow, but by the time he hired Rachmaninoff he was focusing more on new productions of Russian operas featuring talented Russian singers like Chaliapin and Nadezhda Zabela-Vrubel, wife of the artist Mikhail Vrubel. During the 1897–98 season his company presented, in addition to the *Rusalka* conducted by Rachmaninoff (designed by Vasnetsov and Levitan), Rimsky-Korsakov's *Maid of Pskov, or Ivan the Terrible* (designed by Vasnetsov and Korovin, with Chaliapin as Ivan), and also Rimsky's *May Night* (a Moscow premiere conducted by Rachmaninoff, with Chaliapin as the Mayor). Rachmaninoff also conducted Verstovsky's *Askold's Tomb* (incidentally, the first Russian opera performed in the U.S., in New York, in 1869) and Serov's *Rogneda*, as well as Bizet's *Carmen* and Gluck's *Orpheus and Eurydice*. The most anticipated event of the season was the world premiere of Rimsky-Korsakov's *Sadko*, for which the composer came to Moscow at the end of December. Rachmaninoff described *Sadko* in his "Dictated Reminiscences" written in 1932: "I remember very well the first production of *Sadko*, the same *Sadko* that the Metropolitan Opera in New York produced a couple of years ago so brilliantly, and so expertly conducted by Tullio Serafin. The sets, costumes, and makeup in Mamontov's production were all splendid. But the orchestra was poor and the chorus even worse. They were so badly rehearsed that they had to look the whole time at the printed scores, trying to keep the sheet music hidden from the audience in the wide sleeves of their costumes. There were other lapses too... Yet despite that, the success of the new Rimsky-Korsakov opera was enormous. Out of respect for the composer in attendance, even secondary roles were sung by the best artists. Chaliapin sang the part of the Viking Guest, giving another unforgettable performance" (*LN 1*, 56-7).

3.

The company spent the summer of 1898 at Putyatino, the country house of the leading mezzo-soprano in the company, Tatyana Lyubatovich. Rachmaninoff had to prepare the soloists for next season's *Boris Godunov.* He worked intensively with Chaliapin all summer. The standard Rachmaninoff set for "understanding the opera as a whole" meant learning more than just your own part, so Chaliapin learned *all* the parts in the opera, male and female. Rachmaninoff also taught him the elementary rules of music and harmony, and in general tried to educate him musically (*Shaliapin 1960*, 1, 131). After mornings at the piano going over *Boris Godunov* note by note, at midday the two would go for a swim in a nearby river. Chaliapin even worked on his new role during their daily swims: "Swimming out into the river, I would sing a cantilena passage in my part, trying to free my voice to sing in a situation where the rhythms interrupted each other. I remember it was a long time before I could produce the Tsar's calm stance and gait, full of inner dignity and strength. Rachmaninoff died laughing at my ungainly figure as I strolled back and forth along the sandy bank in my birthday suit, looking very important, trying to give my posture a royal bearing. 'You could at least throw a sheet over yourself, Feodor Ivanovich,' Rachmaninoff remarked ironically. 'No,' I answered, 'any fool can look dignified with something draped over him. I want this to work in the nude!'" (*Chaliapin 1960*, 2, 303).

Chaliapin deepened his understanding of Tsar Boris by visiting the historian Vasily Klyuchevsky, who was spending the summer not far from Lyubatovich's dacha. Klyuchevsky was a popular lecturer at Moscow University who combined immense knowledge of historical detail with the talent for reimagining and reenacting events. He suggested to Chaliapin that they take a walk in the woods. "I shall never forget this marvelous walk among the tall pine trees on the sand full of pine needles. The little old man with a pudding-basin haircut and a little white beard, his narrow, wise eyes shining behind his glasses, walked beside me. He stopped every now and then, and in an ingratiating voice, with a cunning grin upon his face, he reenacted for me, just as if he had witnessed the event himself, the dialogue between Shuisky and Godunov, then talked of the police officers as if he knew them personally, of Varlaam, Missail and of the charm of the Pretender. He talked a great deal and it was so wonderfully picturesque that I could see the people he was portraying" (*Borovsky 1988*, 246). Chaliapin always said that if he succeeded in portraying Boris as the tragic, "wicked," and at the same time sympathetic figure created by Pushkin and Mussorgsky, it was Klyuchevsky who had made it possible by showing him Godunov's loneliness and isolation.

At the end of July Chaliapin married Iola Tornaghi, an Italian ballet dancer in the theater. She danced a Gypsy dance in the *Carmen* Rachmaninoff conducted that season, and she later said she had never worked with a more "sensitive" conductor in her life: they communicated in French, and he made sure his tempos were what she wanted for her dance. What struck her was Rachmaninoff's "modesty and nobility" (*Shaliapin 1960*, 1, 530). Rachmaninoff "felt awfully sorry for Fedya [Feodor]" that he was marrying so young, but he would not be dissuaded (*VOR 1*, 275). The entire company celebrated the wedding late into the night. At dawn, outside the bride and groom's window, Mamontov led them in a "bang-on-a-can" concert with stove pipes, iron grills, buckets, and shrill whistles. "Why are you two still in bed?" Mamontov yelled. "People don't come to the country to sleep. Let's go to the woods to look for mushrooms!" The concert resumed. "This pandemonium," Chaliapin recalled, "was being conducted by S. V. Rachmaninoff" (*Shaliapin 1960*, 1, 133-4).

In August, the two worked together on Rimsky-Korsakov's *Mozart and Salieri*. This was the third of Pushkin's four "Little Tragedies" to be set as a small opera (Dargomyzhsky wrote *The Stone Guest* and Cui *A Feast During the Plague*; Rachmaninoff himself would set the fourth when he composed *The Miserly Knight* in 1903-5). The new work was to be premiered by Mamontov's Private Opera in the coming season, and Chaliapin was creating the role of Salieri. It was a new kind of challenge for him, a part that was "all melodic recitative." He turned to Rachmaninoff, who answered all his questions, showing him where he had leeway to change a tempo and where not. "Without distorting the composer's conception, we found the right tone and coloring to portray in three dimensions the tragic figure of Salieri" (*Shaliapin 1960*, 1, 135).

In September, Mamontov arranged a southern tour for Chaliapin and other singers, with Rachmaninoff as accompanist (*VOR 2*, 21). They performed in several Crimean cities including Yalta, where Anton Chekhov attended one of Chaliapin's concerts. During the intermission Chekhov came up to Rachmaninoff and said: "You're going to be a great musician, you know [*bol'shim muzykantom*]." When Rachmaninoff looked surprised at these words, Chekhov added: "You have a very remarkable face" (*LN 1*, 546). After the concert, he and Chaliapin wrote a note to Chekhov, inviting him to join them for dinner in the city garden (*LN 1*, 280).

4.

To the regret of his new friends in Mamontov's theater, Rachmaninoff decided not to sign on for the 1898–99 season. He had gained invaluable experience there as a conductor, but the orchestra and chorus were below par, and Mamontov never gave them enough rehearsal time. In addition, he had no time to give to composition when he was working at the theater. He asked his cousin Alexander Siloti, who had toured America very successfully in 1898, to give him a long-term loan to free him to get back to composition (*LN 1*, 545). He had enjoyed the summer in Putyatino at Tatyana Lyubatovich's country house, and she offered it to him in the fall as a retreat where he could be alone and work without any distractions; she also gave him a dog, Levko, a big Leonberger (a good photo of Rachmaninoff with this shaggy giant may be found in *VOR 1957*, *1*, 288, and other sources). He stayed there during the week, coming back to Moscow for the weekends. Perhaps he saw some of Chaliapin's opening nights at the Bolshoi: 25 November as Salieri, 7 December as Boris Godunov. In November he sent Chekhov an inscribed copy of his orchestral fantasy "The Crag," explaining that Chekhov's story "Along the Road" had inspired him to compose the piece (*T/N*, 48).

Siloti forwarded an invitation to Rachmaninoff from the Philharmonic Society to give a concert in London in April 1899. It was his first foreign concert, and all 2492 seats of the Queen's Hall were filled (*Barber*, 61, 91). He was supposed to play the Second Piano Concerto but it was not yet written, and he declined to play the First because he considered it a "student" work. Instead, he conducted "The Crag" and played his Prelude and another piano work. The critics praised his conducting and *The Times* called his orchestration "superb and original" (*Norris 1993*, 188). He promised to return to London with a new piano concerto. He returned to Russia in time for the centennial of Pushkin's birth: the celebrations included a performance of *Aleko* in the Tauride Palace in St. Petersburg, with Chaliapin singing the lead role. He had never sung it before. Rachmaninoff wrote Slonov about the performance: "...from his first to his last note Aleko sang splendidly. The orchestra and chorus were splendid. The soloists were splendid, not counting Chaliapin, before whom they all fade. He's three heads above them all. I can still hear how he sobbed at the end of the opera. Such sobbing can only come from a great theatrical artist, or a man who has in his own life suffered as deeply as Aleko" (*B/L*, 87).

Rachmaninoff did not overcome his writer's block until he agreed to visit a doctor Nicholas Dahl, whom the Satins knew and who lived nearby. From January to April 1900, Rachmaninoff visited this man every day, telling him of his promise to write a new concerto, and that he had "given up on it in despair." "Consequently I heard the same hypnotic formula repeated day after day while I lay half asleep in an armchair in Dahl's study. 'You will begin to write your concerto... You will work with great facility... The Concerto will be of an excellent quality...' It was always the same, without interruption. Although it may sound incredible, this cure really helped me. Already at the beginning of the summer I began again to compose ... I felt that Dr. Dahl's treatment had strengthened my nervous system to a miraculous degree. Out of gratitude I dedicated my Second Concerto to him" (*Riesemann*, 112-3).

Rachmaninoff spent April and May of 1900 in Yalta, in a villa that belonged to Princess Lieven, a wealthy friend of Mrs. Satina's, who admired him and sympathized with his efforts to recover. There was a brilliant company of artists and writers there who had come down to the Crimea with the Moscow Art Theater as a kind of "spring vacation and huge homage to Chekhov" (*Chekhov 1973*, 385). He saw Chekhov frequently, and met the writers Ivan Bunin, Alexander Kuprin, and Maxim Gorky. He spent July in Italy, helping Chaliapin prepare Boito's *Mephistopheles* in Italian for La Scala: they lived in modest rooms, quit smoking, retired and rose early, and worked intensively (*Gorky 1967*, 145). It was the beginning of Chaliapin's international career as an opera star.

Rachmaninoff worked for the rest of the summer at Krasnenkoye, and by December he had finished two of the three movements of the Second Piano Concerto. He and Chaliapin gave a benefit concert for the student aid fund at Moscow University on 17 December 1900, raising 5930 rubles after expenses (these included rent for the Hall of Nobility 560 R., pay for the orchestra 150 R., two Bechstein pianos delivered and tuned 20 R., and tea for the artists 7 R., 85 K.) The program included Nikolai Rubinstein's Waltz and Tarantella for two pianos played by Rachmaninoff and Alexander Goldenweiser, and Aleko's aria sung by Chaliapin (Shaliapin archive in *RGALI*, f. 912, op. 4, ed. khr. 269). By April 1901 Rachmaninoff finished the concerto and his second suite for two pianos, which he dedicated to Goldenweiser. In the fall, the concerto was performed in its entirety for the first time by Rachmaninoff, with Siloti conducting.

In the spring of 1902 Rachmaninoff went to Novgorod to visit his mother. He had come to ask her blessing for his marriage. His engagement to Natalia Satina was a surprise to everyone, but it needed special dispensation from the church, since they were first cousins. When he had arranged that, he went to Ivanovka to write a set of songs. Gutheil paid handsomely (250 R.) for a song, and he needed money for his honeymoon: he wrote the twelve songs of Op. 21 in two weeks. They include several inspired songs and two of his very greatest and most popular (Songs 38 and 40).

Sergei and Natalia were married in Moscow on April 29, 1902, with Siloti and Brandukov as witnesses. The couple set off for a May-June-July honeymoon in Vienna, Venice, Lucerne, and Bayreuth, where they had tickets to the *Ring* as a wedding gift from Siloti. Then they went to Ivanovka to begin married life in Russia.

34 *Судьба* {К ПЯТОЙ СИМФОНИИ БЕТХОВЕНА} *Fate* {ON BEETHOVEN'S FIFTH SYMPHONY}

Op. 21, No. 1

The impulse behind this song came to Rachmaninoff more than two years before he wrote the other songs in the opus. It stands apart from them in its length (it is his longest song), in its conception as a dramatic monologue demanding "theatrical as well as vocal skills of the highest order" (*Martyn, 122),* and in its performance history, sung as it was on many occasions by Chaliapin (to whom it was dedicated), with the composer at the piano.

The theme of this song goes back to the last line of Pushkin's poem *The Gypsies*, on which the opera *Aleko* was based: "and from the Fates there is no defense." Fate was a theme in Song 18, but Pushkin's theme took on a personal meaning for Rachmaninoff after the failure of his symphony (*Kandinskii-Rybnikov* 1995). In this ballad, Aleksei Apukhtin personifies Fate (*sud'ba*, a feminine noun in Russian) as a malevolent old woman tapping relentlessly with her cane, whose unexpected entrances as an "old friend" bring an end to hopes and happiness. Apukhtin subtitled his poem "On Beethoven's Fifth Symphony," a reference to the belief that the opening notes of the symphony signify Fate knocking at Beethoven's door. This may or may not have been the case (see *Slonimsky 1989*, 166-8), but Rachmaninoff included the subtitle in his song, and used Beethoven's four-note motto repeatedly, beginning with the song's first notes.

The song has been criticized as "ponderous and full of theatrical pathos" (*Challis*, 100), as a "melodramatic showpiece" for Chaliapin which "plumbs the depths of banality" (*Norris 2001*, 142), and as the composer's "one resoundingly banal composition" (*Harrison*, 106). But Barrie Martyn is right to take the song seriously instead of dismissing it: "*Fate* has been much abused by musical commentators, but in fact it is a much better song than they allow" (*Martyn*, 122). The text is less original than those used by Mussorgsky for his "Songs and Dances of Death," but it is in the same genre, and its variety of moods are rendered effectively in the musical setting. The final section depicting the young lover coming to meet his sweetheart after dark is especially dramatic. The success of the song depends on the art of the singer. The Bulgarian bass Raffaele Ariè made an exceptionally eloquent recording of the song in 1954. When the Russian baritone Sergei Leiferkus sang it in 2003 at Salzburg, he was "arresting in his storytelling—chilling" (*Nordlinger*).

Chaliapin, though he did not record the song, sang it with Rachmaninoff, first at Lev Tolstoy's house in Moscow on 9 January 1900, then in a public performance on 9 March 1900, (*LN 1*, 555-6), and again in a concert on 2 December 1900 (the program for this concert is in *Rachmaninoff 1955*, 209). Rachmaninoff recalled the performance at Tolstoy's: Chaliapin sang "indescribably well," but afterwards Tolstoy looked "gloomy and cross," calling Rachmaninoff aside to tell him that Beethoven was "nonsense," and Pushkin and Lermontov were too. Rachmaninoff was annoyed by the remark and never saw Tolstoy again, even though he worshipped him as a writer. When Rachmaninoff later told Chekhov about the incident, Chekhov explained that if Tolstoy had an upset stomach or was having an off day for some reason, he was apt to say "stupid things" (*Swan*, 185-6).

Rachmaninoff's friend Yury Sakhnovsky orchestrated the song. Chaliapin sang it with an orchestra at a concert in 1908: "this transcription, performed for the first time, was done so well and with so much talent that the piece took on a certain symphonic character and, it seems to us, gains much in its new form" (Nikolai Kashkin, *Russkoe slovo*, 18 December 1908).

С своей походною клюкой,
С своими мрачными очами
Судьба, как грозный часовой,
Повсюду следует за нами.
Бедой лицо её грозит,
Она в угрозах поседела,
Она уж многих одолела,
И всё стучит, и всё стучит:
  Стук, стук, стук…
    Полно, друг,
Брось за счастием гоняться!
  Стук, стук, стук…

Бедняк совсем обжился с ней:
Рука с рукой они гуляют,
Сбирают вместе хлеб с полей,
В награду вместе голодают.
День целый дождь его кропит,
По вечерам ласкает вьюга,
А ночью с горя, да с испуга,
Судьба сквозь сон ему стучит:
  Стук, стук, стук…
    Глянь-ка, друг,
Как другие поживают.
  Стук, стук, стук…

Другие праздновать сошлись
Богатство, молодость и славу.
Их песни радостно неслись,
Вино сменилось им в забаву;
Давно уж пир у них шумит.
Но смолкли вдруг, бледнея, гости…
Рукой, дрожащею от злости,
Судьба в окошко к ним стучит:
  Стук, стук, стук...
    Новый друг
К вам пришёл, готовьте место!
  Стук, стук, стук…

Но есть же счастье на земле!
Однажды, полный ожиданья,
С восторгом юным на челе,
Пришёл счастливец на свиданье.
Ещё один он, всё молчит,
Заря за рощей потухает,
И соловей уж затихает,
А сердце бьётся и стучит:
  Стук, стук, стук…
    Милый друг,
Ты придёшь ли на свиданье?
  Стук, стук, стук…

Но вот идёт она, и вмиг
Любовь, тревога, ожиданье,
Блаженство, – всё слилось у них
В одно безумное лобзанье!
Немая ночь на них глядит,
Всё небо залито огнями,
А кто-то тихо за кустами
Клюкой докучною стучит:
  Стук, стук, стук…
    Старый друг
К вам пришёл, довольно счастья!
  Стук, стук, стук…

S svajéj pakhódnaju kljukój,
S svajími mráchnymi achámi,
Sud'bá, kak gróznyj chasavój,
Pafsjúdu sléduyet za námi.
Bedój litsó jejó grazít,
Aná v ugrózakh pasedéla,
Aná ush mnógikh adaléla,
I fsjó stuchít, i fsjó stuchít:
Stúk, stúk, stúk...
Pólna, drúk,
Bróz' za shchástiem ganjátsa!
Stúk, stúk, stúk...

Bednják safsém abzhýlsa s néj:
Ruká s rukój aní guljájut,
Zbirájut vméste khlép s paléj,
V nagrádu vméste galadájut.
Dén' tsélyj dóshch jevó krapít,
Pa vecherám laskájet v'júga,
A nóchju z górja, da s yspúga,
Sud'bá skvos' són jemú stuchít:
Stúk, stúk, stúk...
Glján'-ka, drúk,
Kág drugíje pazhyvájut.
Stúk, stúk, stúk...

Drugíje práznavat' sashlís'
Bagátstva, móladast' i slávu.
Ikh pésni rádasna neslís',
Vinó smenílas' ím v zabávu;
Davnó ush pír u níkh shumít,
No smólkli vdrúk, blednéja, gósti...
Rukój, drazháshcheju ad zlósti,
Sud'bá v akóshka k ním stuchít:
Stúk, stúk, stúk...
Nóvyj drúk
K vám prishól, gatóf'te mésta!
Stúk, stúk, stúk...

No jézd' zhe shchást'je na zemlé!
Adnázhdy, pólnyj azhydán'ja,
S vastórgam júnym na chelé,
Prishól shchaslívets na svidánj'e.
Jeshchó adín ón, vsjó malchít,
Zarjá za róshchej patukhájet,
I salavéj uzh zatikhájet,
A sérttse b'jótsa i stuchít:
Stúk, stúk, stúk...
Mílyj drúk,
Tý pridjósh li na svidán'je?
Stúk, stúk, stúk...

With her walking crutch,
With her somber gaze,
Fate, like a grim sentinal,
Pursues us wherever we go.
Her face spells trouble,
Her hair is white from dire threats,
She's already vanquished many,
And she keeps on tapping, keeps on tapping:
Tap, tap, tap...
Time's up, friend,
Give up chasing after happiness!
Tap, tap, tap...

A poor man's learned to live with Fate:
The two of them walk hand in hand,
Together they harvest grain from the fields,
Together they go hungry as their reward.
Rain pelts him all day long,
His evening comfort is whirling snow,
And at night, in his grief and fear,
Fate comes knocking in his dreams:
Tap, tap, tap...
Take a look, friend,
How other people live!
Tap, tap, tap...

Others gather to celebrate
Riches, youth, and fame.
Merrily their songs ring out,
They pour wine for their pleasure;
The noisy feast has lasted long,
When suddenly the guests fall silent, turn pale...
Trembling with malice, the hand of Fate
Knocks at their window:
Tap, tap, tap...
A new friend
Has come to the feast, set a place for her!
Tap, tap, tap...

But there is happiness on earth!
One day, full of anticipation,
With youthful rapture on his face,
A lucky lad's come to meet his sweetheart.
He's still alone, all is silent,
Twilight darkens behind the grove,
The nightingale finishes its song,
His heart is beating, pounding:
Tap, tap, tap...
Dearest friend,
Will you come to meet me?
Tap, tap, tap...

No vót idjót aná, i vmík
Ljubóf', trevóga, azhydán'je,
Blazhénstva, – fsjó slilós' u níkh
V adnó bezúmnaje labzán'je!
Nemája nóch na níkh gljadít,
Fsjo néba zálita agnjámi,
A któ-ta tíkha za kustámi
Kljukój dakúchnaju stuchít:
    Stúk, stúk, stúk…
        Stáryj drúk
K vám prishól, davól'na shchást'ja!
    Stúk, stúk, stúk…

But here she comes, and in one instant
Love, alarm, anticipation,
Bliss — all flowed together for them
Into one mad kiss!
Mute night watches them,
The whole sky is filled with lights,
When someone softly behind a bush
Taps with her intrusive crutch.
    Tap, tap, tap…
        An old friend
Has come to see you, enough of happiness!
    Tap, tap, tap…

Text. **Alekséi Nikoláyevich Apúkhtin**, 1863. Title: Судьба. К 5-й симфонии Бетховена (Fate. On Beethoven's 5th Symphony). First published in 1886. A sixth stanza (it follows the third stanza of the song text), crossed out in a notebook copy of the poem, is included in recent editions of Apukhtin, but it was not part of the text when Rachmaninoff set it (see the note to the poem in *Apukhtin 1991*, 386). This stanza adds the example of a fighter for human rights and equality who ends up in leg irons—lines which could not have passed the censor in 1886.

Meter. Binary. Iambic tetrameter, with trochees ending each stanza:

Already many has she vanquished,
And still she knocks, and still she knocks:
    Tap, tap, tap...
        Look around,
Give up trying to be happy!
    Tap, tap, tap...

Music. Probably begun summer of 1899 at Krasnenkoye (*VOR 1*, 311), finished Moscow 18 February 1900 (*T/N*, 75). Op. 21, no. 1. C Minor. 4/4, Allegro Moderato, with changes throughout: Marziale, Grave, Con Moto, Andante. For Bass Voice: A flat–e^1 (f^2 in the optional falsetto passage at the end of the fourth stanza). First published separately in April 1900, then with Opus 21 by A. Gutheil in Moscow in 1902.

Dedicated to **Fyódor Ivánovich Chaliápin** (1873–1938). One of five songs Rachmaninoff dedicated to the singer (the others are Songs 64, 68, 71, and 73). For more information about Chaliapin's repertoire of Rachmaninoff's songs, see my note to Song 64.

Recordings. Abdrazakov, Ariè, Burchuladze, Christoff, Furlanetto, Kharitonov, Koptchak, Leiferkus, Mróz, Ognivtsev, Olli, Reizen, Söderström, Suchkova, Sutey.

35 *Над свежей могилой* *By a fresh grave*

Op. 21, No. 2

Semyon Nadson (see Song 33) wrote this poem when he was 17, after the death of a classmate's sister, Natalia Deshevova, whom the poet ardently loved when he was in high school (he later dedicated all his books of poetry to her). It was set to music by more than twenty-five composers between 1879 and 1917.

Rachmaninoff's setting has a declamatory voice part that builds to *forte* on the word "могилой" (grave) at the end of line 4, then softens to a lyrical and tender culmination in the last two lines, sung in 3/2 time. The piano part is very expressive, with "abrupt chromatic figures" (*Norris*, 142) that set the declamatory vocal line in eloquent relief. It is a surprisingly engaging song despite the despondent lyric.

Я вновь один, и вновь кругом
Всё та же ночь и мрак унылый.
И я в раздумье роковом
Стою над свежею могилой!
Чего мне ждать, к чему мне жить,
К чему бороться и трудиться:
Мне больше некого любить,
Мне больше некому молиться!

Ja vnóf' adín, i vnóf' krugóm	I'm again alone, and again surrounded
Fsjó tá zhe nóch i mrák unýlyj.	By the same night and gloomy darkness.
I já v razdúm'je rakavóm	Deep and fateful are my thoughts
Stajú nad svézheju magílaj!	As I stand over a fresh grave!
Chevó mne zhdát', k chemú mne zhýt',	What can I hope for, what can I live for,
K chemú barótsa i trudítsa:	What can I struggle and strive for?
Mne ból'she nékava ljubít',	No longer do I have one to love,
Mne ból'she nékamu malítsa!	No longer do I have one to pray to!

Text. **Semyón Nádson**, 1879. Title: Над свежей могилой (By a fresh grave). Set by Ivan Borodin (1893) and numerous others (*Ivanov 1*, 238).

Meter. Binary. Iambic tetrameter:

Alone again, again surrounded,
The same old night, the same old gloom.

Music. April 1902. Op. 14, no. 2. E Minor. 4/4, Largo. For Low Voice: c–e[1]. First published with Opus 21 by A. Gutheil in Moscow in 1902. No dedication.

Recordings. Burchuladze, Crona, Kharitonov, Koptchak, Leiferkus, Ognivtsev, Olli, Söderström, Suchkova, Tear.

Ivan Borodin: Piotr Slovtsov.

36 *Сумерки* *Twilight*

Op. 21, No. 3

Ivan Tkhorzhevsky published this lyric, a translation from the French of Marie Jean Guyau, in 1901, the year he graduated from St. Petersburg University, in a volume of "philosophical verses" by Guyau. Rachmaninoff luckily found it soon after. Tkhorzhevsky was a poet and translator, remembered mainly for his Russian version of the Rubaiyat of Omar Khayyam (Paris, 1928). Vladimir Nabokov criticized the translator for drawing more on Edward Fitzgerald's famous English translation of the Rubaiyat than on the Persian original, but added "reading these verses as you would read any good Russian poet, one is often struck by their elegance and precision of formulation" (*PRZ*, 392).

This text portrays a moment of union between the evening sky at twilight and a woman witnessing it with a long contemplative gaze. There is a sense of heightened calm, inner peace, and spiritual beauty linking her with the cosmos as the stars gradually come out. Their "bright swarm" is a dynamic image: the starlight seems to hum and vibrate overhead, in communion with her still awareness. It is an unusual image which occurs in another "night song," Tchaikovsky's "Mild stars shone down on us," to a text by Pleshcheyev (Op. 60/12).

Rachmaninoff wrote lovely music for this song. A declamatory and calm opening in the minor key uses the sparest of means in the piano; then triplets put the scene into movement as the woman watches the stars come out. Toward the end, with the "bright swarm," the song moves into the major key and the culmination is reached on the held, highest note in the song, which occurs in line 6 on the word "there" (*tam*). Surprisingly, the song is not well known, but contemporary singers are discovering it for themselves: the Finnish soprano Karita Mattila sang it in recital in London in 2003 and in Helsinki in 2006.

Она задумалась. Одна, перед окном
Склонясь, она сидит, и в сумраке ночном
Мерцает долгий взор; а в синеве безбрежной
Темнеющих небес, роняя луч свой нежный,
Восходят звёздочки бесшумною толпой;
И кажется, что там какой-то светлый рой
Таинственно парит и, словно восхищённый,
Трепещет над её головкою склонённой.

Aná zadúmalas'. Adná pered aknóm,	She's lost in thought. Alone, before the window,
Sklanjás', aná sidít i f súmrake nachnóm	She sits, her head inclined, and in the evening twilight

Mertsájet dólgij vzór;
  i f sinevé bezbrézhnoj
Temnéjushchikh nebés,
  ranjája lúch svoj nézhnyj,
Vaskhódjat zvjózdachki
  besshúmnaju talpój;
I kázhetsa, shto tám kakój-ta svétlyj rój
Taínstvenna parít, i,
  slóvna vaskhishchónnyj,
Trepéshchet nad jejó
  galófkaju sklanjónnyj.

A long gaze radiates from her eyes;
  and in the boundless blue
Of the darkening sky,
  sending down tender rays of light,
Little stars come out
  in a silent throng;
And it seems some kind of bright swarm
Soars there mysteriously, and,
  in heightened excitement,
Trembles high above her
  lowered head.

Text. **Iván Ivánovich Tkhorzhévsky** (1878–1951). Title: Сумерки (Twilight), published in *Guyau 1901*, p. 61. Erroneously identified as M. Tkhorzhevsky in *RPS* and *T/N*. Translation of a French poem by **Marie Jean Guyau** (1854–1888), poet and philosopher. First set by Rachmaninoff.

Meter. Binary. Iambic hexameter:

She sits, her head inclined, at twilight by the window,
As in the boundless blue above the stars appear…

Music. April 1902. Op. 21, no. 3. E Minor–E Major. 4/4, Lento. For High Voice: c^1–g^2 sharp. First published with Opus 21 by A. Gutheil in Moscow in 1902.

Dedicated to **Nadézha Ivánovna Zabéla-Vrúbel** (1868–1913), a coloratura soprano in Mamontov's private opera; she went on to sing at the Mariinsky and was also a noted recitalist. Many composers admired her, including Rimsky-Korsakov, who wrote one of his most beautiful arias for her (Marfa's Act II aria in *The Tsar's Bride*); he dedicated songs to her and her husband, the artist Mikhail Vrubel. Zabela-Vrubel sang the premiere of both this song and "Lilacs," Song 38, accompanied by Rachmaninoff, on 10 February 1903; a month later she premiered Song 40, "Here it's so fine." Rachmaninoff regarded her highly and asked her to sing these new songs (*LN 1*, 327-8, 573).

Recordings. Dodoka, Gerzmava, Guryakova, Isakova, Katulskaya, Levko, Mattila, Naoumenko, Olli, Pusar, Söderström, Suchkova, Sumatchova.

Transcriptions. *Cello:* Mischa Maisky.

Tkhorzhevsky's Source Text, "Lever d'étoiles", Guyau 1881, p. 99:

Pensive, assise au bord de la fenêtre sombre,
Son œil aux longs regards rayonne seul dans l'ombre.
Sur sa tête s'étend sans fin le grand ciel pur.
Les étoiles des nuits se lèvent dans l'azur,
Et par-dessus son front sérieux qui se penche,
Chacune vient sans bruit se ranger, douce et blanche,
Essaim mystérieux dans son vol arrêté,
Qui d'en haut, palpitant, plane sur sa beauté.

37 *Онѣ отвечали* *They answered*

Op. 21, No. 4

The original French lyric by Victor Hugo that is the source of the text of this song, the Russian translation by Lev Mey, and the musical setting by Rachmaninoff are all as close to perfect as can be imagined. Hugo (1802–1885) wrote his "Guitar Song" on 18 July 1838 and published it in *Les Rayons et les Ombres* in 1840 (the original French lyric will be found below).

Lev Mey (1822–1862) was a poet and playwright who wrote historical plays used by Rimsky-Korsakov for his operas *The Maid of Pskov* (1891) and *The Tsar's Bride* (1899), and unusual and interesting original lyrics used by Mussorgksy and Tchaikovsky for songs. He was also an excellent verse translator whose translations Tchaikovsky used for six of his songs, including "None but the lonely heart" (for more on Mey, see *TCS*, 71 and passim).

The play of masculine and feminine in the endings of the third person plural pronoun "they" is the key trick in this lyric: it works both in French (*ils, elles*) and in Russian (*они, онѣ*); this device is crucial to understanding the song. However, when Russian spelling was reformed by the Provisional Government in 1917, the third letter of the feminine pronoun, a vowel written upright as ѣ and in cursive script as *ѣ*, was eliminated because its pronunciation had ceased to have any distinctive features. That did cause a loss in meaning, however, in the case of this pronoun, namely, a distinction between "they" (masculine) and "they" (feminine). In this poem, then, as the typography in pre-reform Russian shows, the three questions are all asked by *men*; the answers are given by *women*. This distinction is lost if the text is printed in the modern Russian alphabet, as it is in the Moscow edition of *RPS*. The text below is printed with the letter ѣ as Rachmaninoff found it in Mey, and as originally published by Gutheil in 1902.

The insistent questions of the men (daring brigands pursued by the Spanish police) are accompanied by surging arpeggios in the piano, while the graceful answers given by the women are *pianissimo*, with three dotted quarter notes that rise an octave and fall back, differently each time; the last answer is very poignant, with a change in key. Even if the distinction between "they" (the men) and "they" (the women) has been lost in the pronunciation of the text, Rachmaninoff makes the distinction abundantly clear through the music. The song was written for soprano or tenor, but there are good recordings by baritones and mezzos too. The Russian soprano Nadezhda Kazantseva gives a crystalline performance.

Спросили *они*: «как, в летучих челнах,
Нам белою чайкой скользнуть на волнах,
  Чтоб нас сторожа не догнали?»
    — Гребите! — *онѣ* отвечали.

Спросили *они*: «как забыть навсегда,
Что в мире юдольном есть бедность, беда,
  Что есть в нём вражда и печали?»
    — Засните! — *онѣ* отвечали.

Спросили *они*: «как красавиц привлечь
Без чары: чтоб сами, на страстную речь,
  Онѣ нам в объятия пали?»
    — Любите! — *онѣ* отвечали.

Sprasíli aní: "Kák v letúchikh chelnákh
Nam bélaju chájkaj skal'zít'
  na valnákh,
Shtop nás starazhá ne dagnáli?"
    — Grebíte! — ané atvecháli.

Sprasíli aní: "Kág zabýt' nafsegdá,
Shto v míre judól'nam jézd bédnast',
  bedá,
Shto jést' v njóm vrazhdá i pecháli?"
    — Zasníte! — ané atvecháli.

Sprasíli aní: "Kák krasávits privléch
Bes cháry: shtop sámi, na strásnuju
  réch,
Ané nam v abjátija páli?"
    — Ljubíte! — ané atvecháli.

The men asked: "how, in swift boats,
Can we glide over the waves
  like white seagulls,
To escape the guards who pursue us?"
    Row! — the women answered.

They asked: "how can we forget for good,
That in this vale of tears there's poverty
  and trouble,
Malice and sorrow?"
    Sleep! — they answered.

They asked: "how can we win pretty women
Without spells: so our passionate words
  alone
Will make them fall into our arms?"
    Love! — they answered.

TEXT. **Lev Aleksándrovich Mey**, 1862. Untitled. First published in 1862 in *Modnyi magazin* (Fashion Shop). First set in Russian by M. M. Ivanov (1849–1927) in 1899. After Rachmaninoff, set by V. A. Zolotarëv (1872–1964) for male choir (Op. 26/2, 1909). Victor Hugo's French poem was set by Liszt (1842), Lalo (1856), Bizet (1866), Saint-Saëns (1870), and Massenet (1886).

METER. Ternary. Two amphibrachs of four feet, two of three:

The mén asked: "and hów can we túrn pretty héads
With pássionate speéches alóne, without spélls,
To máke them fall ínto our árms?
  By lóving! — the wómen replíed.

MUSIC. April 1902. Op. 21, no. 4. D-flat Major. 12/8, Allegro vivace. For High Voice: e^1 flat–b^2 flat. First published with Opus 21 by A. Gutheil in Moscow in 1902.

Dedicated to **Yeléna Yúliyevna Kreutzer** (1875–1961), Rachmaninoff's piano pupil for many years, and friend of both the composer and his wife Natalia. Her surname in Russian is spelled Kreitser; her married name was Zhukovskaya. Under that name she wrote a valuable memoir about the composer (*VOR 1*, 251-342).

Rachmaninoff spent a portion of the summers of 1899–1901 with the Kreutzer family at their country house in Krasnenkoye. He was evidently happy and quite at home at the Kreutzers' summer house; in that setting he found both inspiration and the freedom he needed to do solid work. Even in the arid year of 1899 he wrote Songs 9 and 34 there. The next year, when he returned from Italy in August 1900, he worked there through October writing the second and third movements of his Second Piano Concerto, Op. 18 (see *LN 1*, 557). In 1901 at Krasnenkoye he proofed his Second Suite for Two Pianos, Op. 17 (*LN 1*, 564-5), and composed his Sonata for Cello and Piano, Op. 19 (*LN 2*, 97).

Recordings. Arkhipova, Atlantov, DeGaetani, Dnishev, Dolukhanova, Furdui, Galante, Gedda, Gerzmava, Hvorostovsky, Izotova, Kazantseva, Kennedy, Korshunov, Larin, Lee, Lemeshev, Makarina, Milcheva, Naoumenko, Olli, Price, Pusar, Rautio, Shtoda, Siniavskaya, Söderström, Suchkova, Tcheresky, Tear, Tourel, Vishnevskaya, Zelenina.

Mey's source text, "Autre Guitare" by Victor Hugo, 1838

Comment, disaient-ils,
Avec nos nacelles,
Fuir les alguazils?
— Ramez, disaient-elles.

Comment, disaient-ils,
Oublier querelles,
Misère et périls?
— Dormez, disaient-elles.

Comment, disaient-ils,
Enchanter les belles
Sans philtres subtils?
— Aimez, disaient-elles.

38 *Сирень* *Lilacs*

Op. 21, No. 5

This beautiful song, one of Rachmaninoff's masterpieces, uses a short lyric by Ekaterina Beketova (1855–1892). In the Beketov family several of the women as well as the men were writers (*RP 1*, 202-4). Yekaterina's father, the rector of St. Petersburg University, was a botanist who wrote fiction and criticism as well as books about plants and animals. One of her nephews was the Symbolist poet Alexander Blok (see Song 78), who was a boy of eleven when she died. She wrote works for children, lyrics about nature, and translations from five languages (*Ledkovsky*, 70-1). Underlying the lovely spring-morning images in "Lilacs" is the Russian superstition that it is good luck to find a five-petal lilac flower (usually there are four). The word счастье (shchastje), which in Russian means both "good luck" and "happiness," occurs three times in the lyric.

The initial impulse in the song, in both the opening piano phrase and the repeated, three-note phrase of the voice part, is a mimetic gesture of stepping out for a walk: it is comparable to the opening section of Mussorgsky's "Pictures at an Exhibition" which is entitled "Progulka," a stroll. This is not a promenade in a public place, however, but a private walk to be sung "sempre tranquillo." This gentle forward motion impels the first half of the song toward the goal, the luck waiting in the lilac blossom, a happiness which may be "poor," meaning modest, but is one's own. There is a tremor of alarm in the piano as the second part of the song begins. The goal is reached in the last line of the song. The "gentle twinge of chromaticism" on the three-syllable Russian word for "poor"—an F-flat-E-flat-A-flat phrase—has been remarked by David Jackson (*Jackson*, 175), and Yury Keldysh also mentions this "piquant" touch (*Keldysh*, 238). The song ends in the major, but there is an aura of *grust'* in it, that "sadness" which Rachmaninoff said was the "mother of music" (*LN 2*, 343).

Many singers have found the song appealing, not just women but men, and not only tenors but baritones and basses too (Sergei Leiferkus, Kim Borg). Of the more than sixty recordings I have heard, many are very fine, though it is not easy to find a perfect recording of it. Tamara Siniavskaya sings it beautifully, but with a string orchestra instead of a piano the song loses a great deal. Nezhdanova's recording is charming, but it was done at a glacial pace and late in her life. Of other singers of older generations, Oda Slobodskaya, Kyra Vayne, Maria Kurenko, Zara Dolukhanova, and Irina Arkhipova are all good. Lucia Popp sings it with a clear, bright vibrato but reverses the last two verbs, a small blemish in an otherwise inspired live performance at Salzburg. Nicolai Gedda sings it brightly too but with two wrong notes in the fourth and fifth lines of the second stanza. Dmitri Smirnov sings it very well, but ends on a high A-flat instead of C, which spoils it. Isobel Baillie and Jussi Björling sing it well in English, though the translations are old-fashioned. There are very good modern recordings by Elisabeth Söderström and Joan Rodgers.

The melodic material is modest but so lovely in its development, with a piano part that supports and "converses" with the voice so winningly, that it is not surprising Rachmaninoff decided to transcribe the song for piano. Rachmaninoff's 1942 recording of the transcribed song (on CD RCA Victor 7766-2-RG) is described by Robert Philip in his insightful book *Performing Music in the Age of Recording*: "The way the lines sing out, the way the different strands of the texture are subtly layered, so that the prominence of each line comes and goes, the way in which he separates a melodic line from its accompaniment by subtly dislocating it rhythmically, particularly by playing melody notes fractionally late: these are all vintage Rachmaninoff" (*Philip*, 33).

Поутру, на заре,
По росистой траве,
Я пойду свежим утром дышать;
И в душистую тень,
Где теснится сирень,
Я пойду своё счастье искать…

В жизни счастье одно
Мне найти суждено,
И то счастье в сирени живёт;
На зелёных ветвях,
На душистых кистях
Моё бедное счастье цветёт…

Pa utrú, na zaré,	In the morning, at dawn,
Pa rasístoj travé,	Through dewy grass,
Ja pajdú svézhym útram dyshát';	I walk and breathe the fresh morning air;
I v dushýstuju tén',	And to the fragrant shade,
Ĝde tesnítsa sirén',	Where lilacs cluster,
Ja pajdú svajo shchástje iskát'…	I'll go in search of my happiness…
V zhýzni shchástje adnó	Only one happiness
Mne najtí suzhdenó,	Am I destined to find in life,
I to shchástje f siréni zhyvjót;	And that happiness lives in the lilacs;
Na zeljónykh vetvjákh,	On green branches,
Na dushýstykh kistjákh	In fragrant clusters,
Majo bédnaje shchástje tsvetjót…	My poor happiness blossoms…

Text. **Yekaterína Andréyevna Bekétova**, 1878. Published in a posthumous volume of her poetry *Stikhotvoreniia* (Poems), St. Petersburg, 1895, p. 45. Set in 1900 by Andrei Shcherbachov, a pupil of Felix Blumenfeld and Rimsky-Korsakov; but by Goldenweiser's dating below, Rachmaninoff was the first to set it. His setting is the only one remembered today.

Meter. Ternary. Anapest, lines of two and three feet, with masculine endings. The sample below is taken from *Slonimsky 1949-51*, vol. 2, p. 33:

At the dawn, with the sun,
On the dew sprinkl'd lawn,
I would go for a breath of fresh air.
In the fragrant retreat,
Where the lilacs are sweet,
I will look for my happiness there...

Music. The end of the manuscript of Op. 21 is dated April 1902 (*Bortnikova*, 33 and *T/N*, 77). However, Alexander Goldenweiser, who saw the composer frequently during his dry period between 1897 and 1899, writes that "Lilacs" was written then (*VOR 1*, 407); and according to a memoir by Yelena Vinter, the niece of Tatyana Lyubatovich, "Lilacs" was composed at Putyatino in the summer of 1898 (*VOR 2*, 24; for details about that summer, see p. 91 above).

Op. 21, no. 5. A-flat Major. 9/4, Allegretto. For High Voice: e^1 flat–g^2. First published with Opus 21 by A. Gutheil in Moscow in 1902.

Transcribed for piano by the composer, who played it for the first time in a recital in Kiev 19 October 1913 (*LN 2*, 412). On publication date of the transcription (1914?), see *T/N*, 77-8. No dedication.

Recordings. Arkhipova, Baillie (in English), Bandrowska-Turska, Björling (in English), Borele, Borg, Borisenko, Borodina, Celine, Cernay (in French), Christova, Davtian, DeGaetani, Dionne, Dodoka, Dolukhanova, Farrar (in English), Firsova, Furdui, Furlanetto, Gedda, Gerzmava, Gorchakova, Guleghina, Guryakova, Izotova, Karnobatlova-Dobreva, Kasimova, Kazarnovskaya, Kelessidi, Kharitonov, Kolomyjec, Kontra, Koshetz, Kurenko, Lapina, Larin, Lear, Leiferkus, Lemeshev, Makarina, Makarova, Mishura, Mkrtchyan, Nezhdanova, Olli, Orda, Popp, Pusar, Rautio, Rodgers, Rudenko, Semenchuk, Shpiller, Shtoda, Shumskaya, Silja, Siniavskaya, Slobodskaya, Smirnov, Söderström, Suchkova, Sumatchova, Tourel, Troyanos, Vallin (in French), Vayne, Viting, Weiler, Zhadan, Zimmermann.

Transcriptions. *Cello:* Anthony Elliott, Dmitri Ferschtman, David Geringas, Brian Stucki. *Piano:* Vladimir Ashkenazy, Idil Biret, Boris Bloch, Edward Eikner, Victor Eresko, Morton Estrin, Sergio Fiorentino, Robert Hamilton, Olga Kern, Evgeny Kissin, John McArthur, Benno Moiseiwitsch, Alexei Nasedkin, Sergei Rachmaninoff, Howard Shelley, Yevgeny Sudbin, Simon Trpceski. *Piano trio:* Bekova Sisters.

39 *Отрывок из А. Мюссе* *Fragment from A. Musset*

Op. 21, No. 6

The source of this fragment by Alfred de Musset (1810–1857)—in an excellent translation by Alexei Apukhtin—is "Le nuit de mai" (1835), the earliest of Musset's cycle of four longer "night" poems, which are a dialogue between the poet and his muse. The lines are spoken by the poet early in the poem. The muse tries to persuade the poet to use his grief for his art, to turn it into poetry, "to accept suffering and to go on living and writing" (*Furst*, 520). The dramatic final line of the song—"Oh loneliness, oh poverty!"—is not a generalized outcry but a reference to the sometimes anguished state of solitude and poverty which the poet must learn to live with in order to practice his art. A recent study of the problem of Fate in Rachmaninoff's music suggests that disastrous or difficult outcome is the theme of both the earlier song "Fate" and this song, and that it was a theme that took on a personal meaning for the composer after the failure of his First Symphony. As a counterbalance to it is the theme of happy or lucky outcome in Song 38, "Lilacs," and Song 40, "How fair this spot" (*Kandinskii-Rybnikov*, 94).

Like "Fate," the present song calls for a highly dramatic performance, but in this song the music is more original and its impact stronger, partly because it is much shorter. It is a dramatic soliloquy that moves and pauses and resumes from line to line; the stage is set in space and time: the poet's "cell" at midnight, with chimes heard in the piano part before the singer names them. The pacing and the dynamics change continually, and there is a long pause in line 8 (after the words "Someone's entered…") before the song resumes.The piano plays a very active role in the pacing of the performance and even in providing sound effects, and it ends the song with a passionate coda.

The soprano Nina Dorliak gives a brilliant performance of it, accompanied on the piano by her husband Sviatoslav Richter.

Что так усиленно сердце больное
Бьётся, и просит, и жаждет покоя?
Чем я взволнован, испуган в ночи?
Стукнула дверь, застонав и заноя…
Гаснущей лампы блеснули лучи…
Боже мой! Дух мне в груди захватило!
Кто-то зовёт меня, шепчет уныло…
Кто-то вошёл… Моя келья пуста,
Нет никого, это полночь пробило…
О, одиночество, о, нищета!

Shtó ták usílenna sérttse bal'nóje
B'jótsa, i prósit, i zhàzhdet pakóje?
Chém já vzvalnóvan, ispúgan
  v nachí?
Stúknula dvér', zastanáf i zanója…
Gásnushchej lámpy blesnúli luchí…
Bózhe mój! Dúkh mné v grudí
  zakhvatíla!
Któ-ta zavjót menjá, shépchet unýla…
Któ-ta vashól… Majá kél'ja pustá,
Nét nikavó, éta pólnach prabíla…
Ó, adinóchestva, o, nishchetá!

Why does my sick heart so violently
Beat, and beg, and thirst for peace?
Why am I troubled, afraid
  in the night?
A door slammed, groaning and whining…
Rays of the sputtering lamp glittered…
My God! It takes my breath
  away!
Someone calls me, in a pitiful whisper…
Someone entered… My cell is empty,
I'm alone, that was midnight striking…
Oh loneliness, oh poverty!

Text. **Alekséi Apúkhtin**, 1856. Title: Отрывок. *Из А. Мюссе* (Fragment. *From A. Musset*). First published in the 1886 edition of Apukhtin's poems. A translation of part of Alfred de Musset's "Le nuit de mai" (1835). The French text is at the end of the song below.

Set by several other composers before and after Rachmaninoff, including Vladimir Rebikov ("rhythmo-declamation," 1905) and Nikolai Kharito ("melo-declamation," 1913).

Meter. Ternary. Dactylic tetrameter:

Why am I troubled, afraid in the night?
Slam went a door, with a groan and a whine…

Music. April 1902. Op. 21, no. 6. F-sharp Minor. 12/8, with 9/8 and 6/8 passages, Allegro non tanto. For High Voice: c^1 sharp–a^2. First published with Opus 21 by A. Gutheil in Moscow in 1902.

Dedicated to **Princess Aleksándra Andréyevna Lieven**. Princess Lieven (correctly transliterated Liven, d. 1914) was head of the Women's Prison Committee and other charitable organizations. Natalia and Sophia Satina's mother, Varvara, did charity work with her, and probably introduced Rachmaninoff to Princess Lieven. He took part in many charity concerts for her over the years. After he completed his treatment with Dr. Dahl, she invited him to stay on her estate in the Crimea, where he went in April 1900 with Chaliapin, spending time with Chekhov and Stanislavsky's theater in Yalta.

Recordings. Amaize, Arkhipova, Burchuladze, Chaiter, Christoff, Davtian, Dodoka, Dorliak, Furdui, Gedda, Guleghina, Hvorostovsky, Kabaivanska, Koptchak, Korshunov, Koshetz, Kurenko, Larin, Lee, Lemeshev, Lisitsian, Makarova, Mattila, Mishura, Obraztsova, Ognivtsev, Olli, Petrov, Piavko, Pusar, Rautio, Rodgers, Rozum, Shtoda, Silja, Söderström, Suchkova, Vassilieff.

Transcriptions. *Cello:* Dmitri Ferschtman.

Apukhtin's Source Text:

Pourquoi mon coeur bat-il si vite?
Qu'ai-je donc en moi qui s'agite
Dont je me sens épouvanté?
Ne frappe-t-on pas à ma porte?
Pourquoi ma lampe à demi morte
M'éblouit-elle de clarté?
Dieu puissant! tout mon corps frissone.
Qui vient? qui m'appelle? — Personne.
Je suis seul, c'est l'heure qui sonne;
Ô solitude! ô pauvreté!

40 *Здесь хорошо* *Here it's so fine*

Op. 21, No. 7

The lyric for this lovely song came from a first book of poetry by the poet and children's writer Glafira Mamoshina (1870–1942), also known as Countess Einerling after her first marriage, who adopted the pseudonym "G. Galiná." Galina was one of those poets (like Apukhtin) whom serious intellectuals cited as examples of Rachmaninoff's bad taste in poetry (*LN* 2, 44), a criticism recalled in Catriona Kelly's "very short introduction" to Russian literature (*Kelly*, 103). He had accepted the criticism with good nature, but had stuck by his choices of lyrics. Rachmaninoff's three Galiná songs (40, 45, 56) are among his best. Her lyrics had a musicality that attracted many composers. Alexander Kuprin, a good writer of fiction and follower of Chekhov, reviewed Galiná's book when it came out in 1902. He criticized her "civic" poetry on current events (like women in the Boer War), but he liked the freshness and sincerity of her purely lyric poems, "not large in their dimensions, but so musical and graceful in their form" (*Kuprin 1902*).

Rachmaninoff changed the first word of the poem from "*how* fine it is" to "*here* it's so fine," a small emendation that anchors the moment in the here and now, making it more concrete. If the opening phrase of "Lilacs"—two quarter notes and a dotted half note, repeated—is a melodic gesture that suggests stepping out, here the opening melodic phrase of three eighth notes and a half note "is like a broad gesture pointing out to the view in the distance" of river, meadows, and clouds (*Vasina-Grossman*, 328). The elaboration of this opening melodic figure, falling gradually in the first half, then back up the register to the sustained high B and A on the first two words of the last line, is deeply satisfying; the vowels, predominantly long "ah" sounds in the rhymes, also give definition to the exquisite lyricism of this perfect song. The piano writing is very fine: Rachmaninoff "never excelled these twenty-two bars of lyrical outpouring, [and] in the reflective piano postlude, it is the intensity of such moments that confirms the conviction that the essence of Rachmaninoff lies here rather than in the keyboard athletics beloved by the public" (*Martyn*, 142).

It is not an easy song to sing well, because of the "cruelly difficult *pianissimo* top B natural, which has to appear as from nowhere, and if the singer cannot bring this off, then the whole effect of the song is spoiled" (*Jackson*, 175-6). The many beautiful modern recordings include those by Kathleen Battle, Heidi Grant Murphy, and Elena Bryleva, and two readings by Nicolai Gedda with Gerald Moore (1965) and Alexis Weissenberg (1969). Of the older singers, Oda Slobodskaya and Nadezhda Kazantseva are thrilling and true. For singers, the song is a pure gift. In addition, it has been transcribed for cello, violin, trumpet, and piano.

Здесь хорошо… Взгляни: вдали
  Огнем горит река,
Цветным ковром луга легли,
  Белеют облака.

Здесь нет людей… Здесь тишина…
  Здесь только Бог да я.
Цветы, да старая сосна,
  Да ты, мечта моя…

Zdés' kharashó… Vzgljaní: vdalí	Here it's so fine… Look: in the distance
Agnjóm garít reká,	The river glitters like fire,
Tsvetným kavróm lugá leglí,	The meadows are a carpet of color,
Beléjut ablaká.	There are white clouds overhead.
Zdés' nét ljudéj… Zdés' tishyná…	Here there are no people… It's so quiet…
Zdés' tól'ka Bógh da já.	Here are only God and I.
Tsvetý, da stáraja sasná,	And the flowers, and the old pine tree,
Da tý, mechtá majá…	And you, my dream…

Text. **G. Galiná (Glafíra Adól'fovna Einerling)**. Untitled. First published in *Galina 1902*, p. 79. First set by Rachmaninoff, later by some minor composers.

Meter. Binary. Alternating Iambic tetrameters and trimeters:

It's lovely here… A distant view,
The river gleams like fire…

Music. April 1902. Op. 21, no. 7. A Major. 4/4, Moderato. For High Voice: d^1– b^2. First published with Opus 21 by A. Gutheil in Moscow in 1902.

Dedicated to "**N**," Rachmaninoff's wife Natalia.

Recordings. Bandrowska-Turska, Battle, Borele, Borodina, Bryleva, Chaiter, Christoff, Delunsch, Dilber, di Tullio (in English), Dnishev, Dodoka, Domnich, Dorliak, Fagan, Farrar (in English), Firsova, Fiset, Fleming, Galante, Gedda, Gerzmava, Gruberova, Guleghina, Hendricks, Hvorostovsky, Karnobatlova-Dobreva, Katulskaya, Kazantseva, Kolomyjec, Korshunov, Koshetz, Kovaleva, Kozlovsky, Kurenko, Lapina, Larin, Lee, Lemeshev, Makarina, L. Maslennikova, McCormack (in English), Milcheva, Mirakian, H. Murphy, Nesterenko, Netrebko, Nezhdanova, Ognivtsev, Oleinichenko, Olli, Pons, Pusar, Rautio, Rodgers, Rudenko, Silja, Siniavskaya, Siparis, Slobodskaya, Söderström, Souzay, Suchkova, Talvela, Urmana, Zelenina.

Transcriptions. *Cello:* Dmitri Ferschtman, David Geringas, Mischa Maisky, Brian Stucki, Moray Welsh. *Piano:* Vladimir Ashkenazy, Victor Babin and Vitya Vronsky (piano duo), John McArthur, Earl Wild. *Trumpet:* Sergei Nakariakov. *Violin:* Andrés Cardenes, Sherry Kloss, Itzhak Perlman, Aaron Rosand, Vladimir Spivakov.

41 *На смерть чижика* / *On the death of a siskin*

Op. 21, No. 8

Keeping songbirds was a widespread custom in Russia; there were "bird markets" in the towns; Mikhail Glinka liked having birds in his apartment, in and out of cages, trilling away. This bird is called a *chizh* in Russian, and its diminutive *chizhik*, translated in English as "siskin" (or sometimes "linnet"), is a type of finch common in northern Europe but not native to Britain. The English word "siskin" goes back to the Russian *chizh* via Dutch *sisiken* (in German, *Zeisig*); a citation in the *OED* from 1768 calls the siskin "an irregular visitant, said to come from Russia." Vladimir Dahl identifies *chizh* in his famous *Reasoned Dictionary of the Living Great-Russian Language* (four volumes, 1864–8) by its Latin name "Fringilla Spinus." Thomas Bewick, in his *History of British Birds*, describes the song of *Fringilla Spinus* as "pleasing and sweetly various," like a canary's, though not as loud. It is "familiar, docile, and chearful," beginning its song early in the morning, and it "breeds freely with the Canary." Perhaps the "little winged friend" of the songbird in this charming early 19th-century poem by Vasily Zhukovsky (1783–1852) was a canary; at any rate, the siskin is known for devotion to its mate, and this one dies of heartbreak when he loses her.

Rachmaninoff probably found this text in the 1895 edition of Zhukovsky's poems, where the editors explain that Zhukovsky wrote two "Siskin" poems, but published only this one. They call the poem a "joke," but give no explanation of what prompted Zhukovsky to write it; in the 1959 Soviet edition of the poems, the poem is excluded altogether. To be sure, it is a trifle, no doubt occasioned by the loss of someone's favorite songbird. But the conceit is a pretty one and the writing of it shows tender sentiment and wit. Rachmaninoff's *Allegretto* setting of it is perfectly in keeping with this tenderness. The voice part conveys the elegiac theme with sympathetic feeling, but not ponderously, and there is a graceful contrapuntal piano part which lends it an early 19th century period flavor.

В сем гробе верный чижик мой!
Природы милое творенье,
Из мирной области земной
Он улетел, как сновиденье.

Он для любви на свете жил.
Он нежной песенкой приветной
За ласку нежную платил
И подлетал к руке приветной.

Но в свете страшно и любить:
Ему был дан дружок крылатый;
Чтоб милого не пережить,
Он в гробе скрылся от утраты.

F sjém [sjóm] gróbe vérnyj chízhyk mój!
Piródy mílaje tvarén'je
Iz mírnaj óblasti zemnój
Ón uletél, kak snavidén'je.

In this coffin lies my faithful siskin!
Dear little creature of nature,
From earth's peaceful province
He flew away like a fleeting dream.

Ón dlja ljubví na svéte zhýl.
Ón nézhnaj pésenkaj privétnaj
Za lásku nézhnuju platíl
I padletál k ruké privétnaj.

He lived in this world for love.
With a tender little song of greeting
He'd return tender affection
And fly into my friendly hand.

No f svéte stráshna i ljubít':
Jemú být dán druzhók krylátyj;
Shtob mílava ne perezhýt',
Ón v gróbe skrýlsa at utráty.

But it can be frightening to love:
A little winged friend was given to him;
Rather than survive his beloved,
He hid in the coffin when he lost her.

Text. **Vasíly Andréyevich Zhukóvsky**, 1819. Title: На смерть чижика (On the death of a siskin). First published in 1827. Set only by Rachmaninoff. He changed the adjective in the first line from *milyj* (dear) to *vernyj* (faithful); he also changed *otvetnoj* (in reply) in line 6 to *privetnoj* (in greeting). Most singers pronounce the second word of the text сем (this) as *sjem*, an archaic pronunciation, but some singers use the modern pronunciation *sjom*.

Meter. Binary. Iambic tetrameter:

And with a tender song of greeting
He flew into my friendly hand.

Music. April 1902. Op. 21, no. 8. C Minor. 4/4, Allegretto. For High Voice (but in *Gutheil* for Middle Voice): c^1–f^2. First published with Opus 21 by A. Gutheil in Moscow in 1902.

Dedicated to **Ólga Andréyevna Trúbnikova** (1877–1942), Rachmaninoff's first cousin. When she was a girl, her mother took her to Red Square on Palm Sunday every year and bought her a siskin in a cage, which Olga would take care of until the warm days of late spring, when they went out to the country and set the bird free. Sometimes the bird did not fly away but perched on a nearby branch and sang a farewell song. When her siskin died in its cage one year, Rachmaninoff shared his cousin's grief (*VOR 1*, 122-3). He knew the family well, because he had lived with them as a young man in St. Petersburg before being sent to Zverev at the Moscow Conservatory, and later saw them often when they lived in Moscow.

Recordings. Davydova, Dolukhanova, Izotova, Koptchak, Kurenko, Lemeshev, Mishura, Olli, Popescu, Söderström, Suchkova, Wild (piano).

Transcriptions. *Cello:* David Geringas. *Piano:* Earl Wild.

42 *Мелодия*
Melody

Op. 21, No. 9

This song is Rachmaninoff's third and last setting of a poem by Semyon Nadson (see also Songs 33 and 35). Like his much greater predecessor Mikhail Lermontov, Nadson was a Romantic. A frequent starting point in their poetry is a wish that stands in contrast to the imperfect world as it is. The theme of this lyric is a wish for a certain kind of death, imagined not as something full of regret and tears, but as a passage to a better, higher form of consciousness. The theme recalls Lermontov's late poem of 1841 "I walk out alone onto the road," where the poet wishes for a death that would be like falling asleep, not losing consciousness or sensation, but hearing music and the rustling above him of a dark oak, forever green—an image Nadson echoes in this poem with its "canopies of dark lindens dreaming overhead." The theme has a force in the lives of both poets, who knew they were likely to die soon, Nadson already ill, Lermontov on dangerous military duty fighting Chechen horsemen in the Caucasus mountains, a veteran of one duel and soon to be killed in another.

It may be that the music Rachmaninoff wrote for this song was, as Max Harrison suggests, "conceived in a single breath of inspiration" (*Harrison*, 108). The song is masterfully written to bring out the confident, exalted mood of Nadson's poem, and concludes with a lovely piano postlude that has that quality of beauty, that sense of endless melody, that made Rachmaninoff's works for piano and orchestra so popular throughout the twentieth century. It is alive to nuances of feeling in individual words (like the *pianissimo* top B flat on the word "silence" in the voice part) or passages in the text (like the rippling sextuplets in the piano when the "nearby stream murmurs mysteriously"). The whole song moves with a kind of flowing grace, at a "comodo" (leisurely) pace, yet ever alive and impelled forward. This forward movement has something in common with another song about a passage to a higher realm of music, Tchaikovsky's Song 17, "Carry my heart away into distant harmony" (*TCS*, 52-4).

The recording made by Elisabeth Söderström and Vladimir Ashkenazy is especially beautiful. Transcriptions of the song have been made by Jascha Heifetz (for violin, 1956, pub. 1958) and Arcadi Volodos (for piano, rec. 1996).

Я б умереть хотел на крыльях упоенья,
В ленивом полусне, навеянном мечтой,
Без мук раскаянья, без пытки размышленья,
Без малодушных слёз прощания с землёй.

Я б умереть хотел душистою весною,
В запущенном саду, в благоуханный день,
Чтоб купы тёмных лип дремали надо мною
И колыхалася цветущая сирень.

Чтоб рядом бы ручей таинственным журчаньем
Немую тишину тревожил и будил,
И синий небосклон торжественным молчаньем
Об райской вечности мне внятно говорил…

Чтоб не молился я, не плакал, умирая,
А сладко задремал, и чтобы снилось мне,
Что я плыву... плыву, и что волна немая
Беззвучно отдаёт меня другой волне…

Ja b umerét' khatél na krýl'jakh upajén'ja,	I would like to die on inspiration's wings,
V lenívam palusné, navéjannam mechtój,	In light slumber brought on by a dream,
Bez múk raskájan'ja, bez pýtki razmyshlén'ja,	With no regrets, tormenting second thoughts,
Bez maladúshnykh sljós prashchánija z zemljój.	Faint-hearted tears of parting with the earth.
Ja b umerét' khatél dushýstaju vesnóju,	I would like to die in fragrant spring,
V zapúshchennam sadú, v blagaukhánnyj dén',	In an overgrown garden, on a sweet-scented day,
Shtob kúpy tjómnykh líp dremáli nada mnóju	With canopies of dark lindens dreaming overhead
I kalykhálasa tsvetúshchaja sirén'.	And blossoming lilacs swaying back and forth.
Shtob rjádam by ruchéj taínstvennym zhurchán'jem	With a nearby stream murmuring mysteriously
Nemúju tishynú trevózhyl i budíl,	To disturb and alarm the mute stillness,
I sínij nebasklón tarzhéstvennym malchán'jem	With the blue sky above in its mysterious silence
Ab rájskaj véchnasti mne vnjátna gavaríl…	Telling me of eternity in words I understand…
Shtob ne malílsa ja, ne plákal, umirája,	Let me not be praying or weeping as I die,
A slátka zadremál, i shtoby snílas' mne,	But slumbering sweetly, having a dream
Shto ja plyvú… plyvú, i shto valná nemája	That I'm floating… floating, and a mute wave
Bezzvúchna addajót menjá drugój valné…	Soundlessly hands me over to another wave…

Text. **Semyón Nádson**, 1880. Title: Мелодия (Melody). Written in Tiflis. First published in the sixth edition of Nadson's poems in 1887. Rachmaninoff made small changes to the text, improving it by eliminating two redundant conditional particles, unneeded labial sounds unfriendly to singers.

Set by a dozen other composers, before and after Rachmaninoff. Among them was an amateur composer Rachmaninoff might have known but certainly knew of through his Gypsy friends, the Lodyzhenskys. The man was an Armenian tenor whose name was Karapetyan but who took the stage name Davydov (Alexander Davidovich, 1849–1911). He was very popular in Moscow, where he sang in operettas, at the Bolshoi, and in Gypsy revues, eventually devoting himself to singing Gypsy songs: he was known in Moscow as "the king of the Gypsy romance" (*ME*, 127, *TE*, 264). Davydov shortened Nadson's poem by removing the last stanza, and published his setting of it in 1895 (the text is in *Petrovsky 1997*, No. 251). It must have been well known because there is a recording of it by the contralto Varvara (Varya) Panina, one of the greatest of the Gypsy singers, much admired by Lev Tolstoy, Chekhov, and Blok. The recording, made in 1903, is on the Russian "Grammofon" label, No. 23531 (*Ianin*, 394).

Meter. Binary. Iambic hexameter, with a caesura after the third foot:

My wish would be to die on inspiration's wings,
In dreamy consciousness of airy slumber light…

Music. April 1902. Op. 21, no. 9. B-flat Major. 4/4, Non allegro. For High Voice: b flat–b^2 flat. First published with Opus 21 by A. Gutheil in Moscow in 1902.

Dedicated to **Natália Nikoláyevna Lánting**, a cousin of Natalia Satina. Lanting's mother was the sister of the Satin children's father. There is a photograph of her in the back seat of Rachmaninoff's open-topped four-cylinder "Loreley" model H4A, 24 hp., taken at Ivanovka around 1912. The car was made in Germany by Rudolf Ley's son Alfred, hence the pun on Lorelei. These models, famous in Russia for winning races from Warsaw to St. Petersburg, Moscow, and Kiev, had the steering wheel on the right: the composer is at the wheel. Rachmaninoff took great pleasure in driving his cars and speaks about this several times in his letters. The photograph is in *VOR 1957*, vol. 1, opposite p. 161. A different photo, less good, of Rachmaninoff in this car is in *B/L*, between pp. 22 and 23.

Recordings. Arkhipova, Guleghina, Korshunov, Kurenko, Lee, Milashkina, Naumenko, Olli, Pusar, Shpiller, Söderström, Suchkova.

Transcriptions. *Cello:* Brian Stucki. *Piano:* Patrick Rapold, Arcady Volodos. *Violin:* Sherry Kloss, Itzhak Perlman, Aaron Rosand.

43 *Пред иконой* *Before the icon*

Op. 21, No. 10

This text by Count Golenı́shchev-Kutúzov depicts a woman praying before an icon of the Savior. In the Orthodox tradition, an icon is not merely an image representing the holy figure, but an imprint of the divine face, looking out from transcendent reality into earthly reality. From the point of view of the woman at prayer before the icon, the Savior is *present* in the scene, looking down in sorrow at her as she offers up her prayer. This prayer is not for herself, but for some unspecified other person; implicit in this are her love, and also the suffering of another. The poem is a recognition of earthly limits, because what she is asking for is "impossible"; her prayer cannot be answered, but the sorrow and compassion portrayed here are nevertheless real and felt.

Rachmaninoff recognized the genuine Orthodox spirituality in this scene, and he set the text with tender eloquence and laconic dignity. The piano part is restrained, confined mostly to brief chords, "respectfully discreet… [with a passage in] an insistently repeated B flat… like a bell tolling to summon the faithful" (*Martyn*, 144). The voice part is declamatory, with arcs of melody for the different phrases that avoid tunefulness. Two brief piano interludes pause the voice part in its adagio movement forward. It ends as simply as it began. It is not a well-known song, but it is so well written it deserves another look.

Она пред иконой стояла святою;
Скрестилися руки, уста шевелились;
Из глаз её слёзы одна за другою
По бледным щекам жемчугами катились.

Она повторяла всё чьё-то названье,
И взор озарялся молитвенным светом;
И было так много любви и страданья,
Так мало надежды в молении этом!

Она преклонилась и долго лежала,
Прильнув головою к земле безответной,
Как будто в томленьи немом ожидала,
Что голос над нею раздастся приветный.

Но было всё тихо в молчании ночи,
Лампада мерцала во мраке тревожном,
И скорбно смотрели Спасителя очи
На очи, просящие о невозможном.

Aná pred ikónaj stajála svjatóju; Skrestílisa rúki, ustá shevelílis'; Iz glás jejo sljózy adná za drugóju Pa blédnym shchekám zhemchugámi katílis'.	She stood before the holy icon; Her hands were crossed, her lips were moving; Tears, one after the other, fell from her eyes, Rolling down her pale cheeks like pearls.
Aná paftarjála fsjo chjó-ta nazván'je, I vzór azarjálsa malítvennym svétam; I býla tak mnóga ljubví i stradán'ja, Tak mála nadézhdy v malénii étam!	She kept repeating the name of someone, Her face glowed with a prayerful light; And there was so much love and suffering, So little hope in her prayers!
Aná preklanílas' i dólga lezhála, Pril'núv galavóju g zemlé bezatvétnaj, Kag bútta f tamlén'je nemóm azhydála, Shto gólas nad néju razdástsa privétnyj.	She knelt down and lay there long, Pressing her head to the silent ground, As if in mute weariness expecting A loving voice above her to call out.
No býla fsjo tíkha v malchánii nóchi, Lampáda mertsála va mráke trevózhnam, I skórbna smatréli Spasítelja óchi Na óchi, prasjáshchije a nevazmózhnam.	But all was quiet in the night's silence, The icon-lamp flickered in the anxious darkness, And the Savior's eyes gazed down with sorrow At her eyes that were beseeching the impossible.

Text. **Arsénii Goleníshchev-Kutúzov**, between 1868 and 1878. Title: Молитва (Prayer). First published in 1878 in *Затишье и буря* (1868–1878) (Calm and Storm, [poems of] 1868–1878), page 98: from Section II (of 2) entitled "Затишье" (Calm). Set only by Rachmaninoff, who changed the title and rewrote the last line, which read "На ту, что с моленьем пришла невозможным!" (At the woman who had come with an impossible prayer!).

Meter. Ternary. Amphibrach, 4-foot:

One name she repeated again and again,
Her face all aglow with the light of her prayer...

Music. April 1902. Op. 21, no. 10. E-flat Minor. 9/8, Adagio. For Middle Voice: b flat–f². First published with Opus 21 by A. Gutheil in Moscow in 1902.

Dedicated to **Maríya Aleksándrovna Ivanóva** (1885–1925). She worked as housekeeper, cook, and nanny for Rachmaninoff and Natalia after their marriage. She is referred to as "Marina" in letters and memoirs (there is interesting material about her in *Ermakov*, 75-6 and notes). She joined them in Europe before the war, and they invited her to Dresden in 1924. When leaving the country in 1917, Rachmaninoff left his Moscow apartment on Strastnoi Boulevard in her keeping and from time to time sent her money. She is mentioned in memoirs about Rachmaninoff as a resourceful, intelligent, and indispensable servant, utterly devoted to the composer and his family.

Recordings. Koptchak, Leiferkus, Levko, Milcheva, Olli, Popescu, Söderström, Suchkova.

Transcriptions. *Cello:* Brian Stucki.

44 *Я не пророк* *No prophet, I*

Op. 21, No. 11

The author of this short text, Aleksandr Kruglov (1852–1915), began publishing poems, stories, and newspaper articles in the 1870s after moving to St. Petersburg, where he worked as a librarian. He destroyed the manuscript of an early novel after Dostoyevsky told him it was bookish and showed no knowledge of life. A radical in his youth, he became a moderate and a middling writer most admired for his poems and stories for children. He told Chekhov "I can write weakly, but I always wrote sincerely." Vladislav Khodasevich, a stern critic of other poets, writing in Paris in the 1930s, said of these poems "they somehow radiate light; they're not sweet or mawkish, they don't condescend to the young reader, and they don't moralize." The ideal he held out to his audience was not a life of heroic glory but of dedicated work (a value he shared with Chekhov), a life of steady labor to establish one's own honest and rational kind of happiness (*RP 3*, 168). Rachmaninoff found this poem in a commemorative volume dedicated to a respected pedagogue who had done just that: D. I. Tikhomirov (1844–1915), a pioneer in Russian elementary education and organizer of the first evening schools for workers in Russia.

The voice part of this short song is in two parts, followed by the closing flourish of the piano coda. The first stanza is marked *fortissimo*, "sempre marcato e resoluto," culminating on the word певец (singer or poet). The second half diminishes gradually to *pianissimo*, "tranquillo," then the last line of the text rises to *mezzo forte*, with a long final two-note phrase on F and E-flat that a good singer can hold for ten seconds or more. The piano coda is "piu vivo"and suggests a plucked instrument (though it is not played glissando), a harp, or the "lyre" of the text. The song is written for high voice; among the excellent recordings are those by sopranos Joan Rodgers, Elisabeth Söderström, and the American Heidi Grant Murphy.

Я не пророк, я не боец,
Я не учитель мира;
Я — Божьей милостью — певец,
Мое оружье — лира.

Я волю Господа творю;
Союза избегая с ложью,
Я сердцу песней говорю,
Бужу в нем искру Божью.

Ja ne prarók, ja ne bajéts, Ja ne uchítel' míra; Ja — Bózhjej mílast'ju — pevéts, Majó arúzhje — líra.	I am not a prophet, I am not a warrior, I am not a teacher of the world; I am — by the grace of God — a poet, My weapon is the lyre.
Ja vól'ju Góspada tvarjú; Sajúza izbegája s lózhju, Ja sérttsu pésnej gavarjú, Buzhú v njom ýskru Bózhju!	I create what the Lord wills; Rejecting every kind of lie, With my song I speak to the heart, Igniting there the divine spark of God.

Text. **Aleksándr Vasíliyevich Kruglóv**, by 1901. Untitled. First published in 1901 on p. 199 of *На трудовом пути. К тридцатипятилетию педагогической деятельности Д. И. Тихомирова 1866–1901* (On labor's path. For the 35th anniversary of the pedagogical activity of D. I. Tikhomirov 1866–1901, Moscow, A. V. Vasiliev and Co., 1901). Set only by Rachmaninoff.

To verify Rachmaninoff's song texts, and to learn if he made any changes in wording when setting them, I tried to find the sources he used. Locating this book was particularly difficult and took visits to many libraries in Moscow over several years. I finally found it in the Lenin Library in April 2004. The problem was that Ivanov names the book (*Ivanov 1*, 167) but adds that this is a volume of poems by Kruglov. I could never find this title among Kruglov's many published books, so I looked in all of them for this poem, but unsuccessfully. I found the title in the Lenin catalogue, but ruled it out because it was not by Kruglov, and its full title made it seem unlikely as a source for this poem. Finally I ordered the book to see what it was—and there, alongside works by many hands, including a story by Chekhov, was this poem. Part II of the volume was drawings by artists, and Part III musical compositions—among which was a little chorus for two women's or children's voices by Rachmaninoff's close friend Mikhail Slonov (see the dedication of Song 17). Perhaps Rachmaninoff came across this poem because Slonov showed him the volume.

Meter. Binary. Iambic tetrameter, with some lines of three feet:

No prophet I, nor warrior,
No teacher of the world;
A poet by the grace of God,
My weapon is the lyre.

Music. April 1902. Op. 21, no. 11. E-flat Major. 4/4, Moderato. For High Voice: e^1 flat–a^2 flat. First published with Opus 21 by A. Gutheil in Moscow in 1902.

No dedication.

Recordings. Burchuladze, Dionne, Furdui, Guleghina, Guliayev, Kharitonov, Koptchak, Korshunov, Larin, Leiferkus, Morozov, H. Murphy, Nortsov, Olli, Piavko, Pusar, Rodgers, Shevelev, Söderström, Storozhev, Suchkova, Tear.

45 *Как мне больно* *Sorrow in springtime*

Op. 21, No. 12

This song completes the Op. 21 set of songs which Rachmaninoff wrote in an intense burst of work in April 1902 before his marriage later that month. He took them with him on his honeymoon, because they were written quickly and he wanted to make improvements. After Vienna and Italy they went to the Hotel Sonnenberg by Lucerne at the end of June; there Rachmaninoff decided to work on the songs. Writing his trusted friend Nikita Morozov, whom they invited to visit them in Switzerland, he said: "We've taken two rooms on the top floor (there's a lift!). We've made the outer room into a sort of salon. In Lucerne we rented an upright piano, brand new, which I got for 50 francs for two months and an 18-franc delivery charge. That's very cheap, I think, and the piano isn't at all bad. I've started to work, and so far I'm glued to the romances: they were written so hastily, they're quite unpolished and they're not at all attractive—something like Malashkin or Prigozhii" (*LN 1*, 317, letter of 17/30 June 1902). By comparing his songs to the popular songs of L. D. Malashkin (1842–1902) or those of Yakov Prigozhii (1840–1920), the arranger at the Gypsy night club "Yar" in Moscow, Rachmaninoff was saying that musically they lacked a certain sophisticated finish. The three weeks in Lucerne were spent polishing them.

It might seem odd that a man on the eve of his wedding would choose a poem so full of anguish as the present one, the second of three romances to texts by Galina (the others are Songs 40 and 56)—this "black and cheerless theme" in the words of Barrie Martyn. Finding the song a disappointment, Martyn goes on to say that "perhaps because it does not reflect personal experience its gesturing fails to convince" (*Martyn*, 144). However, Galina's theme of the tormenting and conflicted emotions of spring is familiar material in the Russian romance and need not be an expression of the mood of the composer at a given moment, or even of his personal experience. What matters is the sincerity of the music. It is a well-shaped song, rising to its culmination in the first line of the last stanza, and ending with a short "appassionato" coda. In a fine performance like that of Pavel Lisitsian's, it is unmistakably "an inspired song" (*Harrison*, 108). There are many good recordings of it, and transcriptions for clarinet and for piano.

Как мне больно, как хочется жить...
Как свежа и душиста весна!
Нет! Не в силах я сердце убить
В эту ночь голубую без сна.

Хоть бы старость пришла поскорей,
Хоть бы иней в кудрях заблестел,
Чтоб не пел для меня соловей,
Чтобы лес для меня не шумел,

Чтобы песнь не *рвалась* из души
Сквозь сирени в широкую даль,
Чтобы не было в этой тиши
Мне чего-то мучительно жаль!

Kák mne ból'na, kak khóchetsa zhýt'...	How painful this is, how I yearn to live...
Kák svezhá i dushýsta vesná!	How fresh and fragrant is spring!
Nét! ne f sílakh ja sérttse ubít'	No! I can't silence my heart
V étu nódzh galubúju bes sná.	On this pale blue sleepless night.
Khad' by stárast' prishlá paskaréj,	If only age would come quickly,
Khad' by ínej f kudrjágh zablestél,	Thread my curls with silver frost,
Shtob ne pél dlja menjá salavéj,	Make me deaf to the nightingale singing,
Shtoby lés dlja menjá ne shumél,	To the sounds of the forest murmuring,
Shtoby pésn' ne rvalás' iz dushý	So no song would burst from my soul
Skvos' siréni f shyrókuju dál',	Through lilacs to the wide horizon,
Shtoby né byla v étaj tishý	So there would not be, in the hushed stillness,
Mne chevó-ta muchítel'na zhál'!	This excruciating feeling of sorrow!

Text. **G. Galiná (Glafíra Adól'fovna Einerling)**. Title: Весенняя ночь (Spring night). First published in *Galina 1902*, p. 37. Set only by Rachmaninoff. For Galina's verb in line 1 of the last stanza (лилась, flow), the composer substituted рвалась (burst out), italicized in the Russian text above.

Meter. Ternary. Anapest, 3-foot:

Make me deaf to the nightingale singing,
To the sounds of the murmuring forest...

Music. April 1902. Op. 21, no. 12. G Minor. 6/8, Allegro mosso. For High Voice: d^1–b^2 flat. First published with Opus 21 by A. Gutheil in Moscow in 1902. Arranged for salon orchestra by L. Leonardi (*T/N*, 78). Transcribed for piano (Earl Wild, 1981), clarinet (Wagner Campos, 1998), and cello (Mischa Maisky, 2005). Dedicated to **Vladímir Aleksándrovich Satín** (1881–1945), the composer's brother-in-law, the younger brother of Rachmaninoff's wife Natalia.

Recordings. Aleksandrovich, Arkhipova, Atlantov, N. Bolshakov, Borisenko, Borodina, Dickson (in English), Dnishev, Dodoka, Domnich, Furdui, Grishko, Guleghina, Hvorostovsky, Korshunov, Kurenko, Kushpler, Larin, Lee, Lemeshev, Lisitsian, Magomayev, Makarova, L. Maslennikova, Mirakian, Nikitina, Oja, Olli, Orda, Piavko, Leontyne Price, Pusar, Rautio, Rodgers, Rozum, Seleznev, Serkebayev, Söderström, Storozhev, Suchkova, Tourel, Urmana.

Transcriptions. *Cello:* Maisky. *Clarinet:* Campos. *Piano:* Wild.

46 *Ночь* *Night*

Unlike Songs 1 through 9, which Rachmaninoff chose not to publish, he did approve the publication of the present song in a charity anthology to benefit widows and orphans of musicians in Moscow. The paper on which the fair copy was made was used by the composer in the second half of 1900, and the manuscript bears that date, but the song was probably composed earlier in 1899. In the fall of that year, Vera Skalon decided to marry her childhood friend Sergei Tolbuzin, burning more than a hundred of Rachmaninoff's letters to her. They remained friends, and she was a matron of honor in Rachmaninoff's wedding in 1902, but she never stopped loving him, according to her sister Lyudmila's memoir (*VOR 1*, 247). Rachmaninoff's own tender feelings for Vera are thought to be behind this text which he presumably chose at about this time. The third stanza is an intimate appeal to her in the present, and he wisely decided to remove it.

The text is from that same debut book of poems by Daniil Ratgauz that Tchaikovsky used in 1893 to write his last songs, Op. 73, and the mood is the same: "I am alone, but you are with me, darling, even though we're apart." The song begins softly as a Largo, then in the second stanza, with arpeggios, becomes more animated, with volume varying from *piano* to *forte*; there is anger and self-pity in the third stanza; then a pause as it slows down and becomes quieter and more somber by the end. It has a strong sincerity to it: performances by Valentina Levko and Dmitri Hvorostovsky bring out its power well.

Снова сон на усталые очи нейдёт.
Я один… Но в немой тишине
Кто-то тихо мне скорбные песни поёт,
Наклоняется нежно ко мне.

Замирает душа… Очарованный слух
Ловит звуки знакомых речей…
То не ты ли, желанный, неведомый друг,
Грёза детских, умчавшихся дней?

Истомилася грудь от вседневных тревог,
Гаснет в сердце желаний всех пыл…
И давно уже мне мой насмешливый рок
Все дороги к блаженству закрыл.

Догорает свеча… Ночь глухая плывёт.
Я один… И в немой тишине
Кто-то тихо мне скорбные песни поёт,
Наклоняется нежно ко мне.

Snóva són na ustályje óchi nejdjót.	Once more sleep does not come to my tired eyes.
Já adín… No v nemój tishyné	I am alone… But in the quiet stillness
Któ-ta tíkha mne skórbnyje pésni pajót,	Someone softly sings me mournful songs,
Naklanjájetsa nézhna ka mné.	Tenderly bending down to me.
Zamirájed dushá… Acharóvannyj slúkh	My heart stops… Thrilled, I seem to hear
Lóvid zvúki znakómykh rechéj…	The loving sounds of a familiar voice…
To ne tý li zhelánnyj nevédamyj drúk,	Is that you, my heart's desire, my secret friend,
Grjóza détskikh umcháfshykhsa dnéj?	My dream of bygone childhood days?
Istamílasa grúť' at fsednévnykh trevók,	My breast is weary from everyday worries,
Gásnet f sérttse zhelánij fsékh pýl…	All my heart's ardent desires are burned out…
I davnó uzhé mné mój nasméshlivyj rók	And long ago a mocking fate
Fsé darógi g blazhénstvu zakrýl.	Closed all paths to happiness for me.
Dagarájet svechá… Nódzh glukhája plyvjót…	The candle's burning down… Dull night comes on.
Ja adín… I v nemój tishyné	I am alone… But in the quiet stillness
Któ-ta tíkha mne skórbnyje pésni pajót,	Someone softly sings me mournful songs,
Naklanjájetsa nézhna ka mné.	Tenderly bending down to me.

Text. **Daniíl Maksímovich Ratgáuz**, 1893. Title: Под шепот мечты (Whispers of a dream). First published in *Stikhotvoreniia* (Poems), Kiev, 1893, pp. 76-77. Set only by Rachmaninoff, who changed the title and omitted the third stanza from the song (shown below).

Meter. Ternary. Anapest, alternating 4-foot and 3-foot lines:

Someone sings to me softly a song that is sad,
I'm alone, in the stillness of night…

Music. The manuscript is dated Moscow, 1900, a date confirmed by examination of the paper (*Cannata 1995*, 67). A Minor. 12/8, Largo. For Middle Voice: c^1–a^2. Without opus. First published in 1904 by Jurgenson in a "Collection of compositions by contemporary Russian composers, vol. 2" (*Rytsareva*, 33 and *LN 1*, 553). No dedication.

Recordings. Del Grande, Hvorostovsky, Levko, Lisovsky, Oja, Popescu, Söderström, Suchkova.

Third stanza of the poem, omitted by Rachmaninoff from the song:

То не ты-ли к кому тщетно рвусь я всегда	Could it be you, whom I seek unceasingly,
И к кому я взываю с мольбой,	You, whom I beg to be with me,
О, подруга души, то не ты-ль? — если да,	O, darling girl of my heart, is it you? — if so,
То явись поскорей предо мной!	Then appear before me right now!

Fifteen Romances, Opus 26 (1906)

1.

When, at the end of their honeymoon in July 1902, Sergei and Natalia Rachmaninoff arrived in Bayreuth for the Wagner festival, they joined a party of fellow Russians led by Konstantin Stanislavsky (on Rachmaninoff's relationship with Stanislavsky, see Song 62). Together they visited Liszt's grave, met Cosima Wagner, and attended performances of *The Flying Dutchman*, *Parsifal*, and *The Ring*. They sent a postcard to Siloti, who was at Ivanovka, and another longer greeting to Anton Chekhov, who was spending the summer with his wife the actress Olga Knipper in Stanislavsky's house outside Moscow. The message to Chekhov read: "Russian pilgrims in Bayreuth, inspired by the majesty of art and the theater, send sincere feelings of tribute to a great talent, and pride in our compatriot" (*LN 1*, 320). This message from his enthusiastic friends might have brought a hearty laugh from Chekhov, whose idea of theater was a far cry from Wagner's "Gesamtkunstwerk" about gods, giants, and a gold ring. Yet if there was irony in the implied comparison, the message was quite sincere—in a way all its own, a Chekhov play at the Moscow Art Theater could also be an overwhelming experience of theater as great art.

Rachmaninoff's interest in Wagner's music was deepened in Bayreuth, and he remembered scenes from *Das Rheingold* when he was writing *The Miserly Knight* the following year. As a student he was sarcastic about the interminable length of *Tristan* when he, Scriabin, Goldenweiser, and Taneyev were taking turns playing through the score, but he liked playing his own favorite passages from *The Ring* for friends, skipping the "boring" parts, then announcing "all right now, granddad Wagner, show your stuff!" (*VOR 1*, 245). In concerts Rachmaninoff conducted between 1905 and 1912 he included orchestral music from *Lohengrin*, *Die Walküre*, and the "Siegfried Idyll," as well as the marvelous "Wesendonk-Lieder." In concerts after he left Russia, he played piano transcriptions of Wagner right up to his very last recitals in Louisville and Knoxville in 1943, playing Liszt's arrangement of the "Spinning Chorus" from *The Flying Dutchman* and a transcription of the "Magic Fire" music from *Die Walküre* (details of Rachmaninoff's concert seasons from 1909 to 1943 are in *LN 3*, 439-67).

2.

With Stanislavsky at Bayreuth were some singers and musicians from the Bolshoi Theater, including a double-bass virtuoso a year younger than Rachmaninoff named Sergei Kusevitskii (1874–1951), later famous as Serge

Koussevitzky, conductor of the Boston Symphony from 1924 to 1949 and founder of the music festival at Tanglewood in 1940. Rachmaninoff had first met him when they were students; they would work together over the next fifteen years. Koussevitzky was born in Vyshny-Volochok, a canal town on the Volga. His father Alexander was a Jewish musician who served his twenty-five years of compulsory military service in an army band; when his service ended, he married and started a family. Alexander could play many instruments, and his wife and all their children were musically talented. He formed a family klezmer-band which played at weddings and in taverns, and also toured the province, performing at fairs and carnivals (*Iuzefovich*, 25-28). Young Sergei could play all the stringed instruments as well as the trumpet and the tuba, but his favorite was the double-bass. He was determined to play it better than anyone else. At seventeen he ran away to Moscow, where he managed to talk his way into the Musical Academy of the Moscow Philharmonic. To study in Moscow, a Jew had to convert to Russian Orthodoxy, a step Koussevitzky undertook in 1893 (ibid., 35). For two years he studied and practiced constantly, gaining experience playing nights in the orchestra of the Italian opera. As his mastery grew, he began giving solo recitals: he "solo-tuned" his bass a whole tone higher in order to play pieces written for cello, which he included in his recitals. Koussevitzky joined the Bolshoi in 1895, and by the time he went to Bayreuth in 1902 he was leader of the ten-man double-bass section of the orchestra, with a salary of 1,200 rubles a year (ibid., 49).

3.

From 1902 to 1904 Rachmaninoff devoted himself to composition. He had no regular income and was living off the money Siloti had loaned him earlier. He earned a small income from his pedagogical activities and an occasional fee for concerts, but money was an issue which would have to be addressed. In May 1903 Natalia gave birth to their first daughter, Irina.

In 1902–03 Rachmaninoff composed his first long work for piano, the Variations on a Theme of Chopin, Op. 22, and his Ten Preludes for Piano, Op. 23. Max Harrison has described the Chopin Variations as "an initial presentation, almost a systematization, of most of his own keyboard discoveries, the pianistic textures that particularly characterize his music for the instrument" (*Harrison*, 110-11). As a performance piece it is rather long, and the composer wanted to edit it down; he even recommended some cuts. For this reason, it has remained largely "in the shadows" (*Martyn*, 148). In 2005 Yevgeny Sudbin made a lucid recording of it with some of Rachmaninoff's cuts; it shows the piece to be "a structurally cohesive, scintillating kaleidoscope of invention" (Geoffrey Norris, *Daily Telegraph*, 12 Nov. 2005).

The ten Op. 23 Preludes are small pieces four to eight pages long, each in a different key. Together with the thirteen Op. 32 Preludes of 1910, and the early Prelude in C-sharp minor, Op. 3, No. 2, they constitute a full set in each of the twenty-four keys. With their "melancholy introspection" (*Fanning 2008*), so keenly felt in No. 1 in F-sharp minor, and their singing lines, as in No. 6 in E-flat major and No. 10 in G-flat major, some of them in the slower tempi share colors from Rachmaninoff's song palette.

After publication of the ten Op. 23 Preludes in 1903, Boris Asafiev, then still a student at the St. Petersburg Conservatory, played them for Vladimir Stasov (1824–1906), the grand old champion of the "Mighty Handful," the Russian national school of composers (his principled stance had often brought criticism of the Moscow composers). After hearing No. 2 in B-flat Major, Maestoso, Stasov bestowed words of approval, describing Rachmaninoff's talent as "very fresh, bright, and supple, stamped with a special modern Moscow quality—it rings from a new bell-tower, with new bells in it" (*VOR* 2, 386). Stasov invited Asafiev to come with him to "Penaty" (the Penates), the painter Ilya Repin's summer house in Finland, in 1904. At Stasov's request, Asafiev played the Op. 23 Preludes and several of Rachmaninoff's songs in the presence of Repin and Maxim Gorky, who was visiting Repin at the time. (There is a fine photograph of Stasov, Repin, and Gorky at Penaty in 1904 in *Valkenier*, 163.) The listeners "immediately grasped the Russian sources of the music" and especially the "landscape (*paysage*) quality" of it, not what a painter would see but what a musician, listening keenly in his soul, would "overhear" in the surrounding landscape. Repin thought he noticed something new in the way the melody was shaped, something post-Glinka, post-Tchaikovsky: "It doesn't come out of Italian cantilena, but out of Russian impressions, and there isn't anything French about it." He called No. 4 in D Major, Andante cantabile, "a lake in spring flood, a vast Russian field of water." Gorky said simply: "How well he hears the silence" (*VOR* 2, 386).

There are fine recordings of the complete Op. 23 Preludes by Moura Lympany, Peter Katin, Vladimir Ashkenazy, Howard Shelley, Nikolai Lugansky, Steven Osborne, and others. Emil Gilels, Sviatoslav Richter, and Van Cliburn recorded many of them. Among these are Van Cliburn's No. 4 in D Major, Andante cantabile (Repin's "lake in spring flood"), and his No. 6 in E-flat Major, a radiant Andante with joyous hops and skips at the end, which, as Rachmaninoff told Elena Gnesina, "really came to me all at once on the day my daughter was born" (*Martyn*, 151).

4.

In August 1903 Rachmaninov began work on a short opera *The Miserly Knight*, Op. 24, to the text of one of Pushkin's four "little tragedies." These are short works in blank verse that dramatize fatal passions—in this case, greed. This was the last of the four to be made into a chamber opera, following Dargomyzhsky's *The Stone Guest* (1866–9, completed by Cui and Rimsky-Korsakov in 1872), Cui's *A Feast During the Plague* (1895–1900), and Rimsky-Korsakov's *Mozart and Salieri* (1897). Rachmaninoff especially admired the Rimsky-Korsakov setting and knew it well, having rehearsed Chaliapin in the role of Salieri five summers earlier. But instead of adopting Rimsky-Korsakov's arioso-recitative style, Rachmaninoff created a more symphonic style, giving each character "his own kind of music," with a "core motif" for the miserly Baron (*Frolova-Walker*). He also gave greater prominence to the orchestra, starting with the shimmering tones in the introduction that recall the opening of Wagner's *Das Rheingold*. The leitmotifs and the way the orchestra is used suggest that the Bayreuth *Ring* was on Rachmaninoff's mind when he set Pushkin's text, with its powerful monologue scene of the greedy Baron guarding his chests of gold. The work has been called "a connoisseur's piece," not often performed except in concert (*Holden*, 828). But it can be effective on the stage, as in the striking production I saw at Glyndebourne in 2004, with Sergei Leiferkus singing the role of the Baron.

As it turned out, *The Miserly Knight* was first performed with another opera Rachmaninoff wrote during this period, *Francesca da Rimini*, Op. 25, begun in 1900 and completed in 1904–5. The composer was so frustrated, however, by delays and serious flaws in Modest Tchaikovsky's libretto for *Francesca da Rimini* that the result was much shorter than intended (for details, see *T/N*, 84-86). This double bill was finally produced and given five performances during January 1906, with Rachmaninoff conducting. By this time he was in his second season as conductor at the Bolshoi Theater, with responsibility for all the Russian operas.

5.

When Rachmaninoff came to the Bolshoi in September 1904, the theater was recovering from a long period of neglect of Russian opera in favor of French and Italian composers. In 1861, the Bolshoi had been leased to an Italian opera company for performances four or five times a week, an arrangement which lasted twenty years and meant that Russian operas were performed only rarely. When Tchaikovsky was dazzled by the singing of Adelina Patti in 1871 and again the next season, the general manager in charge of operas at the Bolshoi was an Italian, Eugenio Merelli, son of Bartolomeo Merelli, who knew Verdi and had managed La Scala. By the eighties, Tchaikovsky's operas were being performed at the Bolshoi; Mussorgsky and Rimsky-Korsakov came late in the decade; Borodin's *Prince Igor* was not performed there until 1898.

By that time Vladimir Telyakovsky (1861–1924) was managing the theater, and a new age was under way. Telyakovsky was Director of the Imperial Theaters in Moscow from 1898 to 1901, and from 1901 until the Revolution he administered the imperial theaters in both capitals (the dramatic as well as the musical theaters). It was a court position, unique in the Russian bureaucracy. He reported directly to the Tsar, without intermediaries, discussing with the Tsar (and the various Grand Dukes who had opinions on these matters) everything to do with the theaters: calendar, repertoire, designs and costumes, individual artists, even who would sing or dance what roles. When in St. Petersburg, he was expected to be in attendance whenever the Imperial family went to the theater. He was the general manager for all productions, and had a decisive voice in all questions, artistic and financial. He was also in charge of performances at jubilees, parades, and charity events. He was the personnel manager for the whole huge administrative apparatus, from conductors and choreographers to stage directors, casts, and writers and translators of librettos. He assigned duties, negotiated salaries, wrote and signed contracts, and granted vacations. He shuttled back and forth between the two capitals every week. To his job he brought intelligence, an understanding of theater people, and seasoned experience in the ins and outs at court and in the imperial bureaucracy. And he kept detailed diaries, writing down conversations and comments on performances. These are only now being published in full (three volumes have been issued, covering the years 1898–1906).

Telyakovsky was well aware of the modernist production ideas being tried out by artists and actors in Mamontov's Private Opera and Stanislavsky's Art Theater, and he willingly supported these new directions. He brought Korovin, Golovin, Benois, Bakst, Dobuzhinsky and others in the World of Art movement into new productions of ballets and operas. He also supported the younger generation of extraordinary singers at the Bolshoi—Leonid Sobinov, Antonina Nezhdanova, Feodor Chaliapin. The theatrical world was divided about these new trends. Modernism was a threat to the older establishment, to conductors like Nápravník and Altani, to singers like Nikolai Figner, and to many in the press and public, including some of the Romanovs, who considered it "decadence" and called it that. But to those working for innovation in both performance craft and stage design, Telyakovsky's support was essential. Together they brought the theater into the twentieth century, which, thanks to them, started out as a great age of Russian theater. (In a rare case of misjudgment, Telyakovsky thought Diaghilev, who kept pestering him for a job in the Directorate, was interested only in himself and could bring nothing of any value to the theater. Merezhkovsky agreed, saying to him in 1902 that Diaghilev, then at World of Art, "has already done everything he is capable of, and is no longer of any interest whatsoever": *Teliakovskii 2002*, 209.)

Looking back on his time at the Bolshoi, Rachmaninoff described Telyakovsky as "intelligent and progressive, a man with whom it was easy to work and who welcomed every reasonable suggestion" (*LN 1*, 60). Telyakovsky, in turn, saw in Rachmaninoff a conductor who might be able to break through ossified routine and bring Russian opera to a high level at the Bolshoi. Chaliapin introduced them in 1901 (*Teliakovskii 2002*, 113, 546), but it was not until the spring of 1904 that Telyakovsky persuaded Rachmaninoff to sign a contract. The contract was for five months starting that year (the season ran from September 1 to Lent). Rachmaninoff was torn. He needed the income and welcomed the financial security it would bring him. But the job would take him away from composition for half the year, at a time when he had not yet finished *The Miserly Knight* or *Francesca da Rimini*. In addition, he would have to begin preparing that summer in order to learn operas scheduled for the coming season that he had never conducted, including Glinka's *A Life for the Tsar*, Borodin's *Prince Igor*, and Tchaikovsky's *Oprichnik*, *Eugene Onegin*, and *The Queen of Spades*. Even after he signed the contract, he joked to his close friend Nikita Morozov that he would give a 2,000-ruble reward to anyone who could get him out of his promise to work for the Bolshoi, adding that he felt like putting a notice in the papers: "Lost—peace of mind, due to contract signed this spring; reward to the finder, please return to this address" (*LN 1*, 345).

Rachmaninoff's responsibility was for the Russian operas only; the resident conductor, long in place, would conduct the Western operas. His name was Ippolit Karlovich Altani (1846–1919), often called "the Italian," though he was Italian only by family origin: born in Ukraine, he was educated there and in Petersburg (he was a pupil of Anton Rubinstein), and worked in Russia all his life. He was principal conductor at the Bolshoi from 1882–1906. Rachmaninoff knew Altani (he had conducted the premiere of *Aleko*), and, respecting his seniority, tried his best not to cross paths with him. But a conflict immediately arose over the placement of the conductor's podium. By tradition at the Bolshoi, the conductor was placed near the proscenium, facing the stage, with the members of the orchestra behind him. This was rationalized on the grounds that the conductor's main job was to direct and cue the singers, and the orchestra could follow from behind. But Rachmaninoff knew that his first and hardest job would be to bring the orchestra to a high level previously unknown or at least long forgotten at the Bolshoi. He ordered the podium to be moved back to what is its normal position today so that he could see the orchestra between himself and the stage, and he had the chairs for the musicians rearranged accordingly. Altani objected that the singers and chorus would not be able to see him so far away, but Rachmaninoff held his ground and the changes were made. It caused some grumbling at the theater, because Altani had everything changed back again whenever he was conducting. Rachmaninoff's arrangement was soon recognized as logical and adopted permanently.

For the singers to be coached in their parts in detail, Rachmaninoff rehearsed with each of them individually, with himself at the piano. Incredible as it sounds, many of them had never worked this way before. It brought new confidence and professionalism to the singers. With the orchestra there was the obstacle of the dead weight of tradition, handed-down performance scores with passages cut, expressive dynamic markings unnoticed or ignored in favor of fermatas and rubatos and other liberties taken, all of which had become habit. Rachmaninoff respected the original score and tried to play what the composer had written. Moreover, discipline was lax in the orchestra, with noisy intrusions instead of whispering or tiptoeing, and spontaneous smoke breaks; between sessions, foul language backstage was the rule. It reminded Rachmaninoff of a "tavern" (*traktir*). He knew the score by heart and heard every instrument: he insisted, quietly, on getting it right. He coaxed out of the orchestra a cleanness of sound that no one could remember having heard at the Bolshoi. The critics remarked, as they had when he conducted for Mamontov, that the orchestra sounded like a first-rate orchestra at a symphonic concert—the highest possible praise. Koussevitzky, who led the double-bass section in the Bolshoi orchestra in the 1904–05 season before striking out on his own as a soloist, said that under Rachmaninoff he realized that he had never before played with a conductor who led the music, the performers on stage, and the orchestra—all the forces of the production—in such a single, unified whole (*Iuzefovich*, 55).

In his two seasons at the Bolshoi, Rachmaninoff conducted 89 performances of 11 different Russian operas. Chaliapin sang Boris in *Boris Godunov* and the Miller in *Rusalka*. At a charity gala in February 1905, scenes from three different operas were performed: the Inn scene from *Boris Godunov*, Rachmaninoff's own *Aleko*, and two scenes from Act I of *Eugene Onegin*, with Chaliapin singing all three parts, Varlaam, Aleko, and Onegin, a part written for baritone, not bass. The tessitura was high for him but he sang it so well that the aria in the garden had to be repeated. It was the only time Chaliapin ever sang Onegin on the stage (*Kotliarov 1*, 2 Feb. 1905).

For the Glinka centenary in 1904 the Bolshoi mounted a new production of *A Life for the Tsar* with sets and costumes by Konstantin Korovin, who made a special study of peasant costumes of the Kostroma district. The cast included Chaliapin as Susanin and Nezhdanova as Antonida. Rehearsing the scene of the ball in Act II, where fifty pairs of dancers come on stage to dance the "Krakowiak," Rachmaninoff was suddenly unable to hear the orchestra because the spurs the men were wearing made such a din. He asked that they be removed, but the Bolshoi bureaucracy refused, saying "Polish officers are required to be wearing spurs." Telyakovsky intervened and issued an order to have the spurs removed for this scene (all of this had to be certified on paper with stamps and signatures). One evening during the forest scene in Act IV, when Susanin is on stage alone in a glade, a cat appeared at the back of the stage and slowly ambled toward the prompter's box; Chaliapin, singing the role, sat off to one side "asleep," with eyes closed. Rachmaninoff feared what Chaliapin would do if he saw the cat, and also that the audience might not be able to keep from laughing. Out of respect for Chaliapin, they kept still. The prompter waved his arm, and the cat raised its tail and shot off stage running right past Chaliapin. Chaliapin did not stir, but after the performance he said in the calmest tone of voice to Rachmaninoff: "What realism we achieve in our sets—the forest even has wild animals in it!" (*LN 1*, 59-60).

On 27 September 1905 Rimsky-Korsakov's *Pan Voyevoda* had its Moscow premiere. The composer came down to Moscow for the performance. He wrote of it in his memoirs: "The talented Rachmaninoff conducted. The opera proved to have been well rehearsed.... Orchestra and choruses went splendidly. I was pleased with the sound of the opera in both voices and orchestra. What had sounded fair at the private opera house [in St. Petersburg, at the premiere a week earlier] gained manifoldly with a large orchestra. The whole orchestration had hit the mark squarely, and the voices sounded beautiful" (*Rimsky-Korsakov*, 415). The unrest of 1905 was in full swing then: printers were on strike, there were no newspapers or posters, and the house was only a third full (*Teliakovskii 1926*, 146). But Rimsky-Korsakov was given an ovation, with added warmth for his outspoken protest earlier that year against government inaction after Bloody Sunday—a protest which had led to his dismissal from the faculty of the St. Petersburg Conservatory. This "disgrace to Russia's greatest musician" had brought a widespread outcry, including a letter of protest from prominent musicians in Moscow, which Rachmaninoff signed (*LN 1*, 356-7).

6.

The crisis of 1905 only aggravated all the conditions at the Bolshoi that troubled Rachmaninoff as principal conductor. The discipline and professionalism he wanted in the orchestra were impossible to attain without firing some members and hiring others. Telyakovsky explained to him that this would involve pensions and other personnel and financial issues and was out of the question.

The salaries the theater paid to top performers were quite generous, especially considering the short season—a little over six months, with summers free and a long break during Lent when the theaters were closed. During these breaks, stars could earn money giving performances in Europe. (Or Rachmaninoff could take his family to Italy for vacation, as he did in the spring of 1906.) At the lower end, annual salaries for singers or dancers ranged from 400 to 1,200 rubles, incomes comparable to what male clerks and officers earned, and twice what a governess or teacher might earn (*Buckler*, 232). When

Nezhdanova signed her first yearly contract in 1902 as a singer of leading and secondary roles, her salary was 1,200 rubles (*Nezhdanova*, 74), exactly what Koussevitzky earned as principal double bass in the orchestra. She soon became a favorite of the Moscow public and her salary rose; Koussevitzky's did not. He resigned in protest, with an indignant letter to Telyakovsky (*Teliakovskii 1926*, 142-5), but not until after his marriage to Natalia Ushkova, the daughter of a millionaire tea merchant.

A typical salary for a top singer in the imperial theaters was 3,600 rubles per year (*Frame*, 48). Famous singers, however, often got much more. In 1899 Telyakovsky wooed Chaliapin away from Mamontov's Private Opera, where he was making 6,000 rubles a season, to the Bolshoi, at double the salary. (Six thousand rubles was a reasonably comfortable income; that is what Tchaikovsky received annually from his patron Mme. von Meck: see *TCS*, 268). The contract Chaliapin signed three years later, however, was for 36,800 rubles, paid over eight months at 4,600 per month, plus special perks and benefits he negotiated with the management (*Teliakovskii 2002*, 257).

Rachmaninoff was not in this league (no one was), but he had a comfortable income during his two years at the Bolshoi. When Telyakovsky urged him to sign a contract for the 1906-07 season, the offer was for 8,000 rubles (*LN 1*, 374). In Telyakovsky's ideal scenario, Rachmaninoff would become the general manager of the opera in Moscow, just as Nápravník would in Petersburg. They were the two best conductors of opera in the imperial theaters (and also the only two conductors whose musical decisions Chaliapin never challenged).

In addition, Rachmaninoff also earned from 300 to 450 rubles every time he conducted a concert for the Philharmonic society, or took part in the concerts produced by his friends the Kerzins. Arkady Kerzin and his wife Maria, a pianist, were a sympathetic couple who organized concerts of Russian music, mostly chamber music, every season—concerts very popular with the public. Rachmaninoff grew fond of the Kerzins and took part in their concerts. He took his concert work just as seriously as his work for the Bolshoi. Nikolai Medtner recalled a performance of Tchaikovsky's Fifth Symphony conducted by Rachmaninoff in 1905. He went back to the original score, getting rid of the "sentimental slowing of tempi" and other stylistic distortions Arthur Nikisch had introduced, which had become customary over the years. It was as if they were hearing the symphony for the first time. "Particularly striking was the shattering impetuosity of the finale as a counterbalance to Nikisch's pathos" (*Martyn*, 520).

With the money he was now making, Rachmaninoff could afford a new apartment, and in the fall of 1905 he moved his family to Strastnoi Boulevard, a lovely old tree-lined boulevard in central Moscow. He no longer had any debts, and was able to put money into his beloved country estate at Ivanovka.

For the first time in his life he was financially secure, with contracts in hand for a third season at the Bolshoi, ten concerts at the Philharmonic, and three with the Kerzins, adding up to an income of 13,400 rubles for the 1906–07 season (*LN 1*, 374). He had the esteem of the musical world and was productively engaged at the center of cultural life in Moscow, where he knew everyone and everyone knew him.

Yet all this came at the cost of what mattered most—time of his own and the freedom to compose. Rachmaninoff pondered his decision through the spring and summer of 1906. He finally told Telyakovsky "categorically" that he could never remain in the theater, whatever his title and salary. And Telyakovsky understood him: "He wants fame, but a different fame, that of a composer and a concert artist; he wants freedom and independence" (*Teliakovskii 1926*, 149-50).

It was harder to turn down the Philharmonic and the Kerzins. Yet if he spent the season in Moscow, his time would continually be taken up. True, he had summers at Ivanovka to compose, but they were too short to take on major new work, and besides, Ivanovka was a place to restore body and soul. He had several opera projects in mind, but above everything else he wanted to write a new symphony. If this was a deep inner need, after the failure of his first symphony, it was understandable. But to do it, he needed "freedom." He would have to leave Moscow and all its demands, and go somewhere for fall, winter, and spring where he would be completely undisturbed. He was thinking of Leipzig or Dresden (*LN 1*, 398).

7.

In the spring of 1906, Rachmaninoff was already discussing with the Kerzins a new group of songs for the upcoming season. Perhaps the idea came from them. It was welcome, as a way to help fund the sabbatical he hoped to take during the coming year; it was also a task that could be completed in a short space of time (the songs were composed between 14 August and 17 September). Maria Kerzina supplied some poems, for which he thanked her in a letter to Arkady Kerzin from Florence in April (*LN 1*, 370). Back home at Ivanovka on 2 August 1906, Rachmaninoff wrote asking her to send him some more poems, if she didn't mind; there weren't quite enough, and so far they all required minor keys: "Couldn't you send some that are a little more 'major'? It would make me very glad and endlessly grateful to you" (ibid, 397). She did send more, but even so, of the fifteen songs only five are in major keys.

In style and theme, Opus 26 is in many instances a new departure for Rachmaninoff's songs. Some of the lyrics Mrs. Kerzin sent the composer have a philosophical force unusual in the earlier songs: Romanticism is turning into Realism. The passage of time and its cost is a strong theme, as in the last song in the set, "All things depart never to return" (Song 61), and in Feodor Tyutchev's powerful four-line lyric "All-punishing God has taken everything from me" (Song 48). What was passionate and full of longing in the earlier love songs is seen in an entirely new light in Yakov Polonsky's dramatic monologue "Yesterday we chanced to meet" (Song 59), with its shocked realization of the merciless toll of the years, and its sudden feeling of pity for a woman once loved but long forgotten.

The merging of the inner world with the natural world in fine earlier songs 38, 40, 42 ("Lilacs," "How fine it is here," "Melody," all in major keys), is present here, but only in one song, "At my window" (Song 56, A Major), to a text by Galina; it has a "big tune," a melody that soars then falls in ravishing conclusion. The theme of "Sorrow in springtime" from Op. 21 (another Galina poem) is reimagined concretely in Op. 26 in Ivan Bunin's complex and much more modern lyric "I'm alone again" (Song 55, D minor), where everything is ironic and both love and spring are equally deceptive. As for Bunin's poetic merging of soul, night, steppe, dreams, and the road leading into the distance in "The night is sad" (Song 58, B minor), the composer himself warned that the burden of expressing the music of this song lay on the pianist rather than the singer. "Christ is risen" (Song 52) is a powerful indictment of the world should Christ rise to see it as it is today. These seven songs have been the most frequently performed of the fifteen.

The other songs include declamatory settings such as the prose text from Sonya's final monologue in Chekhov's *Uncle Vanya* (Song 49), and the very first song in the set, "Many are the sounds" (Song 47), which has gone quite unappreciated; it is about artistic creation, a new theme for Rachmaninoff, to be taken much further in Op. 34. Song 53, to words by Aleksei Khomiakov, the Orthodox philosopher, addressed to his sons who died in infancy ("To the children"), is almost unknown in Russia owing to bowdlerization of its religious language; it was a favorite in English through the 1950s, but the circumstances to which it refers were lost in translation and sentimentalized. Two of the songs are technically difficult to perform: "Two partings" (Song 53), which calls for a baritone and a soprano, and "The ring" (Song 60), which has an *ossia* piano part to make things easier for the accompanist. As a result, Op. 26 had a mixed reception with performers and the public.

Rachmaninoff finished the songs in early autumn, and gave them to his publisher in Moscow on his way to Dresden. When Gutheil published the fifteen songs early in 1907, they were all dedicated to Maria and Arkady Kerzin.

47 *Есть много звуков*
Many are the sounds

Op. 26, No. 1

Rachmaninoff begins Opus 26 with this slow Adagio in D-flat major. The song gave a cheerless start to the concert when the Kerzins premiered the new songs in February 1907. Tchaikovsky's colleague, Nikolai Kashkin, who was present, found it disappointing. Reviewing it, he wrote that its "declamatory manner" was ill-suited to a lyric that calls for "an integral poetic mood" (*Kashkin*, 20 Feb. 1907). Other critics sympathetic to the composer have called the music "ponderous" (*Martyn*, 171), finding "it exudes a kind of fatigue, a Chekhovian mood" not present in the lyric (*Grigorii Prokof'ev 1910*, 783-4). As the opening number in a recital of intimate songs, it was perhaps doomed to failure in the Great Hall of the Nobility, with its seating capacity of two thousand.

Others have seen the song as a kind of masterpiece. Max Harrison writes that it has "exactly the right stoical demeanour" (*Harrison*, 128). Boris Asafiev wrote a paean to the song, saying that here Rachmaninoff shows "how music takes on form in the consciousness, with all its willed beauty, its manfulness, the confidence of every sound it strikes" (*VOR* 2, 387). The introspective lyric by Aleksei Tolstoy is an elegy for "whisperings of the heart"—thoughts, poems, songs unsung—that are drowned out by daily cares and worries: unwritten music, if you will. This suggests that the words had a personal significance for Rachmaninoff. Unlike Aleksei Tolstoy's folk-style "Harvest of sorrow" (Song 14), this lyric is not a lament that sums up the failure of a whole life. Rather, it is a reckoning of losses along the way, on a journey in progress, "nel mezzo di cammin di nostra vita." There is regret, but no consolation, and yet the music Rachmaninoff created for the lyric is so convincing in its simplicity, in its sense of truth achieved with laconic means, that the music itself becomes the consolation, a stay against the losses.

It is among the composer's half dozen least recorded songs, although there are fine recordings by Pavel Lisitsian and Maria Popescu. We follow the spare melodic contour (four notes, E-flat to A-flat) as it unfolds and is elaborated, while legato chords keep time: the tolling of a bell. On the word "songs" in line 2 there is marked tenderness. The quiet intensity is varied by gradations from *piano* to *forte* and back, with small crescendos and diminuendos. There is a key shift in the last line of the first stanza, and another shift follows. The voice rises in struggle in the second stanza, but then slows down to stately calm, ending in sober sadness. The song ends with six *cantabile* measures on the piano—slow, soaring lyric flight, falling downward into silence. Howard Shelley brings this out beautifully in his accompaniment to Maria Popescu.

Есть много звуков в сердца глубине,
Неясных дум, непетых песней много;
Но заглушает вечно их во мне
Забот немолчных скучная тревога.

Тяжёл её непрошеный напор,
Издавна сердце с жизнию боролось,
Но жизнь шумит, как вихорь ломит бор,
Как ропот струй, так шепчет сердца голос.

Jest' mnóga zvúkaf f sérttsa glubiné, Nejásnykh dúm, nepétykh pésnej mnóga; No zaglushájet véchna ikh va mné Zabót nemólchnykh skúshnaja trevóga.	Many are the sounds deep in the heart, Thoughts never formed, songs unsung; But they are muted and lost within By incessant cares and tedious anxiety.
Tjazhól jejó nepróshenyj napór, Izdávna sérttsa z zhýzniju barólas', No zhýzn' shumít kak víkhar' lómid bór, Kak rópat strúj, tak shépchet sérttsa gólas.	This unwelcome pressure weighs heavily, My heart is in a struggle with life, But life roars like a gale that breaks tall pines, While, like streams that murmur softly, the heart's voice whispers low.

Text. **Alekséi Tolstóy**, 1859. Untitled. First published in *Русская беседа* (Russian Colloquy) in 1859. Set earlier by Palladius Bogdanov, director of the Court Choir, and by A. S. Taneyev.

Meter. Binary. Iambic pentameter:

This uninvited pressure weighs me down,
The dulling worries and incessant cares.

Music. Written 14 August 1906 at Ivanovka. Op. 26, no. 1. D-flat major. 4/4, Adagio (♩ = 46). For Middle Voice: e^1 flat–f^1. First published by A. Gutheil in Moscow in 1907.

Dedicated to **Maria Semyónovna Kérzina** (1864–1926) and **Arkády Mikháilovich Kérzin** (1856–1914). Kerzin, a lawyer, and his wife Maria, a pianist trained at the Moscow Conservatory, organized in Moscow in 1896 a "Circle of Devotees of Russian Music," which presented more than a hundred concerts from 1896 to 1912. The concerts were given first in private houses, then at the Slaviansky Bazaar restaurant, and from 1902 at the Great Hall of the Nobility (near the Bolshoi Theater). After 1904 some of the concerts were with full symphony orchestra (see *ME 3*, 67). Rachmaninoff appeared in his first "Kerzin" concert in January 1904, when he and Brandukov performed his Sonata for piano and cello, Op. 19 (*LN 1*, 576). In 1905 he conducted four concerts for them, including one in which his Second Piano Concerto was played by Konstantin Igumnov (the programs are in *LN 1*, 577).

Recordings. Lisitsian, Nortsov, Popescu, Söderström, Suchkova.

48 *Всё отнял у меня*
All was taken from me

Op. 26, No. 2

Leading 19th-century writers like Lev Tolstoy, Turgenev, Dostoyevsky, and Pushkin were quick to realize that Feodor Tyutchev (1803–1873) was a great and original lyric poet. Pushkin knew some early poems of Tyutchev and published them in his magazine *The Contemporary*. Tyutchev was an unusual case, a diplomat who worked abroad the first half of his life; his correspondence was in French and his two wives were German. He used Russian mainly for poetry, a Russian that had its own slightly archaic but colloquial feeling. He jotted down his lyrics as they came to him subliminally wherever he was, sitting in a meeting or riding in a carriage—like those "heart's whispers" of the preceding song—then put the scraps of paper in a drawer and forgot about them. Some by way of friends found their way into magazines. Tyutchev did not object, but he took no interest in their publication. In mid-century Turgenev collected those he liked, sometimes making "corrections" to the meter, and published them in a book. And yet Tyutchev's poetry was never widely recognized in his lifetime, a fact Lev Tolstoy noted with regret, saying "our whole intelligentsia has forgotten him, or is trying to forget him, because they consider him 'outdated,' you see" (quoted in *Blagoi*, 552).

This explains to some extent why Tyutchev's poems were rarely used for songs by 19th-century composers. There are a few exceptions, most notably Tchaikovsky, with two songs and a duet: one of them, "As over darkly glowing embers," Op. 25/2, 1875, is a remarkable song (*TCS*, 62-3). But it was in the 1890s, after the philosopher Vladimir Solovyov pointed out Tyutchev's original ideas of nature and the cosmos, that the Symbolists discovered him; since then, Tyutchev's greatness has been universally recognized. Rachmaninoff and his contemporaries—Taneyev, Grechaninov, Nicolas Tcherepnin, and especially Nicolai Medtner—wrote songs to Tyutchev's lyrics, and interest in him has continued into the 20th-century with composers like Georgi Sviridov.

Of the five Tyutchev poems set by Rachmaninoff (Songs 32, 48, 57, 71, 72), this text is the shortest. It is ingenious, like a biting epigram, but without the underlying satire. It is considered Tyutchev's final poem, addressed to his wife after he had his first stroke, a few months before he died. What is characteristic about it is the way it is built around the singularity of a moment in time: this is the moment when he has lost every reason to pray but one. Some of Tyutchev's most striking lyrics get their rhetorical power from this strategy. In a poem entitled "I like the Lutheran service" (1834) Tyutchev expresses a similar sentiment: "I like the Lutheran service—and understand the sublime doctrine of these severe, plain walls... but don't you see? Faith is ready to depart; she has not yet walked out the door, but her house is already empty and bare. Pray to God: you are praying for the last time."

Rachmaninoff's brief but powerful song—a minute, more or less—is in two parts: a sweeping crescendo at the outset, *agitato, forte*, expressing a strong outcry to the end of line 2; then a dramatic transition to the lyrical and tender concluding two lines, a marked slowing down to *comodo*, gentle and not too loud, "outwardly calm but inwardly tense" in the words of the Leningrad accompanist and pedagogue Yevgeny Shenderovich (1918–1999). Between these two parts is a single syncopated bar for piano alone that falls diatonically, then rises chromatically; the chromaticism dissolves by the end, with two final notes of the postlude that seem to "sum up the grievous tale" (*Shenderovich*, 177). The recording Shenderovich made with the Russian bass Yevgeny Nesterenko is one of the best among the many fine performances of this song.

Всё отнял у меня казнящий Бог, —
Здоровье, силу воли, воздух, сон.
Одну тебя при мне оставил Он,
Чтоб я Ему ещё молиться мог.

Fsjó ótnjal u menjá kaznjáshchij Bókh:	Chastising God has taken everything away from me:
Zdaróv'je, sílu vóli, vózdukh, són.	Health, willpower, breath, sleep.
Adnú tebjá pri mné astávil Ón,	You alone are all that He has left me,
Shtob já Jemú jeshchó malítsa mók.	That I might still find strength to pray to Him.

Text. **Feódor Ivánovich Tyútchev**, February 1873. Untitled. Dedicated to Ernestine Pfeffel, the poet's second wife. Set only by Rachmaninoff.

Meter. Binary. Iambic pentameter:

And you alone are all that I have left,
That I might still find strength to pray to Him.

Music. 15 August 1906. Op. 26, no. 2. F-sharp Minor. 4/4, Tempo Moderato (♩ = 96). For Middle Voice: f^1 sharp–e^2. First published with Opus 26 by A. Gutheil in Moscow in 1907. Dedicated to **Maria and Arkady Kérzin**.

Recordings. Amaize, Burchuladze, Chaiter, Christoff, Crona, Del Grande, Furdui, Guliayev, Hvorostovsky, Koptchak, Kurenko, Kushpler, Larin, Leiferkus, Levko, Magomayev, Milcheva, Mkrtchyan, Morozov, Murzayev, Nesterenko, Ognivtsev, Orda, Piavko, Pirogov, Popescu, Rautio, Seleznev, Shaposhnikov, Söderström, Storozhev, Suchkova, Vassilieff, Vladimirov, Weiler.

49 *Мы отдохнём* *We shall rest*

Op. 26, No. 3

Rachmaninoff admired Chekhov and Tchaikovsky as men above all the other artists he knew. About the composer, he said in an interview in 1930: "I was introduced to Tchaikovsky some three years before he died.... [A]t that time [he] was already world-famous, and honoured by everybody, but he remained unspoiled. He was one of the most charming artists and men I ever met. He had an unequalled delicacy of mind. He was modest, as all really great people are, and simple, as very few are. I met only one other man who at all resembled him, and that was Chekhov" (*Rachmaninoff 1930*, 557). The composer's admiration for Anton Chekhov (1860–1904) is everywhere attested, but this description in his own words of the qualities Chekhov shared with Tchaikovsky states it best.

Rachmaninoff met Chekhov in Yalta in 1898, and they came to know each other much better in the spring of 1900. Chekhov even made plans to go with Rachmaninoff and Chaliapin on their trip to Italy in June, but he changed his mind and stayed in Yalta. (Chekhov was slow to realize that he had tuberculosis, but by 1897 it had been diagnosed in an advanced stage: *Chekhov 1973*, 292). Chekhov was perhaps drawn to the two younger men because he liked musicians and sometimes thought that, of all his readers, musicians and painters understood him best. In Moscow, Rachmaninoff attended the Art Theater regularly and was present at the premiere of *The Cherry Orchard* on 17 January 1904, in honor of Chekhov's name day. In these last years of Chekhov's life, he and Rachmaninoff spoke about collaborating on opera projects, including Chekhov's play *Uncle Vanya* (see Arnold McMillin's article "Russian Music in and around Chekhov," *McMillin 2004-2*).

Rachmaninoff found the words for the present song in *Uncle Vanya*. The passage, very well known, is taken from Sonya's last speech to Uncle Vanya which ends the play: "We shall rest" (Nicolas Slonimsky translated it as "We shall have peace" in his metrical translation, *Slonimsky 1949-51*). It is a promise of peace after a life of fruitless labors and disappointed hopes. Subliminally, it is also a response to an "it's stifling!" motif (*dushno*!) that runs through the play, sharing as it does the etymological root for "breathe": "we will breathe freely" (*Chekhov 2006*, 814). A common Soviet interpretation of Sonya's words is that before the Revolution they could only be understood as "sentimental solace," but in the new Soviet world they proclaim an "unshakeable faith in the future" (*Senelick 1997*, 201). The religious import of Sonya's words, however, is employed by Chekhov without irony and without sentimentality; coming from Sonya, the words convey a pure and loving consolation.

The composer understood the special challenge this text presented: if the song came across as sentimental, Chekhov's lyrical intent would be distorted. In his letters to Maria Kerzina he cautioned that a bad performance would be a "caricature" (*LN 1*, 425). He wrote music designed to prevent that, setting the words as plain declamation, to be performed without histrionics. Rachmaninoff had seen *Uncle Vanya* at the Art Theater and knew how the words ought to come across in performance. He might have had in mind the actress Vera Komissarzhevskaya, whom he knew. (He later dedicated a song to her memory, Song 69.) She won fame as Nina in Chekhov's *Seagull*, where she solved the difficult problem of the monologue in Act I ("Humans, lions, eagles") by modulating her voice musically, treating the words as poetry, not parody, so that the audience did not laugh, as the director had feared: "Anton was won over by her musicality" (*Rayfield 1998*, 394). Rachmaninoff met her in St. Petersburg at his cousins' house, where she was temporarily living. There he heard her perform Arensky's melodeclamation to Turgenev's poem "How fresh the roses were": "she spoke the words simply, but it seemed that she was singing" (*VOR 2*, 74). That kind of natural delivery, words spoken simply but producing a musical effect, is what Rachmaninoff was aiming for in this song.

Nikolai Kashkin was present when the Kerzins premiered the songs at a concert in February 1907. In his review, he singled out this song as an example of a poetic mood perfectly sustained (*Russkoe slovo*, 20 Feb. 1907). Soviet writers criticized the song for not conveying the "bright hope" of Sonya's words: it is "sad, tired, timid, and unsure of itself" (*Briantseva*, 371-2); it is "gloomy, with heavy bell sounds and the rhythm of a funeral march" (*Keldysh*, 301). But these criticisms assume a kind of socialist-realist optimism alien to Chekhov's poetics. The piano part works to diminish any tendency to sentimentality in the words (*Harrison*, 129). The song can be effective in performance, often by a bass or baritone (it was written for low voice). Sergei Leiferkus brings it to life by fluid pacing, and, with his warm delivery, shapes the monologue into a whole. In recordings she made for the Rachmaninoff Society in 1950, the soprano Maria Kurenko gives a finely judged performance in which the words are sung with perfect clarity and expressiveness.

Мы отдохнём!
Мы услышим ангелов,
мы увидим всё небо в алмазах,
мы увидим, как всё зло земное,
все наши страдания
потонут в милосердии,
которое наполнит собою весь мир,
и наша жизнь станет тихою,
нежною, сладкою, как ласка.

Я верую, верую...
Мы отдохнём...
Мы отдохнём...

My addakhnjóm!
My uslýshym ángelaf
my uvídim fsjo néba v almázakh,
my uvídim, kak fsjo zló zemnóje,
fse náshy stradánija
patónut v milasérdii,
katóraje napólnit sabóju ves' mír,
i nasha zhýzn' stánet tíkhaju,
nézhnaju, slátkaju, kak láska.
Já véruju, véruju...
My addakhnjóm...
My addakhnjóm...

We will rest!
We will hear the angels sing,
we will see heaven shining like a jewel,
we will see the evil of the world,
all our suffering banished,
redeemed by love,
love that will fill all creation,
and our life will be as peaceful,
and tender, and sweet as a caress.
I have faith, I have faith...
We will rest...
We will rest...

Text. **Ánton Pávlovich Chékhov**. Prose excerpt from Act IV of *Uncle Vanya*, first published in 1897. Set only by Rachmaninoff.

Music. 14 August 1906. Op. 26, no. 3. D Minor. 4/4, 3/2, 2/4. Lento (♩ = 48). For Low Voice: a–d^2. First published with Opus 26 by A. Gutheil in Moscow in 1907. Dedicated to **Maria and Arkady Kérzin**.

Recordings. Baturkin, Hvorostovsky, Karolik, Khromchenko, Koptchak, Kozlovsky, Kurenko, Leiferkus, Oja, Pirogov, Rautio, Silja, Söderström, Suchkova.

50 *Два прощания* (*Диалог*) *Two partings* (*Dialogue*)

Op. 26, No. 4

The declamatory style of some of the songs in Opus 26 surprised Kashkin and others who first heard them in 1907. But there is a logic to this in terms of the composer's development, if we remember that he had just finished setting Pushkin's dramatic poem *The Miserly Knight* in a style that employs extensive recitative within a melodic framework established by the orchestra. In this new set of songs he further explores declamatory style in the Russian romance, going in a direction that takes him closer to Dargomyzhsky, Mussorgsky, and Rimsky-Korsakov than to Tchaikovsky. In 1908, during his Dresden period, Rachmaninoff would set to music the most prosaic of texts, a telegram to Stanislavsky, Song 62.

The present text, a literary folk song by Aleksei Koltsov written in very short four-syllable lines, some of them rhymed, would seem to be the opposite of prose. A glance at the text shows it to be as metrical as a nursery rhyme, though the subject is an adult theme handled ironically. It is a rare romance for two voices, not one, a baritone and a soprano; many phrases are short melodies, others are repeated notes in declamatory style. It is not a duet like Tchaikovsky's duets for high and middle voice singing together (see *TCS*, 287-96), but two voices singing separately back and forth in dialogue. The man (Voice 2) begins the song, asking the girl (Voice 1) about two lads who romanced her, now that she has lost them both. The dialogue tells a revealing story, first of innocent cruelty and then of experience and regret. It is playful but it has an underlying gravity. Rachmaninoff varies the pacing and emotional shading with changes of tempo throughout, marked in the text. To heighten the contrast at the halfway point of the song (Voice I, piu mosso), some sopranos sing the three optional higher E naturals on the phrase "the other one."

Voice 2 [Moderato]
— Так ты, моя
Красавица,
Лишилась вдруг
Двух молодцов?
Скажи же мне,
Как с первым ты
Рассталася,
Прощалася?

Voice 1 [un poco piu mosso]
— Рассталась с ним
Я весело;
Прощалася —
Смеялася...
[Meno mosso]
А он ко мне,
Бедняжечка,
Припал на грудь
Головушкой;

И долго так
Лежал, молчал;
Смочил платок
Горючими...
Ну — Бог с тобой! —
Промолвил мне.
[un poco piu mosso]
Схватил коня,
Поехал в путь —
В чужих краях
Коротать век.

Voice 2 [Tempo I]
— И ты над ним
Смеялася?
Его слезам
Не верила?
Скажи ж теперь,
Мудрёная,
Как ты с другим
Прощалася?

Voice 1 [Piu mosso]
— Другой не то…
Не плакал он,
А и теперь
Всё плачу я.
[Ancora un poco piu mosso]
Ах, обнял он
Так холодно,
Так сухо речь
Повёл со мной:
[Piu vivo]
— Я еду, вишь,
Не надолго;
Ещё с тобой
Увидимся,
И вволюшку
Наплачемся…
[a tempo]
По сердцу ли
Такой ответ?
[sempre piu mosso]
Махнул рукой,
Не кланяясь,
В моё лицо
Не смотрючи,
[Piu vivo (Presto)]
Пустил коня
И был таков!

Voice 2 [Tempo I]
— Кто ж памятней
Останется
Душе твоей,
Красавица?

Voice 1
— Мне первого,
Конечно, жаль,
Люблю же я
Последнего!

Voice 2 [Moderato]	Voice 2 [Moderato]
— Tak tý, majá	And so my dear,
Krasávitsa,	My beautiful,
Lishýlaz' vdrúk	How did you lose
Dvúkh mólattsaf?	Two lads so soon?
Skazhý zhe mné,	How was it with
Kák s pérvym tý	The first of them,
Rastálasja,	You said farewell,
Prashchálasja?	You said goodbye?
Voice 1 [un poco piu mosso]	Voice 1 [un poco piu mosso]
— Rasstálas' s ním	— I sent him off,
Ja vésela;	My heart was gay;
Prashchálasja —	I said farewell —

Smejálasja...
[meno mosso]
A ón ka mne,
Bednjázhechka,
Pripál na grút'
Galóvushkaj;
I dólga tak
Lezhál, malchál;
Smachíl platók
Garjúchimi...
Nú — Bókh s tabój! —
Pramólvil mné.
[un poco piu mosso]
Skhvatíl kanjá,
Pajékhal f pút' —
F chuzhýkh krajákh
Karótat' vék.

Voice 2 [Tempo I]
— I tý nad ním
Smejálasja?
Jevó slezám
Ne vérila?
Skazhý sh tepér',
Mudrjónaja,
Kák tý z drugím
Prashchálasja?

Voice I [piu mosso]
— Drugój ne tó...
Ne plákal ón,
A i tepér
Fsjo pláchu já.
[Ancora un poco piu mosso]
Ákh, óbnjal ón
Tak khóladna,
Tak súkha réch
Pavjól sa mnój:
[Piu vivo]
— Ja jédu, vísh,
Ne nádalga;
Jeshchó s tabój
Uvídimsja,
I vvóljushku
Napláchemsja…
[a tempo]
Pa sérttsu li
Takój atvét?

I laughed away...
[meno mosso]
But he poor lad,
He dropped his head
And fell so sad
Upon my breast;
And long like that
He silent lay;
Upon my scarf
He poured hot tears.
Well — go with God! —
He said to me.
[un poco piu mosso]
He took his horse,
And rode away —
To languish long
In lands far off.

Voice [Tempo 1]
— And so it was
You laughed at him?
You mocked his tears
In disbelief?
Then tell me now,
Oh maid so wise,
How did you leave
The other lad?

Voice I [piu mosso]
The other one was different...
He did not weep,
And now it's I
Who weep all day.
[Ancora un poco piu mosso]
Ah, in his arms
I felt so cold,
The words he spoke
Were dry as dust:
[Piu vivo]
— I shall be gone
But for a while;
And then again
We'll be as one,
And shed sweet tears
To our heart's content…
[a tempo]
Is that an answer
From the heart?

[sempre piu mosso]	[sempre piu mosso]
Makhnúl rukój,	He waved his arm,
Ne klánjajas',	Without a bow,
V majó litsó	With not one look
Ne smótrjuchi,	Into my eyes,
[Piu vivo (Presto)]	[Piu vivo (Presto)]
Pustíl kanjá	He spurred his horse
I býl takóf!	And left for good!
Voice 2 [Tempo I]	Voice 2 [Tempo I]
— Któ sh pámjatnej	— Now who, fair maid,
Astánetsa	Of these two lads
Dushé tvajéj,	Is closer to you,
Krasávitsa?	Heart and soul?
Voice 1	Voice I
— Mne pérvava,	— The first of them,
Kanéshna, zhál',	I pity, sure,
Ljubljú zhe já	But I love
Paslédneva!	The last one!

Text. **Alekséi Vasílyevich Koltsóv**, 1837; first published in 1838. Title: Два прощанья (Two partings). Rachmaninoff respelled and added the subtitle.

First set by Alexander Dubuque in 1853. His setting sounds like one of Alexander Varlamov's simpler songs, with repeated short melodic phrases. The elegant Ukrainian bass Boris Gmyria sang both voices in a charming live recording that has the feeling of an Alexander Vertinsky cabaret scene in period style.

Meter. Ternary. A four-syllable line beginning as an amphibrach and ending as a dactyl. The obligatory strong downbeat is on the second syllable, but an optional second stress may fall on the fourth syllable:

In his embrace
I felt so cold,
The words he spoke
Were dry as dust.

Music. 22 August 1906. Op. 26, no. 4. C Minor. 4/4, 2/4, Moderato (♩ = 69), with a Presto section (♩ = 168). For Soprano and Baritone: d^1–g^2, e flat–d^1. First published with Opus 26 by A. Gutheil in Moscow in 1907. Dedicated to **Maria and Arkady Kérzin**.

Recordings. Fomina and Nesterenko, Kurenko and Gontsov, Lapina and Murzayev, Rodgers and Leiferkus, Söderström and Shirley-Quirk, Suchkova (both voices).

Dubuque: Boris Gmyria (Recital in Leningrad 1.13.69 on a Melodia LP M 10 36766).

51 *Покинем, милая…* *Beloved, let us fly…*

Op. 26, No. 5

This plea to escape to the countryside to greet the arrival of spring is the third of three lyrics by Arsenii Golenishchev-Kutuzov set to music by Rachmaninoff (the others are Songs 15 and 43). The poet titled this lyric "Sonnet," but it has only ten lines instead of fourteen, and is written in iambic hexameters rather than the usual iambic pentameters of the Russian sonnet. If any lines were cut by the censor, there is no evidence of it, nor do cuts seem likely given the innocent nature of the text. There is even a rude enjambment at the end of the fourth line which destroys the integrity of the quatrain expected in the classical sonnet. In other words, this is not a conventional sonnet. It nonetheless has its own poetic life as a tender moment of pleading in a romantic relationship.

In this song the voice line moves continually in melodic phrases that express reverie, haunting yet seductive, "molto cantabile," varied with diminuendos, crescendos, and ritardandos. The piano part is beautifully supportive. There is a dramatic transition "più vivo" on the enjambed phrase at the end of line 4, followed by a shift in key for the phrase "or have you lost your love for fields of yellow grain." The voice falls lightly, only to rise again, culminating in the highest note in the song, a sustained a^2–flat, sung *pianissimo*, on the word *vzor* (gaze) in the last line.

Mstislav Rostropovich remarked upon Rachmaninoff's use of *piano* in climaxes. In her book about the great cellist as teacher, Elizabeth Wilson recalls a class devoted to Rachmaninoff's cello sonata, Op. 19: "'In the culminations,' Rostropovich taught, 'the higher you go the quieter it gets, and the more vibrato you need. This is a uniquely beautiful feature of his music'" (*Wilson 2008*, 263). This song, like "Sing not to me, beautiful maiden" and "Here it's so fine," shows Rachmaninoff employing the *pianissimo* climax in a song.

Despite its beauty, the song has not been widely performed. Among the fine recordings are those by the Soviet tenor Georgi Vinogradov, with Rachmaninoff's friend Alexander Goldenweiser on the piano, and the English soprano Joan Rodgers, who sings it with ravishing tenderness, with pianist Howard Shelley. Wagner Campos has transcribed the delicate melody for clarinet, and Brian Stucki for cello.

Покинем, милая, шумящий круг столицы.
Пора в родимый край, пора в лесную глушь!
Ты слышишь? — нас зовет на волю из темницы
Весны победной шум и пенье птиц... К чему ж

Нам усмирять души волшебные порывы?
Иль разлюбила ты желтеющие нивы,
И рощи свежие, и хмурые леса,

Где, помнишь, мы вдвоём задумчиво блуждали
В вечерний час, когда темнеют небеса,
И молча бродит взор в тумане спящей дали?

Pokínem, mílaya, shumjáshchij krúk
stalítsy.
Pará v radímyj kráj, pará v lesnúju
glúsh!
Ty slýshysh?—naz zavjót na vólju is
temnítsy
Vesný pabédnaj shúm i pén'je
ptíts… K chemú sh

Nam usmirját' dushý valshébnyje parývy?
Il' razljubíla ty
zheltéjushchije nívy,
I róshchi svézhyje i khmúryje lesá,

Gde, pómnish, my vdvajóm zadúmchiva
bluzhdáli
V vechérnij chás, kagdá temnéjut nebesá,
I mólcha bródit vzór f tumáne spjáshchej
dáli?

Darling, let's quit the noisy
capital,
Escape to the countryside we love,
to the quiet forest!
Can you hear it? — they're calling us
to break free,
These sounds of spring triumphant
and singing birds… Why, then,

Suppress the magic outbursts of the soul?
Or have you lost your love
for fields of yellow grain,
And fresh groves and darkling woods,

Where the two of us, — remember? —
wandered pensively
One evening hour, as the sky grew dark,
And gazed in silence at the sleepy misty
distance?

Text. **Arsénii Arkád'evich Goleníshchev-Kutúzov**, 1878. First published as "Sonnet" in his collection of poems *Затишье и буря* (Calm and Storm, 1878), p. 35. Set only by Rachmaninoff, who dropped the title, made two minor changes in word endings, and in line 5 substituted волшебные (magical) for блаженные (blessed).

Meter. Binary. Iambic hexameter:

We wandered pensively, the two of us — remember? —
And gazed in silence at the sleepy misty distance…

Music. 22 August 1906. Op. 26, no. 5. A-flat Major. 4/4, Moderato (♩ = 52). For High Voice: g^1–a^2 flat. First published with Opus 26 by A. Gutheil in Moscow in 1907. Dedicated to **Maria and Arkady Kérzin**.

Recordings. Dolukhanova, Kozlovsky, Larin, Obraztsova, Piavko, Rodgers, Söderström, Suchkova, Sumatchova, Tear, Vinogradov.

Transcriptions. *Cello:* Brian Stucki. *Clarinet:* Wagner Campos.

52 *Христос воскрес* *Christ is risen*

Op. 26, No. 6

At midnight on Russian Easter the priest announces "Christ is risen!" and the people reply, "Truly, He is risen!"; the same words are spoken when greeting others on Easter Sunday morning. Yekaterina Beketova, the author of "Lilacs" (Song 38), wrote a children's poem with this title in 1888, which celebrates the traditional Easter of Russian Orthodox believers (*Beketova*, 129-30). Here is her final stanza:

В семьях друг друга все дарят	All in the family exchange gifts
Яичком ярко-красным,	Of Easter eggs dyed bright red,
И все, ликуя, говорят,	And, celebrating the clear morning,
Встречаясь утром ясным:	Greet each other with the words:
Христос воскрес! Христос воскрес!	Christ is risen! Christ is risen!
Пришла нам весточка с небес!	Heaven has sent us good tidings!

The present lyric by Dmitry Merezhkovsky is a somber contrast to this domestic picture, throwing an ironic light on Easter in order to shock the reader into seeing the truth about the world. He challenges the complacent pieties, saying that if Christ were among us to see the human condition, he would see that the world is soaked in the blood and tears of oppression. His response to the triumphant cry "Christ is risen" could only be tears, not joy.

Rachmaninoff's setting of Merezhkovsky's lyric is a powerful monologue which "grows in intensity as it unfolds" (*Harrison*, 129). Two bars of repeated bell-like chords on the piano quickly establish a dramatic sense of expectation. The first two lines of the text are sung not very loudly in somber declamatory style; then comes the *forte* third line, each word strongly emphasized with tenuto marks, and lines 4 and 5 follow *fortissimo*. The emotional power rises rapidly in these first five lines, with emphatic marks on key words, and the same pattern follows in the second half of the song, which begins softly but by crescendos rises to a loud conclusion.

The song has attracted singers with its emotional power and somber beauty. There are many good performances. The Polish contralto Ewa Podleś has published three recordings of it and has sung it often in recital, as she did in Jordan Hall in Boston in February 2006. Recordings by Boris Christoff and Martti Talvela are also powerful. The composer wrote three optional notes in the seventh bar, the first two down a fifth and the last down a third: Talvela and Christoff sing this third optional note to fine effect.

"Христос воскрес!" — поют во храме;
Но грустно мне… душа молчит.
Мир полон кровью и слезами,
И этот гимн пред алтарями
Так оскорбительно звучит.
Когда б Он был меж нас и видел,
Чего достиг наш славный век,
Как брата брат возненавидел,
Как опозорен человек,
И если б здесь, в блестящем храме
"Христос воскрес" Он услыхал,
Какими б горькими слезами
Перед толпой Он зарыдал!

"Khristós vaskrés!" pajút va khráme;
No grúsna mné… dushá malchít.
Mir pólan króv'ju i slezámi,
I étad gímn pred altarjámi
Tak askarbítel'na zvuchít.
Kagdá b On býl mezh nás i vídel,
Chevó dastík nash slávnyj vék,
Kag bráta brát vaznenavídel,
Kak apazóren chelavék,
I jésli b zdés', v blestjáshchem khráme
"Khristós vaskrés" On uslykhál,
Kakími b gór'kimi slezámi
Peret talpój On zarydál!

"Christ is risen!" — they sing in church;
But I am sad… my soul is mute.
The world is soaked in blood and tears,
And this hymn sung before the altar
Sounds so insulting and unjust.
If He were among us and could see
What our glorious age has wrought,
How brother looks on brother in hatred,
How man has fallen in disgrace,
And here among us, in this glittering church,
If He heard the words "Christ has risen,"
What a bitter flood of tears
He would shed before the crowd!

Text. **Dmítry Merezhkóvsky**, 1887. Untitled. First published in Стихотворения (Poems) in 1888. Set only by Rachmaninoff.

Originally Merezhkovsky wrote eight more lines to the effect that only when tyrants are brought down and slaves are freed will it be possible for all the peoples (nations) of the world to say "Truly, Christ has risen." Sentiments like this were unacceptable in print in Tsarist Russia and the lines were cut by the Imperial censor; they were not published until 1925 (*Merezhkovskii 2000*, 775). The censored lines will be found below.

Meter. Binary. Iambic tetrameter:

But I am sad… my soul is mute.
The world is soaked in blood and tears…

Music. 23 August 1906. Op. 26, no. 6. F Minor. 4/4, with 3/2 passages, Moderato (♩ = 58). For Middle Voice: d^1 flat–f^2. First published with Opus 26 by A. Gutheil in Moscow in 1907. Dedicated to **Maria and Arkady Kérzin**. Threlfall and Norris list a transcription for cello and piano, or cello and salon orchestra by L[eonidas?] Leonardi, published by A. Gutheil in 1923 (*T/N*, 89).

Recordings. Burchuladze, Cehanovsky, Christoff, Dawson (in English), DeGaetani, Gedda, Gryzunov, Guleghina, Hvorostovsky, Isachenko, Karolik, Keenlyside, Kharitonov, Kontra, Koptchak, Koshetz, Kozlovsky, Labinsky, Larin, Leiferkus, Milcheva, Murzayev, Nesterenko, Oja, Orda, Piavko, Podleś, Popescu, Rautio, Shevelev, Söderström, Storozhev, Suchkova, Talvela, Yourenev.

Concluding lines of the poem, cut by the censor:

Пусть на земле не будет, братья,	Brothers, may there no longer be
Ни властелинов, ни рабов,	Tyrants or slaves on the earth,
Умолкнут стоны и проклятья,	Then groans and curses will grow still,
И стук мечей, и звон оков, —	And clashing swords and rattling chains, —
О лишь тогда, как гимн свободы,	O only then, like a hymn of freedom,
Пусть загремит: "Христос воскрес!"	Let the cry resound: "Christ is risen!"
И нам ответят все народы:	And all the nations will answer us:
"Христос воистину воскрес!"	"Truly, Christ is risen!"

53 *К детям*
To the children

Op. 26, No. 7

A father addresses his two little infants in this tender, well-paced, and beautifully composed song. In the first two stanzas he recalls his midnight visits to their room, to keep watch as they sleep, to bless them, to rejoice in thoughts of their innocence and hopes for their future happiness. With the third stanza there is a dramatic shift to a more linear declarative line, away from quiet joy, to the very different reality of the present: the room is dark, the icon lamp is no longer lit, and the children "are no more." Their absence is permanent. In the last stanza, he asks the children to pray for him now, as he used to pray for them: it is understood that as innocent souls in heaven, their prayers will have a purity which is consolation for their death as little infants. The poem was written by the well-known Russian Orthodox theologian and philosopher Aleksei Khomiakov (1804–1860), soon after his two infant sons died in their first year of life.

There have been curious avenues of resistance to this text, with the result that the understanding and appreciation of the song have been skewed both in Russia and in the English-speaking world. In the standard modern Soviet edition of the songs (*PSR*), Khomiakov's words have been *rewritten* to purge all traces of religious language from the text. Tchaikovsky's songs were in some cases reworded in performance (see *TCS*, 175, 282), but his texts were not tampered with in their published form. Here, in the "academic" edition of Rachmaninoff's songs, the text has been altered with no indication that it departs in any way from the original poem set by the composer. Soviet commentators say nothing about this. Yury Keldysh, who has excellent insights into the song, admires it for its "vocal intonations that are not declamatory, but sincere, intimate speech, with pauses and reflection"; he points out the "deep spiritual anxiety and concern" in the shift from major to minor in the final cry "Oh, children!" (*Keldysh*, 302); but he is silent about the altered text. Briantseva avoids the issue, calling the song a "lyric-philosophical monologue" (*Briantseva*, 371); Vasina-Grossman does not discuss the song at all. Soviet singers, perhaps aware of the corrupt text, avoided recordings and performances of it (the only Soviet recording known to me is the one by Andrei Ivanov). In Rachmaninoff's day, the song was performed with its original text: Nina Koshetz sang it with the composer at the piano in their 1916 recitals, for example. Today, however, the song is virtually unknown among the Russian public.

"To the children" has had a quite different fate in English. David Jackson, in his well-judged survey of recordings of Rachmaninoff's songs, wrote of it in 1988 that "with the possible exception of 'Lilacs' this is probably the most widely popular of the songs" (*Jackson*, 177). There are recordings of it in English by John McCormack (who made the song famous in English), Eileen Farrell, Elisabeth Schwarzkopf, and other fine singers; there is even a video performance by Risë Stevens. They all use the English translation by Rosa Newmarch (1857–1940), which is included in the Gutheil Russian-English edition of 1922, reprinted by Boosey & Hawkes and others many times, and still used in the English-speaking world. The main problem with the Newmarch translation is in the fourth line of the third stanza "малюток моих уже нет!" (my infants are no more), which she renders misleadingly as "the children are children no more!" This suggests that the children have grown, perhaps been sent away to school, and are missed at home. Out of Rosa Newmarch's translation has come a reading of the text which is more comforting than the thought that the children might have died in infancy: "the poem tells of a parent's sense of loss as the years pass and infant children grow up and leave home" (*Martyn 1990*, 173); the song is about "a mother's nostalgia at the growing up of her family" (*Norris 2001*, 143); the text is "a most touching expression of a mother's regret that her children have grown up and left home" (*Harrison 2005*, 129). The critic Richard Dyer, writing notes for Jan DeGaetani's recording in 1979, suggested the speaker in the song is the nanny: "The song returns us to the nursery, this time viewed from the emotional perspective of a nanny, who surveys a dark and silent room and realizes, with renewed anguish, that the children are no longer there; they have grown up."

Performances of this misconstrued English version of the song were common through the mid-twentieth century. In an affecting early television performance by Risë Stevens for the "Voice of Firestone," the scene shows mother in her living room, sitting next to framed photos of a little girl and boy, both already of school age. As the song is introduced by the orchestra, she reads a letter which begins "Dear Mommy, We're having a wonderful time in school. We are both O. K."

Today, performers outside Russia sing the song in Russian, using (almost always) the original Khomiakov-Rachmaninoff text, still in print outside Russia in the Gutheil edition. There are good recordings of it by Nicolai Gedda, Robert Tear, Jan DeGaetani, Elisabeth Söderström, and, perhaps best of all, the Russian baritone Dimitri Kharitonov, with pianist Leif Ove Andsnes. Only in performances that use the real Russian text—exactly half of the recordings listed here—do we have Rachmaninoff's original song.

Бывало, в глубокий полуночный час,
Малютки, приду любоваться на вас;
Бывало, люблю вас крестом знаменать,
Молиться, да будет на вас благодать,

Любовь Вседержителя Бога.

Стеречь умиленно ваш детский покой,
Подумать, о том, как вы чисты душой,
Надеяться долгих и счастливых дней
Для вас, беззаботных и милых детей.
Как сладко, как радостно было!

Теперь прихожу я: везде темнота,
Нет в комнате жизни, кроватка пуста;
В лампаде погас пред иконою свет…
Мне грустно, малюток моих уже нет!
И сердце так больно сожмётся!

О, дети! В глубокий полуночный час,
Молитесь о том, кто молился о вас,
О том, кто любил вас крестом знаменать;
Молитесь, да будет и с ним благодать,
Любовь Вседержителя Бога.

Byvála, v glubókaj palúnachnyj chás,
Maljútki, pridú ljubavátsa na vás;
Byvála, ljubljú vas krestóm
znamenát',
Malítsa, da búdet na vás blagadát',
Ljubóf' Fsederzhýtelja Bóga.

Time was when I loved at a late midnight hour,
To see you asleep in your room, little children,
My joy was to bless you
with the sign of the cross,
And to pray that peace and grace be upon you,
And the love of Almighty God.

Steréch umiljónna vazh détskij pakój,
Padúmat' a tóm, kak vy chísty dushój,
Nadéjatsa dólgikh i shcháslivykh dnéj
Dlja vás, bezzabótnykh i mílykh detéj.
Kak slátka, kak rádasna býla!

To keep watch over your childish rest,
To think how pure you are in soul,
To hope for long and happy days
For you, my carefree, beloved children.
How sweet and how joyous it was!

Tepér' prikhazhú ja: vezdé temnatá,
Nét f kómnate zhýzni, kravátka
pustá;
V lampáde pagás pred ykónaju svét…
Mne grúsna, maljútak maíkh uzhe nét!
I sérttsa tag ból'na sazhmjótsa!

Now when I come it's dark all around,
There's no life in your room, the little bed
is empty;
The light in the icon lamp has gone out…
I am sad, my little ones are no more!
My heart is crushed so painfully!

O, déti! V glubókaj palúnachnyj chás,
Malítes' a tóm, kto malílsa a vás,
A tóm, kto ljubíl vas krestóm
znamenát';
Malítes', da búdet i s ním blagadát',
Ljubóf' Fsederzhýtelja Bóga.

Oh, children! At this late midnight hour,
Pray for him who prayed for you,
Whose joy was to bless you
with the sign of the cross;
Pray that all blessings be upon him too,
And the love of Almighty God.

Text. **Alekséi Stepánovich Khomyakóv**. Written in 1838 or 1839 after the death of his two infant sons, Stepan (1837–38) and Feodor (June–October 1838). Published in 1844 with the title "К детям" (To [my] children); in the 1910 edition of his poems it has the title "На кончину двух первых детей" (On the death of my first two children). For details see *Khomiakov 1900*, vol. 4, and *Khomiakov 1969*, 561. The English pastor William Palmer (1811–1879) corresponded with Khomiakov and translated some of his poems into English, including this one (see *Birkbeck 1895* and *Khomiakov 1995*). As is clear from the sample stanza below, Palmer correctly has the absent children dead, not grown up. Set only by Rachmaninoff.

Meter. Ternary. Amphibrachs, four-foot, with a three-foot line at the end of each stanza. The sample below is from William Palmer's translation in *Khomiakov 1900*, vol. 4, p. 413 (the first word in the last line should be omitted to preserve the metrical pattern):

But now, if I go, all is silence, all gloom;
None sleep in that crib, nothing breathes in that room;
The light that should burn at the image is gone:
Alas! so it is, children, now I have none,
And my heart how it painfully throbs!

Music. Ivanovka, 9 September 1906. Op. 26, no. 7. F Major. 12/8, Lento (♩ = 52). For Middle Voice: e^1–f^2. First published with Opus 26 by A. Gutheil in Moscow in 1907. Dedicated to **Maria and Arkady Kérzin**. Transcribed for piano by Earl Wild (1981).

Recordings. Crooks (in English), DeGaetani, Del Grande, Farrell (in English), Gedda, Hislop (in English), An. Ivanov (emended text), Kharitonov, Koshetz, Lloyd (in English), McCormack (in English), Melton (in English), Pelle, Popescu, Pusar, Schwarzkopf (in English), Slobodskaya, Söderström, Risë Stevens (video, in English), Suchkova (emended text), Tear, Zimmermann (partially emended text).

Transcriptions. *Piano:* Earl Wild.

54 *Пощады я молю*
I beg for mercy

Op. 26, No. 8

Songs about spring are typically bright and joyful: spring is the season that brings renewal, and often love. In Tchaikovsky's songs these associations are present in the three children's songs about spring (Songs 54, 60, 64 in *TCS*, Op. 54, nos. 3, 9, 13); in his Heine setting "Little blue eyes of spring" (Song 18, (without opus number); and in one of his best-known songs, "It was in early spring" (Song 40, Op. 38/2), which celebrates spring and first love.

There is a more modern, ironic counter-theme to this affirmation of spring, which might be called "spring can be cruel." The one example in Tchaikovsky's songs is "Отчего" (Why, Op. 6/5), a setting of a lyric Heinrich Heine wrote in 1822. Its irony is that, now that the poet is abandoned, "spring is here, but it feels like winter now." A modern variation on Heine's counter-theme is the well-known song by Richard Rodgers and Lorenz Hart "Spring is here! Why doesn't my heart go dancing?" (1938). Another modern song that takes this counter-theme as its starting point, but develops it with witty irony, is Fran Landesman's "Spring can really hang you up the most" (1956), with its rich, self-mocking narrative, conveyed definitively by artists like Ella Fitzgerald and Betty Carter.

The present lyric by Dmitri Merezhkovsky is another variation on the theme of "cruel spring." Merezhkovsky knew Heine's poetry well, but he also knew Russian urban romances: his lyric for one of Rachmaninoff's early songs is an imitation "cruel romance" (Song 10). In the fin-de-siècle urban romances, spring often brings passionate love—but once spring passes, it leaves only a painful memory of love that has been lost. Badly wounded by spring once, Merezhkovsky now pleads that spring not punish him again. The lyric has ambiguity, but little irony.

Rachmaninoff's response to Merezhkovsky's lyric is an impassioned, driven song, which has a "marvelous urgency" and an "excitingly invigorating piano accompaniment"; Barrie Martyn judges it "one of Rachmaninoff's most splendid settings" (*Martyn*, 173). In a letter to Maria Kerzina, the composer noted that the piano part is "extremely important" and that the singer "will barely have time to take a breath," adding nevertheless that it should be performed faster than the metronome mark indicates (Dresden, 7 December 1906, *LN 1*, 411). Its pacing and the notes themselves make it difficult to sing: it is among the composer's least performed songs. Nevertheless, in a fine performance like the one by the dramatic tenor Georgi Nelepp, it has arresting intensity and conviction.

Пощады я молю! Не мучь, меня, Весна,
Не подходи ко мне с болезненною лаской,
И сердца не буди от мертвенного сна
Своей младенческой, но трогательной сказкой.

Ты видишь, как я слаб, — о сжалься надо мной!
Меня томит и жжёт твой ветер благовонный.
Я дорого купил забвенье и покой, —
Оставь же их душе, страданьем утомлённой...

Pashchády ja maljú! Ne múch menjá, Vesná,	I pray for mercy! Do not torment me, Spring,
Ne patkhadí ka mné z baléznennaju láskaj,	Do not approach me with your sickly caresses,
I sérttsa ne budí at mértvennava sná	Nor stir my heart from deathly slumber
Svajéj mladéncheskaj no trógatel'naj skáskaj.	With your infantile but poignant fairy-tale.
Ty vídish kak ja sláp! — o, zzhál'sa nada mnój!	You see how weak I am — oh take pity on me!
Menjá tamít i zhzhót tvoj véter blagavónnyj!	I am burnt and withered by your wind sweet and fragrant!
Ja dóraga kupíl zabvénje i pakój...	Dearly have I paid for oblivion and peace...
Astáv' zhe íkh dushé, stradán'jem utamljónnaj...	Grant them to a soul, weary with suffering...

Text. **Dmitri Merezhkóvsky**, 1886. Title in the manuscript "Отрывок" (Fragment), but later crossed out; first published in 1888 in Merezhkovsky's "Стихотворения (1883–1887)" (Poems 1883–1887) without a title. Set first by Rachmaninoff, later by Felix Blumenfeld (Op. 41/1, 1910).

Meter. Binary. Iambic hexameter:

So dearly have I paid for this forgetful sleep...
Then grant oblivion to a weary suffering soul...

Music. Ivanovka, 25 August 1906. Op. 26, no. 8. A Minor. 3/2, 4/4, Allegro con fuoco (♩ = 104). For High Voice: g^1 sharp–a^2. First published with Opus 26 by A. Gutheil in Moscow in 1907. Dedicated to **Maria and Arkady Kérzin**.

Recordings. Christoff, Kurenko, Naoumenko, Nelepp, Söderström, Suchkova, Tear.

55 *Я опять одинок*
Again I am alone

Op. 26, No. 9

The lyric of this unusual song was written by Rachmaninoff's contemporary Ivan Bunin (1870–1953). It is an original lyric, not a translation from Shevchenko, as is mistakenly indicated in the score (see notes on the text below). Both in his lyrics and in his prose (for which he is better known), Bunin is a gifted landscape painter, a *paysagiste*. But he sees nature for what it is, whether it maps his state of being, as we shall see in Song 58, or stands in contrast to it, as it does here.

In this song we have Heine's theme of "cruel spring" once again, but it is expressed in a new way. The poet greets spring with a happy shout, but his joy is followed by a painful awareness that he and his lover are in fact separating. Bunin "sketches out the facts" (*Aikhenval'd*, 420), meaning the psychological facts: they gain immediacy because this is not a memory but a realization occurring now, in real time. The song expresses this powerfully. It begins and ends in extreme intensity, with the slower intervening phrases (lines 2, 3, 4, 5) conveying both the release of tension and the passage of time. Then the intensity resumes, rising to the optional high note on the verb in line 7, a B flat which most singers prefer. There is true lyric daring and vulnerability in the declamatory voice part, to which the piano gives eloquent support.

The creative rapport between composer and lyricist here is not an accident. Rachmaninoff met Bunin in May of 1900 in Yalta, where they were spending time with Chekhov and members of the Moscow Art Theater as described earlier (see page 94). They seem to have taken an instant liking to each other. Bunin recalled in 1950 in a note he wrote in memory of Rachmaninoff that the two of them stayed up most of the night walking on the beach, quoting Pushkin and Lermontov, Fet and Tyutchev. At dawn Rachmaninoff embraced Bunin and said "Let's be friends forever!" (*Bunin 2003*, 56). There were not many meetings after that, although Rachmaninoff did manage to give some financial support to Bunin in the 1930s. The two superb songs he wrote to Bunin's lyrics are a fitting outcome to the artistic rapport they felt in Yalta.

Although written for high voice, some of the best performances of the song are by baritones; especially fine is Aleksei Ivanov, who forgoes the optional B flat on the second syllable of line 7.

Как светла, как нарядна весна!
Погляди мне в глаза, как бывало,
И скажи: отчего ты грустна,
Отчего ты так ласкова стала?

Но молчишь ты, слаба, как цветок…
О, молчи! Мне не надо признанья:
Я узнал эту ласку прощанья, —
Я опять одинок!

Kak svetlá, kak narjádna vesná!
Pagljadí mne v glazá, kak byvála,
I skazhý: atchevó ty grusná,
Atchevó ty tak láskava stála?

How bright spring is, how festively adorned!
Look me in the eyes, as you often used to,
And tell me: why are you sad,
Why this sudden loving caress?

No malchísh ty, slabá kak tsvetók...
Ó, malchí! Mne ne náda priznán'ja:
Ja uznál étu lásku prashchán'ja, —
Ja apját' adinók!

But you're silent, fragile as a flower...
Oh, don't speak! No confession is needed:
I recognize this farewell caress, —
Once again I'm alone!

Text. **Iván Alekséyevich Búnin**, 1899. Untitled. First published in *Zhurnal dlia vsekh* (Everybody's Magazine) in December 1900, No. 12, p. 1424. I found the journal in the Historical Library in Moscow. In that issue, this lyric by Bunin is printed alongside some of Bunin's translations of Shevchenko. In the Index of the journal for 1900 the author of "Я опять одинок" is given as Bunin, not Shevchenko. On the page, however, it might have been taken for one of Bunin's Shevchenko translations, a mistake Rachmaninoff apparently made. Ever since, the poem has been erroneously attributed to Shevchenko in all editions of Rachmaninoff's songs, in commentaries and recordings, and in authoritative sources like the *New Grove* and WorldCat. The error has, however, been noted by Bunin scholars in Russia: see *Logvinov* 1973, 299-301.

Set first by Reinhold Glière (Op. 14/4, 1905); other settings by Viktor Pergament, Yuly (Joel) Engel (Op. 5/2, 1906), the tenor Viktor Sadovnikov (Op. 1/5, 1911), and Rachmaninoff's friend Yury Sakhnovsky (Op. 4/5, 1909).

Meter. Ternary. Anapest, three-foot, with a chopped-off two-foot last line:

But you're silent, and weak as a flower...
Oh, don't speak! No confession is needed...
This affection at parting I know, —
Once again I'm alone!

Music. Ivanovka, 4 September 1906. Op. 26, no. 9. D Minor. 12/8, Allegro (♩ = 100). For High Voice: e^1–a^2 (b^2 flat). First published with Opus 26 by A. Gutheil in Moscow in 1907. Dedicated to **Maria and Arkady Kérzin**. Transcribed for cello by Moray Welsh.

Recordings. Atlantov, Gedda, Ghiaurov, Gmyria, Golovin, Guliayev, Hvorostovsky, Al. Ivanov, Korshunov, Kurenko, Larin, Lear, Lemeshev, Lisitsian, Magomayev, Milcheva, Mishura, Nelepp, Nortsov, Ognivtsev, Piavko, Rodgers, Rozum, Shevelev, Slovtsov, Söderström, Suchkova, Tear, Zlatogorova.

Transcriptions. *Cello:* Moray Welsh.

56 *У моего окна*
Before my window

Op. 26, No. 10

This is Rachmaninoff's third and last lyric by Countess Einerling, better known by her pen-name Galiná. As we saw in "Here it's so fine" (Song 40), Galiná's poems were criticized as too lightweight to be taken seriously, but were admired for their musicality and graceful sincerity. In "Sorrow in springtime" (Song 45) there was resistance to spring, but here there are no conflicting emotions. The image of a cherry tree in blossom (actually a "bird cherry," the Eurasian *Prunus padus*, with clusters of small fragrant white flowers) is a diaphanous emblem of spring, which intoxicates the poet and suggests to her a music of "love songs without words."

The lyrical beauty of Rachmaninoff's song carries the listener forward from the very first notes. The voice part, marked *cantabile*, leads the way at the outset and throughout the song. With the fifth bar (line 3 of the text), the piano part (*la melodia ben marcato*) follows the melodic lead, becomes an independent voice, and gains even more prominence in the second stanza of the lyric. For a moment the piano is silent as the voice rises to a high B on the word "дыханье" (breath) at the end of line 6; this is immediately followed by a rich piano phrase marked by a long *legato* slur over the entire seventh line "their sweet aroma clouds my senses." Yevgeny Shenderovich sees the song as a kind of "duet" for voice and piano, where the pianist has to make the chords "sing" in a prolonged, unbroken *legato* flow to bring out a "ravishing" sound of string instruments (*Shenderovich 1996*, 176). In the lovely postlude the piano withdraws almost reluctantly from the poetic mood created by the song.

The song has a rich recording history. A beautiful early recording was made by the tenor Dmitry Smirnov in 1912 in Paris; he recorded it later that year in St. Petersburg, and again in 1929 in Berlin (*TRC 42/3*, Sept. 1997). Ivan Kozlovsky also recorded it three times, the last time around 1964 with the Bolshoi Theater Orchestra, in a lush arrangement for strings by Vladimir Yurovsky that illustrates Shenderovich's notion of how the piano part is supposed to sound. Of the many fine pianists who have recorded it, some of those who come closest to this *legato* ideal are Alexis Weissenberg (with Nicolai Gedda), Ivari Ilya (with Maria Guleghina), Vladimir Ashkenazy (with Elisabeth Söderström), and Shenderovich himself (with Galina Kovaleva). Most singers take the three optional higher notes in bars 4 and 12, especially the high B mentioned above, but some do not (Jennie Tourel, Albert Orda, Evelyn Lear). In English, Dame Isobel Baillie recorded it with Gerald Moore in 1943, singing the Rosa Newmarch translation. John McCormack made a recording in 1924, changing a phrase in the translation, as he often did, to suit himself. For "The cherry blossoms sing *a wordless song of love,*" he substitutes "*a tender song to me.*" Fritz Kreisler joined him on this date, appropriating some of the best piano phrases for his violin, leaving the pianist Edwin Schneider with little to do; the sound is sweet but it rather spoils the song.

У моего окна черёмуха цветёт,
Цветёт задумчиво под ризой серебристой...
И веткой свежей и душистой
Склонилась и зовёт...

Её трепещущих воздушных лепестков
Я радостно ловлю весёлое дыханье,
Их сладкий аромат туманит мне сознанье,
И песни о любви они поют без слов...

U majevó akná cherjómukha
tsvetjót,
Tsvetjód zadúmchiva pad rízaj serebrístaj...
I vétkaj svézhej i dushýstaj
Sklanílas' i zavjót...

Jejó trepéshchushchikh vazdúshnykh lepestkóf
Ja rádasna lavljú vesjólaje dykhán'je,
Ikh slátkij aramát tumánit mne saznán'je,
I pésni a ljubví aní pajút
bes slóf...

The cherry tree's in flower outside
my window,
In silver robe it blossoms pensively...
And with a fresh and fragrant bough
It bends to me and beckons...

Lovely are its trembling airy blossoms,
In rapture I inhale their happy breath,
Their sweet aroma clouds my senses,
They are singing love songs
without words...

Text. **G. Galiná (Glafíra Adól'fovna Einerling)**. Untitled. First published in *Zhurnal dlia vsekh* (Everybody's Magazine) in July 1902, No. 7, p. 813. Set only by Rachmaninoff.

Meter. Binary. Iambic, 6-foot, with two shorter lines:

A cherry tree is blossoming outside my window,
With fresh and fragrant bough it bends to me and beckons ...

Music. Ivanovka, 17 September 1906. Op. 26, no. 10. A Major. 4/4, Lento (♩ = 50). For High Voice: e^1–a^2 (b^2). First published with Opus 26 by A. Gutheil in Moscow in 1907. Dedicated to **Maria and Arkady Kérzin**.

Recordings. Arkhipova, Baillie (in English), Borele, Del Grande, Dionne, Dodoka, Domnich, Firsova, Galante, Gedda, Gerzmava, Guleghina, Korshunov, Kovaleva, Kozlovsky, Kurenko, Larin, Lear, Lee, McCormack (in English), Melton (in English), Ognivtsev, Oleinichenko, Orda, Pusar, Rodgers, Rudenko, Shtoda, Smirnov, Söderström, Suchkova, Sumatchova, Tourel, Woytowicz (in Polish), Zhadan.

Transcriptions. *Cello:* Anthony Elliott, Brian Stucki.

57 *Фонтан*
The fountain

Op. 26, No. 11

Rachmaninoff evidently took a mimetic approach to this lyric by Feodor Tyutchev, giving musical expression to the motion of water in a fountain as it sprays up in a misty cloud and falls back to earth. It is a short song, less than ninety seconds long, but it takes a lot of notes to imitate the movement and visual effects of a fountain. The song succeeds as a musical picture, "carried out with a fluid delicacy in the treble sextolets that suggest the play of the fountain's jets, while deep bass octaves imply an underlying power" (*Harrison*, 130). The entire song, with its "surging" accompaniment and octave leap on the word "height" (*Martyn*, 173), comes across effectively in the recording by the tenor Alexandre Naoumenko with Howard Shelley at the piano.

Tyutchev's purpose, however, went well beyond this: in a second stanza, he speaks of human thought, striving heavenward in its quest but ordained inevitably to come falling back to earth. There is more than the physics of water drops and light at stake here, as the word "doomed" at the end of the first stanza warns. The composer's omission of the second, metaphysical stanza has met with objections from several critics (see *Blagoi*, 572 and note). Poetically, the second stanza is very fine, with its use of "solemn, archaic" language (*Liberman*, 215) to express the philosophical notion that human thought, however it strives upward, falls short of the highest summit and can go no further. In his copy, Lev Tolstoy marked the poem "profound." The omitted stanza will be found below.

Смотри, как облаком живым
Фонтан сияющий клубится;
Как пламенеет, как дробится
Его на солнце влажный дым.
Лучом поднявшись к небу, он
Коснулся высоты заветной
И снова пылью огнецветной
Ниспасть на землю осуждён...

Smatrí, kak óblakam zhyvým	See how like a living cloud
Fantán sijájushchij klubítsa;	The shining fountain shoots up;
Kak plamenéjet, kag drabítsa	How its damp cloud of mist
Jevó na sónttsa vlázhnyj dým.	Flames as it sprays in the sunlight.
Luchóm padnjáfshys' k nébu, ón	Soaring skyward like a ray of light
Kasnúlsa vysatý zavétnaj	It reaches its topmost height
I snóva pýl'ju agnetsvétnaj	And again like fire-colored dust
Nispást' na zémlju asuzhdjón...	Is doomed to fall back to earth...

Text. **Fyódor Ivánovich Tyútchev**, by 1836. Untitled. First published by Aleksandr Pushkin in his journal *Современник* (The Contemporary) in the fall of 1836 in a group of poems entitled "Poems sent from Germany." Set only by Rachmaninoff.

Meter. Binary. Iambic tetrameter:

Again, in rainbow-colored spray,
Is doomed to fall back down to earth…

Music. Ivanovka, 6 September 1906. Op. 26, no. 11. D Major. 4/4, Maestoso (♩ = 56). For High Voice: d^1–b^2 flat. First published with Opus 26 by A. Gutheil in Moscow in 1907. Dedicated to **Maria and Arkady Kérzin**.

Recordings. Del Grande, Farrar (in English), Kurenko, Kuuzik, Naoumenko, Shumskaya, Söderström, Suchkova, Tear.

Second stanza of the poem, omitted by Rachmaninoff from the song:

О смертной мысли водомёт,	Oh mighty fountain of mortal thought,
О водомёт неистощимый!	Oh fountain inexhaustible!
Какой закон непостижимый	What law incomprehensible
Тебя стремит, тебя мятёт?	Impels you on, inspires you?
Как жадно к небу рвёшься ты!..	How avidly you strive toward heaven!..
Но длань незримо-роковая,	But a Hand invisible and preordained,
Твой луч упорный преломляя,	Refracting your stubborn ray of light,
Свергает в брызгах с высоты.	Casts you down in spray-drops from on high.

58 *Ночь печальна* *The night is mournful*

Op. 26, No. 12

Following the striking dramatic monologue of "Again I am alone" (Song 55), Rachmaninoff chose the present lyric as the second of two settings to words by Ivan Bunin. This time the lyric is an internal monologue, in which the poet ponders his own situation, voicing his thoughts aloud to himself and to the reader. We have noticed before in discussing Rachmaninoff's songs that even the most discerning critics are sometimes quicker to understand the merits of the music than of the lyric itself. In the case of this song, the lyric has been seen as "despairing" (*Martyn*, 174), or even as "a discouraging poem" whose "pessimism" is countered only by the inventive piano writing Rachmaninoff devised for the song (*Harrison*, 130). Both scholars are right to draw attention to the wonderful piano part the composer wrote for this song, but there is more to this lyric than a pessimistic outlook.

First, the poem is not a disembodied complaint, but set in a concrete world: the lyric voice is situated clearly both in space (the vast steppe, a path, a distant light), and in time (night, the beginning of a journey). Next, the verse form, the musical shape of the lines, is trochaic pentameter, a rare meter in Russian literary practice (Pushkin, for example, did not write a single line in this meter: see *Unbegaun 1963*, p. 30). For this reason, it stands out and calls attention to itself, as Bunin would have understood instinctively. Mikhail Lermontov used the five-foot trochee in 1841 in one of his last and most famous lyrics "Выхожу один я на дорогу," which begins "I walk out alone onto the road. Through the mist the stony path glistens; the night is quiet, the wilderness is listening to God, and star is talking to star." Lermontov's poem, famous as such but also as a very popular Russian song after it was set to music in 1861 by E. S. Shashina, turned out to be the first in a loose cycle of related lyrics written by poets after him. Formally, they are all written in trochaic pentameter lines, initiated by a verb of motion in the first line. Thematically, they share the common idea of the beginning of a difficult journey, perhaps a fateful or final journey, undertaken at night or close of day; there is a questioning of why the journey is difficult and what the outcome will be. One example is Feodor Tyutchev's "Вот бреду я вдоль большой дороги," written on the first anniversary of the death of Yelena Denisieva, his last love, in 1865: "I walk along the highway in the peaceful light of fading day; my heart is heavy, my legs are numb… My darling, do you see me?" Lermontov's theme was taken up in the twentieth century too. In 1920 Osip Mandelstam wrote "В Петербурге мы сойдемся снова," a poem about the uncertain future of poetry and poets in the early years of Soviet power: "We shall come together again in Petersburg as though we had buried the sun [a reference to the death of Pushkin], and utter the blessed and meaningless word... in the black velvet of the Soviet night." In 1946, Boris Pasternak took up the theme in "Гул затих. Я вышел на подмостки," the first of his *Zhivago* poems, called "Hamlet": "The hum has died down. I walk out on the stage... In the distant echo I seek to grasp what will happen during my life. The darkness of night is aimed at me through a thousand opera-glasses." These examples, like Lermontov's original poem, show the seriousness of the theme by virtue of the questions it raises about destiny, death, and eternal life.

Bunin could not have known these other poems (Tyutchev's lyric was not published until 1903), but his lyric has its own place as a variation on Lermontov's verses in this rare trochaic meter—a poem he would have known by heart. In this lyric, taking as his starting point Lermontov's five-foot trochaic line and the images of night, the path, and the journey to be undertaken alone, Bunin personalized the theme in his own terms. It is not about death and eternal life, but about a different journey. It is a young man's poem; it lacks the conclusive finality of the Lermontov text, but Bunin shares Lermontov's resolute determination to take his own journey under its own terms. He is not discouraged or pessimistic. The poet accepts "sadness" and "dreams," and affirms the heart's "love and melancholy." There is sadness here, but a sadness that contains love and the compelling power of dreams.

A year before Rachmaninoff wrote this song, Reinhold Glière wrote a setting of the poem for solo voice and piano. It is a well-made declamatory song in three parts that begins with somber chords, then becomes agitated and passionate in the second stanza before slowing to a resigned, serene conclusion. Rachmaninoff's song is a Largo in B minor which is a more satisfying poetic whole, and never somber. The piano quintuplets broaden quickly into melody: the composer warned that the song demands an even greater singing effort from the pianist than the singer (letter of 24 Nov.1906, *LN1*, 411.) The voice part is declamatory yet continuously lyrical, with tenuto marks to place emphasis on the words of the questions in lines 5 and 6: each sung note counts. The piano part is lyrical too, but has a commanding mastery and added weight that bring out the resolute quality in the lyric. The result is one of Rachmaninoff's most beautiful and poetic songs. There are many fine recordings, including one made by the tenor Georgi Vinogradov, with the composer's friend Alexander Goldenweiser at the piano. Goldenweiser was the accompanist for the singers at the premiere of Opus 26 in Moscow on 12 February 1907.

Ночь печальна, как мечты мои…
Далеко, в глухой степи широкой,
Огонёк мерцает одинокий...
В сердце много грусти и любви.

Но кому и как расскажешь ты,
Что зовёт тебя, чем сердце полно?
Путь далёк, глухая степь безмолвна,
Ночь печальна, как мои мечты.

Nóch pechál'na, kak mechtý maí…	Mournful is the night, and sad my dreams…
Dalekó, v glukhój stepí shyrókaj,	Far off, in the wide deserted steppe,
Aganjók mertsájet adinókaj…	A solitary light is flickering…
F sérttse mnóga grústi i ljubví.	Your heart brims with melancholy and love.
No kamú i kák rasskázhesh tý,	But to whom and how would you express
Shtó zavjót tebjá, chem sérttse pólna?	What summons you, what fills your heart?
Púd' daljók, glukhája stéb' bezmólvna,	The way is long, the empty steppe is silent,
Nóch pechál'na, kak maí mechtý.	The night is sad, like my dreams.

Text. **Iván Alekséyevich Búnin**, 1899. Untitled. First published in *Zhurnal dlia vsekh* (Everybody's Magazine) in August 1900, No. 8, p. 917. Set earlier by Reinhold Glière (Op. 14/1, 1905).

Meter. Binary. Trochaic pentameter:

Mournful is the night, and sad my dreams,
Going forth along a lonely road,
Dark and silent the deserted steppe,
Solitary gleams a distant light…

Music. Ivanovka, 3 September 1906. Op. 26, no. 11. B Minor. 4/4, Largo (♩ = 48). For High Voice: e^1–f^2 sharp. First published with Opus 26 by A. Gutheil in Moscow in 1907. Dedicated to **Maria and Arkady Kérzin**. Arranged for piano, voice, and cello by the composer with bowing by Brandukov: see *Rytsareva 1980*, 35, and *T/N*, 88-9.

Recordings. Arkhipova, Baturkin, Christoff, Del Grande, Dodoka, Dolukhanova, Firsova, Furdui, Guleghina, Hvorostovsky, Isakova, Izotova, Kharitonov, Korshunov, Kurenko, Larin, Lee, Lemeshev, Levko, L. Maslennikova, Milcheva, Murzayev, Ognivtsev, Piavko, Pirogov, Rautio, Rodgers, Rozhdestvenskaya, Semenchuk, Silja, Siniavskaya, Söderström, Suchkova, Sumatchova, Talvela, Tear, Vinogradov, Vishnevskaya.

Glière: Elena Prokina.

Transcriptions. *Cello:* Dmitry Ferschtman, Mischa Maisky.

59 *Вчера мы встретились* *When yesterday we met*

Op. 26, No. 13

Like Aleksei Tolstoy and Afanasy Fet, Yakov Polonsky (1819–1898) was a successor in lyric poetry to Pushkin and Lermontov. All three were contemporaries of the great realist novelists—Turgenev, Dostoevsky, Lev Tolstoy—born in the decade from 1818 to 1828. The aims and strategies of narrative prose were never far from Polonsky's mind. He charted the passage of time in concrete images taken from the world around him. He had a knack for storytelling in the short confines of the lyric poem. Tchaikovsky used a Polonsky lyric for his popular "Song of the Gypsy Girl" (Op. 60/7, 1886), a lyric that is intensely musical in its verse form but tells a Romantic story with exotic local color.

The Polonsky lyric chosen for the present song also tells a story, but here time's passage is described in a prosaic, though very dramatic way. This chance encounter between the poet and a woman he knew some time ago is consciously unmusical: the long enjambed hexameter lines obscure the rhymes, so that it reads like a short prose passage from a longer story. It is "a little glimpse into lives in progress," as the Tchaikovsky specialist Donald Seibert remarked after we had listened to Chaliapin's recording of the song.

The song is one of Rachmaninoff's most successful essays in giving musical expression to ordinary phrases of human speech. It is less rhetorical than that other declamatory masterpiece, "Fragment from Musset" (Song 39). He finds truncated speech-like melodies for each of the short phrases; they are separated by pauses, and made emphatic with tenuto markings that highlight the drama and emotional intensity in Polonsky's narrative. The piano marks time in the "simple syncopated accompaniment familiar from many of Rachmaninoff's songs" (*Norris*, 143). The singer has to act out the lines gently, without overplaying the part. It has a finely designed forward movement: the melodic phrases gradually connect as the song rises to its *pianissimo, dolce* "farewell." The very last phrase, shown in italics, is taken from "The Feast During the Plague," one of Pushkin's "Little Tragedies": the reference is to Mary, an urban prostitute with "a heart of gold," "fallen" but pitiable and good (*Pushkin 2000*, 210).

Despite the metronome marking, the song is most engaging if not taken too slowly. Besides Chaliapin, there are fine performances by Lisitsian, Koptchak, Hvorostovsky, and many others. Leiferkus, though slow, sings it expertly.

Вчера мы встретились: она остановилась,
Я также… Мы в глаза друг другу посмотрели…

О, Боже! как она с тех пор переменилась,
В глазах потух огонь, и щёки побледнели…
И долго на неё глядел я, молча, строго…
Мне руку протянув, бедняжка улыбнулась;
Я говорить хотел, она же, ради Бога
Велела мне молчать, и тут же отвернулась,
И брови сдвинула, и выдернула руку,
И молвила: «Прощайте, до свиданья»!
А я хотел сказать: «На вечную разлуку
Прощай, *погибшее, но милое созданье*».

Fcherá my fstrétilis': aná astanavílas',
Ya tágzhe… Mý v glazá drug drúgu
pasmatréli…
O, Bózhe! kák aná s tekh pór
pereminílas'…
V glazákh patúkh agón', i shchóki
pablednéli…
I dólga na nejó gljadél ja, mólcha,
strόga…
Mne rúku pratjanúv, bednjáshka
ulybnúlas';
Ja gavarít' khatél, aná zhe,
radi Bóga
Veléla mne malchát', i túd zhe atvernúlas',
I brόvi zdvínula, i ýdernula rúku,
I mólvila: "Prashchájte, da svidán'ja!"
A ja khatél skazát': "Na véchnuju razlúku
Prashcháj, pagípsheje, no mílaje sazdán'je."

Yesterday we chanced to meet; she stopped,
So did I… We looked into each other's
eyes…
Good God! how she has changed
since our last meeting,
Her eyes have lost their light, her cheeks
their color…
For a long time I gazed at her, in silence,
sternly…
The poor thing offered me her hand,
and gave me a smile;
I was about to speak, but she bade me
for God's sake
To be still, and quickly turned away,
And frowned, and withdrew her hand,
And spoke: "Farewell… goodbye…!"
And I wanted to say: "So we part forever,
Farewell, thou being, ruined, but still dear."

Text. **Yákov Petróvich Polónsky**, 1844. Title: Встреча (Encounter). First published in Polonsky's debut volume of verse "Гамма" (Scale) in 1844. Set only by Rachmaninoff, who dropped the title in lieu of the first phrase.

Meter. Binary. Iambic hexameter:

I was about to speak, but she prevented me,
And quickly turned away, and frowned, withdrew her hand…

Music. Ivanovka, 3 September 1906. Op. 26, no. 13. D Minor. 4/8, Moderato (♩ = 56). For Middle Voice: d^1–e^2. First published with Opus 26 by A. Gutheil in Moscow in 1907. Dedicated to **Maria and Arkady Kérzin**.

Recordings. Amaize, A. Bolshakov, Chaiter, Chaliapin, Christoff, Del Grande, Grishko, Guliayev, Hvorostovsky, Kharitonov, Koptchak, Koshetz, Kurenko, Larin, Leiferkus, Lemeshev, Lisitsian, Maslennikov, Milcheva, Ognivtsev, Politkovsky, Popescu, Rozum, Seleznev, Serkebayev, Sheremet, Souzay, Söderström, Suchkova, Talvela, Vassilieff, Zimmermann.

60 *Кольцо* *The ring*

Op. 26, No. 14

Sometimes the least known songs are the most interesting. Here is one. Its extreme language and the folkish lilt of the short dactylic line endings are strange at first, but we soon realize this is the old theme of "the man that got away," a common plaint in songs, and not only Russian songs.

Rachmaninoff's brilliant setting of this folk song by Aleksei Koltsov instantly conveys the incantatory power of the words. The lyric was common in songbooks after 1850, a specimen of the category "*russkaia pesnia*" (Russian song), and many composers wrote music for it. Rachmaninoff's song is the most original, however, with its extraordinary piano part, "restlessly twitching... like the fluttering flame of a taper" (*Martyn*, 174). For pianists not up to its demands, the composer wrote an unusual easier "ossia" part. Yelena Kreutzer recalled Rachmaninoff's playing it for her soon after it was written: "When he demonstrated a new romance, he always hummed along with it... 'The Ring' made an enormous impression. The piano accompaniment literally took my breath away. What a pity it is that owing to the extraordinary difficulties of the voice and piano parts, the song has been consigned to total oblivion" (*VOR 1988*, 1, 325). The piano part is powerfully executed by Vladimir Ashkenazy (Söderström) and Howard Shelley (Popescu); to hear the words sung with artistic feeling and crystalline clarity, the performance by Maria Kurenko is unmatched.

Я затеплю свечу
Воску ярого,
Распаяю кольцо
Друга милого!

Загорись, разгорись,
Роковой огонь!
Распаяй, растопи
Чисто золото!

Без него для меня
Ты не надобно,
Без него на руке
Камень на сердце.

Что взгляну, то вздохну,
Затоскуюся.
И зальются глаза
Горьким горем слёз.

Возвратится ли он?
Или весточкой
Оживит ли меня,
Безутешную?

Нет надежды в душе,
Ты рассыпься же
Золотой слезой,
Память милого!

Невредимо, черно
На огне кольцо,
И звенит по столу
Память вечную…

Ja zatéplju svechú Vósku járava, Raspajáju kal'tsó Drúga mílava!	I will light a candle Of pure white wax, I will melt the ring Of my beloved friend.
Zagarís', razgarís', Rakavój agón'! Raspajáj, rastapí Chísta zólata!	Flare up, burn bright Fateful fire! Grow soft and melt, Pure yellow gold!
Bez nevó dlja menjá Ty ne nádabna, Bez nevó na ruké Kámen' ná serttse.	If I don't have him I don't need you, If I don't have him, You're a stone on my heart.
Shto vzgljanú, to vzdakhnú, Zataskújusa. I zaljútsa glazá Gór'kim górem sljos.	I stare, then sigh, I'm filled with despair. My eyes spill over In bitter tears of grief.
Vazvratítsa li ón? Ili véstachkaj Azhyvít li menjá, Bezutéshnuju?	Will he ever come back? Or send some word To revive me, Inconsolable?
Net nadézhdy v dushé, Ty rassýp'sa zhe Zalatój slezój, Pámjat' mílava!	My soul has lost hope, So melt away too, Like a golden tear, All memory of him!
Nevredíma, chernó Na agné kal'tsó, I zvenít pa stalú Pámjat' véchnuju...	The ring is indestructible, Blackened in the fire, It jangles on the table, A memory that will not die...

Text. **Alekséi Vasílyevich Koltsóv**, 1830. Title: Перстень (Ring). First published in *Литературная газета* (Literary Gazette) in 1831. Set by ten composers, including Gurilyov (1850), Peter P. Bulakhov (1854), Dargomyzhsky (1856), and A. N. Koreshchenko (Op. 2/2, 1893).

Meter. Mixed. Odd lines are two-foot anapests of six syllables; even lines of five syllables have a trochaic foot followed by a dactyl (see *Unbegaun*, 50):

Now I stare, then I sigh,
Inconsolable...

Music. Ivanovka, 10 September 1906. Op. 26, no. 14. B Minor. 12/8, 9/8, Allegro (♩= 104) with slower sections. For Middle Voice: b^1–g^2. First published with Opus 26 by A. Gutheil in Moscow in 1907. Dedicated to **Maria and Arkady Kérzin**.

Recordings. Kurenko, Levko, Oja, Popescu, Söderström, Suchkova.

61 *Проходит всё*
All things pass away

Op. 26, No. 15

Working at Ivanovka in August and September 1906, Rachmaninoff wrote the fifteen songs of Opus 26 in a little more than a month. He arranged them in nearly chronological order, but placed this song at the end, even though it is dated a few days before nos. 10 and 14. The text by Daniil Ratgauz is a philosophical lyric about the transience of life, illustrated with brief examples in lines 2 to 7, but suddenly personalized—"I can sing no happy songs!"—in its final line. This melancholy declaration is very much in character for Ratgauz, who does not offer it as a plea for pity but rather as a fact of his artistic credo. The epigraph to his first book is a quote from Edgar Allan Poe: "Melancholy is the most legitimate of all the poetical tones" (*TCS*, 269-70). For Rachmaninoff, melancholy was never an artistic credo nor a defining trait of his personality, but, as we saw in the case of "Lilacs" (Song 38) and have seen elsewhere in these songs, he did believe that "sadness" (*grust'*) was the "mother of music."

As philosophical poetry, Ratgauz's lyric offers no very striking images for reflection; the song, however, is not facile, but has a confident power. It has been a favorite of singers. It builds in lapidary phrases to the final line, with its top note on the third syllable and its final sustained E flat marked *ad libitum*. Its tonality of E-flat minor, "the key of seclusion and aristocratic retreat from the common elements of harmony" (*Slonimsky 1989*, 144), comes across with a kind of unchallengeable force. With this statement, Rachmaninoff brought Opus 26 to a conclusion.

From the letters Rachmaninoff wrote to Maria Kerzin before and after the songs were premiered in February 1907 (*LN 1*, letters 312, 318, 323, 328), it is clear the composer had definite ideas about who should perform them. He may have had particular singers in mind when he wrote the songs. The singers he named were all artists of the first rank. For nos. 1, 2, 3, 6, 7, 13, and 15 he had in mind the lyric baritone George Baklanov (1881–1938), but since Baklanov did not take part in the Kerzins' concerts, he agreed on another good baritone, Ivan Gryzunov (1879–1919). He asked the great lyric tenor Leonid Sobinov (1872–1934) to sing nos. 5, 8, 11, and 12, warning him that they were difficult. Sobinov prepared them, but a conflict prevented him from taking part in the premiere; Rachmaninoff offered to drop them from the program, but they were sung instead by a lesser artist, Alexander Bogdanovich (1874–1950). For soprano, he recommended Nadezhda Salina (1864–1956), an outstanding concert singer, but the Kerzins offered Anna Kiselevskaya. She sang only "We shall rest" (which was a failure, as he had warned), "At my window" (the only song in the set really written for a soprano), and the soprano part in "Two partings." As he had feared, "The Ring," sung by a lesser mezzo-soprano, was "awful," but he managed to laugh about it. Since Goldenweiser was the pianist, at least the piano part was given its due. Reviews and letters all diplomatically conveyed the message that the songs were a flop and the audience was cruelly disappointed.

When Rachmaninoff started writing Opus 26, and was still finishing the long fourth song, "Two partings," he referred to them in a letter to Morozov as "trifles" necessary to finance his move to Dresden (*LN 1*, 398). After they were all written, however, he had a different opinion of them, and did not agree with the critics or those in the audience who found them disappointing (ibid., 425). The songs show genuine inspiration and ready invention. They break new ground in their style of declamation, or at least carry it much further, giving it new variety; they show what melodic and dramatic power the declamatory style can possess, and still retain his own personal signature. The piano is integrated with even greater mastery than before, giving laconic support to the voice but also elaborating the song as a lyrical whole. In 1916, when the composer and Nina Koshetz gave a recital to introduce the new Opus 38 songs, the first half of the program included three of the Opus 26 songs, "At my window," "To the children," and "Many are the sounds," an overlooked masterpiece rarely performed today (RGALI, programs from the V. A. Kiselev collection, F. 2985, op. 1, ed. khr. 638).

To the extent that the success of a song, at least for singers and the public, can be measured by the number of times it is performed on a recording, seven of the Opus 26 songs are among the top twenty most frequently recorded songs by Rachmaninoff. They are, in ascending order, "Again I am alone," "All was taken from me," "When yesterday we met," "At my window," "Christ is risen," "Night is mournful," and the present song.

Проходит всё, и нет к нему возврата.
Жизнь мчится вдаль мгновения быстрей.
Где звуки слов, звучавших нам когда-то?
Где свет зари нас озарявших дней?

Расцвёл цветок, а завтра он увянет,
Горит огонь, чтоб вскоре отгореть...
Идёт волна, над ней другая встанет...
Я не могу весёлых песен петь!

Prakhódit vsjó i nét k nemú vazvráta.	All things depart never to return.
Zhýzn' mchítsa vdál' mgnavénija bystréj.	Life speeds away faster than an instant.
Gde zvúki slóf, zvucháfshykh nám kagdáta?	Where are the sounds of words we once heard?
Gde svét zarí nas azarjáfshykh dnéj?	Where is the light of dawn that lit our days?

Rastsvjól tsvetók, a záftra ón uvjánet,	The flower blooms, tomorrow it will fade,
Garít agón', shtop fskóre adgarét'...	The flame burns bright but soon burns out...
Idjót valná, nad néj drugája fstánet...	As one wave rises up another overtakes it...
Ja ne magú vesjólykh pésen pét'!	I can sing no happy songs!

Text. **Daniíl Maksímovich Ratgáuz**, by 1902. Title: Проходит всё, и нет к нему возврата (All things pass away never to return). First published in Ratgauz's book *Песни любви и печали* (Songs of love and sadness), St. Petersburg, 1902, page 27. Set first by Rachmaninoff; later by Viktor Sadovnikov (1914).

Meter. Binary. Iambic pentameter:

The flower blooms, tomorrow it will fade,
The flame burned bright, but now is burning out...

Music. Ivanovka, 8 September 1906. Op. 26, no. 15. E Flat Minor. 4/4, Adagio (♩ = 52). For Bass Voice: e^1 flat–f^2. First published with Opus 26 by A. Gutheil in Moscow in 1907. Dedicated to **Maria and Arkady Kérzin**.

Recordings. Atlantov, Burchuladze, Cehanovsky, Chaiter, Christoff, Gmyria, Guliayev, Hvorostovsky, Kharitonov, Koptchak, Koshetz, Kozlovsky, Laptev, Larin, Leiferkus, Lisitsian, Magomayev, Milcheva, Murzayev, Nortsov, Ognivtsev, Oja, Orda, Piavko, Podleś, Pogossov, Rautio, Reizen, Rosing, Rozum, Serkebayev, Shevelev, Siniavskaya, Söderström, Storozhev, Suchkova, Tourel, Woytowicz (in Polish).

62 *Письмо К. С. Станиславскому от С. Рахманинова* *Letter to K. S. Stanislavsky from S. Rachmaninoff*

The professional friendship between Rachmaninoff and Konstantin Stanislavsky, who was ten years his senior, goes back to 1897, when the composer got his first conducting job in Savva Mamontov's private opera company. They got to know each other better in Yalta in the spring of 1900, seeing Chekhov every day, and by the time they met in Bayreuth for Wagner's *Ring* in 1902 they were friends. Rachmaninoff attended the premiere of *The Cherry Orchard* on 17 January 1904, in honor of Chekhov's name day. He was a "devoted worshipper" of the Moscow Art Theater, in the words of Sergei Bertensson, and felt for Stanislavsky "extraordinary admiration—I may even say tenderness" (*B/L*, 229). Bertensson observed this at first hand when Stanislavsky was in New York with the theater in 1922-23; Rachmaninoff saw every play in their repertory several times, visited the performers backstage, and entertained them in his "hospitable home on Riverside Drive" (ibid.)

His acquaintance with Stanislavsky coincides with the beginning of his close friendship with Chaliapin. On 14 October 1908, the Moscow Art Theater celebrated its tenth anniversary at a grand evening party with readings, speeches, and a cantata sung in chorus by opera stars. That evening, after a day of rehearsals at the Bolshoi for *Boris Godunov*, Chaliapin arrived at the Art Theater and announced that he had a letter from his friend Rachmaninoff in Dresden which he intended to *sing* to the assembled company. With Arseny Koreshchenko sat the piano, Chaliapin performed the song, whereupon Stanislavsky and Nemirovich-Danchenko embraced him and asked him to sing it again, which he did. All this made the Moscow papers the next day (*LN 1*, 623-4; see also October 1908 entries in *Kotliarov*).

The text of Rachmaninoff's letter is very plain, but musically it is both sophisticated and convincing in its sincerity. There are witty touches, as when the composer mentions the stunning recent success of "The Blue Bird" in line 4 of the text (Stanislavsky had created and mounted the world premiere of Maeterlinck's play the preceding month). Rachmaninoff quotes, in the piano accompaniment of the twelfth bar, a polka that Ilya Sats had written for the play, and combines it with the solemn church motif of "many years," an absurd combination that amused Stanislavsky (*LN 1*, 624). The pacing of the song is well calculated to convey the warmth of feeling behind the words. It begins "rather slowly" (Довольно медленно), speeds up and slows down again, until, by the end, it moves "rather quickly" (Довольно скоро) and "majestically" (Величественно). The directions to the singer are to sing "warmly" (Тепло) and "with great feeling" (С большим чувством), then, on the phrase "Blue Bird," "very softly" (Очень мягко); the repeated ecclesiastical chant "многая лета" (many years) is to be sung with animation (Оживлённо) and "brightly" (Бодро). After this enthusiastic paean, the flat signature and date, with postscript, are comical in a deadpan way. The letter was post-dated in Dresden to coincide with the event in Moscow, where Chaliapin would sing it.

Sergei Leiferkus sang this "singing telegram" (Thomas Hodge) at Salzburg in 2003 (*Nordlinger*). Leiferkus, an exceptionally skilled actor-singer of Russian songs, has made a fine recording of it.

> Дорогой Константин Сергеевич,
> я поздравляю Вас от чистой души, от всего сердца!
> За эти десять лет Вы шли всё вперёд, вперёд и вперёд,
> и на этом пути Вы нашли "Синюю птицу!"
> Она Ваша лучшая победа!
> Теперь я очень сожалею, что я не в Москве,
> что я не могу, вместе со всеми, Вас чествовать,
> Вам хлопать, кричать Вам на все лады:
> "Браво, браво, браво!"
> И желать Вам многая лета, многая лета, многая, многая лета!
> Прошу Вас передать всей труппе мой привет, мой душевный
> привет.
> Ваш Сергей Рахманинов.
> Дрезден.
> Четырнадцатое октября тысяча девятьсот восьмого года.
> Post scriptum. Жена моя мне вторит.

Daragój Kanstantín Sergéjevich!
ja pazdravljáju Vás at chístaj dushý,
at fsevó sérttsa!
Za éti désjat' lét Vý shlí fsjó
fperjót, fperjót i fperjót,
i na étam putí Vý nashlí "Sínjuju ptítsu!"
Aná Vásha lútshaja pabéda!
Tepér' já óchen' sazhaléju, shto já ne
v Maskvé,
shto já ne magú, vméste sa fsémi,
Vás chéstvavat',
Vám khlópat', krichát' Vám
na fsé ladý:
"Bráva, bráva, bráva!"
I zhelát' Vám mnógaja léta, mnógaja
léta, mnógaja, mnógaja léta!

Dear Konstantin Sergeevich,
I congratulate you in all sincerity,
with all my heart!
For these ten years you have moved ever
forward, forward, and forward,
and on the way you found "The Blue Bird"!
It is your greatest triumph!
Today I'm very sorry that I'm not
in Moscow,
that I can't join with all the others
to honor you,
to applaud you, to shout to you
in all registers:
"Bravo, bravo, bravo!"
And to wish you many more years,
many years, many, many years!

Prashu Vás peredát' fséj trúppe
 mój privét, mój dushévnyj privét.
Vásh Sergéj Rakhmáninaf.
Drézden.
Chetýrnattsataje aktjabrjá týsacha
 devjatsót vas'móva góda.
Postskríptum. Zhená majá mné ftórit.

Please convey to the whole company
 my greetings, my heartfelt greetings.
Yours, Sergei Rachmaninoff.
Dresden.
On the fourteenth of October in the year
 one thousand nine hundred eight.
Postscript. My wife seconds me in this.

TEXT. **Sergéi Vasílyevich Rachmáninoff**, October 1908.

MUSIC. Dresden, October 1908. E-flat Major. 12/8, with 4/4 and 6/8 parts. For Bass Voice: B flat–e^1. Without opus number.

According to *Rakhmaninov 1955*, 353, Rachmaninoff's Moscow publisher Karl Gutheil published the song in a separate edition after the jubilee performance; in *PSS* it is among "romances published during Rachmaninoff's lifetime" (*Rakhmaninov 1957*, 326). This is presumably the four-page edition of the score for voice and piano, printed in Moscow by V. Grosse, without a date, listed in the catalogue of the Russian State Library in Moscow. The publication would have been soon after the jubilee and certainly prior to 1914. Gutheil did not have his own printing house, contracting out his work to the musical typography firm of V. Grosse, who also had a music store in Moscow. The edition now used by singers was published in *PSS* in 1957. The score from that edition is reproduced in *B/L*, 148-52.

A manuscript in Rachmaninoff's hand is in the archives of the Moscow Art Theater; a reproduction of it is in *Rakhmaninov 1955*, between pages 352-3.

RECORDINGS. Del Grande, Demianov, Guliayev, Leiferkus, Söderström, Suchkova, Yakovenko.

Fourteen Romances, Opus 34 (1912–1915)

1.

In October 1906 Rachmaninoff moved with Natalia and their daughter Irina to Dresden, where they lived for the next three years, visiting Russia rarely except in the summers, which he always spent at his Ivanovka estate. Dresden was more costly than Moscow, but they found a sunny townhouse where he could work undisturbed. He attended a production of Richard Strauss's *Salome* and was dazzled by the orchestration, though he had mixed feelings about that opera, and *Elektra* (*Cannata 2000*, 34). Every year he traveled to German cities to attend concerts. He wanted to hear programs and master classes of Arthur Nikisch, a conductor he admired: in Leipzig he heard Brahms's First and Tchaikovsky's Sixth Symphonies, "a program of genius" (*LN 1*, 423), and in Berlin he heard Nikisch conducting an "amazing" performance of Brahms's Second Symphony—"what a beautiful symphony it is!" That evening he heard Pablo Casals for the first time, with the talented young Portuguese cellist Guilhermina Suggia (who appeared as Mme. P. Casals-Suggia, though they were not married); he found their playing "remarkable and well worth hearing" (*LN 1*, 462).

Rachmaninoff was taking a long leave from other activities to devote himself to composition. Opera had been high on his list of priorities, but Rachmaninoff paid for his good luck with *Aleko* with bad luck thereafter. *Francesca da Rimini* (1904-5) ended up as fragments because of Modest Tchaikovsky's weak libretto. As soon as the composer reached Dresden, he sought to enlist his friend Mikhail Slonov as librettist for an opera based on Maeterlinck's *Monna Vanna*, but copyright problems prevented them from going past draft scores. Ideas for *Salammbô* came to nothing. After *Aleko*, only his one-act opera *The Miserly Knight* (1903-5) was a realized success.

The Dresden years were nevertheless very productive. In his time there and his summers at Ivanovka, Rachmaninoff wrote his Second Symphony (op. 27, 1906–7), his First Piano Sonata (op. 28, 1907), a symphonic poem *The Isle of the Dead*, (op. 29, 1909), his Third Piano Concerto (1909), Thirteen Preludes for Piano, (op. 32, 1911), and the first of his two sets of Études Tableaux for piano, op. 33 (1911).

As soon as Rachmaninoff reached Dresden in October he began his Second Symphony, in E minor. He finished it there in the spring of 1907, orchestrated it in the summer and fall, and conducted the premieres in St. Petersburg and Moscow himself at the beginning of 1908 (*T/N*, 90). The symphony is known for its sweeping melodies and powerful, elaborate orchestration, in which the

Dies irae theme appears briefly in clarinets and violas and then prominently as the opening theme of the Scherzo. "The great romantic song of the slow movement [Adagio] is also derived, albeit at one remove, from *Dies irae,* ... a natural continuation of the clarinet melody and also later a counterpoint to it,... which ends with the same harmonies as at the conclusion of 'The Heart's Secret' [Song 47, 'Many are the sounds'], suggesting that this movement is indeed about the intimate secrets of the soul" (*Martyn*, 184-5). Running some sixty minutes, the symphony was thought for many years to require cuts in performance, but the composer had serious reservations about any cuts when they were proposed: "it is like cutting a piece out of my heart." Rachmaninoff's Second, adds Barrie Martyn, "like Schubert's 'Great' C major Symphony, is a very expansive work and one that cannot satisfactorily be pruned without ruining the architecture" (ibid., 186). Nowadays the symphony is performed without cuts. Whether or not the listener is aware of the "architecture" in detail, enjoyment of the Second Symphony is widespread among audiences in England and North America. In a poll of over 140,000 classical music listeners taken by the BBC in 2005, it was twelfth in the top twenty favorites, in a list including Beethoven's Ninth, Beethoven's Fifth Piano Concerto, Barber's Adagio for Strings, Bizet's Pearl Fishers' Duet, Mozart's Clarinet Concerto in A, the Pachelbel Canon, and "Finlandia" by Sibelius. Remarkably, at the top of the list was Rachmaninoff's Second Piano Concerto, and in twentieth place his Rhapsody on a Theme of Paganini, reinforcing Rachmaninoff's unquestionable popularity as a mainstream composer today (*Pettifor*).

In May 1907 Rachmaninoff interrupted his composing with a trip to Paris to take part in Diaghilev's first "Paris Season" of Russian music. In the concert devoted to Rachmaninoff's works, the composer conducted Chaliapin in the "Spring" cantata and played the Second Piano Concerto. He saw his cousin Félia Litvinne, a great favorite with Paris audiences, who sang in one of Rimsky-Korsakov's operas. Rimsky received ovations and was the toast of the city. When Rachmaninoff returned with his family to Ivanovka, in June, Natalia gave birth to their second daughter Tatiana.

2.

After Serge Koussevitzky married Natalia Konstantinovna Ushkova, daughter of a millionaire tea merchant, in September 1905, he quit his job as lead bass player at the Bolshoi Theater, but continued to give solo concerts in Russia and Europe. During Rachmaninoff's Dresden years, the Koussevitzkys lived in lavish style in Berlin, where Serge dreamed of becoming a director of musical performances on a grand scale. Ultimately, he wanted new repertoire for his concerts, a priority he carried over to Paris and Boston for the rest of his life. In 1909 in Berlin he established the "Russkoe Muzykal'noe Izdatel'stvo" (RMI, Russian Music Publishers) at a cost of one million marks. He signed up, among other composers, Scriabin, who was nearly destitute after the death of his publisher Mitrofan Belaiev in 1904. Rachmaninoff stayed with his publisher Gutheil, but he was on the editorial board of RMI with Scriabin, Medtner, and Koussevitzky (*Iuzefovich*, 101-3, 131-3). When the war started in 1914, Koussevitzky bought Gutheil, becoming Rachmaninoff's publisher as well.

To realize his ambition of being an entrepreneur of musical concerts, Koussevitzky understood that he would have to learn to conduct. Like Rachmaninoff and others, he looked to Arthur Nikisch as a model, attending his concerts and master classes. Rachmaninoff also coached him. His debut as a conductor took place in January 1908 in the Beethoven Hall in Berlin, with the Berlin Philharmonic. In addition to Tchaikovsky's "Romeo and Juliet" and instrumental music to Taneyev's trilogy "Oresteia," he conducted Rachmaninoff in his Second Piano Concerto. In the audience were Nikisch, Ferruccio Busoni, Reinhold Glière, and Joseph and Rosina Lhévinne. The audience showed enthusiasm, but the German reviews were mixed. Recalling that debut later, Glière wrote: "Koussevitzky led the orchestra insecurely, and the only thing that saved it was the high professionalism of the musicians in the orchestra. Rachmaninoff, seated at the piano, assisted the conductor with nodding of his head, leading the orchestra with his extraordinarily energetic, rhythmically exact playing" (ibid., 116).

The following year, Koussevitzky returned to Russia and established his own orchestra. He led concert seasons in Moscow and St. Petersburg, and, during the summers, took his orchestra back to his roots, to towns along the Volga, in a specially equipped steamboat. As the 1914 war and the two Revolutions of 1917 curtailed these activities, he held on until 1920, when he returned to Berlin, then Rome, then Paris, where he led the "Concerts Koussevitzky" and continued his publishing activities. When he came to Boston to lead the Boston Symphony in 1924, he pursued his goal of performing new repertoire, including many new American works commissioned by him.

3.

Contemporaries of Rachmaninoff who dropped in on him when he happened to be practicing remarked on the unusual way he would slow down a particular phrase and repeat it innumerable times until it was "right." Whenever he was performing, he made sure to allot generous practice time before a performance. During the composer's years in Dresden, he performed only his own works in concerts in Europe and Russia, because he could not afford to spend time practicing while trying to compose. He conducted the Moscow premiere of his new symphony in February 1908, and followed that up with a recital of his own solo piano works at the Great Hall of the Moscow Conservatory. In May, he played his Second Concerto in London with Koussevitzky. The *Times* critic praised the "deep feeling" of the slow movement and "brilliant finale" as played by the orchestra (Koussevitzky was clearly much more confident than he had been in his debut in January). About Rachmaninoff he wrote that "the extraordinary precision and exactitude of his playing, and even the strict economy of movement of arms and hands which M. Rachmaninov exercises, all contributed to the impression of completeness of performance." He added that "the freedom from extravagance of any kind was the most remarkable feature" (*B/L*, 146).

Concerts in London and other European cities gave him some income, but he still was not comfortable financially. On New Year's Day 1909 he confessed in a letter to Mikhail Slonov from Dresden: "In past years I used to borrow money, and I'm borrowing again now. In May I borrowed 3,500 R. from Koussevitzky… The truth is, so far in my life, with the possible exception of my two years at the Bolshoi Theater, I've never had any extra money. I regret it often, and very often think about my children and what they will do without me."

In the first three months of the New Year he composed his symphonic poem *Isle of the Dead*, op. 29, then in April left Dresden for good and returned to Ivanovka. He joked how he would miss life in his Dresden villa, but "by contract" with his wife not to live abroad more than three years, he had no choice. Then a solution to Rachmaninoff's immediate financial worries came when, after months of on and off negotiations, he got a contract to go to America in October 1909 to play and conduct his own works on a three-month tour.

Rachmaninoff had promised to write a new piano concerto for the American tour. Home at Ivanovka, he spent June through September writing the new concerto, his Third, in D minor, op. 30. The concerto was barely finished one week before leaving for New York in October. The manuscript travelled with him, together with a "dumb piano" for practicing the concerto on board ship; "I believe it is the only time that I have resorted to this mechanical toy, which, however, at the time proved very useful" (*Riesemann*, 158). Disembarking at the pier in New York, the first thing he wanted to know was when rehearsals would begin.

On 4 November 1909 Rachmaninoff gave his first American recital at Smith College in Northampton, Massachusetts, a solo concert where he played his own piano works. In three months, he gave some thirty concerts, as soloist and conductor; he conducted his Second Symphony, *Isle of the Dead*, and Mussorgsky's "Night on Bald Mountain," and performed his own Second Piano Concerto with various conductors in Boston, Hartford, Philadelphia, Baltimore, Cincinnati, Chicago, Pittsburgh, Buffalo, Toronto, and New York, sometimes giving more than one concert in the same city. He got on especially well with Max Fiedler, the German conductor of the Boston Symphony. Rachmaninoff's success in Boston induced the orchestra to offer him the position of successor to Fiedler, but the thought of being away from Moscow for long periods with or without his family struck him as "absurd" (ibid.). The world premiere performance of the Third Piano Concerto was held on 28 November with the New York Symphony Orchestra, conducted by Walter Damrosch. On 16 January 1910, in Carnegie Hall, he played the concerto with the New York Philharmonic with Gustav Mahler conducting. At that time Rachmaninoff considered Mahler second only to Nikisch as a conductor, but after witnessing Mahler's rehearsals, Mahler won first place in his esteem. "He touched my composer's heart straightaway by devoting himself to my Concerto until the accompaniment, which is rather complicated, had been practiced to the point of perfection, although he had already gone through another long rehearsal. According to Mahler, every detail of the score was important—an attitude which is unfortunately rare amongst conductors." After forty-five minutes, Mahler announced that they would repeat the first movement. "My heart froze within me. I expected a dreadful row, or at least a heated protest from the orchestra. This would certainly have happened in any other orchestra, but here I did not notice a single sign of displeasure. The musicians played the first movement with a keen or perhaps even closer application than the previous time" (ibid., 158-160).

If Rachmaninoff's Second has come to be thought of as the most popular of the twentieth-century piano concertos, his Third has acquired the reputation of being the most difficult to play, a kind of "ultimate" in Romantic piano concertos (*Martyn*, 216). With its two cadenzas "of unprecedented magnificence" (the longer one is an *ossia*, or alternative), it has a "more subtle structure" than the Second, and is one of the composer's "most completely integrated large-scale works" (ibid., 210-12). Even though it was dedicated to Josef Hofmann, Hofmann never played it, possibly owing to its difficulty for his smaller hands. Rachmaninoff played it for him in 1911. Hofmann thought it lacked form, and was more a *fantaisie* than a concerto. This "snap judgment" kept the work much less known internationally than it might have been, had Hofmann taken it up (ibid., 216). Then, when Vladimir Horowitz first came to New York in 1928, Horowitz immediately asked to meet Rachmaninoff, and he played the concerto in the Steinway showroom on West 57th Street, with the composer playing the orchestra part on an adjacent grand piano. From that day on, the composer felt that the Third Piano Concerto "belonged" to Horowitz and gladly told him so.

4.

With the money he earned on his American tour, Rachmaninoff was soon able to pay off his debts and, fulfilling an old dream, to buy his first car. In 1911, Mr. and Mrs. Satin turned the Ivanovka estate over to their three children. Natalia's share went to her and Rachmaninoff, and Sophia yielded her interest to her brother Vladimir, so that henceforth the two brothers-in-law managed the estate. Vladimir was in charge of the crops and Rachmaninoff in charge of the animals. The estate had been mortgaged three times and had large debts. Rachmaninoff's fees were by this time considerable, and he decided to try to save Ivanovka if he could. He invested all his extra income over the next years in keeping up the estate and buying new farm machinery (*LN* 2, 384-5). In the summers, he continued to compose at Ivanovka. There in 1910 he composed his first work for church choir, the Liturgy of St. John Chrysostom, op. 31, and finished writing his set of twenty-four preludes with the Thirteen Preludes, op. 32.

After returning from America in February 1910, Rachmaninoff kept a busy schedule of performances in major cities in Russia, England, Germany, Poland, and Finland. In 1911 he began (in London) a new European season of thirty-three performances as soloist and conductor, including, for the first time in several years, the performance of a work not his own—Tchaikovsky's First Piano Concerto (*Martyn*, 234-5). In February 1912 he conducted six performances of *The Queen of Spades* at the Mariinsky Theater in St. Petersburg. This turned out to be his last appearance on the podium as a conductor of opera.

While he was at the Mariinsky conducting Tchaikovsky's opera, he received a letter from a stranger, a woman, who signed herself simply as "Re" (the note D in the musical scale). She wrote that she was an avid supporter of his music, that she had friends who were also eager supporters of his music, and that she only hoped she would have a chance to talk to him during the *Queen of Spades* engagement. This letter apparently touched him, and he replied that he would be glad to talk to her after the engagement, but now was too busy even to think. The correspondence continued without their meeting, she writing many letters to each of his replies, sharing with him everything that was going on in her intellectual life. She copied into notebooks poems she liked and recommended to him as song lyrics. When he found some of her own "oriental" verses published under her own name, he understood who she actually was, but he continued to call her "Re." In December 1912 they finally met.

Her name was Marietta Shaginian (1888–1982). She was born in Moscow in a Russified Armenian family: her father was a doctor and her mother a musician. She was schooled in Moscow in an excellent girls' *gymnasium*. She was interested in music and was conscious from an early age that she was an "intellectual" interested in ideas and in literature. While still in school, she and her girl friends organized discussion topics like "The decline of musical thinking as a symptom of the death of culture."

The reference books describe Shaginian as a poet, novelist, playwright, journalist, and memoirist, which is true, but she was essentially an enthusiast. She was also an explainer. She began by telling Rachmaninoff that his music was *necessary* (the opposite of what Tolstoy had said), and that its progressive character was worth a thousand times more than the formal tricks of the modernists. She explained to him that he should not be so eager to write songs to doggerel like Galina's poems, and should not go after cheap stage effects (*LN* 2, 44). He defended himself on the first charge by saying he had only used two or three of her poems out of fifty-one songs, and denied the second. She explained that he was not as confident a composer as he should be, and with this he agreed. Rachmaninoff's correspondence with Marietta opened up a line of conversation with an intelligent, interesting younger woman, which he apparently needed and had missed from the days of writing to the Skalon sisters. He enjoyed her letters and they stayed in touch, mostly by mail, until he left Russia in 1917.

One month after "Re" first wrote him, Rachmaninoff asked her to send him some poems suitable for songs. He added that they ought to be more on the sad side than happy—"bright tones don't come to me very easily!" (ibid., 43). Among the poems she sent him in the spring of 1912, the composer chose thirteen excellent texts from classical nineteenth-century Russian poets beginning with Pushkin and Tyutchev and running up to Fet, Polonsky, Maikov, Khomiakov, and one early Symbolist poem by Konstantin Balmont. He wrote the songs at Ivanovka between 4 and 19 June 1912, and Gutheil published them in 1913. Two years later, he added "Vocalise" to the opus, making it fourteen songs. The first song, Pushkin's "Muse," he dedicated to "Re."

63 *Муза* *The muse*

Op. 34, No. 1

For the Greek and Roman poets, and their successors in the Western tradition, it is through the "muse," as everyone knows, that the poetic word is transmitted from its source of inspiration, divine and all-knowing, to the mortal poet, who renders it in the human language of an earthly time and place. Music and poetry come through her; she is descended from Mnemosyne, the goddess of memory. In their epics, Homer and Virgil and later, Dante and Milton, all address the Muse, invoking her for instruction and guidance in telling their stories truthfully. After Homer, Hesiod named nine muses, variously able to inspire in literature, the arts, philosophy, and mimic performance: these are the muses of heroic or epic poetry (Calliope), history (Clio), choral dancing and singing (Terpsichore), tragedy (Melpomene), comedy (Thalia), love and erotic poetry (Erato), sacred song, oratory, pantomime (Polyhymnia), astronomy (Urania), and flute-playing, or lyric poetry (Euterpe).

Alexander Pushkin (1799–1837) knew this tradition well and turned to it often in his lyric and narrative poetry, but, bringing to it the freedom of his creative imagination, he fashioned a portrait of his own Euterpe, personal to him. As a St. Petersburg poet, reared in settings where sculptures of the muses and other classical figures are everywhere at hand, Pushkin knew how to put to graceful use the neo-classical, more public faces of the muse, as in *Eugene Onegin* at the end of Chapter Seven, where Tatiana, during her debut season in Moscow, attends the theater: there we have sightings of Melpomene, with her "howl of lamentation," and Thalia, "quietly napping," and Terpsichore, "the only one still able to amaze." In contexts of his own identity as a lyric poet, however, Pushkin took the figure of the muse less conventionally, elaborating it and personalizing it, so that the portrait of *his* muse, limned in detail particular to his own creative life, is not to be confused with others. He gave her human, girlish qualities, describing her as a "loving" (ласковая) and "playful maid" (резвая дева); when he was young, she was the "girl-friend of my days, innocent, simple, somehow so dear, an enchantress with a mind of her own" ("О боги мирные," 1824). As he enters the wider world she is a companion to him, accompanying him on his southern exile, wearing Circassian battle dress and fascinated by rude village life (epilogue to *Prisoner of the Caucasus*), or with him at night by the Black Sea, "on Taurida's shores," listening to the sea roar. The last chapter of *Eugene Onegin* begins with a log of her journeys with him from his school days on, until at last she appears as a provincial maiden in his garden, with a French novel in her hands—the very heroine of his novel. In her open nature, receptive, independent, true to what she knows, Pushkin's muse and Tatiana are versions of a single ideal personality. Out of her origins as a mysterious Greek maiden, the Muse becomes a companion to Pushkin wherever his imagination takes him, an accomplice and confidante, as well as the source of poetic inspiration.

The hallmark of intimacy is already present in this lyric of 1821, written soon after Pushkin was exiled to the south. He portrays her at the time he was just a boy. She is his teacher, supervising his first solo flights on the lyric panpipes. She is not a stylized, passive classical figure but fully alive, a lovely maiden who tosses back her hair; they have a close and special relationship. Her visits are not at night, but during the day, from dawn to dusk, in the shade of oak trees. In these manifestations, after his weak fingers try to make music on the "seven-reeded pipe," she rewards his efforts by taking the flute into her own hands and playing on it a divine music that fills his heart with sacred "enchantment" (очарованье). The word is common in Zhukovsky and other Romantic poets of the Golden Age, but Pushkin used it sparingly; it has, in this context, a sacral power.

Rachmaninoff brought to this marvelous lyric the stylistic approach he had consciously developed in Opus 26. It is a style John Reed, in the context of Schubert's great song "Der Doppelgänger," has called "neither song nor recitative, but lyrical declamation" (*Reed*, 263). The music is *lento*, *dolce*, flute-like. Opening piano notes, delicate and gently stepping down, outline a descent to earth, with arpeggios and trills affirming an incarnate physical presence. The voice part is almost naive, very unadorned, mimicking the first unsure trials of fingers on the flute, in contrast with the sure mastery of the piano phrases given to the Muse. Confidence begins. In the middle of the song, after the word "shepherds," there are five bars of piano interlude, arresting movement, assessing progress; then movement resumes and confidence builds, *piu vivo*. Major chords in the piano reinforce the rising movement, as the Muse takes the flute from his hands and breathes into it her own divine music. The voice part soars to its top height in the penultimate line before it falls away. The song ends where it began, with the delicate piano figures and arpeggios of the beginning. Thus the song's graceful ascent and restrained, balanced finish describe an Apollonian arc.

In gratitude for her advice in choosing poems for Opus 34, Rachmaninoff dedicated the song to Marietta Shaginian. She showed it to Nicolai Medtner (1880–1951), a younger composer Rachmaninoff admired. The Medtner family was a center of Moscow intellectual life in the Symbolist period: Andrei Bely (1880–1934), the poet Rachmaninoff would set in Song 79, and his friend the poet Vladislav Khodasevich (1886–1939) frequented the Medtner circle, as did Shaginian herself. She recalled how Khodasevich once recited, unforgettably, this very poem of Pushkin's, conveying its Orphic power. Medtner decided

Rachmaninoff's song was a failure and that he could do it better: in Shaginian's words, "he understood it more deeply, showing its progression from quiet pastoral mode to triumphant dithyramb" (*Shaginian 1975*, 437-39). Her opinion was the first round in a debate about which composer did a better job setting Pushkin's poem (see *Martyn 1990*, 236, *Martyn 1995*, 103, *Harrison*, 181, and *Boyd*, 23). Medtner's approach is more literal: from a decorous and graceful beginning the music swells to frenzied rapture. Some pianists who admire the way Medtner's songs are fastidiously worked out have praised it, but the emphatic piano writing in his Dionysian hymn becomes by the end too strenuous. Sergey Prokofiev liked Medtner's sonatas, but felt that "his songs are not good because ... he lacks a sense of the individual words in the text" (*Prokofiev 2008*, 168). There are recordings by Joan Rodgers and Elisabeth Schwarzkopf (in English, with the composer at the piano), but no Russians have recorded it.

Rachmaninoff's Apollonian approach works much better, although it is difficult to perform well: the singer must convey the declamatory phrases with expression and warmth, and the pianist must lead gently but firmly, not allowing the song to stall. There are good recordings by Konstantin Lisovsky, Joan Rodgers, Nicolai Gedda, and others. The performance by Elisabeth Söderström and Vladimir Ashkenazy, with their ravishing ensemble work, dispels any doubts that this is one of Rachmaninoff's finest songs.

В младенчестве моём она меня любила
И семиствольную цевницу мне вручила;
Она внимала мне с улыбкой и слегка
По звонким скважинам пустого тростника
Уже наигрывал я слабыми перстами
И гимны важные, внушённые богами,
И песни мирные фригийских пастухов.
С утра до вечера в немой тени дубов
Прилежно я внимал урокам девы тайной,
И, радуя меня наградою случайной,
Откинув локоны от милого чела,
Сама из рук моих свирель она брала.
Тростник был оживлён божественным дыханьем
И сердце наполнял святым очарованьем.

V Mladénchestve majóm aná menjá ljubíla	She favored me from my early childhood,
I semistvól'nuju tsevnítsu mne vruchíla;	Handing me the seven-reeded panpipes;
Aná vnimála mne s ulýpkaj i slekhká	She listened with a smile, as haltingly
Pa zvónkim skvázhynam pustóva trastniká	Along resonant openings in the hollow reeds
Uzhé naígryval ja slábymi perstámi	I improvised with unskilled fingers
I gímny vázhnyje, vnushónnymi bagámi,	Solemn hymns, inspired by the gods,
I pésni mírnyje frigíjskikh pastukhóf.	And peaceful songs of Phrygian shepherds.

S utrá da véchera v nemój teni dubóf	From dawn to dusk in the silent shade of oaks
Prilézhna já vnimál urókam dévy tájnaj,	I heeded eagerly the lessons of the mysterious maiden,
I, ráduja menjá nagrádaju slucháјnaj,	And, gladdening me with an occasional reward,
Atkínuf lókany at mílava chelá,	Tossing her locks back from her dear brow,
Samá iz rúk majíkh svirél' aná bralá.	She would take the flute from my hands into her own.
Trastník byl azhyvljón bazhéstvennym dykhán'jem	Then the reeds would come alive with her divine breath
I sérttse napalnjál svjatým acharaván'jem.	And fill my heart with sacred enchantment.

Text. **Aleksándr Sergéyevich Púshkin**. Written in Kishinev, 5 April 1821. Title: "Муза" (The Muse). First published in *Сын отечества* (Son of the Fatherland) in 1821, no. 23; in Pushkin's first collection of lyrics (1826), it is included in a group of poems entitled "Подражания древним" (Imitations of the Ancients).

The last word in line 8, дубов ("of oak trees"), is incorrectly printed as дубров ("of oak groves") in *Gutheil 1922* and subsequent reprints based on it. The misprint is slight but singers should be aware of it.

The poem was first set (as a "cantata for voice and piano") by Pushkin's contemporary A. N. Verstovsky (*Vinokur*, 184). Composers who have set it for voice and piano include Glazunov (Op. 59/1, 1898), Medtner (Op. 29/1, 1914), Vladimir Deshevov (1938), and the renowned pianist Tatiana Nikolayeva.

Meter. Binary. The poem has been described as a sonnet (*Kahn 2008*, 52), but sonnets in Russian are written in iambic pentameter and arranged in quatrains and tercets (*Unbegaun*, 83). Pushkin wrote this poem in six-foot rhyming couplets with a caesura in the middle of the line, the Russian equivalent of the French Alexandrine perfected by Racine and the 17th-century dramatists:

She first appeared to me when I was still a youth,
And placed into my hands the seven-reeded flute.

Music. Dated 6 June 1912, Ivanovka. Op. 34, no. 1. E Minor. 4/4, with modifications, Lento. For High Voice: e^1–a^2. First published by A. Gutheil in Moscow in 1913.

Dedicated to **Mariétta Sergéyevna Shaginián** (1888–1982).

Recordings. Del Grande, Dionne, Dolukhanova, Gedda, Kurenko, Lee, Lisovsky, Mattila, Michaels Bedi, Naoumenko, Rodgers, Savenko, Söderström, Suchkova, Tear.

Medtner: Peter Del Grande, Joan Rodgers, Elisabeth Schwarzkopf (in English).

Glazunov: Mikhail Lukonin.

Transcriptions. *Piano:* John McArthur, Earl Wild.

64 *В душе у каждого из нас* *In the soul of each of us*

Op. 34, No. 2

For Opus 34 Rachmaninoff chose works by Pushkin, Tyutchev, Polonsky, Khomiakov, Maikov, Fet, and Konstantin Balmont—"foremost representatives of Russian Romanticism" (*Norris 2001*, 143). The one exception to this is the author of the present text, Apollon Korinfsky (1868–1937), who was never a major figure like the others and is largely forgotten today. To learn more about him, we have to turn to the good chroniclers of Russian literature.

His name, literally "Apollo Corinthian," sounds like a *nom de plume*, but it was not. His Mordvinian-peasant grandfather, Mikhail Varentsov (1788–1851), walked, like Lomonosov, to St. Petersburg, to study architecture, won a gold medal for his diploma project "in the Corinthian style," and changed his surname to "Korinfsky." He went on to design churches and university buildings in the Empire style in Kazan and other Volga towns. A second curious fact of Korinfsky's biography is that he was born in Simbirsk, where he was a high-school classmate, though not a close friend, of another boy born in that Volga town, whose name was Vladimir Ulyanov. The Korinfsky family had a good library, which young Ulyanov is thought to have used when the two boys were in school together. Ulyanov later turned out to be the man known by his Bolshevik party nickname of Lenin. Korinfsky apparently did not realize that his classmate and Lenin were one and the same person until Lenin started making public speeches in 1917 (*Bialyi*, 414-16; see also *RP 3*, 70-71).

He worked all his life writing reviews and essays for the intellectual journals. He made his debut as a poet in 1894, issuing volumes of verse every year or two with titles like *Songs of the Heart*, *Black Roses*, *Gleams of a Dream*, and *Hymn to Beauty* (where Marietta Shaginian found the present lyric). Reviewing *Black Roses* in 1896, Akim Volynsky called him "a mediocre versifier, not unaware of the market for decadence among contemporary readers" (*RP 3*, 71). Composers found his poems attractive as a ready source of sentimental song lyrics for popular romances. Glazunov set three of them in 1899 and 1908, and two other notable composers wrote songs using Korinfsky's words: Nikolai Sokolov (1859–1922), a teacher of Shostakovich, and Aleksei Taskin (born 1871), a music-hall pianist who was Chaliapin's favorite rehearsal partner. Taskin was accompanist to the famous Anastasia Vialtseva, and he discovered the great popular singer of the Soviet period Izabella Yurieva (1899–2000), whose performances of Russian folk songs and popular romances are considered classics today and can be heard on Russian radio and TV, and on YouTube.

Shaginian apparently took Korinfsky seriously as a poet, and Rachmaninoff evidently liked the poem enough to write music for it. Perhaps he was drawn to the "spring of sadness" found within every soul. The poem is not specific enough to be "decadent": the "fire of passions" lacks poetic detail or even any hint of something experienced or actual. The images and epithets are a series of generalities, most of them clichés—"sacred moment," "blessed hour," "fleeting attraction," and "unending oblivion." The basic idea of the poem, that love equals sadness, is a common cliché in Russian romances.

The lack of any true poetry in this text notwithstanding, the music Rachmaninoff created for the song is genuine and powerful. The piano part is a chordal accompaniment with striking harmonies and harmonic progressions (*Norris 2001*, 145); it is spare but eloquent, without prelude or postlude. Accompanied by these laconic chords, the song is a somber recitative for low voice that seems a precursor (as music, not text) of Shostakovich's cycle of poems by Michelangelo. There are fine recordings by Sergei Leiferkus and Sergej Koptchak.

В душе у каждого из нас
Журчит родник своей печали.
Из ближних стран, из дальной дали
Её приливы пробегали
В заветный миг, в блаженный час
В душе у каждого из нас.

Огнём страстей опалена,
Душа не верит упоенью,
Ни мимолётному влеченью,
Ни бесконечному забвенью
Не покоряется она,
Огнём страстей опалена...

Моя любовь — печаль моя,
В ней солнца свет, в ней мрак неволи,
В ней жизнь, в ней крик предсмертный боли,
В ней глубина паденья воли,
В ней путь к вершинам бытия;
Моя печаль — любовь моя!..

V dushé u kázhdava iz nás	In the soul of each of us
Zhurchít radník svajéj pecháli.	Flows a spring of our own sadness.
Iz blízhnikh strán, iz dál'noj dáli	From lands near or far away,
Jejó prilívy prabegáli	Its tides have rushed by
V zavétnyj mík, v blazhénnyj chás	In a sacred moment, in a blessed hour,
V dushé u kázhdava iz nás.	In the soul of each of us.

Agnjóm strastéj apalená,	Scorched by the fire of passions,
Dushá ne vérit upajén'ju,	The soul does not believe the rapture,
Ni mimaljótnamu vlechén'ju,	Not to fleeting attraction
Ni beskanéchnamu zabvén'ju	Nor to unending oblivion
Ne pakarjájetsa aná,	Does it submit,
Agnjóm strastéj apalená…	Scorched by the fire of passions…
Majá ljubóf' — pechál' majá,	My love and my sadness are one,
V nej sóntssa svét,	The sun's light is in it,
v nej mrák nevóli,	the darkness of bondage,
V nej zhýzn', v nej krík	The shout of pain
pretsmértnyj bóli,	before death,
V nej glubiná padén'ja vóli,	Within it is the depth of the fall of the will,
V nej pút' k vershýnam bytijá;	And the path to the pinnacle of being;
Majá pechál' — ljubóf' majá!..	My sadness and my love are one!..

Text. **Apollón Apollónovich Korínfsky**, between 1896 and 1898. Untitled. First published in *Гимн красоте и другие новые стихотворения* (Hymn to beauty and other new poems), St. Petersburg, 1899, page 95. Set only by Rachmaninoff.

Meter. Binary. Iambic tetrameter:

My sadness and my love are one,
The dark within, the light of sun…

Music. Dated 5 June 1912, Ivanovka. Op. 34, no. 2. C Major. 4/4, with modifications, Non allegro. For Low Voice: c–e^1. First published by A. Gutheil in Moscow in 1913.

Dedicated to **Feódor Ivánovich Shalyápin (Chaliapin)** (1873–1938). One of five songs Rachmaninoff dedicated to his lifelong friend; the others are Songs 34, 68, 71, and 73. Of the songs dedicated to Chaliapin, the only one he is known to have sung is Song 34, "Fate"; he also sang Song 62, the letter to Stanislavsky, which he introduced, and Songs 47 ("Many are the sounds"), 52 ("Christ is risen"), and 59 ("When yesterday we met"). For Chaliapin's concert repertoire, see *Shaliapin 1960*, vol. 2, 498-508.

Recordings. Del Grande, Koptchak, Leiferkus, Söderström, Suchkova, Sutey, Zakharov.

Transcriptions. *Bass trombone:* John Rojak.

65 *Буря* *The storm*

Op. 34, No. 3

This short Pushkin lyric of 1825, with its image of a maiden in white high on a cliff viewing a violent storm at sea, is not well known, although many composers have noticed it. *The Singer's Rachmaninoff*, remarking that Rachmaninoff wrote his song in the same key of E minor as "The Muse," notes that the song "progresses in powerful chromatic passages in the piano accompaniment to create the image of wind and waves surging at the feet of the Muse" (*Challis*, 169).

There is something puzzling and intriguing about Pushkin's text. A maiden (дева, a poetic word for девушка, a young woman) stands on a cliff by the sea during a spectacular storm: is she a memory, or an imagined figure? Pushkin lived by the Black Sea coast from 1823 to 1824, before returning to Russia (where he wrote the poem). After the lyrics of his southern period, with their frequent classical associations, the Georgics ("Primety"), the free rendition of the idyll "Earth and Sea" by Moschus of Syracuse, the sea-nymph ("Nereida"), and the "Muse" of Song 63, one wonders if this maiden seen on a cliff is a woman he loved, or perhaps the Muse herself; yet she is not personalized or otherwise identified as muse, but just a figure dressed in white, her shawl blowing in the wind. Is the poem an unfinished fragment? Evidently not, since Pushkin gave it a title and published it; he did not, however, include it among the "Imitations of the Ancients" when he compiled his first book of lyrics in 1826.

The description of the storm, dramatically lit, is also unusual: Pushkin never describes a storm simply for its own sake, but puts it to apt narrative or lyric use. For Pushkin, the image of a storm (буря) is associated with alarm, trouble, the intrusion of a destructive force into a peaceful life (a private life). The storm in *The Bronze Horseman* is the most famous example. In two of his best-known lyrics, "Winter Evening" (Зимний вечер, 1825) and "Premonition" (Предчувствие, 1828), the only consolation the poet can find to counter the threat of these very different storms is the company of a *woman close to his heart*: in the first poem it is his old nanny, the "good friend of my poor youth," and in the second it is his "angel," his beloved. In the lyric of the present song, the storm is described in its awesome beauty, "the sea in stormy darkness, the azureless sky exploding in flashes," with the maiden as centerpiece, lit up and buffeted by the elements; then, suddenly, the poet brings the poem to an abrupt and unexpected end: "but trust me: the girl on the cliff is more fair than waves, sky, and tempest." The turn here away from the storm and back to the girl is a consolation aimed at warming the heart.

When Pushkin wrote this lyric, he was also writing *Eugene Onegin* (which he had begun in the South). In these years an argument was going on in Pushkin's mind about beauty, framed in terms of the *ideal* versus the *actual* (*Lotman*, 622-23). "The Storm" reads like a diary entry in that internal dialogue, a kind of lyric postcard. The contrast is between a Romantic ideal of beauty (the storm) and beauty as it actually exists (the girl on the cliff). He discussed the rejection of Romanticized ideals of beauty in the Appendix to *Eugene Onegin*, in stanzas written between 1825 and 1830 ("Onegin's Journey"): "I thought then I couldn't live without desert wastelands, cresting waves of pearl, the roar of the sea, massive cliffs, and the ideal of a 'proud maid'; those feelings are gone now; Muse! forget the past." The message on the postcard is that the girl in white, like Tatiana, may be vulnerable, her shawl blown in the wind, but she is fairer by far than the romantic backdrop. The subject is beauty and inspiration, but in the light of a chastened and sober understanding to which Pushkin calls on his Muse to bear witness. The Muse, then, although not explicitly present in "The Storm," is implicitly present in the choice the poet makes in the last two lines, an aesthetic choice as well as a choice of the herat.

Rachmaninoff understood the raw power of the forces at work in this lyric, and gave eloquent expression to them. He brings out the violence of the storm with a powerful staccato piano part, written with subtle coloration to suggest the crash and ebb of the waves, the splash of water, the strikes of lightning. The clarion notes of the voice part declaim the first eight lines in rapid Allegro, and then everything slows down delicately to Andante, on the phrase "without azure." There, after a piano interlude which brings a pause, a lovely lull, to the storm, the last two lines of the voice part fall serenely, yielding to recognize true beauty, with the final word "storm" held for two long measures, on a four-note, slowly falling phrase. The song ends with a complex piano postlude, *pianissimo* reflection, then, accelerating and growing louder, a return to Allegro, to the storm, to the staccato crash of waves against the cliff.

This tour de force is difficult to perform and remains a rarity among Rachmaninoff's songs. There is only one Soviet recording of it, a strong performance by the tenor Konstantin Lisovsky. Other good recordings are by Nicolai Gedda (with Alexis Weissenberg) and Elisabeth Söderström (with Vladimir Ashkenazy). Like Song 60, "The Ring," another ambitious song which has been overlooked, it awaits discovery by a new generation of artists.

Ты видел деву на скале,
В одежде белой, над волнами,
Когда, бушуя в бурной мгле,
Играло море с берегами.
Когда луч молний озарял
Её всечасно блеском алым,

И ветер бился и летал
С её летучим покрывалом!
Прекрасно море в бурной мгле,
И небо в блёстках, без лазури.
Но верь мне: дева на скале
Прекрасней волн, небес и бури.

Ty vídel dévu na skalé,
V adézhde bélaj, nad valnámi,
Kagdá, bushúja v búrnaj mglé,
Igrála móre z beregámi.
Kagdá lúch mólnij azarjál
Jejó fsechásna bléskam álym,
I véter bílsa i letál
C jejó letúchim pakryválam!
Prekrásna móre v búrnaj mglé,
I néba v bljóstkakh, bez lazúri.
No vér' mne: déva na skalé
Prekrásnej vóln, nebés i búri.

Did you ever see a maiden high on a cliff
Dressed in white, above the waves,
When the sea, surging in stormy darkness,
Played with the beaches, pounding them.
While lightning kept illuminating
Her in flashes of scarlet light,
And the whipping wind flew,
Blowing her shawl like wings!
Fair is the sea in stormy darkness,
And the sky in explosive flashes, without azure.
But believe me: the maiden on the cliff
Is fairer far than waves, sky, and tempest.

Text. **Aleksándr Sergéyevich Púshkin**, 1825. Title: Буря (Storm, or Tempest). First published in *Московский вестник* (Moscow Herald) in 1827, no. 2. First set by N. S. Titov in 1830, later by Pauline Viardot (1865), Anton Rubinstein (Op. 78/4, 1868), and several Soviet composers including Vera Gerchik, Igor Belorusets, Ashir Kuliev, and Mark Karminsky (see *Vinokur*).

Rachmaninoff changed Pushkin's rare archaic form "в блесках" in line 10 (meaning "in flashes") to the modern form "в блёстках." I have retained Rachmaninoff's punctuation, but Pushkin's original text shows a comma after line 4, and a question mark at the end of line 8.

Meter. Binary. Iambic tetrameter:

You've seen a maiden on a cliff,
All dressed in white, above the waves…

Music. 7 June 1912, Ivanovka. Op. 34, no. 3. E Minor. 4/4, 3/4, Allegro (lines 1-10); Andante (last two lines). For High Voice: c^1–a^2. First published by A. Gutheil in Moscow in 1913.

Dedicated to **Leoníd Vitáliyevich Sóbinov** (1872–1934), Russian lyric tenor and major star at the Bolshoi in the first quarter of the 20th century. Rachmaninoff dedicated five songs to him, all in Opus 34: Songs 65, 66, 67, 72, 74. Although Sobinov did not record any of Rachmaninoff's songs, "Night is sad" (Song 58) is said to be the last song he sang in public (*L'vov*, 76). He is in *Record of Singing*, vol. 1.

Recordings. Del Grande, Gedda, Lisovsky, Naoumenko, Söderström, Suchkova.

66 *Ветер перелётный* *The migrant wind*

Op. 34, No. 4

In the cosmic contest between world-extinguishing night and life-renewing day acted out in this short lyric, day emerges victorious. Even if the outcome is a bit too easy and obvious, it works. What makes it winning is the way it is told, its naive directness and the exuberance and playfulness of the language—it could almost be a little fable for audiences of all ages. The vehicle is the wayward wind caught in flight, a poetic image that inspired Rachmaninoff's delicate, restrained piano accompaniment; the wind (ветер) was a favorite image of the author, the Symbolist poet Konstantin Balmont (1867–1942), who earlier provided the excellent translation from Shelley for Song 23. A third text by Balmont (Song 83) will conclude, brilliantly, Rachmaninoff's last set of songs, Opus 38.

Balmont was a poet with an all-embracing vision, who found in the world-defining ideas of Symbolism—the four elements, the dualisms of night and day, time and eternity, and so on—a framework for his own poetic gifts. The map of his imagination was centered on Russia but went well beyond it. He travelled the world (he even lectured at Oxford), and translated expertly from many languages (he published two volumes of poems and stories by Poe, where Rachmaninoff found his text for "The Bells," Op. 35, 1913). Later critics who prized exactitude in "word and sense" (*Mirsky 1979*, 192) criticized him for being diffuse, verbose, "drunk on words" (*Aikhenval'd*, 373); Ilya Ehrenburg, who, like nearly everyone, had been under Balmont's spell (*Èrenburg 1*, 122-27), later wrote of him: "he sailed all the seas and travelled all the roads, but noticed nothing in the world except his own soul" (quoted in *Orlov*, 10). Yet for ten years between *Under a Northern Sky* (1894) and *Let's Be Like the Sun* (1903) the reading public could not get enough of him, nor, it seems, could Russian composers: by 1917, Balmont had more texts set to music (280) than any other Russian poet, including Pushkin. (Pushkin was a close second, however, and after 1917 he overtook Balmont, in part because of his popularity among Soviet composers, but also because the Soviet literary establishment dropped Balmont almost immediately after the Revolution.)

This lyric comes from Balmont's second "Symbolist" collection called "In Boundlessness" (*В безбрежности*, 1895). He placed it in the first section of the book entitled "Beyond Limits" (За пределы), and as an epigraph to that section he cited Goethe's "Spirit of the Earth": "Unceasing motion is my realm; death and birth the fabric of existence." The lyric works with three of the four elements (air, water, fire) and the dualism of night and day. The rest is word-play, sound instrumentation (*звукопись*), alliterations, labials and liquids, the contrast of "hushings" and velars, and the triumph of the rhyming vowel "o" in the second half of the poem, where the sun, the "fiery eye," appears, to defeat night.

Balmont wrote the poem in trochaic lines of six feet, with a caesura in the middle of the line, an unusual meter. Taking some liberties, my translation replicates this odd meter (but not the rhymes) in order to convey the sense of headlong forward movement in this line. In Rachmaninoff's song, he marks the line endings clearly, as well as the full stop at the caesura in line seven, after "Night reigned supreme in the world." The clear lyrical shape of the song is one of the reasons it works so well in performance. Of the sixteen recordings, there are many very good ones: Joan Rodgers, in crystalline voice, sings it slowly; Nicolai Gedda gives a dramatic reading of it; and Georgi Vinogradov sings it with tender lyricism.

Ветер перелётный обласкал меня
И шепнул печально: "Ночь сильнее дня."
И закат померкнул.Тучи почернели.
Дрогнули, смутились пасмурные ели,

И над тёмным морем, где крутился вал,
Ветер перелётный зыбью пробежал.
Ночь царила в мире. А меж тем далёко
За морем зажглося огненное око.

Новый распустился в небесах цветок,
Светом возрождённым заблистал восток.
Ветер изменился и пахнул мне в очи,
И шепнул с усмешкой: "День сильнее ночи!"

Véter pereljótnyj ablaskál menjá	Rippling gusts of migrant wind caressed my face,
I shepnúl pechál'na: "Nóch sil'néje dnjá."	Voices said in whispers: "Night defeats the day."
I zakát pamérknul. Túchi pachernéli.	Then the sunset darkened. Rain clouds turned to black,
Drógnuli, smutílis' pásmurnyje jéli,	Somber firs grew troubled, trembled in dismay.
I nad tjómnym mórem, gde krutílsa vál,	O'er the darkling sea, across a looming wave,
Véter pereljótnyj zýb'ju pra-bezhál.	Rippling wind slipped past and raced along the swell.
Nóch tsaríla v móre. A mesh tém daljóka	Night now reigned supreme in the colossal world. Meanwhile,
Zá marem zazhglósja ógnennaje óka.	Far across the sea a fiery eye ignited.

Nóvyj raspustílsa v nebesákh tsvetók,	Radiantly in heaven a flower opened wide,
Svétam vazrazhdjónnym zablistál vastók.	Light was resurrected in the glowing east.
Véter izmenílsa i pakhnúl mne v óchi,	Then the shifting wind blew straight into my eyes,
I shepnúl s usméshkaj: "Dén' sil'néje nóchi!"	Whispering with a grin: "The day defeats the night!"

Text. **Konstantín Dmítriyevich Balmónt**, Winter, 1895. Untitled. First published in *В безбрежности* (In boundlessness), 1895, page 70. Republished in a second edition in 1896; the only difference is that the word "east" (восток), capitalized in 1895, is not capitalized in the 1896 edition. Rachmaninoff's text may have come from this second edition where the word is not capitalized.

Set only by Rachmaninoff.

Meter. Binary. Trochaic hexameter, with a caesura (word boundary) in the middle of the line. The lines below show the metrical pattern:

Rippling gusts of migrant || *wind caressed my face,*
Voices said in whispers: || *"Night defeats the day."*
Then the sunset darkened. || *Rain clouds turned to black,*
Somber firs grew troubled, || *trembled in dismay.*

Music. 9 June 1912, Ivanovka. Op. 34, no. 4. A Minor — C Major. 3/4, Andante. For High Voice: c[1]–a[2]. First published by A. Gutheil in Moscow in 1913. Dedicated to **Leoníd Vitáliyevich Sóbinov** (see Song 65).

Recordings. Arkhipova, DeGaetani, Del Grande, Dodoka, Gedda, Gerzmava, Izotova, Kurenko, Lee, Lemeshev, Levko, Pusar, Rodgers, Söderström, Suchkova, Vinogradov.

Transcriptions. *Clarinet:* Wagner Campos.

67 *Арион* *Arion*

Op. 34, No. 5

This text is the third of three lyrics by Pushkin that Marietta Shaginian cleverly, and to brilliant outcome, chose for Opus 34, each different, but having in common the theme of art, inspiration, and the ways in which the poet is engaged in acts of creation. "Arion" illustrates the difference between the poet (the singer) and the ordinary man. Historically, Arion was a Greek poet of the 7th century B.C. Legend has it that he escaped a crew of sailors intending to rob him by singing a song that was so inspired it charmed both the sailors and the dolphins swimming around the ship; Arion leapt overboard, and rode safely to shore on the back of one of the dolphins.

Pushkin uses the legend here for his own purposes, changing the story. He omits the dolphin, telling a simpler account of a storm at sea in which a ship and all its crew perish, while he alone, taken on the voyage to sing to the oarsmen as they row, is cast ashore as sole survivor. The poem has been read in Russia as an allegory about Pushkin as the only member of the Decembrist circle to escape punishment after the failure of the revolt of December 1825. The Decembrists were men of Pushkin's class, many of them friends; he shared their political goals—the abolition of serfdom and establishment of a liberal democracy—but he did not take part in their attempted coup. Of course, the harsh punishment of the Decembrists wounded Pushkin deeply, as it did other Russians, but even if such a parallel was in Pushkin's mind when he wrote this lyric, it stands on its own independently of that.

Pushkin reimagines the Arion legend as a story about the survival of the poet, who is one of the many on board ("we were many" is the opening phrase). He is set apart from them in his "mystical" or "mysterious" (таинственный) gift; as such, he alone survives the storm, as do his "hymns," which exist in a reality separate from the fate of ordinary men and their labors. The theme is the immortality of art, which outlives time and tragic circumstance by the divine power invested in its creation. There is a direct line here from the poet first taught by the Muse when still a boy, to Arion, a mature singer (певец), who miraculously survives, and whose songs also will survive.

The song is a superb musical realization of the lyric. Its eight pages contain some of the strongest piano writing in all Rachmaninoff's songs and call for an extraordinary pianist: it is a joy to hear this song with piano performances by Leif Ove Andsnes (Kharitonov), Vladimir Ashkenazy (Söderström), and Alexis Weissenberg (Gedda). Both piano and voice parts bring out well the drama in the compact lyric. There are seven or eight sections in all, from the opening piano bars which establish the motion over deep ocean waters, still calm, *molto marcato il basso*, to the heroic opening voice phrase culminating in a high A on the word "depths" in line 4, with instructions to the pianist to "follow the voice yieldingly" (*colla parte*) on the phrase "powerful oars"; then the song slows down for a dreamy nine bars that convey the peaceful motion of the boat before returning to Allegro in line 7, and a *forte* "I sang to the sailors." Seven bars of piano interlude follow that recall the virtuoso demands of Rachmaninoff's own piano concertos. The storm section leads rapidly to the slowing down in the last three lines, to be sung *comodo*, at an easy pace. The voice part concludes in a slow reverie on the final two syllables that run for six bars *ad libitum*: these two notes can be sung with an alternative ending that goes up to D in the second octave, instead of down to D in the first octave (Söderström and Naoumenko sing this *ossia* option, which is very beautiful). The song has "vast energy, being one of Rachmaninoff's finest inspirations as a songwriter" (*Harrison*, 182). Again, Medtner wrote his own "Arion," and again it seems he tried too hard: his song, which ends in a "piano rampage," is "severely taxing" to both pianist and vocalist (*Martyn 1995*, 131). The only performance I have heard is by the tenor Ivan Kozlovsky.

Нас было много на челне;
Иные парус напрягали,
Другие дружно упирали
В глубь мощны вёслы. В тишине
На руль склонясь, наш кормщик умный
В молчаньи правил грузный чёлн;
А я, — беспечной веры полн, —
Пловцам я пел… Вдруг лоно волн
Измял с налёту вихорь шумный…
Погиб и кормщик, и пловец!
Лишь я, таинственный певец,
На берег выброшен грозою,
Я гимны прежние пою,
И ризу влажную мою
Сушу на солнце под скалою.

Nás býla mnóga na chelné;	There were many of us in the boat;
Inýje párus naprjagáli,	Some kept the sail taut,
Drugíje drúzhna upiráli	Others in unison dipped
V glúp' móshchny vjósla. F tishyné	Powerful oars into the deep. In the silence,
Na rúl' sklanjás', nash kórmshchik úmnyj	Leaning on the tiller, our skilled helmsman
V malchán'je právil grúznyj chóln;	Silently steered the laden vessel;
A já — bespéchnaj véry póln, —	And I, — full of carefree trust, —
Plaftsám já pél… Vdrúk lóna vóln	Sang to the oarsmen… Suddenly the cradle of the waves

Izmjál s naljótu víkhar' shúmnyj…	Was sundered by a roaring whirlwind…
Pagíp i kórmshchik i plavéts!	The helmsman perished, and all the crew!
Lish já, taínstvennyj pevéts,	I alone, the mysterious singer,
Na bérek výbrashen grazóju,	Cast ashore by the storm,
Já gímny prézhnije pajú	I sing my former hymns,
I rízu vlázhnuju majú	And dry out my damp garment
Sushú na sónttse pat skalóju.	In the sun under a cliff.

Text. **Aleksándr Sergéyevich Púshkin**, 16 July 1827. Title: Арион (Arion). First published in *Литературная газета* (Literary Gazette) in 1830, no. 43, page 52, unsigned.

There is a small discrepancy in line 4 between Pushkin's archaic form for the plural word "oars" (веслы, pronounced vjésly), and the modern form вёсла (pronounced vjósla), used by Rachmaninoff in his song. *PSR* prints Pushkin's form, but Gutheil prints the modern form the composer preferred. In recordings, only Söderström sings Pushkin's form *vjésly*; all the others sing Rachmaninoff's *vjósla*, except Suchkova, who follows *PSR* but gives it a modernized pronunciation *vjósly*. Medtner kept Pushkin's form, but in his recording of Medtner's song Kozlovsky also modernized the vowel to *vjósly*.

First set by Rachmaninoff; later by Nicolai Medtner (Op. 36/6, 1919) and several Soviet composers, including Vano Muradeli and Vissarion Shebalin.

Meter. Binary. Iambic tetrameter:

I sing the hymns I sang before,
And on a rock beneath a cliff
I dry my garment in the sun.

Music. 8 June 1912, Ivanovka. Op. 34, no. 5. D Minor. 4/4, Allegro. For High Voice: d^1–b^2 flat. First published by A. Gutheil in Moscow in 1913.

Dedicated to **Leoníd Vitáliyevich Sóbinov** (see Song 65).

Recordings. Del Grande, Gedda, Kharitonov, Kilchevsky, Kurenko, Larin, Naoumenko, Savenko, Söderström, Suchkova.

Medtner: Ivan Kozlovsky.

Transciptions. *Cello:* Brian Stucki.

68 *Воскрешение Лазаря*
The raising of Lazarus

Op. 34, No. 6

Aleksei Khomiakov (1804–1860) was an important Russian Orthodox theologian who wrote poems and historical verse dramas in the somewhat old-fashioned but powerful and authoritative style of Pushkin's rhetorical poetry. Two of his poems set by Tchaikovsky, one about the splendor of the night sky and the other about courage, eloquently reveal his style; Tchaikovsky thought them to be among the best songs of his later years (see *TCS*, Songs 74 and 84). D. S. Mirsky considered Khomiakov's intensely felt 1858 poem "The Laborer" ("Труженик") to be "the summit of Khomiakov's verse and of Russian religious poetry in general" (*Mirsky 1979*, 180).

Like Song 53 ("To the Children"), the other song Rachmaninoff wrote to a poem by Khomiakov, this poem was also occasioned by a death, in this case that of the poet's wife, who died in January 1852, after which he was grief-stricken for many months. Even though his wife's death and subsequent despondency are not mentioned in the poem, Khomiakov was unable to write until he finally wrote this poem of regeneration in October of that year. In manuscript, he called it "Verses for Lazarus Saturday," the day before Palm Sunday, a holiday observed in a spirit of joy in the Russian and other Orthodox churches of the Byzantine rite.

Rachmaninoff's song has a restrained, minimal solemnity, in keeping with Khomiakov's lyric. The voice part, with its occasional chromatic hints of losing direction, then finding it, expresses real travail in a convincing way, and its spare chords and short coda to be played *molto marcato* convey release and final triumph. Geoffrey Norris points out that the song is "notable for its effective harmonic progressions, particularly at the sublime resolution of bar 13," with the words of resurrection in line 6 (*Norris*, 146). Max Harrison rightly finds in the harmony and in the song's "masterly postlude" a reminder of Mussorgskian "revelation" (*Harrison*, 182). Barrie Martyn reads the coda as a "peremptory sequence of harsh chords" that "sums up the composer's astringent new tone of voice" (*Martyn*, 238). There are powerful recordings by Alexander Welitsch, Sergei Leiferkus, Elisabeth Söderström, and others.

О, Царь и Бог мой! Слово силы
Во время оно Ты сказал,
И сокрушён был плен могилы,
И Лазарь ожил и восстал.

Молю, да слово силы грянет,
Да скажешь "Встань!" душе моей,
И мёртвая из гроба встанет,
И выйдет в свет Твоих лучей!
И оживёт, и величавый
Её хвалы раздастся глас
Тебе — сиянью Отчей славы,
Тебе — умершему за нас!

O Tsár' i Bókh moj! Slóva síly	Oh Tsar and God of mine! A mighty word
Va vrémja óna Tý skazál,	You spoke in ages past,
I sakrushón býl plén magíly,	And shattered was the grave's prison,
I Lázar' ózhyl y vasstál.	And Lazarus rose from the dead.
Maljú, da slóva síly grjánet,	I pray, may your mighty word ring out,
Da skázhesh "fstán'!"dushé majéj,	May you say "Arise!" to my soul,
I mjórtvaja iz gróba fstánet	May my soul rise up from the grave,
I výjdet f svét	And come forth into the light
Tvajíkh luchéj!	of your radiance!
I azhyvjót, i velichávyj	And returned to life again, its voice
Jejó khvalý razdástsa glás	Will resound in solemn praise
Tebé — sijánju	Of you — the shining light
Ótchej slávy,	of the Father's glory,
Tebé — umérshemu za nás!	Of you — who gave his life for us!

Text. **Alekséi Stepánovich Khomiakóv**, October 1852. Title: Воскресение Лазаря (The resurrection of Lazarus). Rachmaninoff's spelling, which differs in one letter, is a literary and Church Slavonic form of the word for "resurrection," a form not used in conversation. First published in Khomiakov's *Poems* of 1861. Set only by Rachmaninoff.

Meter. Binary. Iambic tetrameter:

Oh God, my King! When long ago
You summoned Lazarus from the grave…

Music. 4 June 1912, Ivanovka. Op. 34, no. 6. F Minor. 4/4, Grave. For Low Voice: c^1–f^2. First published by A. Gutheil in Moscow in 1913.

Dedicated to **Feódor Shalyápin (Chaliapin)** (see Song 64).

Recordings. Del Grande, Leiferkus, Murzayev, Nesterenko, Söderström, Suchkova, Sutey, Welitsch.

Transcriptions. *Bass trombone:* John Rojak.

69 *Не может быть!* *It cannot be!*

Op. 34, No. 7

Rachmaninoff wrote this song soon after the unexpected death of the celebrated actress Vera Komissarzhevskaya, who died suddenly of smallpox in 1910 at the age of forty-five. Many of her most famous roles were in contemporary plays: Nora in Ibsen's *Doll's House*, Nina in Chekhov's *Seagull*, and Sonya in his *Uncle Vanya*, and other roles in plays by Maeterlinck, Ibsen, and Chekhov. In 1896 during rehearsals of *The Seagull*, Chekhov wrote a friend that she was "marvelous," adding that at one of the rehearsals "many people wept as they watched her, and they said she is the best actress in all Russia today" (*Chekhov 1973*, 284). Chekhov's sense of her greatness was justified in the years that followed, although he did not live to witness her most innovative and creative years. On the eve of his death in 1904, Komissarzhevskaya resigned from the Imperial theaters and founded her own theater in St. Petersburg, bringing in the young director Vsevolod Meyerhold and attracting the excited attention of the Symbolists, including the poet Alexander Blok. After her death, Blok eulogized her as the "Promised Spring" of the modern Russian theater (*Blok 1960-63*, vol. 5, 417–20).

Rachmaninoff knew Komissarzhevskaya personally, as we saw earlier ("We shall rest," Song 49, Op. 26/3). Like everyone, he admired the musicality and incomparable freshness of her voice. In the wave of tributes to her after her death, Rachmaninoff wrote this song to words by Apollon Maikov (originally written on the death of Maikov's young daughter), adapting the lyric freely to his own purposes. He did not publish it separately, but saved it for the new opus of songs that would come two years later, when he dedicated it to her memory.

In its freshness and sincerity of feeling, the song is a small masterpiece. It accomplishes exactly what it sets out to do, beginning with an agitated, full-voiced, spontaneous outburst (Allegro), then slowing down gradually to the conclusion (Lento), where the final six words are sung softly, *piano* and sweetly, *dolce*—reluctant falling phrases, like falling tears. The piano support is eloquent, from agitated shock to tender lyricism to final reflection.

There are fine recordings by Sergej Larin, Elisabeth Söderström, and others, but perhaps the most moving performance is the one by Ivan Zhadan (Jadan), the sweet-voiced Russian tenor of the old school, who performed it when he was already past fifty and living in the United States.

Не может быть! Не может быть!
Она жива!.. сейчас проснётся…
Смотрите: хочет говорить,
Откроет очи, улыбнётся;
Меня увидевши, поймёт,
Что неутешный плач мой значит,
И вдруг с улыбкою шепнёт:
"Ведь я жива! О чём он плачет!.."

Но нет! Лежит… тиха, нема,
Недвижна…

Ne mózhet být'! Ne mózhet být'!	It cannot be! It cannot be!
Aná zhyvá!.. sejchás prasnjótsa…	She is alive!.. in a moment she'll wake up…
Smatríte: khóchet gavarít',	Look: she wants to speak,
Atkrójet óchi, ulybnjótsa;	She'll open her eyes, she'll smile;
Menjá uvídevshy, pajmjót,	When she sees me, she'll understand,
Shtó neutéshnyj plách mój znáchit,	What my inconsolable lament means,
I vdrúk s ulýpkaju shepnjót:	And suddenly with a smile she'll whisper:
"Vit' já zhyvá! A chóm ón pláchet!.."	"But I'm alive! What's he weeping for!"
No nét! Lezhýt…tikhá, nemá,	But no! She lies there… quiet, silent,
Nedvízhna…	Not moving…

Text. **Apollón Nikoláyevich Máikov** (1821–1897), 23 April 1866. Title: Дочери (To my daughter), a cycle of three poems, this being the third. First published in the journal Заря (Dawn), 1869, no. 11, in a cycle entitled "Заметки и мгновения" (Notes and moments). Written in memory of the poet's daughter Vera, who died in 1866 at the age of 11. Rachmaninoff made several slight changes to the text.

Set before Rachmaninoff by three minor composers, including the St. Petersburg pedagogue and music critic Nicolai Soloviev (1904).

Meter. Binary. Iambic tetrameter:

It cannot be! It cannot be!
She is alive!.. she wants to speak…

Music. 7 March 1910, Moscow; revised 13 June 1912, Ivanovka. Op. 34, no. 7. E flat Minor. 4/4, Allegro; Lento. For Middle Voice: e^1 flat–a^2 flat. First published by A. Gutheil in Moscow in 1913.

Dedicated to the memory of **Véra Feódorovna Komissarzhévskaya** (1864–1910).

Recordings. Del Grande, Kozlovsky, Larin, L. Maslennikova, Ognivtsev, Popescu, Pusar, Söderström, Suchkova, Zhadan.

70 *Музыка* *Music*

Op. 34, No. 8

Here is Yakov Polonsky again, in a very different vein from his arresting dramatization of a moment of chance encounter, "When yesterday we met" (Song 59). "Music" is a metaphorical description of the effect music has on the poet's consciousness, a sense of being transported on a wave of sounds to a vision of otherworldly beauty. It has much in common with a lyric by his friend Afanasy Fet, "Carry my heart away," which Tchaikovsky had earlier set to music (see his Song 17, *TCS*, 52-54).

There is a sense of exploration about both Tchaikovsky's song and this one. Rachmaninoff finds tentative phrases that lead to an unusual melody, then a counter-melody, inverted in an odd way. We don't know where the song is going—as if we really are being borne up on a wave, carried away by "music." With line 5, *molto cantabile*, a sense of destination and resolution begins that touches the bottom of the range of the voice part at the end of line 8, then rises to the high point in the remainder of the song, to end on the crest of the wave. The harmonies and flexible time signatures give it a "disembodied feel" (*Martyn*, 238); the harmonies in the piano, especially in the brief postlude, are striking.The song shows that Rachmaninoff can conjure haunting beauty, even when reducing his means, particularly in the piano, to an absolute minimum.

Perhaps because of its originality, there have been very few recordings of the song. No one has conveyed its quiet power with such clean clarity as Galina Vishnevskaya, who recorded it in Germany in 1976, with the laconic, finely judged accompaniment of Mstislav Rostropovich. She sings lines 9 and 10 in reverse order, giving the final quatrain alternate rhymes instead of enclosing rhymes; but in terms of the meaning of the lyric, this makes no difference at all.

И плывут, и растут эти чудные звуки!
Захватила меня их волна…
Поднялась, подняла и неведомой муки
И блаженства полна...
И божественный лик, на мгновенье,
Неуловимой сверкнув красотой,
Всплыл, как живое виденье,
Над этой воздушной, кристальной волной, –
И отразился,
И покачнулся,
Не то улыбнулся…
Не то прослезился…

I plyvút, i rastút, éti chúdnyje zvúki!	They flow and they grow, these wonderful sounds!
Zakhvatíla menjá ikh valná…	I am carried on their wave…
Padnjalás', padnjalá i nevédamaj múki	As it swelled, it lifted me, filling me
I blazhénstva palná…	With strange torment and bliss…
I bazhéstvennyj lík, na mgnavénje,	And, for an instant, a divine face,
Neulavímaj sverknúf krasatój,	In a flash of elusive beauty,
Fsplýl, kak zhyvóje vidénje,	Floats like a living vision,
Nad étaj vazdúshnaj, kristál'naj valnój,–	Over this airy, crystal wave, –
I atrazílsa,	And is reflected,
I pakachnúlsa,	And sways,
Ne tó ulybnúlsa…	Almost with a smile…
Ne tó praslezílsa…	Almost with a tear…

Text. **Yákov Petróvich Polónsky**, between 1870 and January 1876. Title: "Музыка" (посв. П. И. Чайковскому) – "Music" (dedicated to P. I. Tchaikovsky). First published in *Озими*, Ч. I, Новый сборник стихов Я. П. Полонского (*Winter Wheat*, Part I, Newly Collected Poems of Ya. P. Polonsky), printed by V. S. Balashev in St. Petersburg in 1876, page 162. Set only by Rachmaninoff.

Meter. Ternary. Anapest, lines varying from four to two feet (first five lines); then dactyls and amphibrachs, four feet diminishing to two feet:

How they flow, how they grow, these magnificent sounds!
And I'm caught, lifted up, on a wave…
And a visage divine
Floats, like a vision that's living,
And is reflected,
And seems to sway,
Perhaps it is smiling…
Perhaps it is weeping…

Music. Ivanovka, 12 June 1912. Op. 34, no. 8. E-flat Minor. 6/8, 9/8, 12/8. Andante mosso. For Middle Voice: b^1 flat–g^2 flat. First published with Opus 34 by A. Gutheil in Moscow in 1913.

Dedicated to **P. Ch.** [Pyotr Tchaikovsky]. When Lamm's 1957 edition of the Complete Romances (*RPS*) was published in Moscow, the index of the names of persons to whom the songs were dedicated (compiled by Zarui Apetian) glossed the initials "P. Ch." with the words "no information." This shows that Rachmaninoff's Soviet editors (unlike Tchaikovsky's editors in 1940) made no attempt to find and verify the original sources of Rachmaninoff's lyrics. Had they looked at Polonsky, it would have been obvious whose the initials were.

Recordings. Del Grande, An. Ivanov, Kurenko, Popescu, Söderström, Suchkova, Vishnevskaya. (Zara Dolukhanova did not record this song, despite *Bennett*, 459; the only Soviet recording is by Andrei Ivanov.)

71 *Ты знал его* *You knew him*

Op. 34, No. 9

Rachmaninoff wrote this song for Feodor Chaliapin, and he must have imagined an ideal performance of it in Chaliapin's masterly declamatory style. So far as is known, however, Chaliapin did not sing it (*Shaliapin* 2, 506), and later singers have avoided it. In the Soviet period only the excellent Andrei Ivanov recorded it. It is a difficult song, but effective in a good performance.

The theme of the lyric by Feodor Tyutchev is the Romantic distinction between the poet and the ordinary man. Pushkin was drawn again and again to the theme, (one striking example is "Arion," Song 67), and it was revived with imaginative force in the twentieth century by Vladislav Khodasevich in his *Heavy Lyre* (1923). Tyutchev treats the theme with almost epigrammatic brevity, contrasting the pale moon in daytime (the poet as an ordinary man, observed in society, and "disdained" as such) with the moon at night, wherein the poet, a "god of light" who shines radiantly, is revealed. The lyric shows genuine feeling (perhaps the first stanza has some features of self-portraiture), and it has Tyutchev's appealing mixture of solemn and colloquial styles.

The shape of the song is faithful to the text, rising to a strongly felt rhetorical climax at the end of each stanza. The style is somber throughout. It begins with a piano introduction of heavy descending chords in "harsh and wayward harmonies" (*Martyn*, 239). The voice part finds no sure melodic or lyrical footing. The postlude is a release, slight and tender, which does find lyricism; it is an instance of the *pianissimo* culmination Rostropovich spoke of as a mark of Rachmaninoff's style. A performance that illustrates this well is the recording by the Macedonian baritone Alexander Welitsch, who really does sing the final syllable of the text *pianissimo*, as indicated in the score (this effect was one of Chaliapin's specialties). In addition to Ivanov's and Welitsch's solid performances, Sergei Leiferkus gives a convincing reading of the song, with fine piano accompaniment by Howard Shelley.

Ты знал его в кругу большого света,
То своенравно весел, то угрюм,
Рассеян, дик иль полон тайных дум,
Таков поэт — и ты презрел поэта!

На месяц взглянь: весь день, как облак тощий,
Он в небесах едва не изнемог;
Настала ночь, и светозарный бог,
Сияет он над усыплённой рощей!

Ty znál jevó f krugú bal'shóva svéta,	You knew him in the beau monde,
Tó svajonrávna vésel, tó ugrjúm,	Now blithe, now morose,
Rasséjan, dík il' pólon tájnykh dúm,	Distracted, rude, or full of secret thoughts,
Takóf poét — i tý prezrél poéta!	Such is the poet — and you disdained him!
Na mésjadz vzglján': vez' dén',	Regard the moon: by day,
kak óblak tóshchij,	a scraggy cloud,
On v nebesákh jedvá ne iznemók;	He's faint and barely visible overhead;
Nastála nóch, i svetozárnyj bókh,	But when the night comes, he's a god of light,
Sijájet ón nad usypljónnaj róshchej!	And shines so brightly above the sleeping grove!

Text. **Feódor Ivánovich Tyútchev**, 1829 or early 1830s. Untitled. First published in the periodical *Гражданин* (Citizen) in January 1875. The poem was printed there in two stanzas, and this is the form in which Rachmaninoff found it; modern editors, on the basis of the manuscript, print it as one stanza of eight lines (*Tiutchev 1987*, 382).

Rachmaninoff changed the archaic and somewhat quaint verb in the opening phrase of the poem from "Ты зрел его" (You saw him) to the modern and stylistically neutral "Ты знал его" (You knew him). In doing so, he loses the word play in "Ты зрел" ("you saw," line 1) and "Ты презрел" ("you despised," line 4). The composer then adopted "Ты знал его" as title to the song. In English, "The Poet" is sometimes used as the title. Set only by Rachmaninoff.

Meter. Binary. Iambic pentameter:

Regard the moon: by day, a scraggy cloud,
He's faint and barely visible overhead;
But when the night comes, he's a god of light,
And shines so brightly o'er the sleeping grove!

Music. Ivanovka, 10 June 1912. Op. 34, no. 9. D Major. 4/4, Grave, Marziale. For Middle Voice: c^1 sharp–f^2 sharp. First published with Opus 34 by A. Gutheil in Moscow in 1913.

Dedicated to **Feódor Ivánovich Shalyápin (Chaliapin)** (1873–1938). One of five songs Rachmaninoff dedicated to his friend; the others are Songs 34, 64, 68, and 73.

Recordings. Del Grande, An. Ivanov, Leiferkus, Söderström, Suchkova, Sutey, Welitsch.

72 *Сей день я помню* *I remember that day*

Op. 34, No. 10

This fifth and last song to a lyric by Feodor Tyutchev has been called a "perfect song" which "makes its points quickly, with absolute precision" (*Harrison*, 183). A delicate rise and fall of triplets in the brief piano introduction sets up the lovely melody of the first couplet and the variations that follow. The crescendo of lines 3-6 culminates in the sudden chromaticisms of line 8, as the song slows down to tender *pianissimo* for the conclusion; the last line is a beautiful variation on the original melodic phrase, with a high B-flat on the phrase "new *world*." Here the song ends, with no piano postlude at all.

At about a minute and a half in performance, it is one of Rachmaninoff's shortest songs: only Songs 25, 48, 54, 57, and 77 are as short or shorter. It was dedicated to the great tenor Leonid Sobinov. There is an outstanding recording of the song by Nicolai Gedda, with the pianist Alexis Weissenberg.

Сей день, я помню, для меня
Был утром жизненного дня.
Стояла молча предо мною,
Вздымалась грудь ея.
Алели щёки, как заря,
Всё жарче рдея и горя…
И вдруг, как солнце *золотое*,
Любви признанье *молодое*
Исторглось из груди ея,
И новый мир увидел я!

Séj dén', ja pómnju, dlja menjá,	That day, I remember, was for me
Býl útram zhýznennava dnjá.	The morning of a new life.
Stajála molcha preda mnóju	She stood silently before me,
Vzdymálaz' grút' jejá.	Her bosom heaving.
Aléli shchóki, kag zarjá,	Her cheeks were scarlet as the dawn,
Fsjó zhárche rdéja i garjá…	Glowing red and flaming hotter...
I vdrúk, kak sóntse zalatóje,	And suddenly, like a golden sun,
Ljubví priznánje maladóje	Ardent love's young confession
Istórglas' iz grudí jejá,	Burst out from her heart,
I nóvyj mír uvídel já!	And I saw a new world!

Text. **Fyódor Ivánovich Tyútchev**, 1830. Untitled. First published in the journal *Русский архив* (Russian Archive) in 1879.

Rachmaninoff cut the last word in line 4, "волною" (like a wave). He also reversed the epithets for "sun" and "confession" in lines 7 and 8: he has a *golden* sun and a *young* confession (italicized above in the Russian text of the lyric). In Tyutchev's original lyric it is the other way around: the sun is *young* and the confession *golden*. Rachmaninoff might have reversed these epithets himself; or, what is more likely, he simply used the lyric as printed on page 75 of P. V. Bykov's 1912 edition of Tyutchev's poems, which had just been published when he wrote the song. In that edition (but nowhere else) this erroneous reversal occurs.

The Soviet composer Yuri Shaporin (1887–1966) wrote a song to this same text that restores the missing word in line 4, and uses the epithets *golden* sun and *young* confession from Bykov's 1912 edition.

First set in 1896 and published privately by S. L. Tolstoy (1863–1947), one of Lev Tolstoy's sons. Later settings by Georgi Catoire (1916) and Yuri Shaporin.

Meter. Binary. Iambic tetrameter:

Her cheeks were scarlet as the dawn,
And glowing red and flaming hot…

Music. Ivanovka, 10 June 1912. Op. 34, no. 10. A-flat Major. 4/4, Andante semplice. For High Voice: a^1 flat–b^2 flat. First published with Opus 34 by A. Gutheil in Moscow in 1913.

Dedicated to **Leonід Vitáliyevich Sóbinov** (1872–1934). One of five songs, all in Opus 34, dedicated to the Russian tenor; the others are Songs 65, 66, 67, 74.

Recordings. Del Grande, Gedda, Kozlovsky, Kurenko, Naoumenko, Pusar, Söderström, Suchkova, Tear.

Shaporin: Zara Dolukhanova.

73 *Оброчник* *The true servant*

Op. 34, No. 11

This serious and deeply felt poem is Afanasy Fet's answer to accusations of the "civic irrelevance" of his poetry. In the 1860s, the radical critics began ridiculing Fet for writing lyrics that had no "utilitarian value" in a society that needed drastic reforms. This "howling of wild beasts," as he phrases it in this poem, effectively drove him out of literature until the Symbolists discovered him at the end of the century (see *TCS*, 52).

Fet wrote the poem as a declaration of allegiance to his art as poet, as keeper of the poetic word in service to the Russian tradition and the Russian community of the faithful. The title is a metaphor for this. Historically, the word *obrochnik* means a peasant who has promised to pay a set amount of rent to his master in labor and produce, and hence is free of the onerous *corvée* system, in which he owed all his labor to his master and had little or no freedom of choice. Fet applies it to himself in the meaning of a "free" servant sworn to keep his word; by his honest labor he produces goods of real *spiritual* worth. His service is the sacred art of song, as the text makes clear in the phrases "singing praise," "singing," and "a song on my lips." For this reason, "The herald," or "True servant" are better titles than "peasant" or "sharecropper," which call up misleading associations. The poem was an important statement for Fet. Within a few days of writing it, he sent it to two of his fellow poets who were among his closest correspondents, men deeply sympathetic to Fet's lyric gifts, Yakov Polonsky and "K. R.," the pseudonym of Grand Duke Konstantin Romanov (*Fet 1971*, 727).

Rachmaninoff chose this lyric because it had personal significance for him, too: it was an answer years later to Lev Tolstoy, who challenged the composer in 1900, when he and Chaliapin had performed "Fate" for him, by asking, "Is such music *needed* by anybody?" (*B/L*, 88). The song, marked "Molto marcato" and *pesante*, conveys well the determination and vigor of Rachmaninoff's belief in and fidelity to his artistic path. Critics have found fault with its relentless rhythm (*Martyn*, 239) and the "stirring" but "rather conventional" result (*Harrison*, 183). Fair enough; yet in a nuanced and shaded performance such as the one by Sergei Leiferkus and Howard Shelley it has a winning integrity and force.

Хоругвь священную подъяв своей десной,
Иду. И тронулась за мной толпа живая,
И потянулись все по просеке лесной,
И я блажен и горд, святыню воспевая.

Пою и помыслам неведом детский страх:
Пускай на пенье мне ответят воем звери, —
С святыней над челом и песнью на устах,
С трудом, но я дойду до вожделенной двери.

Kharúkv' svjashchénnuju padjáf
svajéj desnój,
Idú. I trónulaz' za mnój talpá
zhyvája,
I patjanúlis' fsé pa próseke
lesnój,
I já blazhén y górt svjatýnju
vaspevája.

Raising the sacred banner with my
right hand,
I go forth. And a multitude of people
follows me,
And we proceed through the forest
clearing,
And I am blessed and proud, praising
the sacred image in song.

Pajú i pómyslam nevédam détskij strákh:
Puskáj na pénje mné atvétjat
vójem zvéri, —
S svjatýnej nat chelóm
i pésnju na ustákh
S trudóm, no já dajdú
da vazhdelénnaj dvéri.

I sing and am impervious to childish fears:
Even if wild beasts shout my singing down
with their howling, —
With the sacred image above my head
and a song on my lips,
I will overcome every hardship and at last
attain the longed-for portal.

Text. **Afanásy Afanásievich Fet**, 1889. Title: Оброчник (Sworn to keep his word). First published in the journal *Русское обозрение* (Russian Review) in 1890. Set only by Rachmaninoff.

Meter. Binary. Iambic hexameter, with a caesura after the third foot:

I hold the banner high, I know no childish fears,
And I am blessed and proud, and sing a song of praise…

Music. Ivanovka, 11 June 1912. Op. 34, no. 11. C-sharp Minor. 4/4, Non allegro, Molto marcato. For Low Voice: c^1 sharp–e^2. First published with Opus 34 by A. Gutheil in Moscow in 1913.

Dedicated to **Feódor Ivánovich Shalyápin (Chaliapin)** (1873–1938). This is the last of five songs Rachmaninoff dedicated to his friend; the others are Songs 34, 64, 68, and 71. All of them (like the part of the Baron in *The Miserly Knight*, composed with Chaliapin in mind) are written in a dramatic, declamatory, often somber style—a "lyrical recitative" to which the singer brought his great gifts of dramatic expression. There is no evidence that Chaliapin ever sang this song, however: the songs listed in his concert repertoire are Songs 34, 47, 52, 59 and 62 (*Shaliapin 2*, 506). He also sang bass parts in Rachmaninoff's operas *Aleko*, *The Miserly Knight*, and *Francesca da Rimini*, as well as the baritone part in the cantata "Spring" (ibid., 508).

Recordings. Amaize, Bock (in German), Del Grande, Ghiuselev, Leiferkus, Nesterenko, Söderström, Suchkova, Sutey.

Transcriptions. *Bass trombone:* John Rojak.

74 *Какое счастье* *What happiness*

Op. 34, No. 12

If the previous song was a declaration of Afanasy Fet's faith in his art, this last of five songs to his lyrics (the others are Songs 2, 12, 24, 73) brings us back to Fet in glorious lyric flight. The poet and his beloved are alone, just the two of them, under a night sky of brilliant stars reflected in the broad mirror of a river; there is a great depth below them and a great height above. As they look up and take in the enormity of this view of heaven and earth, his excitement is transformed into an ecstatic awareness of his feeling of love for her. Once the magnificent setting is established, Fet conveys his mounting ecstasy not through elaborate metaphors but through colloquial imperatives and jabbing disclaimers: "Call me mad! Call me what you will! I can't keep silent, I'm not going to, I don't know how! All I mean is that I love you, you alone!"

Rachmaninoff's brilliant musical setting of Fet's lyric demands a great deal of both pianist and vocalist. The piano drives the headlong intensity of the ecstasy and finishes it with a long, thrilling postlude: Ashkenazy and Söderström present a perfectly balanced performance in this respect. The exalted mood at the beginning of line three is achieved by one of Rachmaninoff's perfectly judged pianissimos: Sergej Larin's performance captures this moment best. Söderström, Zhadan, and Larin sing the two optional *ossia* notes up an octave in line five on the phrase "call me *crazy*!" as sopranos and tenors usually do, but Karita Mattila sings them as written, low, almost growling, with a fierce intensity.

Какое счастье: и ночь, и мы одни!
Река — как зеркало и вся блестит звездами,
А там-то, голову закинь-ка да взгляни:
Какая глубина и чистота над нами!

О, называй меня безумным! Назови,
Чем хочешь: в этот миг я разумом слабею
И в сердце чувствую такой прилив любви,
Что не могу молчать, не стану, не умею!

Я болен, я влюблён, но, мучась и любя, —
О, слушай! о, пойми! — я страсти не скрываю,
И я хочу сказать, что я люблю тебя,
Тебя, одну тебя люблю я и желаю!

Kakóje shchástje: i nóch, i mý adní:	What happiness: it's night, and we're alone!
Reká — kag zérkala i fsjá blestíd zvezdámi,	The river is like a mirror, all glistening with stars,
A tám-ta, gólavu zakín'-ka da vzgljaní:	And there on high, lean your head back and look up:
Kakája glubiná i chistatá nad námi!	What profundity and purity is overhead!
O, nazyváj menjá bezúmnym! Nazaví,	Oh, call me crazy! Call me
Chem khóchesh: v état mík ja rázumam slabéju	What you will: at this moment reason fails me
I f sérttse chústvuju takój prilíf ljubví,	And in my heart I feel such a surge of love
Shto ne magú malchát', ne stánu, ne uméju!	I can't keep silent, I won't, I'm not able!
Já bólen, já vljubljón, no, múchas' i ljubjá —	I'm sick, I'm in love, but, tormented and loving —
Ó slúshaj! ó pajmí! — ja strásti ne skryváju,	Oh, listen! oh hear me! — I can't hide this passion,
I já khachú skazát', shto já ljubljú tebjá,	And I want to say I love you,
Tebjá, adnú tebjá ljubljú ja i zheláju!	It's you, it's you alone I love and desire!

Text. **Afanásy Afanásievich Fet**, 1853 or 1854. Untitled. First published in *Sovremennik*, (The Contemporary) in 1854.

Set earlier by Karl Davydov in 1874.

Meter. Binary. Iambic hexameter, with caesura after the third foot (in my translation below, the caesura is not observed in the second line). Fet uses "счастие" (luck) in the first line in keeping with the meter, but Rachmaninoff revised it to the more colloquial variant of the same word "счастье":

What happiness I feel: it's night, and we're alone!
The river's like a mirror, glistening with stars,
And lean your head back, see the sky immense and deep…

Music. Ivanovka, 19 June 1912. Op. 34, no. 12. A Major. 4/4, Allegro con fuoco. For High Voice: c^1 sharp–b^2 flat. First published with Opus 34 by A. Gutheil in Moscow in 1913.

Dedicated to **Leoníd Vitáliyevich Sóbinov** (1872–1934). One of five songs, all in Opus 34, dedicated to the Russian tenor; the others are Songs 65, 66, 67, 72.

Recordings. Del Grande, Kozlovsky, Kurenko, Lapina, Larin, Maslennikov, Mattila, Naoumenko, Obraztsova, Söderström, Suchkova, Zhadan.

Davydov: Dmitri Smirnov.

75 *Диссонанс*
Dissonance

Op. 34, No. 13

Rachmaninoff was always drawn to the dramatic potential inherent in an ensemble of two, singer and pianist, performing a song which expressed strong feelings. Despite its length he did not shorten or change a single word of Yakov Polonsky's poem, written in long anapestic tetrameter couplets and subtitled "Motif from the confessions of Ada Christen."

When Polonsky published the poem in 1876, the name Ada Christen signalled to the reader aware of contemporary German literary trends such frank themes as "the fallen woman," "forbidden love," and "survival by sinning" (*Hacken*, 307). Ada Christen (1839–1901) was a Viennese writer who as a teenager had lived a "bordello-like existence" as an actress in traveling German comedy troupes. Her first book, a collection of poems entitled *Lieder einer Verlorenen* (Songs of a Lost Woman), was a sensation when it was published in 1868. It was soon republished, and followed by more poems ("Out of the Ashes" and "Out of the Depths") and sketches and short stories about survival on the edge.

There was no one quite like Ada Christen in 19th-century Russian literature, which explains why poets like Aleksei Pleshcheyev and Yakov Polonsky read her with such interest. Tchaikovsky used Pleshcheyev's translation of her poem "You alone" for his Song 73 (Op. 57/6), which originally was a lyric on the "fallen woman" theme, but which Tchaikovsky altered, elevating it to a statement about a steadfast devotion in which, tragically, there is no love. There are other songs by Tchaikovsky that imply intimate situations and erotic awareness from what is (or could be) the woman's point of view, such as "To forget so soon" (Song 10, by Apukhtin), and "He loved me so," (Song 36, Op. 28/4, by Delphine Gay, translated by Apukhtin). Thematically, "Dissonance" belongs in this group of songs: it is really a scenic dramatic monologue like Tchaikovsky's "To forget so soon," rather than a story of "forbidden love."

To say that Polonsky's verses are "quite daring for their time" (*Harrison*, 183) or "unusually adventurous" (*Martyn*, 240) is to miss the mark. After *Anna Karenina* (1878), the text cannot be read as a diary entry in the life of a woman in an adulterous relationship: seen that way, it becomes ridiculous. Rachmaninoff treats the poem musically as a series of self-revealing emotional gestures—imagined flight, return to a poetic setting, a lovers' tryst revisited, the fantasy of an embrace, "a kiss without fire," and the determined dream, nevertheless, that two souls can again merge into one. Barrie Martyn has rightly said that it is "notable for the musical freedom with which the composer closely follows the strained emotional undertones of the poem—there are six changes of key and thirty-three changes of time signature" (*Martyn*, 240). To this can be added the many different performance marks, initially Non Allegro, Agitato, then Tranquillo, Agitato again and Piu agitato, Andante, slowing down and speeding up: the music continually takes new shapes with these changes in tempo and style to reflect the breakout from the stifling night, the poetic scene of the pond and nightingale's song, the tense meeting in the dark, and so on. The piano is strong, enveloping the voice part and shaping the whole song right up to the long accelerated postlude.

When Nina Koshetz and Rachmaninoff were planning their autumn concert programs in the summer of 1916, she asked the composer to orchestrate this song. It was one of her favorite songs, which required a dramatic performance. He apparently agreed to do it, but no record of it exists (*LN* 2, 408). The two of them performed the song in the Small Hall of the St. Petersburg Conservatory on 30 October 1916, with Rachmaninoff at the piano (*Barber*, 330), and numerous times before and after that through 1917 (*LN* 3, 445).

Пусть по воле судеб я рассталась с тобой,
Пусть другой обладает моей красотой!

Из объятий его, из ночной духоты,
Уношусь я далёко на крыльях мечты.

Вижу снова наш старый, запущенный сад:
Отражённый в пруде потухает закат;

Пахнет липовым цветом в прохладе аллей;
За прудом, где-то в роще, урчит соловей…

Я стеклянную дверь отворила, дрожу,
Я из мрака в таинственный сумрак гляжу,

Чу! там хрустнула ветка, не ты ли шагнул?!
Встрепенулася птичка — не ты ли спугнул?!

Я прислушиваюсь, я мучительно жду,
Я на шелест шагов твоих тихо иду,

Холодит мои члены то страсть, то испуг,
Это ты меня за руку взял, милый друг!?

Это ты осторожно так обнял меня,
Это твой поцелуй — поцелуй без огня!

С болью в трепетном сердце, с волненьем в крови
Ты не смеешь отдаться безумствам любви,

И, внимая речам благородным твоим,
Я не смею дать волю влеченьям своим,

И дрожу, и шепчу тебе: милый ты мой!
Пусть владеет он жалкой моей красотой!

Из объятий его, из ночной духоты,
Я опять улетаю на крыльях мечты,

В этот сад, в эту темь, вот на эту скамью,
Где впервые подслушал ты душу мою…

Я душою сливаюсь с твоею душой —
Пусть владеет он жалкой моей красотой!

Púst' pa vóle sudép ja rastálas' s tabój,
Púzd' drugój abladájet majéj krasatój!

Never mind that fate has parted us,
And another man possesses my beauty!

Iz abjátij jevó, iz nachnój dukhatý,
Unashús' ja daljóka na krýljakh mechtý.

From his embraces, in the stifling night,
I am carried far away on wings of dream.

Vízhu snóva nash stáryj, zapúshchennyj sát:
Atrazhónnyj f prudé patukhájed zakát;

I see again our garden, old and overgrown:
The setting sun reflected in the pond;

Pákhnet lípovym tsvétam f prakhláde alléj;
Za prudóm, gdé-ta v róshche, urchít salavéj…

The air smells of blossoms in the cool linden alleys;
Past the pond, in the grove, a nightingale is warbling…

Ja stekljánnuju dvér' atvaríla, drazhú,
Ja iz mráka f taínstvennyj súmrak gljazhú,

I open the glass door, trembling,
In darkness I gaze into the mysterious shadows,

Chú! tam khrúsnula vétka, ne tý li shagnúl?!
Fstrepenúlasa ptíchka — ne tý li spugnúl?!

Hark! a stick cracked, was that you taking a step?!
A bird flew up — was it you who startled it?!

Ja prislúshyvajus', ja muchítel'na zhdú,
Ja na shélest shagóf tvajíkh tíkha idú,

I listen intently in an agony of expectation,
I tiptoe toward the rustle of your footsteps,

Khaladít maji chlény tó strást', tó ispúk,
Éta tý menjá zá ruku vzjál, mílyj drúk!?

My limbs shiver with passion and fright,
Is it you taking my hand, my darling!?

Éta tý astarózhna tak óbnjal menjá,
Éta tvój patselúj — patselúj bez agnjá!

Is this cautious embrace you,
Is this kiss yours — a kiss without fire!

Z bólju f trépetnam sérttse,
    s valneńjem f kraví
Ty ne sméjesh addátsa
    bezúmstvam ljubví,

I, vnimája rechám blagaródnym tvajím,
Ja ne sméju dát' vólju vlechénjam svajím,

I drazhú, i shepchú tebé:
    mílyj ty mój!
Púzd' vladéjet on zhálkaj majéj krasatój!

Iz abjátij jevó, iz nachnój dukhatý,
Ja apját' uletáju na krýljakh mechtý,

V état sát, v étu tém', vót na étu skamjú,
Gde fpervýje patslúshal ty
    dúshu majú…

Ja dushóju slivájus' s tvajéju dushój —
Púzd' vladéjet on zhálkaj majéj krasatój!

With pain in your trembling heart,
    with excitement in your blood,
You don't dare to surrender
    to mad flights of love,

And, listening to your noble words,
I dare not give vent to my own feelings,

And I tremble, and whisper to you:
    darling of mine!
So what if he possesses my poor beauty!

From his embraces, in the stifling night,
I am carried away again on wings of dream,

To this garden, this darkness, this bench,
Where you first listened secretly
    to my soul…

And again I merge my soul with yours —
So what if he possesses my poor beauty!

Text. **Yákov Petróvich Polónsky**, 1875. Title: Диссонанс (Dissonance); subtitle: "Motif from the confessions of Ada Christen." First published in 1876 in Polonsky's volume of new poems "Озими" (Winter shoots), Part I, pp. 179-80. Set only by Rachmaninoff, who removed the subtitle.

Meter. Ternary. Four-foot anapests:

To this garden, this darkness, this bench we once knew,
Where we merged in our souls for the very first time…

Music. Ivanovka, 17 June 1912. Op. 34, no. 13. E-flat Minor. 4/4, Non allegro, with frequent changes. For High Voice: b flat–b^2. First published with Opus 34 by A. Gutheil in Moscow in 1913.

Dedicated to **Félia Vasíliyevna Litvín (Litvinne**, 1861–1936), Russian dramatic soprano. Born in St. Petersburg as Françoise-Jeanne Schütz, she studied and made her debut in Paris; she sang all over the world, including one season at the Metropolitan Opera (1896–97). She is in the *Record of Singing*, vol. 1, singing arias from *Aida* and *Le Cid*. She was married to a man in the same Litvinov family that Rachmaninoff's grandmother Butakova, née Litvinova, belonged to: hence she and the composer were distantly related by marriage. Rachmaninoff knew her and saw her in Paris in 1907.

Recordings. Borele, Dionne, Kurenko, Lee, Rodgers, Rozhdestvenskaya, Söderström, Suchkova, Urmana.

76 *Вокализ* *Vocalise*

Op. 34, No. 14

1.

Rachmaninoff's "Vocalise" is known everywhere in the musical world. Written in 1915 for soprano with piano accompaniment, Rachmaninoff transcribed the song for soprano with orchestra for its public premiere in January 1916. That same year Mikhail Press, a violin teacher at the Moscow Conservatory, transcribed it for violin and piano. Other transcriptions followed—for orchestra, for piano trio, for cello with piano, for flute and other woodwinds with piano, and so on, to the present day, when transcriptions of "Vocalise" are performed by an astonishing variety of solo instruments and combinations of instruments. In all its versions it has probably been recorded more than any piece Rachmaninoff wrote other than the C-sharp minor Prelude, but the heyday of the Prelude was the first half of the 20th century, whereas the "Vocalise" has been performed ever more widely in the 20th and early 21st centuries. The composer himself, who grew tired of the Prelude because his concert audiences invariably asked him to play it, had a special affection for the "Vocalise" all his life, especially in its arrangements for strings.

The song has become so familiar that it is now hard to imagine what it was like to hear it for the first time. The baritone Sergei Levik heard an early performance by the soprano Antonina Nezhdanova; Rachmaninoff had worked closely with her while he was finishing the song, and he dedicated it to her. Levik had a startling reaction to her performance: "only at the end did I realize there were no words: everything was contained in the music" (*Levik 1962*, 350). A later Russian commentator described it as "a song melody, heard as if from afar, so the words are not intelligible" (*Vasina-Grossman*, 334). The melody has a haunting beauty. The piece lasts for nearly seven minutes, with the first two of its three parts repeated. This "endless" lyric flight suggests a mood or moment that might have a name, yet it has no words.

The song is more than what its title implies. A "vocalise" is a scale or improvised melody, sung to an open vowel sound, usually "ah"; singers use vocalise passages to train the voice in tone and pitch, or as a warm-up exercise. Composing a vocalise to be performed, however, was a novel practice at the time. At the Paris Conservatoire, a voice teacher named A. L. Hettich persuaded his colleagues to compose a "vocalise-étude" for a series he was editing for the publisher Alphonse Leduc. Gabriel Fauré led the first set of ten with a vocalise in E minor written in 1906 (see *Johnson 2009*, 296-7). In 1909 Maurice Ravel wrote his "Vocalise-étude en forme d'habanera" as no. 20 in the series. Unlike most of these rather academic pieces, Faure's lovely vocalise is still sung, and Ravel's became and remains a favorite of performers and audiences. The series went on for decades, and eventually included a contribution by Aaron Copland, published in 1929 as no. 71 in the series: recorded in 1935 by Ethel Luening with the composer at the piano, it is a witty, antic piece, starting out as a scale and moving into wistful song and fancy bel canto. There is no evidence the Paris project had any influence on Rachmaninoff, whose impulse to write a vocalise was quite independent.

2.

Rachmaninoff's "Vocalise" differs from his other songs with opus numbers in that it did not come into being alongside a group of songs all written at the same time, but rather appeared independently. It was written directly after the intense creative period of six weeks that produced the *All-Night Vigil*, Op. 37, composed in January and February 1915. Though obviously different from the *Vigil* in its scope and in its ends and means, the "Vocalise" continues in its own way the creative trajectory that produced the *All-Night Vigil*. Widely considered Rachmaninoff's greatest choral work and the high point of composed Russian liturgical music, the *Vigil* is written for four-part unaccompanied mixed chorus. Its fifteen motets are sung "through the night," from vespers to matins the next morning. (The work is sometimes called, misleadingly, "Vespers"; there is an illuminating discussion of it in *Martyn*, 253-61.) At its center is the fifth motet in which a solo tenor voice sings the text of the *Nunc dimittis*: "Lord, now lettest thou thy servant depart in peace...." The *Nunc dimittis* stands out as the only *solo* number in this choral work. It is "a singularly beautiful melody over pairs of rocking choral chords which evoke a distant echo of *Dies irae*" (ibid., 257).

As a wordless song, the "Vocalise" carries much further the vocalise passages in two earlier songs, "Harvest of sorrow" (Song 14) and "The soldier's wife" (Song 19). These are laments in folk style that use a short vocalise as coda to the song. The "Vocalise" is a lamentation too, but not in folk style, and not tied to any text. In its *zachin*, its initial impulse, the "Vocalise" is like the beginning of the *Nunc dimittis*: it starts abruptly, without preliminaries, and proceeds on a lyric course marked by rhythmic freedom, melodic repetition and variation. It is generally seen as giving expression to a wide array of feelings—longing, tenderness, sorrow, struggle, resolution, and final rest, but the only concrete evidence of a specific meaning is in the *Dies Irae* theme, indicative of death and final judgment.

As soon as the *Vigil* was finished, it went into rehearsal with the choir of the Moscow Synod. The premiere was on 15 March 1915, and that was followed by half a dozen sold-out performances. These performances of the *Vigil* with full choir and soloists were a revelation to the composer. After one of them, he exchanged words with a clerk who was writing out the parts of the score.

Praising the choir, Rachmaninoff said to him: "I had no idea I had written *such* a work as this" (A. P. Smirnov in *VOR 1*, 444).

3.

Soon after the public performances of the *Vigil*, Rachmaninoff came to Nezhdanova with a draft of a new song called "Vocalise," dated 1 April 1915. He must have had Nezhdanova in mind from the time he began working on it. He knew from her peerless recital work, as well as their work together at the Bolshoi, the beauty, warmth, and rare simplicity she would be able to bring to a through-composed "vocalise-lament." They met numerous times in April to rehearse the song, modifying it, adding performance marks, discussing nuances and breathing points, and even changing the key, at her suggestion, from his original E-flat minor to C-sharp minor (these changes are discussed and illustrated in *Nezhdanova*, 261-264). Their work was left unfinished in April. After the sudden death of Scriabin (April 14), Rachmaninoff went to Finland to prepare a program of Scriabin's piano music for the following season. He was in Finland until the beginning of August, after which he went to Ivanovka for the rest of the summer. During that summer, his beloved teacher Sergei Taneyev died (June 6), and there was continual bad news from the war front. When the summer was over, Rachmaninoff had a revised, final version, signing the manuscript "21 September 1915, Moscow" (*Rytsareva*, 37).

The song is shaped into three parts. In the opening section of twenty-four bars, the eight notes of the *Dies irae* theme occur in the opening phrase, not as a stand-alone figure, but transformed rhythmically, with some note values shortened or prolonged. These chopped and dotted notes give the melody a certain lilt, so that in spite of the "Lentamente" tempo, the song has, or can have, given the performance, an Andante forward movement. The disguised *Dies irae* provides a melodic figure with a falling intonation, a figure that, with melodic variation, will rise, fall again, return, repeat, and respond with new patterns. The first six bars, sung *piano*, negotiate a descent from e^2 to c^2, with a final trill. This is followed by a rising intonational figure, which introduces an undercurrent of passion, *poco piu animato*, impelling the melody upward, where it soars and swells before slowing back down to *piano* again. The range is widened here, from f^1 to f^2. This section of twenty-four bars is then to be repeated in its entirety. It is intended to be repeated, and when it is, in some but not all performances, Part I takes up three minutes or more—about half the duration of the whole song.

Part II is half as long as I. It is a response to Part I which establishes a new direction. It rises gently but firmly to the upper end of the register, by *crescendo*, to a *fortissimo* g^2, diminishing to *piano* only at the end. Part II consists of sixteen bars intended, like Part I, to be repeated.

Part III (eight bars, not repeated) takes the song to a culmination by rising *espressivo* all the way from c^1 to c^3, then descending an octave to a prolonged final c^2, marked *tenuto, ad libitum*. Thus the "Vocalise" proceeds out of an initial, rhythmically altered melody derived from the *Dies irae*, elaborates it with a contrasting response in Part II, and then brings it to resolution in Part III.

As written, with Parts I and II repeated, the song takes from six to seven minutes to perform. Its sustained length, the rhythmic and melodic subtlety of its phrases, the continual changes in pacing and dynamics, and its range of two full octaves all make it a song which is unusually difficult to sing. The singer has to do what Nezhdanova did during her rehearsals with Rachmaninoff: find the right initial tempo, not too slow and not too fast, and then work through the vocalization as indicated by all the performance marks, *animato* and *espressivo*, accelerating and slowing down, bringing out subtly the notes marked *tenuto*, and registering gradations in volume from *piano* to *fortissimo*. All this must be put together into a seamless whole that moves fluidly, without any sense of strain or effort. A performance, however beautiful the voice, can fall short of conveying the song's sustained spell if not well judged and carefully prepared.

The recording by the Swedish soprano Elisabeth Söderström (1975, 6:25) sets the standard. Söderström keeps her eye on the score; she brings the music to life, and keeps it alive, without apparent effort, through the repeated parts; she slows down the ending just enough to convey the poignance and vulnerability that are a part of the final resolution. Joan Rodgers (1995, 6:10) is also very fine in her pacing: she slows down and holds back ever so slightly in repeated passages, keeping the reprises fresh and new before returning to tempo. Galina Vishnevskaya (1976, 7:40) sings it very slowly, in dramatic rather than lyric voice; she takes some optional lower notes in the conclusion, but still sounds effortful at times, although her sustained final note is exemplary. Maria Guleghina (2002, 6:37) has controlled vibrato; she sings with expressive phrasing and good legato. Anja Silja (2009, 7:17) includes "Vocalise" in an admirable program of Rachmaninoff and Mussorgsky songs recorded on the eve of her seventieth birthday; she sings it slowly, shaping the phrases well; it is an expert performance, even though the song does not show a voice past its prime to best advantage. Two well-known tenors have recorded it. Nicolai Gedda (1969, 5:04) is in supple voice with a light, perfect high C, but the pace he sets is much too fast. Ivan Kozlovsky with orchestra (1947, 7:01) sings too loudly, forcing some notes and needlessly prolonging others, his later truncated version with piano (1970s, 3:30) is, alas, no better. Suzanne Murphy (1986, 6:51) and Sylvia McNair (1992, 6:50) have recorded beautiful performances of the complete song with orchestra.

Truncated performances run from three to five minutes. They may repeat Part I but not Part II, or vice-versa, or they may be without any repeats. Among the finest are the recordings by Evelyn Lear (1974, 3:40), Ruth Ann Swenson (1994, 4:38), and Kiri Te Kanawa (1989, 5:09) with piano; with orchestra, Natalie Dessay (1998, 5:24), Renée Fleming (1997, 5:44), Kiri Te Kanawa again (1994, 5:17), and the countertenor Brian Asawa (1997, 4:55). Anna Moffo's seductive performance (1964) skips the second repeat, but even so, with Stokowski setting the pace, it lasts well over seven minutes. Lily Pons (1947, 3:52) has an aspiration problem, in which the syllable "ah" turns into an awkward "ha." Kathleen Battle (1991, 4:02), in recital at Carnegie Hall, starts out well, but runs out of breath and cannot sustain the final note. Maria Kurenko (1950, 4:36) defies the years at age 60 (Nezhdanova, Obukhova, and Kurenko all had the same teacher, Umberto Masetti, and were known for longevity of voice). Her tone is not as beautiful as a younger singer's, but she sings briskly and correctly, taking the high notes and not the optional lower ones. There are some recent arrangements of the song for unusual combinations of singers and instruments. These include an original two-man collaboration by the jazz singer Bobby McFerrin and the cellist Yo-Yo Ma (1996, 6:27), with voice and cello trading places on repeats.

4.

"Vocalise" lends itself so well to arrangements for various instruments that it has an even larger life of its own as an instrumental piece, especially for strings. Played by a string orchestra, it is transformed into something like a slow Bach aria—the "Air on a G String" from Bach's Suite in D Major, for example. Rachmaninoff remarked about this in a letter to his friend the cellist Modest Altschuler in January 1918: "I especially liked your idea to perform 'Vocalise' in the style of a Bach aria. That's right, and I've had the same thought myself. I heard it played by ten violins in unison in an arrangement by [Mikhail] Press. It sounded splendid, and I was very pleased. Try to do this yourself, only transpose it into E minor" (*LN* 2, 105).

Later in 1918, Rachmaninoff made his own transcription for orchestra (transposed into E minor). It was for a thirty-seven-piece orchestra that included two horns and nine woodwinds (flutes, oboes, clarinets, bassoons, one English horn), six first and six second violins, six violas, four cellos, and four double basses. The earliest recording of "Vocalise" for orchestra is Rachmaninoff's own orchestral version, with the composer himself conducting the Philadelphia Orchestra in 1929. Owing to the time limitation of a 78 rpm record, the orchestra had to play the song through without repeating I and II. This recording shows Rachmaninoff's mastery as a conductor: it is neither too fast nor too slow; the pace is steady but with subtle rubatos that do not slow down the flow, nor overdo the breath-catching hint of delay before the bass strings are plucked. All this transforms the performance into something magically alive.

Of all the different instruments for which "Vocalise" has been transcribed, performances of it by cello or violin come closest to expressing the lovely legato voice part of the original song. The first recording on cello was made by the Russian-American cellist Gregor Piatigorsky in 1946. Limited by the 78 rpm format, he had to omit both repeats, but his recording set a standard of clarity and eloquence. Of the many fine recordings that have followed, five of them are especially remarkable.

The first and, formally, the most lucid, was made in the early 1950s by Mstislav Rostropovich. He learned "Vocalise" when preparing for the Budapest competition in 1949, as one of several miniatures "where first and foremost one must develop a beautiful singing sound and work on filigree, minute details of color and timbre" (*Wilson 2008*, 42-3). His sound is a clean, singing vibrato, with different shades of color and timbre expressed at every step, but his primary aim is not beauty of tone. Rather, it is lapidary, a conscious shaping of the song, starting with a true *lentamente* tempo and then proceeding to delineate each successive part, now employing a strenuous energy, now falling back to surrender and reflection. The piano support by Alexander Dediukhin is exactly what such an approach calls for: it is there as needed but otherwise hardly noticeable.

In contrast, the recording by Lynn Harrell with Vladimir Ashkenazy (1984) shows the fine ensemble work of two masters of romantic style. Here there is beauty of tone, with lovely vibrato, expressive rubato in the timing, and every note of the piano bringing clarity and support. When the pace slows, their relapse into a slight dreaminess brings out the sense of mystery and quest in the music.

Yehuda Hanani's version (2000) has a higher, lighter tone; he starts from E rather than C. He seems to breathe life miraculously into each phrase. The movement is lilting, with clean vibrato, but, like Rostropovich, his aim is not beauty of tone. His leaner, drier sound sets phrases into relief: now elegiac, now a little sweeter, now laconic, now contemplative. The last held note is exemplary, sustained with a perfect legato stroke of the bow.

Few artists bring out passionate intensity better than Mischa Maisky (2005), who was a student of Rostropovich's from 1966–70. His live recording has ample vibrato and ringing tone; Pavel Gililov's piano is fully engaged and adds to the powerful feeling built up in the first half of the performance. With the repeat of Part II, however, the interpretation becomes reflective and tender. After so much passion, Maisky reaches that *pianissimo* which Rostropovich taught was the culminating point in many of Rachmaninoff's compositions (ibid., 263): this conclusion to the song is thereby extraordinarily moving.

Finally, there is the recording by Moray Welsh (2000), who studied with Rostropovich in Moscow from 1969–71. His vibrato is held back, but his cello sings; the beauty here is in simplicity and serenity. Martin Roscoe's piano yields prominence to the cellist yet leads the way at transition points. Perfectly judged, with no unnecessary details or wasted motion, this performance gives exact voice to the eloquence and beauty inherent in the music as Rachmaninoff wrote it.

Violinists have performed the work almost as often as cellists. There are many notable recorded performances. The earliest I have found (but have not heard) is by Mischa Elman (1928). A decade later, Ruggiero Ricci recorded a singing, sweet-toned version of the transcription by Press (1938, 4:04), nicely paced with a lively flow. He shifts down an octave in the repeat of Part I, then back up for the rest of the song; at the end, he splits the long final note, dropping down an octave halfway through. The recording by Jascha Heifetz (1947, 4:01), like Ricci's, is abbreviated owing to the 78 rpm time limitation, but it stands out from all others in its impeccable reading of the score, with its lean vibrato and variety of tonal colors. Itzhak Perlman, in a thoroughly attractive performance (1995), follows Ricci and Heifetz in playing the reprise of Part I an octave lower, but he divides the final note by shifting *up* an octave halfway through, ending the song *pianississimo*. Vladimir Spivakov (1991) changes octaves up and down in nearly every phrase, which turns a welcome musical variation into something tedious and overdone. The earliest recording with no cuts is by David Oistrakh (1947): it is slow (6:44) but riveting, unadorned but expressive, and free of octave shifts. Maxim Vengerov has made two exemplary recordings, observing Oistrakh's chaste approach to the Press arrangement, once with piano (2001) and once with added strings (2005). Nadja Salerno-Sonnenberg (1992) recorded an original reading different in ways from the others. She omits the second repeat but still times in at 6:47; she plays *lentamente* through and through, but her tempo keeps up an *andante* lope and never drags. Her controlled expressive techniques, including fermatas and the sudden burst of *forte*, steer her performance in the direction of the sublime, with a marked Gypsy temperament. Among other superlative recordings with piano are those by the Israeli violist Rivka Golani (2003), the Georgian violinist Lisa Batiashvili (2010, with Hélène Grimaud), and the recording, expertly dubbed, by the Russian violinist-violist Yuri Zhislin (2005), who plays his own original transcription, alternating violin and viola (I, I repeat, II) then, to fine effect, a viola-violin duet for the second half of the song.

For violin with orchestra, the sweet, energetic, clean vibrato of Nathan Milstein (1962) is inimitable and impossible to match. Isaac Stern (1972) plays with characteristic warmth, *listening* closely in ensemble with the orchestra and playing directly to his audience. Joshua Bell (2006) reminds us that just as a beautiful voice is not enough to make the song succeed, so too a virtuoso instrumental performance has to *sing*: absent *cantabile*, *animato*, *espressivo*, the song is merely beautiful without being moving.

Nathan Milstein understood how "Vocalise," in even the simplest performance, without accompaniment, had to be above all *expressive*. He told the story of dropping by one afternoon in the 1930s to visit Rachmaninoff at his home "Senar" by Lake Lucerne. Gregor Piatigorsky was with him and both had their instruments. Rachmaninoff was taking a late after-dinner nap. On the music stand was the sheet music for "Vocalise," which they both knew well. Without a word, they began playing it very quietly, in unison, an octave apart. Rachmaninoff suddenly came into the room in his pajamas, walked to the piano, and, standing up, accompanied them to the end, whereupon he left the room with moist eyes without saying a single word (*Milstein*, 124).

5.

Before me is a list I have been keeping for several years of transcriptions of "Vocalise" for different instruments. There can be no "complete" list, because new recordings are released on an almost monthly basis. They are published on compact discs, sold in audio format on iTunes and other sites, and posted in video format on YouTube, in surprising variety and sheer numbers. Max Harrison, writing in 2005, noted with evident surprise a transcription of the song *even for saxophone* (*Harrison*, 184). However, a search of WorldCat in September 2010 showed more than fifteen recordings with piano or other accompaniment by professional saxophonists (not counting student recitals), and nine different published scores of "Vocalise" arranged for alto, soprano, and tenor saxophone. One of the recordings is a performance by the jazz saxophonist Branford Marsalis, who plays it in clean legato style with the English Chamber Orchestra in an arrangement by Michel Colombier. More adventurous is a performance on YouTube by the Russian jazz artist Igor Butman playing soprano saxophone with the strings of Yuri Bashmet's Moscow Soloists. Butman improvises freely after playing through Part I, showing that "Vocalise" has a life in jazz improvisation just like any other "standard" song. In 1973 Don Sebesky, one of the finest arrangers in the history of jazz, wrote a remarkable arrangement of the song in which Paul Desmond on alto saxophone and Milt Jackson on vibraphone play the voice part freely, taking turns, backed up by Bob James on piano, Ron Carter on bass, Jack DeJohnette on drums, and a full orchestra.

The list below of instrumental recordings of "Vocalise" is long and varied. Among performances by eminent soloists are those by Gary Karr on double bass, Emma Johnson on clarinet, Philippe Magnan and Eugene Izotov on oboe, Frank Morelli and Daniel Smith on bassoon, James Galway on flute, Andy Findon on multiple flutes, Michel Tirabosco on panflute, Michala Petri on recorder, Micha Makarenko on balalaika, Joe Sakimoto on harmonica, Timofei Dokshitser and Alison Balsom on trumpet, and, in an elegant arrangement, Christian Lindberg on trombone. Even the tuba can be lyrical, as Patrick Sheridan, Hank Feldman, and Daniel Perantoni show. Perhaps the most astonishing and challenging of all are Clara Rockmore on theremin and Jim Turner on the musical saw—rare virtuosos who give performances both strange and unusually moving.

Among ensembles are stellar piano trios like the now-forgotten Andreas Trio and the brilliant Eroica Trio. There are also unusual combinations: "Trio Voronezh," made up of Russian folk instruments (bayan, domra, double bass balalaika); "Répercussion," a group of orchestral percussionists who play the song on marimbas, vibraphone, bass metallophone, tubular bells, and glockenspiel; and a German group called "Musica Variata" (organ, shawm, bagpipe, flute), who play an arrangement for organ and flute.

For pianists, "Vocalise" has been something of a challenge. It was decades before the first piano transcription appeared. Victor Babin first arranged it, for performance by his popular piano duo with his wife Vitya Vronsky (recorded 1940, published 1942). For piano solo, the first published transcription was by the Scottish composer and pianist Alan Richardson (1956). Not knowing or not liking this transcription, the Italian pianist Sergio Fiorentino wrote and recorded his own version in Paris in 1962. Emil Gilels (1977) and Evgeny Kissin (1993), among others, have recorded the Richardson transcription: Kissin is unmatched for perfect finger work, but Gilels brings subtle rubato and a gradually mounting sense of conviction which give the performance life beyond technical perfection. The Hungarian pianist Zoltán Kocsis published a strong, more nuanced transcription in 1981 and recorded it a year later; it has since been recorded by Howard Shelley (1991) and Vladimir Ashkenazy (2002). The American Earl Wild made a sumptuous transcription which assumes, gradually, gorgeous harmonic colors, and employs cascading chords, arpeggios, trills and other features of the Romantic pallette before coming to a spare, laconic conclusion; he recorded it twice (1982, 1991). A new transcription by the Russian arranger Anton Borodin goes back to the simpler score of the original song; it has been recorded in a clean, chaste, lyrical performance by Nadejda Vlaeva (2007). Rachmaninoff himself never mentioned "Vocalise" as a song for piano transcription, nor did he perform it as a piano solo. He had, after all, come to hear it in his mind as a Bach aria played by strings—"the more, the better" (*LN* 2, 107).

6.

Antonina Nezhdanova gave the song its premiere at one of Serge Koussevitzky's concerts in Moscow on 24 January 1916. It was commonly believed that the composer accompanied her on the piano at the premiere (*T/N*, 110). A Koussevitzky specialist has clarified this matter, however, asserting that Nezhdanova sang the composer's own version for *soprano with orchestra*, conducted by Koussevitzky, after which Rachmaninoff came up to the piano and accompanied Nezhdanova in some of his songs (*Iuzefovich 2004*, 331); Nezhdanova herself confirms this (*Nezhdanova*, 172).

Moreover, it seems Koussevitzky was ahead of everyone else in transcribing the song and performing it in public. He performed it on his "solo-tuned" double bass at a Moscow concert conducted by Gregor Fitelberg on 7 December 1915 (*Iuzefovich*, ibid.). Rachmaninoff's old friend Sakhnovsky said of Koussevitzky's performance that "he literally *sang* Rachmaninoff's vocalise." The journal *Muzyka* made light of this transcription, writing that "Mr. Koussevitzky's inclination to popularize the inspirations of Rachmaninoff may cause us very soon to listen to that same vocalise in the majestic register of the trombone, and then perhaps all the other instruments of the orchestra in turn" (*Keldysh*, 383). A century later, of course, this is exactly what has happened—but with many further revelations that the critics at *Muzyka* could not have imagined.

Music. 1915. Op. 34, no. 14. C-sharp Minor. 4/4, Lentamente, Molto cantabile. For High Voice and Piano: c^1 sharp–c^3 sharp. Dedicated to **Antonína Vasíliyevna Nezhdánova** (1873–1950).

There has been confusion in the *dating* because the first thirteen songs of Opus 34 were composed in 1912. The correct date was given by the composer himself in 1917, when, at Boris Asafiev's request, he wrote out a list of his compositions with dates: for songs 1–13 in Op. 34, he gave the date "Summer 1912," but for "Vocalise" he wrote "April 1915" (*LN* 2, 99). The first manuscript of the song, given by Rachmaninoff to Nezhdanova, is dated 1 April 1915 (*Nezhdanova*, 261); the final manuscript is dated 21 September 1915 (*Rytsareva*, 37). The erroneous date "April 1912" is often cited (for example in *B/L*, 415) and persists to the present day, although Russian commentators (*Briantseva*, *Keldysh*) give 1915.

As for the *opus number*, when Rachmaninoff wrote the song, Opus 34/1–13 was already in print (published in January 1913). "Vocalise" was first published in a separate edition in 1916, and subsequently added to Opus 34 as no. 14.

Transcriptions (Selected published musical scores).

Soprano with orchestra: Rachmaninoff, first published 1916.

Orchestra: Rachmaninoff, first published 1919. Later arrangements by Stokowski, Morton Gould, and others, published and unpublished.

Piano trio: Julius Conus. "Transcription pour piano, violin et violoncelle." Leipzig: Breitkoff & Hartel, 1928. Eroica Trio, 1998.

Violin with piano: Mikhail (Michael, Michel) Press: Moscow, Leipzig-Berlin, London, New York, 1916. A revision of the Press transcription was made by the Russian-American violinist Josef Gingold: New York, 1958. Among the violinists who have used the Press arrangement was Jascha Heifetz, who is sometimes mistakenly named as author of the transcription for violin. Heifetz did perform and record "Vocalise," but it is not one of his three transcriptions of Rachmaninoff's songs.

Cello with piano: Anatol Brandukov, 1922. A second arrangement, now widely used, is by the American cellist Leonard Rose (New York, 1960). Rose's students include Lynn Harrell, Yehuda Hanani, and Yo-Yo Ma, who have all performed it.

Recordings (Selected).

Voice with piano: Kathleen Battle, Annette Celine, Dilbèr, Inessa Galante, Nicolai Gedda, Maria Guleghina, Ivan Kozlovsky, Maria Kurenko, Evelyn Lear, Olga Makarina, Moscow Boys Choir, Judith Mok, Joan Rodgers, Anja Silja, Elisabeth Söderström, Natalia Suchkova, Ruth Ann Swenson, Kira Te Kanawa, Galina Vishnevskaya, Maria Zelenina.

Voice with orchestra: Brian Asawa, Natalie Dessay, Renée Fleming, Jane Gilchrist, Ivan Kozlovsky, Nelly Lee, Norman Luboff Choir, Sylvia McNair, Yoshikazu Mera, Anna Moffo, Suzanne Murphy, Galina Oleinichenko, Lily Pons, Kiri Te Kanawa, Stefania Woytowicz.

Voice with other instruments: Terry Barber (with Karl Jenkins's "Adiemus"), Bobby McFerrin (with Yo-Yo Ma, cello).

Orchestra: Academy of St. Martin-in-the-Fields (Neville Marriner), American Symphony (Leopold Stokowski), Berlin Philharmonic (Lorin Maazel), Boston Symphony (Serge Koussevitzky), Budapest Festival Orchestra (Iván Fischer), Budapest Philharmonic (Rico Saccani), Detroit Symphony (Leonard Slatkin), Giant Box Jazz Orchestra (Don Sebesky), Morton Gould Orchestra, André Kostelanetz Orchestra, London Symphony (André Previn), Minnesota Orchestra (Eiji Oue), National Philharmonic (Charles Gerhardt), Philadelphia Orchestra (Eugene Ormandy, Sergei Rachmaninoff), Russian National Orchestra (José Serebrier), St. Louis Symphony (Leonard Slatkin), St. Petersburg Philharmonic (Mariss Jansons, Yuri Temirkanov), Singapore Symphony (Lan Shui), Tchaikovsky Chamber Orchestra (Lazar Gosman), USSR Symphony (Evgeny Svetlanov).

Symphonic band: L'orchestre d'harmonie de la Garde républicaine (Roger Boutry).

Ensembles: Andreas Trio (piano trio), Capital Brassworks (brass and percussion), Eroica Trio (piano trio), London Cellos (Geoffrey Simon), Musica Variata (organ, shawm, bagpipe, flute), Répercussion (marimbas, vibe, bass metallophone, tubular bells, glockenspiel), Quartetto di Venezia (string quartet), Trio Voronezh (bayan, domra, double bass balalaika), Violin Ensemble of the Bolshoi Theater (Yuli Reyentovich).

Unaccompanied Instruments.

Electronic synthesizer: Isao Tomita (Plasma Symphony Orchestra), Hans Wurman (Moog synthesizer).

Organ: Nigel Potts, Todd Wilson.

Piano: Vladimir Ashkenazy, Victor Babin & Vitya Vronsky, Edward Eikner, Tina Faigen, Sergio Fiorentino, Emil Gilels, Cyprien Katsaris, Evgeny Kissin, Zoltán Kocsis, Péter Nagy, Antonio Pompa-Baldi, Howard Shelley, Wonny Song, Nadejda Vlaeva, Earl Wild.

Accompanied Instruments (with piano unless noted).

Acoustic guitar: Duo Bergerac (with cello).

Balalaika: Micha Makarenko.

Bassoon: Frank Morelli, Daniel Smith (with orchestra), Masahito Tanaka.

Cello: Boris Andrianov, Jirí Bárta, Coenraad Bloemendal (with harp), Cesar Bourguet, Gautier Capuçon, Han-Na Chang (with orchestra), Natalie Clein, Roger Drinkall, Anthony Elliott, Pierre Fournier, Ophélie Gaillard (with orchestra), David Geringas, Leonid Gorokhov, Michael Grebanier, Bernard Gregor-Smith, Emanuel Gruber, Yehuda Hanani, Lynn Harrell, Desmond Hoebig, Wolfram Huschke, Robert Irvine, Alexander Ivashkin, Ralph Kirshbaum, Maria Kliegel, Alexander Kniazev, Nina Kotova (with orchestra), Elemér Lavotha, Dorothy Lewis, Feodor Luzanov, Mischa Maisky, Sophie McNestrie, Bejun Mehta (with cello ensemble), Truls Mørk, Andrea Noferini, Miklós Perényi, Gregor Piatigorsky, Carlos Prieto, Mstislav Rostropovich, Eckart Runge, Rebecca Rust, Sara Sant'Ambrogio, Guido Schiefen, Heinrich Schiff, Jeffrey Solow, Vytautas Sondeckis (with orchestra), Luka Šulić, Petja Svensson, Julie Tanner, Wladislav Warenberg, Moray Welsh, Vélitchka Yotcheva, Alexander Zagorinsky.

Clarinet: Daniel Bonade (with orchestra), David Campbell, Martin Fröst, Alexey Gorokholinsky, Emma Johnson, Murray Khouri.

Domra: Tatiana Grachëva.

Double bass: Silvio Dalla Torre (bassetto), Knut Guettler, Gary Karr, Jorma Katrama, Yasunori Kawahara, Daniel Marillier, Milton Masciadri, Mark Morton, Josep Quer i Agustí, Michael Rieber, Klaus Trumpf.

Drums: Bernard Riche (with double bass).

Electric guitar: Slash (with rhythm section).

English horn: Patrick McFarland.

Euphonium: Adam Frey.

Flugelhorn: Sergei Nakariakov.

Flute: Gunilla von Bahr (with chamber ensemble), Christian Delafontaine, Abbie de Quant, Andy Findon (several flutes, multitracked), James Galway (with orchestra), Susan Hoeppner (with chamber ensemble), Sefika Kutluer (with orchestra), Ronda Mains (with guitar and cello), Kenneth Smith.

French horn: Hermann Baumann.

Harmonica: Joe Sakimoto.

Musical saw: Jim Turner.

Oboe: Peter Cooper (with harp), Diana Doherty (with orchestra), Eugene Izotov, Philippe Magnan.

Panflute: Michel Tirabosco (with orchestra).

Recorder: Michala Petri (with guitar).

Saxophone: Greg Banaszak (with orchestra), Arno Bornkamp, Paul Brodie (with harp), Igor Butman (with string ensemble), Paul Desmond (with jazz orchestra), Amy Dickson, Sergey Kolesov, Clifford Leaman, Gary Louie (with orchestra), Joseph Lulloff (with orchestra), Branford Marsalis (with orchestra), Harvey Pittel, Debra Richtmeyer (with orchestra), Timothy Roberts, Iwan Roth (with orchestra), Eugene Rousseau, Adam J. Schattschneider, Brian Sparks.

Theremin: Clara Rockmore.

Trombone: Christian Lindberg, Philip Swanson (with organ).

Trumpet: Ole Edvard Antonsen (with organ), Eric Aubier (with organ), Alison Balsom (with orchestra), Timofei Dokshitser, John Hagstrom (with wind ensemble), Tine Thing Helseth, Raymond Mase, Gerald Webster (with organ).

Tuba: Morton Feldman, Daniel Perantoni, Patrick Sheridan.

Vibraphone: Milt Jackson (with jazz orchestra).

Viola: Rivka Golani, Yuri Zhislin (dubbed duet with violin).

Violin: Joshua Bell (with orchestra), Nicola Benedetti, Lola Bobesco, Benjamin Breen, Eddy Brown, Kim Chee-Yun, Mirijam Contzen, Angèle Dubeau (with string orchestra), Mischa Elman, Rachel Gough (with organ), Jascha Heifetz, Elissa Lee Koljonen, Catherine Manoukian, Alexander Markov, Anne Meyers, Nathan Milstein (with orchestra), David Oistrakh, Dene Olding, Elmar Oliveira, Itzhak Perlman, Ruggiero Ricci, Nadja Salerno-Sonnenberg, Jewgeni Schuck (with guitar), Gil Sharon, Vladimir Spivakov, Isaac Stern (with orchestra), Mela Tenenbaum, Rudens Turku, Maxim Vengerov, Xue Wei, Yuri Zhislin (dubbed duet with viola), Nikolaj Znaider.

77 *Из Евангелия от Иоанна*
(Гл. XV, стих 13)
From the Gospel of John
(Ch. XV, verse 13)

This song, more like one of Brahms's "serious songs" on Biblical texts than a Russian romance, was written to honor the fallen soldiers of the Russian army after the outbreak of World War I. That event, which took place on 19 July 1914 (Old Style) at 4 p.m. Moscow time, turned out to mark the beginning of the end for the Russian empire.

Some in Russia met the news with patriotic élan, but they were few. On 20 July Maxim Gorky wrote to a friend: "For a long time—three years now—I've been convinced a European war was inevitable, I've felt prepared for catastrophe, I've thought about it a great deal, but now that it's begun I feel overwhelmed, as if what's happened is quite unexpected. It's frightening for *Rus* [Russia], for our people, for our future" (*Bialik*, 591). A month later, Anna Akhmatova published her poem "July 1914." In the poem, a lone, one-legged figure in the courtyard speaks, Cassandra-like, in a language that reaches back to archaic, Slavonic words to name the disasters ahead:

Сроки страшные близятся. Скоро	Fearful times draw near. Soon
Станет тесно от свежих могил.	Earth will be crowded with fresh graves.
Ждите глада, и труса, и мора,	Expect famine, earthquakes, pestilence,
И затменья небесных светил.	And eclipse of the heavenly bodies.

For Akhmatova that date marked the beginning of the *real* twentieth century; it held a fateful place in her calendar throughout her life.

For Rachmaninoff, the date was fateful, too, at first in more mundane ways. His children's governess had a German passport: could he take her to a dacha in Finland for summer vacation? (*LN* 2, 79). He was called at least twice for military service, and joked that if he were sworn into the ranks he would probably end up leading a military band. He soon understood, however, that war with Germany threatened the two wellsprings of his life: his family life in Moscow and Ivanovka, and his professional life as a European artist who performed every season in England, Germany, and the rest of Europe. By August 1915 it was becoming clear that the Tsarist Government might be defeated.

Among patriotic activities undertaken soon after the war began, Ivan Bunin and other public figures in Moscow and St. Petersburg—now renamed Petrograd—collaborated in a project to raise money for war victims. It was an album, lavishly produced by A. A. Levenson at his famous Art Nouveau printing house in downtown Moscow. Among the contributions were poems by Balmont and Briusov, who was already off as a war correspondent; artwork by Ilya Repin and Leonid Pasternak; music by Glazunov, Scriabin, and others; and a choice Bunin story "The Grammar of Love." Rachmaninoff led the musical contributions with this setting of a verse from the New Testament. The expensive album, published in April 1915, apparently sold out in a single day (*Bialik*, 612).

The piano triplets that begin and end the song command attention to the two compact lines of text, igniting the air as it were, framing the last three words. These three words, "for his friends," are lengthened and greatly slowed down, to tender effect; rhapsodic piano phrases surround them with luminous color. The whole piece takes little more than a minute.

Among Rachmaninoff's songs, "From the Gospel of John" is virtually unknown: apart from four recordings, each in a set of "complete recorded songs," the song has no known performance history. Overlooked (and forgotten) as an album piece written for the war effort, its Biblical source made it unacceptable in the Soviet era either as a patriotic elegy or a recital song. Now it can be heard for what it is: a moving musical expression of the Church Slavonic text. The recording by Sergei Leiferkus and Howard Shelley brings out its great power.

Больши сея любве никто же имать,
Да кто душу свою положит за други своя.

Bólshy sejá ljubví niktó zhe imát',	Greater love hath no man than this,
Da któ dúshu svojú polózhyd	That he lay down his soul [life]
za drúgi svojá.	for his friends.

Text. **Holy Bible, Russian Church Slavonic Version**. Gospel of John, Chapter XV, Verse 13.

Music. 1914. Although the manuscript Rachmaninoff gave the publisher is dated 16 February 1915, the composer gave Boris Asafiev the date "autumn of 1914" (*LN* 2, 100); in the same list published earlier in *VOR 1957*, vol. 2, p. 260, the date given is "December 1914." A Major (C-sharp minor). 4/4. Довольно медленно (Rather slowly). For Bass Voice: C sharp–e[1]. Without opus.

Published in April 1915 by A. A. Levenson in "День печати. Кличъ. Сборникъ на помощь жертвамъ войны." Подъ редакціей И. А. Бунина, В. В. Вересаева, Н. Д. Мелешова ("Press Day. Appeal. Album for the Aid of Victims of the War." Edited by I. A. Bunin, V. V. Veresaev, N. D. Meleshov.) No dedication.

Recordings. Leiferkus, Nesterenko, Söderström, Suchkova.

Six Poems, Opus 38 (1916)

I.

Nearly a year into the war, the sudden death of Alexander Scriabin on 14 April 1915 came as a cruel shock to the whole nation. Attempts to lance an abscessed boil on Scriabin's upper lip gave him blood poisoning, and three days later he was dead at the age of forty-three.

The artistic world was stunned, and reactions were swift, with poets leading the way. Valery Briusov, Jurgis Baltrushaitis, and other Symbolists wrote poems, including Vyacheslav Ivanov's "Music is orphaned, and with her/Poetry, her sister" (*Iuzefovich*, 280). In Petrograd, Osip Mandelstam's initial thoughts turned into a long unfinished meditation on the whole arc of Russian culture, in which he compared the death of Scriabin with the death of Pushkin in 1837: "Pushkin and Scriabin are two transformations of one sun, two transformations of one heart. Twice the death of an artist has gathered together the Russian people and lighted a sun above them" (see *Brown 1973*, 231).

The Pasternak family—the artist Leonid, his wife Rozalia, a pianist, and their children Boris, Alexander, and Lydia—had known Scriabin for years as a neighbor at their summer dacha, a friend and guest at their musical evenings. For all of them, Scriabin's death was a deeply felt personal loss; for Boris, it was an especially keen loss because Scriabin had been his idol and the source of his inspiration to become a composer (see "Скрябин" in *Pasternak 1961* and, in English, *Pasternak 1959*). In the music world, responses were personal, but had a practical side, too. Scriabin's family had almost no money, and the publisher Jurgenson immediately forgave Scriabin's debts to him. Koussevitzky, Siloti and others gave benefit concerts with proceeds going to Scriabin's survivors.

Rachmaninoff's immediate reaction to Scriabin's death is unclear but was certainly unlike other losses he had experienced. On one hand, the death of Tchaikovsky was the loss of a man he revered and loved; such would be the loss of Sergei Taneyev, who died not long after Scriabin's funeral, from a heart illness brought on by a cold he caught following the coffin to the cemetery. On the other hand, there was no love or personal bond between Rachmaninoff and Scriabin, even though they were "brothers," fellow "cubs" in Zverev's piano school, who owed their formation as keyboard masters to Zverev and their other teachers. According to Matvei Presman, their classmate, the two of them were not close and actually disliked each other from the start; they had nothing in common in character, in disposition, or in the music they liked.

Although Chopin was an early interest for both, neither could find inspiration or sustenance in the direction the other took that interest. A striking difference between them is in their view of Russian songs, which Rachmaninoff loved from the start. Presman once asked Scriabin why he never wrote any romances: "they're one of the most interesting musical forms, and publishers make money on them, which means composers do too!" Scriabin's reply was that he could only write a romance to a text he himself had written, but he was never satisfied with the words (*VOR 1*, 171-2). (He did make one attempt, however, in 1891, "If only I could, like a beautiful dream," Хотел бы я мечтой прекрасной; Zara Dolukhanova has recorded it.) Their boyhood animosity passed, but it turned into a feeling of cool distance. By the time Scriabin died, the two composers had long since ceased to communicate.

Rachmaninoff was in Moscow on April 16, the day of the funeral mass, and went down to the square in the Arbat district where Scriabin lived. It was cold, raining, and thronged with people. The little neighborhood church, Nikola on the Sands, was too small to hold the full Synodical Choir, so the choirmaster had chosen only the most beautiful voices and the best singers. Rachmaninoff knew them well, from recent performances of his *All-Night Vigil* a month earlier. And he also knew the "deep and soul-stirring" music which the choir sang that day "with an almost unearthly beauty." It included, as he described it to a fellow musician, "the Lord's Prayer from the *Oktoechos*, which in reality consists only of the D major triad and its dominant chord, but the lovely sound of these nine- or ten-part harmonies in all grades of strength was so indescribably beautiful that it must have reduced the most obstinate heathen to tears and softened the heart of the most hardened sinner" (*Riesemann*, 180-1). "At that moment" Rachmaninoff resolved to make a concert tour of "all the major Russian towns" and to play "only pianoforte works composed by Scriabin" (ibid.). If he had been puzzled or confused about his feelings when he entered the crowded church that day, by the time he left, music had cleared his head and he knew what he had to do.

Rachmaninoff spent the summer in Finland to learn the Scriabin pieces he would have to play (before that, his custom in solo recitals had been to play only his own compositions). The works he chose were early and middle pieces, including some preludes of Op. 11 and études of Op. 42, the "Satanic Poem," the Second Sonata, with its tender, singing, then dancing Andante movement, and the dazzling Fifth Sonata, a piece driven by excited, forward-thrusting phrases rather than melody (a full list is in *VOR I*, 470-1, and *LN 3*, 444-5). He was a quick learner. A few days before his first solo recital in Moscow (12 October 1915), Rachmaninoff dropped by to see Alexander Goldenweiser. His program seemed short to him and he asked Goldenweiser to suggest some other work to include. Goldenweiser asked if he knew the "Fantasy," Op. 28? No, he did not, whereupon Goldenweiser handed the score to Rachmaninoff. As

Goldenweiser explains, "it is one of the most extraordinarily difficult pieces of Scriabin and quite long." Rachmaninoff played it right through, liked it, and included it in his recital a few days later (*VOR I*, 411). Of Op. 42, no. 5, in the same program, a favorite of Vladimir Horowitz, Rachmaninoff later said "It's a difficult étude—it took me a whole hour to learn it" (quoted in *Martyn*, 377).

Of thirty-seven concerts and recitals given by Rachmaninoff during the 1915–1916 season, sixteen were devoted entirely to Scriabin, and two more to mixed programs of works by both composers. He gave solo recitals of Scriabin's piano pieces in Moscow and Petrograd, Kharkov, Kiev, Saratov, Rostov-on-the-Don, Baku, and Tiflis (Tbilisi). In addition, he played Scriabin's Piano Concerto in F# minor in Petrograd, Moscow, and Tiflis. This was roughly half of his total of thirty-seven concerts that season. Concerts in some of these distant places involved train journeys of twenty-four or thirty-six hours during wartime conditions.

Rachmaninoff received little thanks from the press or the public for his homage to Scriabin. The general comment was that in playing Scriabin he was playing himself. Scriabin played differently, in his own unique way. As the composer Yury Nikolsky explained it, Scriabin had a "magical, soft touch, as if keys were not involved, but the sounds simply rose up and melted in the air." He went on to explain: "From the first sounds of the Second Sonata I understood that, as always, Rachmaninoff was not submitting himself to the composer, but the composer to himself. The whole program was performed not in the way Scriabin played and not in the way everyone else imitating Scriabin played. He played with his own 'Rachmaninovian' sound. It was very convincing in my opinion. His playing always gave me the greatest satisfaction. So it was this time. But during intermission, in the green room, I heard the harsh comments of the Scriabinists. I did not share their opinion and loved the performance. At any rate, I never heard Scriabin performed that way again" (*VOR 2*, 48). Sergey Prokofiev was at one of the recitals when the same angry outcry occurred after the Fifth Sonata. After the concert he tried to pacify Rachmaninoff by saying "'after all, Sergei Vasiliyevich, you did play it extremely well'; to which the master wryly replied, 'and you, I daresay, expected me to play it badly?'" (quoted in *Nice*, 126). Out in the provincial towns, however, some in the audience were virulent and threatening, shouting "*pórcha*"!—a dark word which means to cast a spell so powerful as to bring on illness or death to a living being. The performances of Scriabin by Rachmaninoff were a devilish act to damn Scriabin's music to Hell. He kept an ascetic mien, but he was troubled and disappointed.

After one of his concerts in Rostov, he had dinner with "Re," Marietta Shaginian, who was visiting her mother. He explained to her what he was trying to do: "Scriabin, after all, is a real musician, though he often forgot that and others forgot it during his lifetime. Now, some are trying to establish an occult school of Scriabin performance, and want to bury once and for all what he was born with, his innate musicality. I hear his musicality, I always tried to hear that in him. I see my concerts as simply the duty of one musician, still alive, before another musician, now passed on, to tell people how he hears his music. So here I am, traveling the Russian land, telling everyone about the music I hear" (*VOR* 2, 138-9).

2.

The 1915–1916 concert season was long and exhausting. On top of that, Rachmaninoff was obsessed with news from the front, reading the papers compulsively every day, worried about what the future might bring both to his career and to his Ivanovka estate, where he had been pouring all the money he earned into capital improvement. He joined his family there but was unable to work or concentrate on anything. Suffering with pains in his hands and temple, and encouraged by his wife, he decided to go to Kislovodsk in June to take a cure.

This southern zone, with its mild, sunny climate, fresh mountain air, and views of crags all around and distant high peaks, was gradually brought under Russian control after 1801. In the early 1800s, it was here that an untamed, romantic frontier began, a sort of Russian Wild-West, brilliantly portrayed in Mikhail Lermontov's novel *A Hero of Our Time* (1840). The main towns, originally military settlements, were Pyatigórsk (pyiti-GORSK, 1685 feet, pop. 32,000) and Kislovódsk (kees-lah-VOTSK, 2695 feet, pop. 14,000), both situated around abundant hot springs and numerous sources of famous mineral waters (the figures are from *Baedeker 1914*, 459-61). These towns became the favorite watering place in Russia. By Rachmaninoff's day, they were fully developed in comfortable and rather grand style, served by direct trains from Moscow, with good hotels, parks, concert halls, and bathing galleries staffed with doctors and assistants. Kislovodsk was especially well endowed with first-class amenities. When Rachmaninoff arrived in Kislovodsk in June 1916, he checked into the Hotel Rossiya on Poplar Allée, opposite the Narzan Spring (source of that same prized mineral water, the shortage of which, on a hot day in Moscow, is a bad omen in the opening scene of Mikhail Bulgakov's *Master and Margarita*).

The doctors examined him and recommended he go for treatments to the nearby resort of Essentuki (yes-sen-too-KEY), a dozen miles away, with its cold alkaline springs "efficacious in affections of the stomach and liver" (ibid.). This is where Marietta Shaginian found him when she visited the spa in June. He had asked her to bring him some poems he could use for songs, and she had them with her. She found Essentuki, with its older clientele taking serious treatments, depressing after the more fashionable Kislovodsk. Rachmaninoff was in a sanatorium in the two best rooms (there was a grand piano in one), with lackeys in white gloves standing by to wait on him. The nearby rooms were empty, and in his rooms the shades were lowered. When Marietta entered, he was dressed in a gray hospital robe and looked dreadful; she had seen him worried and discouraged before, but she had never seen tears in his eyes. Her appearance evidently brought him to tears because he felt himself in deep crisis, unable to *work*, unable to *compose*, and here was dear *Re*, his only real confidante to whom he could confess this desperate state, which he could not confess even to his wife. He began a long monologue about how his creativity had been stricken in his youth, like a damaged sapling, irreparably, when his First Symphony failed, how his powers as a composer had greatly waned since that disaster, how he would never be anything but just another well-known pianist and a mediocre composer. Marietta said little but tried to comfort him with sympathy and a supportive gaze. When he calmed down, she brought out a notebook with fifteen poems by Lermontov and twenty-six poems by contemporary Symbolist poets. He disliked modern poets, especially the Symbolists, but she persuaded him to take a serious look at some of their poems. Then and there she began going over the poems with Rachmaninoff, including the Symbolist texts which he eventually used for Opus 38, explaining to him her textual and musical ideas. As she tells it, after she left and while he was still in Essentuki, the composer sketched out the six new songs, finishing them in the autumn back home in Ivanovka (*VOR* 2, 150-2; also in *Shaginian*, 427-30.)

The gloom that Marietta found was quickly dispelled by the arrival of Rachmaninoff's closest friend and musical soulmate Feodor Chaliapin. He was staying at the Novaya Kazyonnaya Hotel in Essentuki, where he spent a few days taking treatments before they both returned to Kislovodsk. Stanislavsky and Koussevitzky were there too. No one could cheer up Rachmaninoff like Chaliapin. He was in great form, entertaining them with stories at a table in the park where they met every day. Rachmaninoff listened with smiles and laughter to Chaliapin's stories, jokes, bursts of song, impressions and funny scenes (*Kotliarov* 2, 121-2). There were little impromptu performances nearly every day.

Among the artists vacationing in Kislovodsk that summer was a young star of the Moscow Zimín Opera, the soprano Nina Koshetz. When Rachmaninoff arrived in Kislovodsk in June, Koshetz sent him a bouquet of roses with a note asking for his wife's address: she wanted to write Natalia a letter. He obliged and thanked her, expressing doubt that with Kislovodsk prices she could afford to spend so much on flowers (*LN* 2, 85). They had met in 1915 at a party, probably at the Silotis.

Nina Pavlovna Koshetz was born in Kiev in 1894 (though other dates—1891, 1892—are found in various sources), the daughter of Ukrainian opera singers, Pavel and Maria Koshits (Porai-Koshyts in Ukrainian). Her father, Pavel, became a leading tenor at the Bolshoi, but lost his voice and, as a result, committed suicide in 1904, when she was ten. As a girl she took piano lessons at the Moscow Conservatory and went on to pursue a complete musical education there. She graduated with distinction in 1913, completing courses in piano with Konstantin Igumnov, in composition with Sergei Taneyev (he also taught her to sing Tchaikovsky's songs), and in singing with Umberto Masetti, who taught such peerless singers as Antonina Nezhdanova and Nadezhda Obukhova. She also studied acting with Stanislavsky.

Rachmaninoff and Koshetz knew each other professionally by 1916. On 10 February of that year, he accompanied her at a recital in Moscow when she sang some of his songs, chosen by him, including "All was taken from me," Song 48, and "Dissonance," Song 75—dramatic songs which express devotion in very strong terms. A reviewer wrote: "Koshetz's voice sounded so fresh and full, her performance so musical and sincere, that the loud success that accompanies her appearances is completely understandable" (*VOR* 2, 494).

Natalia (in Ivanovka) and Nina (in Kislovodsk) had a friendly exchange of letters in the summer of 1916 in which they discussed their health, Nina's weight worries, and her preparation to sing Tatiana in *Eugene Onegin*. Natalia wrote Nina on 22 July, a week after Rachmaninoff was already home from the Caucasus: "I received your letter and the postcard [with your photo], which gave me great pleasure. The Caucasus has plainly been good for your health, and you seem rested, judging by your happy expression on the card. I asked Seryozha to tell me about you in every detail. I learned that you sang his romances frequently, that he accompanied you, and that everyone always liked your performance. I'm not surprised and am very glad to hear it. I was also interested to hear you sang some of Tchaikovsky's arias. I look forward to hearing you in *Onegin* next winter, and in any other opera you like. Restore your health and build up your strength as much as you can while you're in the Caucasus, since you're going to have an interesting winter, I think, and there will be a lot of work ahead. Seryozha, of course, is much better after Essentuki. Alas, in just one week he's already lost some of his tan. Our weather this summer has been sunless, rainy, and cold ...." (*LN* 2, 406-7).

Working in ensemble as singer and accompanist, Koshetz and Rachmaninoff proved to be ideal partners from the time they first performed together in February 1916. When she turned up in Kislovodsk that summer, Rachmaninoff was overjoyed. She was, as Koussevitzky described her, "a Chaliapin in petticoats" (*Nice*, 135). What could be better? She had musical brains and the best training the Moscow Conservatory could give. Her career after graduation was a brilliant success, proving her to be a very good singer and a good actress, who played her roles on the opera stage with flair (at times, some felt, excessive), and who was an incomparable recitalist. She had the allure and charm of a beautiful, stylish, talented woman completely at home in the world of Russian music, which is to say, in Rachmaninoff's world. It is no wonder that she captivated him.

Soon after meeting her in Kislovodsk, he wrote her a perfectly correct letter in which he addresses her in the formal "you," but which shows how relaxed and even intimate he feels with her: "Dearest Nina Pavlovna, I've had my bath and now I'm resting. Last night Stanislavsky unexpectedly dropped by and stayed the whole evening. I'm very sorry I wasn't able to come see you! I hoped to see you today, but 'it rained, and stopped, and rained again' [a quote from *The Miserly Knight*]. Maybe we'll see each other at 5.30 in 'our' pavilion at Spring No. 3, by fountain No. 4? Or maybe you'll come to my place at 4.30? Shall we have supper? All plans are good! Which do you prefer? I'm sending you your umbrella to keep away the rain and prying eyes. I kiss your dear hands. S. R." (*LN* 2, 86).

Among their plans, "all of them good," there would be many happy hours spent going through Rachmaninoff's book of songs. She would sing them, he would accompany her, and their invited friends, like Stanislavsky, would come by to listen. During these days together, the songs coming into being as Opus 38 already began to be associated with Koshetz, the artist who would perform them. If Rachmaninoff had sketched out the Opus 38 songs in Essentuki after listening to Marietta's textual preparation and musical ideas, as Marietta stated he had done, he might have shown Nina these sketches in Kislovodsk. She was a composer of romances herself, an accomplished pianist, and would certainly have had reactions to any work he showed her. Nina always maintained afterwards that they worked together on the songs. At some point, the composer gave her his sketches of the songs. Pencil drafts of all six songs (arranged in a different order) plus two other "unpublished songs" that were not included in the opus (they will be found below on pages 259-60) are among Rachmaninoff's papers at the Library of Congress. They are part of an undated notebook "from the collection of Nina Koshetz" (*T/N*, 121). Before Rachmaninoff left Kislovodsk that summer, they had already agreed that they would give at least one recital together in the coming season.

Rachmaninoff was still working on the songs in Ivanovka on 1 September when he wrote her saying: "You *must* sing the new songs, which I'll give you when I get to Moscow" (*LN* 2, 88). The recital program would consist of eighteen songs in all, six in each of three parts, with Opus 38 as the middle group. When the final schedule for the season was drawn up, there would be not one recital, but five. When the dates were eventually set, the recitals would be in Moscow (24 October), Petrograd (twice, 30 October and 2 December), Kharkov

(17 December), and Kiev (20 January). In addition to Opus 38, the songs in the program were "Many are the sounds" (Song 47), "The muse" (Song 63), "All was taken from me" (Song 48), "Arion" (Song 67), "The migrant wind" (Song 66), "What happiness" (Song 74), "At my window" (Song 56), "Excerpt from A. Musset" (Song 39), "I remember the day" (Song 72), "It cannot be" (Song 69), "To the children" (Song 53), "Dissonance" (Song 75). Possible encores were "Spring waters" (Song 32), "Lilacs" (Song 38), and "On the death of a siskin" (Song 41; see *LN* 2, 445, and 407-8).

The reviews were not only good, but the reviewers had difficulty finding a suitable precedent for such artistic excellence. The fact that the accompanist not only played with matchless beauty but was the composer himself put the recital in a class of its own. As for Koshetz, Rachmaninoff had made the best possible choice of partners, as Leonid Sabaneyev, among others, pointed out: "It would be hard to find a more suitable performer in terms of rare musicality, enormous artistic tact, and sheer power of expression, at times so shattering that many have come to the realization that in her we have an artist of the first rank" (*Keldysh*, 405). Boris Asafiev began by singling out her "simplicity, sincerity, directness," all very positive words in the Russian context. He went on to say that in her "deep inner spirituality and truth of human feeling" she could only be compared with Chaliapin. "One does not want to compare Koshetz with Chaliapin, but to say that they are phenomena of the same order—one may, one must. In their singing flows the direct, unmediated stream of life itself, so that terms like vocal school and technique and even artistic awareness are out of place" (ibid.). Asafiev made a special point of praising her acting, the skill with which she accompanied her singing with subtle facial and bodily gestures, naturally, and always expressive of the dramatic content of the romance. He argued that inherent dramatic content was a distinctive feature of Russian romances as opposed to a song or *Lied* (*Muzykal'nyi sovremennik*, No. 9-10, 9 Dec. 1916, pp. 14-15). He found her performance "the natural continuation of Chaliapin's great method of interpreting the Russian romance," adding that "it is no surprise that, like him, Koshetz is an opera singer."

After the Petrograd recital on 30 October 1916, Siloti gave a dinner party for the artists who had taken part in two evenings of concerts he had arranged. Among them was Sergey Prokofiev, who had conducted his "Scythian Suite" the night before. After the party, Prokofiev wrote in his diary: "[Rachmaninoff's] latest cycle, to words by new poets, is sheer delight. Nina Koshetz, who sang them, is an artist who merits the closest attention. But she was so unbearably full of herself at the Siloti supper party afterwards that I could not avoid getting at loggerheads with her. We exchanged a few caustic remarks." The songs, however, and her performance of them, inspired him to spend the next few days "in a rare degree of absorption, fluency and love composing Op. 27," his songs to five poems by Anna Akhmatova (*Prokofiev 2008*, 148). When Prokofiev heard Koshetz again in January 1917, he noted her "flaming temperament and ... striking ability to vary gradations of tenderness in her interpretation [of songs]." He was still annoyed by her vanity, but confessed "I rate her very highly as a singer, and I must admit as a woman—it is no wonder she captivated Rachmaninoff" (ibid., 168-9). By the summer, in Kislovodsk, Prokofiev was himself captivated by her, and had to collapse after two days trying to keep up with the "fantastic, volcanic Koshetz." She was in a frenzy, suddenly packing all her trunks and boarding a train to Moscow, having just said goodbye to Rachmaninoff. She gave Prokofiev her picture, signing it with the words "Tout passe, tout casse, tout lasse"—everything passes, everything breaks, everything tires one out (ibid., 218).

In material about Koshetz during this period, it is common to find assertions, always undocumented, to the effect that "her romance with Rachmaninoff became the talk of artistic Russia" (ibid., 148). Rachmaninoff never commented on this rumor nor gave any sign that it was true; Koshetz herself, however, as creator of her own legend, did not deny it, and gradually led others to believe that it was true. Today, one is free to believe her or not. In an artistic sense, however, what is certain, and what truly matters, is that they shared a rare musical rapport that shaped the creation of six of Rachmaninoff's finest songs. This creative burst was followed by the Opus 39 Études-Tableaux, composed immediately after the songs.

When Opus 38 was finished, Rachmaninoff dedicated all the songs to Nina Koshetz. Marietta Shaginian, as his *textmeister* who had given him the poems, was offended that the songs were not dedicated to her. She even made an excuse for not attending the recital after the composer had pleaded with her to come.When Marietta later told him she was hurt, he made a joke of it in the hope she would laugh it off, because he knew his debt to her and he did not want her to be hurt (*VOR 2*, 154). Nevertheless, she did not forget it, and in all the redactions of her memoir of Rachmaninoff she scoffs at Koshetz's lack of true style, citing the Medtners, who could not bear to sit through her recitals owing to her intolerable "gypsy" mannerisms. (Perhaps Marietta was unaware that as a young man Rachmaninoff was drawn to gypsy themes, gypsy style, and at least one gypsy woman). In her reminiscences of Rachmaninoff, Shaginian expresses her animosity towards Koshits but reduces it somewhat in a second edition (*VOR 1957*, vol. 2, 191 and *VOR 1988*, vol. 2, 146-7). In the end, both women had been essential to the success of Opus 38, not only materially, but spiritually: Marietta had dried his tears, and Nina had given him back his inspiration.

78 *Ночью в саду у меня* *In my garden at night*

Op. 38, No. 1

As soon as he read the text of this song, Rachmaninoff found music in it waiting to be written down. "It's remarkable," he told Marietta Shaginian, "that this Armenian poet has such a musical feeling for nature. If every poet writing about nature could do what he does, then we musicians would simply have to touch the text—and the song would be ready" (*VOR* 2, 153).

There is nothing "Armenian" about Alexander Blok's excellent Russian translation of Avetik Isahakian's original poem, but Rachmaninoff gives the music a hint of something "vaguely eastern" in the C natural of the fourth syllable of the voice part (*Martyn*, 264). The piano remains spare and laconic in the first half of the song, with an arpeggio break, then gives elaborate support to the lamentation with a second arpeggio followed by a filigree of thirty-second notes under the voice as the word "bitterly" is sung in a long, falling melisma.

The text has the timeless feel of folk poetry. The lines are short two-foot dactyls with a strong line-end marked by a rhyme. Within the line every third vowel is stressed to give an array of changing colors as the vowels are sung—O, U, A, and so on—a pattern the composer emphasizes with tenuto marks. The key word in the poem, *willow* (*íva*) is used in each quatrain in the diminutive form (*ívushka*), which heightens the feeling of intimacy and tenderness. Blok expertly uses a second diminutive form (*dévushka-zór'ka*, maiden-dawn) to set up a rhyme with *gór'ko*, "bitterly," in the beautiful falling four-note passage in line 7 that is the culmination of the song.

Alexander Blok (1880–1921) told a contemporary he was "excited" by the talent of Isahakian. He translated about twenty of Isahakian's poems (*Orlov 1980*, vol. 2, 164). Isahakian is remembered in Armenia today both as a poet and a patriot (his portrait is on the 10,000 dram banknote). Vladimir Nemirovich-Danchenko wrote Blok in November 1916, mentioning this song: "Musicians in Moscow… are giving high praise to Rachmaninoff these days. They're saying he recently wrote a romance to one of your poems that's almost the best thing he's written" (*VOR* 2, 516).

Ночью в саду у меня
Плачет плакучая ива,
И безутешна она,
Ивушка, грустная ива.

Раннее утро блеснёт—
Нежная девушка-зорька
Ивушке, плачущей горько,
Слёзы кудрями сотрёт.

Nóchju f sadú u menjá Pláchet plakúchaja íva, I bezutéshna aná, Ívushka, grúsnaja íva.	At night in my garden A weeping willow weeps, And nothing will console her, Sad willow, sad willow tree.
Ráneje útra blesnjót— Nézhnaja dévushka-zór'ka Ívushke, pláchushchij gór'ka, Sljózy kudrjámi satrjót.	With morning's first light— Dawn, tender maiden, From the willow, weeping bitterly, Will wipe away the tears with her tresses.

Text. **Aleksándr Blók**, 1916. Translation of a poem by **Avetik Isahakian** (1875–1957), Armenian poet (in Russian, his surname is spelled Исаакян). Untitled. First published in 1916 in *Sbornik armianskoi poezii* (Anthology of Armenian poetry), a publication of Maxim Gorky's "Parus" publishing house in Petrograd.

Set only by Rachmaninoff. Rachmaninoff changed the last word in the poem from отрёт to сотрёт, perhaps to make it easier to sing; the meaning "will wipe away" is unaffected.

Meter. Ternary. Dactyls of three feet:

Dáwn will consóle her sad wéeping,
Wípe away téars with her trésses…

Music. Op. 38, no. 1. G Minor. Varying time signatures, Lento. For High Voice: e^1–b^2 flat. The finished manuscript is dated 12 September 1916. First published with Opus 38 by Russian Music Publishers in Moscow and Petrograd in 1916.

Dedicated to **Nína Pávlovna Kóshetz**.

Recordings. Borele, Bryleva, Cahill, Del Grande, Dodoka, Furdui, Galante, Gerasimova, Izotova, Kasimova, Kazantseva, Kelessidi, Khromchenko, Kudriavchenko, Kurenko, Lapina, Larin, Lee, Maslennikov, Mok, H. Murphy, Orfenov, Pusar, Rautio, Rodgers, Söderström, Suchkova, Upshaw, Zamiatina.

79 *К ней*
To her

Op. 38, No. 2

The Symbolists were drawn to the "Orphic" quality of verse, to the myth that the power of poetry lies in its "music." Andrei Bely (1880–1934) was one of the most consciously musical of the Russian Symbolist poets, trained as a mathematician and a philosopher, the first to study Russian prosody statistically in order to understand its "laws," or at least the ways it behaves. He was incredibly diverse as a poet and prose writer and went through many phases.

In this poem Bely works with associated sounds that recur in repetition. The unit is a dactylic couplet, the first line with two stresses, the second with only one. For these pairs of five-syllable phrases, Rachmaninoff found a chromatic five-note piano phrase which sets the song in motion (*Martyn*, 265). The piano intensifies the emotion with rhapsodic passages that end each of the three parts.

The verbal material is as carefully designed as the ternary metrics: everything is in threes. The text expresses frustration and unfulfilled longing, just as the previous song "At night in my garden" expressed inconsolable sadness, but here we are presented with a classical image, the river Lethe. It implies a passage from life to death from which there is no return. In this poem addressed "To her," a beloved who is "washed away by Lethe's pale streams," the poet is like Orpheus, trying to be reunited with his Eurydice through music. It is an Orphic moment in the life of the poet.

Rachmaninoff turned it into a ravishing song. He retains the three-part structure of the lyric but elaborates it gradually, culminating in a three-part *cantabile* phrase on the repetition of the word "streams." The rather lingering postlude suggests the mystery implicit in such a text; Vladimir Ashkenazy brings this out well in the excellent recording he made of the song with Elisabeth Söderström.

Травы одеты
Перлами.
Где-то приветы
Грустные
Слышу, — приветы
Милые...

Милая, где ты, —
Милая!..

Вечера светы
Ясные, —
Вечера светы
Красные...
Руки воздеты:
Жду тебя...

Милая, где ты, —
Милая?

Руки воздеты:
Жду тебя
В струях Леты
Смытую
Бледными Леты
Струями...

Милая, где ты, —
Милая?

Trávy adéty	The grasses are adorned
Pérlami.	In pearls.
Gdé-ta privéty	Somewhere greetings
Grúsnyje	Sorrowful
Slýshu, — privéty	I hear, — greetings
Mílije...	Dear...
Mílaja, gdé tý, —	Dear one, where are you, —
Mílaja!..	Dear one!..
Véchera svéty	Lights of the evening are
Jásnyje, —	Visible, —
Véchera svéty	Lights of the evening are
Krásnyje...	Beautiful...
Rúki vazdéty:	Arms uplifted:
Zhdú tebjá...	I wait for you...
Mílaja, gdé tý, —	Dear one, where are you, —
Mílaja?	Dear one?
Rúki vazdéty:	Arms uplifted:
Zhdú tebja	I wait for you
F strújakh Léty	In streams of Lethe
Smýtuju	[You are] washed away
Blédnymi Léty	By Lethe's pale
Strújami...	Streams...
Mílaja, gdé tý, —	Dear one, where are you, —
Mílaja?	Dear one?

Text. **Andréi Bély (Borís Nikoláevich Bugáev)**, written in April 1908 in Moscow, and published in *Urna* (Urn) in 1909. Set only by Rachmaninoff.

Meter. Ternary. Dactyls of two feet, alternating with one:

Lights of the evening
Visible...

Music. Op. 38, no. 2. F Major. Few time signatures, 9/8, 6/8, Andante. For High Voice: f^1–b^2 flat. The finished manuscript is dated 12 September 1916. First published with Opus 38 by Russian Music Publishers in Moscow and Petrograd in 1916. Dedicated to **N. P. Kóshetz**.

Recordings. Asawa, Bryleva, Cahill, Del Grande, Dodoka, Evtodieva, Gerasimova, Kudriavchenko, Kurenko, D. Kuznetsova, Lee, Maslennikov, H. Murphy, Rodgers, Shpiller, Söderström, Suchkova, Tear, Upshaw, Woytowicz (in Polish).

80 *Маргаритки* *Daisies*

Op. 38, No. 3

The author of this exuberant declaration of love to the daisy (or "marguerite," as the Eurasian oxeye daisy is called) was a Russian poet who used the pseudonym Igor-Severianin (1887–1941), written with a hyphen to call attention to the literal meaning of his pen name: "Igor-Northman" (*Severianin 1999*, 5). He was a native of St. Petersburg, but liked spending time in an Estonian village near the Gulf of Finland, where he could fish. He wrote this poem there, at a farmhouse called, coincidentally, "Ivanovka," on a day in July, 1909 (ibid., 25). After years of publishing pamphlets with titles that evoke the days of Rurik and heroic exploits, then coming under various more modern influences, in 1911 he was finally recognized as a poet by Briusov and Blok. In 1913, the poet Feodor Sologub (see Song 82), his neighbor at a *dacha* in Estonia, wrote a warm introduction to his first major book, *The Thundering Cup*, which included "Daisies." It went through ten printings in five years.

He called himself the leader of "Egofuturism," which set out to rid poetry of bourgeois morality and starchy conventions; to this, he added a passion for neologisms, funny or strange. He was soon travelling the country with other like-minded rebels like Mayakovsky, Burliuk, and the Futurist crowd. Like them, he was one of the first poets to recite his poems to large audiences in lecture halls and auditoriums. He played to the gallery, some thought too much; for Sergey Prokofiev, that "vulgarized and diminished the effect of the brilliant flashes with which he peppers his verse" (*Prokofiev 2008*, 195). The public, especially the young public, loved him. His musicality (and irony, and whimsical overreach) caught the ear of Alexander Vertinsky, the renowned cabaret artist, who made some of his poems into musical cabaret acts. Prokofiev read all his poems, saying he found elements of musical composition, including counterpoint, at work in them (*Severianin 1999*, 8).

"Exuberance is beauty" said William Blake, a rule that may apply to small things, too, like this lyric in praise of daisies. The poet is surrounded by them, by their abundance; he compares their petals with white silk wings, their inner force with the elemental power of summer, their numbers with a "shining army," or "regiment" in Russian, an image that evokes Alexander Nevsky and the glorious past. His excitement mounts. In the last stanza, he orders earth to "fix the flowers drinks of dew and let the sap flow"; these daisies are living, sensual creatures. From there it is not far to adorable creatures, "girls" (not little girls, but *devushki*, young women), so beautiful you could fall in love: "Girls, I love you!" The poem is nothing less than a declaration of love. None of this romantic extravagance would work as well with *romashka*, the common Russian word for "daisy"; *margaritka* is more poetic, and also a girl's name.

Rachmaninoff subdues Severianin's exuberant means to his own different ends. Musically, he imagined this declaration of love not as a tempo Allegro, but as a slow Lento, a delicate and tender love song, decorated with trills and demisemiquavers. Max Harrison describes "Daisies" as "another perfect song, conceived all of a piece, in a single breath of subdued stillness" (*Harrison*, 203). Rachmaninoff reportedly said that in parts of the song, the singer was *accompanying* him, that is, supporting him, as he led the way on the piano. When he made a piano transcription of "Daisies," very little had to be done because so much of the song was in the piano part already.

In 1918 Severianin and others held another round of readings of their poems at the Polytechnic Museum in Moscow. A public vote was taken for "King of the Poets:" Balmont came in third, Mayakovsky second, and Severianin won the title. He went to Estonia, declaring himself King of Poets upon arrival. He never came back to Russia again. He did not consider himself an émigré, but a *dachnik* in Estonia. This, of course, was unrealistic, financially and politically. He tried to survive by giving readings in Europe, in places where Russian émigrés lived: Riga, Warsaw, Berlin, Paris, Bucharest, Bessarabia, Belgrade. The readings were successful, but most of the proceeds went to paying expenses. He continued to write. He never considered himself anti-Soviet, so he was not understood in the émigré press; the Soviets considered him a renegade and banned his works. In the sad and often tragic fate of the Russian diaspora, he was a loner on the periphery.

Hearing of his plight in 1926, Rachmaninoff sent money to him. Severianin replied: "Shining Colleague! You have acted as a true artist. I thank you from my heart for the gift of forty-five days of lyrical concentration, a period of time that these days means something" (*LN 3*, 406). Today, Severianin's works are published in Russia in both scholarly and penny editions and once more he has a large audience of readers.

О, посмотри! — как много маргариток
    И там и тут...
Они цветут; их много; их избыток;
    Они цветут.

Их лепестки трёхгранные — как крылья,
    Как белый шёлк.
В них — лета мощь, в них — радость изобилья,
    В них — светлый полк.

Готовь, земля, цветам из рос напиток
    Дай сок стеблю...
О, девушки, о, звёзды маргариток,
    Я вас люблю!

O, pasmatrí — kak mnóga margarítak	Oh, look! how many are the daisies
I tám i týt...	Here, and over there…
Aní tsvetút; íkh mnóga; íkh izbýtak;	They're in flower; so many; an abundance;
Aní tsvetút.	And all in flower.
Íkh lepestkí trjókhgránnyje —	Their three-edged petals are
kak krýl'ja,	like wings,
Kak bélyj shólk.	Like white silk.
V níkh — léta mósch, v níkh —	They have the power of summer,
rádast' izabíl'ja,	the joy of abundance,
V níkh — svétlyj pólk.	They're a shining army.
Gatóv', zemljá, tsvetám iz rós napítak	Earth, fix the flowers a drink of dew,
Dáj sók stebljú...	Give the stems juice…
Ó, dévushki, ó, zvjózdy margarítak,	Oh, girls, oh, starry daisies,
Já vás ljubljú!	I love you!

Text. **Igor Severiánin** (**Igor Lotarëv**), July 1909. First published in a St. Petersburg monthly in January 1910, it came out in book form in 1913 in his first collection of poems *Громокипящий кубок* ("A cup seething with thunder," a title taken from Tyutchev's poem "Spring thunderstorm"). First set in 1914 by the composer Nikolai Roslavets, but only Rachmaninoff's setting is well known.

Meter. Binary. Iambic, alternating lines of five and two feet:

They have the summer's power, abundant joy,
An army bright.

Music. Op. 38, no. 3. F Major. 3/4, Lento. For High Voice: f^1–a^2 flat. The finished manuscript is not dated. First published with Opus 38 by Russian Music Publishers in Moscow and Petrograd in 1916. Dedicated to **N. P. Kóshetz**.

Transcribed for piano by the composer; first performed in London in 1922. Transcribed for violin and piano by Fritz Kreisler; published in 1926. Transcribed for violin and piano by Jascha Heifetz in 1945; published in 1947 (on dating, see *T/N*, 122-3).

Recordings. Borele, Bryleva, Cahill, Davtian, Del Grande, Dionne, Dodoka, Furdui, Gerasimova, Kasimova, Kelessidi, Koshetz, Kudriavchenko, Kurenko, D. Kuznetsova, Larin, Lee, Maslennikov, I. Maslennikova, H. Murphy, Nortsov, Price, Pusar, Rodgers, Shpiller, Söderström, Suchkova, Upshaw, Woytowicz (in Polish), Zamiatina.

Transcriptions. *Piano:* Vladimir Ashkenazy, Idil Biret,Viktor Eresko, Morton Estrin, Sergio Fiorentino, Emil Gilels, Olga Kern, Aleksey Nasedkin, Sergei Rachmaninoff, Howard Shelley, Yevgeny Sudbin, Simon Trpceski, Arcady Volodos. *Piano Trio*: Bekova Sisters. *Violin:* Andres Cardenes, Friedemann Eichhorn, Jascha Heifetz, Sherry Kloss, Fritz Kreisler, Lydia Mordkovitch, David Oistrakh, Itzhak Perlman, Alexander Sitkovetsky.

81 *Крысолов*
The pied piper

Op. 38, No. 4

This fresh variation on the Pied Piper theme is by Valery Briusov (1873–1924), prolific Moscow poet, prose writer, publisher, editor, and translator (noted for his translations of Armenian poets, including Avetik Isahakian). The tale of the Pied Piper, or Rat Catcher, goes back to the brothers Grimm, and the subsequent poem by Goethe, who added that the Piper sometimes catches girls, too. This is the version that Franz Schubert and Hugo Wolf set to music.

Briusov expands Goethe's theme into a bold, boastful seduction, after which the girl is sent to the pasture to be with the lambs. What does the exchange of rings mean? It is taunting, even cruel, but the "tra-la-la" in every quatrain does not allow us to dwell on it.

Rachmaninoff wrote brilliant *scherzando* (playful) music for the song, starting with spiky staccato notes on the piano. The voice part is continually changing: now *dolce*, now *cantabile*, again *scherzando*, speeding up and slowing down. Hearing the song, we do not notice any cruelty in the lyric, because the music conveys capricious, playful, erotic seduction that is quite innocent.

Reportedly, Rachmaninoff told Koshetz that performing the song ought to come naturally to her, since she was the Pied Piper (*Martyn*, 265). With "Daisies," it was one of his two favorite songs in Opus 38 (*Shaginian*, 431).

Я на дудочке играю,
Тра-ля-ля-ля-ля-ля-ля,
Я на дудочке играю,
Чьи-то души веселя.

Я иду вдоль тихой речки,
Тра-ля-ля-ля-ля-ля-ля,
Дремлют тихие овечки,
Кротко зыблются поля.

Спите, овцы и барашки,
Тра-ля-ля-ля-ля-ля-ля,
За лугами красной кашки
Стройно встали тополя.

Малый домик там таится,
Тра-ля-ля-ля-ля-ля-ля,
Милой девушке приснится,
Что ей душу отдал я.

И на нежный зов свирели,
Тра-ля-ля-ля-ля-ля-ля,
Выйдет, словно к светлой цели,
Через лес, через поля.

И в лесу под дубом тёмным,
Тра-ля-ля-ля-ля-ля-ля,
Будет ждать в бреду истомном,
В час, когда уснёт земля.

Встречу гостью дорогую,
Тра-ля-ля-ля-ля-ля-ля,
Вплоть до утра зацелую,
Сердце лаской утоля.

И, сменившись с ней колечком,
Тра-ля-ля-ля-ля-ля-ля,
Отпущу её к овечкам,
В сад, где стройны тополя.
Тра-ля-ля-ля!

Já na dúdachke igráju,
Tra-lja-lja-lja-lja-lja-lja,
Já na dúdachke igráju,
Chí-ta dúshy veseljá.

Já idú vdol' tíkhaj réchki,
Tra-lja-lja-lja-lja-lja-lja,
Drémljut tíkhije avéchki,
Krótka zýbljutsa paljá.

Spíte, óftsy i baráshki,
Tra-lja-lja-lja-lja-lja-lja,
Za lugámi krásnaj káshki
Strójna fstáli tapaljá.

Málуј dómik tám taítsa,
Tra-lja-lja-lja-lja-lja-lja,
Mílaj dévushke prisnítsa,
Shto jéj dúshu óddal já.

I na nézhnyj zóf sviréli
Tra-lja-lja-lja-lja-lja-lja,
Výjdet, slóvna ksvétlaj tséli,
Cheres sát, cheres paljá.

I vlesú paddúbam tjómnym
Tra-lja-lja-lja-lja-lja-lja,
Búded zhdát' v bredú istómnym,
Fchás, kagdá usnjót zemljá.

Fstréchu góst'ju daragúju,
Tra-lja-lja-lja-lja-lja-lja,
Fplód' daútra zatselúju,
Sérttse láskaj utaljá.

I, smenífshys' snéj kaléchkam,
Tra-lja-lja-lja-lja-lja-lja,
Atpushchú jejó kavéchkam,
Fsád gde strójny tapaljá.
Tra-lja-lja-lja.

I play upon my little pipe,
Tra-la-la-la-la-la-la,
I play and play my little pipe,
Making merry many a soul.

I walk along the quiet stream,
Tra-la-la-la-la-la-la,
Gentle lambs are dozing,
Softly the fields are waving.

Sleep away, sheep and rams,
Tra-la-la-la-la-la-la,
Beyond meadows of red clover,
Shapely poplars rise.

A little house is hidden there,
Tra-la-la-la-la-la-la,
A darling girl will have a dream
That I gave my soul to her.

And to the tender call of a flute,
Tra-la-la-la-la-la-la,
She'll come to keep a rendezvous,
Through the woods, through the fields.

And in the forest under a dark oak,
Tra-la-la-la-la-la-la,
She'll wait in a daze, delirious,
For the hour when the earth sleeps.

I will meet my dear guest,
Tra-la-la-la-la-la-la,
Cover her till dawn with kisses,
Slake my heart's desire for caresses.

Then, exchanging rings with her,
Tra-la-la-la-la-la-la,
I'll let her join the lambs,
In the garden with the shapely poplars.
Tra-la-la-la!

TEXT. **Valéry Yákovlevich Briúsov**, 1904. Set only by Rachmaninoff.
METER. Binary. Trochaic, four-foot:

To a rendezvous she'll come,
Through the woods and through the fields.

Music. Op. 38, no. 4. C Major. No time signatures, Non allegro, scherzando. For High Voice: e^1–a^2. The finished manuscript is dated 12 September 1916. First published with Opus 38 by Russian Music Publishers in Moscow and Petrograd in 1916. Dedicated to **N. P. Kóshetz**.

Recordings. Bryleva, Cahill, Davtian, Del Grande, Dionne, Dodoka, Dolukhanova, Domnich, Gerasimova, Hendricks, Izotova, Kudriavchenko, Kurenko, Lee, Lemeshev, Maslennikov, H. Murphy, Rodgers, Shpiller, Söderström, Suchkova, Tear, Tourel, Upshaw, Zamiatina.

Transcriptions. *Tuba:* Gene Pokorny.

82 *Сон* *Sleep*

Op. 38, No. 5

Feodor Sologub (1863–1927) was born in St. Petersburg. His parents were serfs; a few years after Emancipation (1861) his father died of tuberculosis, and his mother was left to take care of two young children. His mother worked as a servant in a gentry house run by a widow who used corporal punishment on the boy for any dereliction. Despite this cruel childhood, he was gifted in mathematics and philosophy, finished school and higher education, and eventually became a teacher in a good school in St. Petersburg. He wrote numerous books of poetry, fiction, plays, and translations. He was revered by his contemporaries as one of the greatest Symbolist poets.

The poem shows Sologub as a master of language used not just to describe or represent reality, but to "create" it. Its title is sometimes translated as "dream" but the text makes it clear this is "sleep" as an oneiric state; in Russian, *son* means both. I have used the pronoun "he" rather than "it" in my translation, since "sleep" is a masculine noun, and appears here as a kind of being with eyes, lips, wings, and shoulders. The poem is last in a series of poems in which the image of *son* is very frequent, sometimes meaning death. (There is a song by Hugo Wolf, "An der Schlaf," which employs that idea, but playfully.) The meter is unusual, compact. The first word in the second line is a rare Old Slavic verb meaning "wish for," in an antiquated participial comparative form one might find only in a poem by Tyutchev; it makes a strong, almost magical effect.

As a song this is one of Rachmaninoff's most beautiful. It is divided into two parts, with a long postlude. In the first half of the song, the piano part is terse, but sets the terms with two notes on the right hand, an A flat and B flat, repeated, "like the half-heard sound of a distant bell ringing." In the second half, the piano enters richly, anticipating the voice phrases "like a pre-echo from the unconscious mind" (*Martyn*, 266). The recording by Zara Dolukhanova is one of the most remarkable: the singing is thrilling and the words crystal clear.

В мире нет ничего
Вожделенее сна,—
Чары есть у него,
У него тишина,
У него на устах
Ни печаль и ни смех,
И в бездонных очах
Много тайных утех.

У него широки,
Широки два крыла,
И легки, так легки,
Как полночная мгла.
Не понять, как несёт,
И куда, и на чём,
Он крылом не взмахнёт,
И не двинет плечом.

V míre nét nichevó	Nothing in the world
Vazhdelénneje sná, —	Is more wished for than sleep,—
Cháry jést' unevó,	He has powers to charm,
Unevó, tishyná.	He has stillness.
Unevó naustákh	On his lips there is
Ni pechál' i ne smékh,	Neither sorrow nor laughter,
I vbezdónnykh achákh	And in his fathomless eyes
Mnóga tájnykh utékh.	Are many secret pleasures.
Unevó shyrakí,	He has wide,
Shyrakí dvá krylá,	Two wide wings,
I lekhkí, tak lekhki,	And they're light, as light
Kak palnóchnaja mglá.	As midnight darkness.
Ne panját', kak nesjót,	How you're borne is unknown,
I kudá, i nachóm,	And whence, and on what,—
Ón krylóm ne vzmakhnjót,	He won't flap his wing,
I ne dvínet plechóm.	And he won't move his shoulder.

Text. **Feódor Sologúb** (**Feódor Kuzmích Tetérnikov**), May 1886. First published in *Тени:* "Рассказы и стихи" (*Shadows:* "Stories and poems"), St. Petersburg, 1896, p. 108; in *Collected Works* 1913, vol. 1, p. 118. Set only by Rachmaninoff.

Meter. Ternary. Anapest, two feet:

Nothing's wished for like sleep,
More devoutly desired,
Neither laughter nor grief
In his fathomless eyes.

Music. Op. 38, no. 5. D-flat Major. 3/4, Lento. For High Voice: f^1–b^2 flat. The finished manuscript is dated 2 November 1916. First published with Opus 38 by Russian Music Publishers in Moscow and Petrograd in 1916. Dedicated to **N. P. Kóshetz**.

Recordings. Borele, Bryleva, Cahill, Del Grande, Dionne, Dodoka, Dolukhanova, Fleming, Gerasimova, Keenlyside, Kozlovsky, Kudriavchenko, Kurenko, Lapina, Lee, Makarina, Maslennikov, H. Murphy, Rodgers, Shpiller, Söderström, Suchkova, Upshaw.

Transcriptions. *Cello*: Brian Stucki. *Clarinet:* Wagner Campos. *Piano:* Earl Wild.

83 *Ay!* *A-oo!*

Op. 38, No. 6

Sometimes translated as "The Quest," this is a perfect song to end a cycle of songs that (except for "Sleep") take up various aspects of love. Balmont is a poet who uses extravagant metaphors and, by taking them seriously, makes them do the work.

The central metaphor here is the title "a-oo." This is a phrase you shout when you've lost track of each other in the woods hunting for mushrooms, or any similar situation: "hello, is anyone there? where are you? I'm over here! A-oo! I'm looking for you!" The poet is looking for the woman with "gentle laughter," a fleeting vision, a fairy tale of a woman who connected with him, then disappeared, leaving only a memory of her soft laughter deep inside him. Climbing the mountain together apparently indicates how arduous their union might have been. The line "a flower lit a candle for a flower in daylight" is a metaphor for the singularity and beauty of their encounter. The whole poem is hyperbolic, and almost comical in its ineffability. It is fun, but we take it seriously, if we are Symbolists, because these things have a higher meaning.

Balmont was a very attractive and charismatic bard: of all the famous people Sergey Prokofiev knew, he was most thrilled to meet Balmont (who told him his name was stressed on the second syllable: Balmónt). In Prokofiev's diary for the summer of 1917, he tells the story of encountering Balmont in Kislovodsk. Balmont was visiting a gorgeous twenty-three-year-old admirer who, perched on the edge of "The Rock of Perfidy and Love," inspired by her love for the poet, felt she could fly, but crashed to the ground, breaking a leg. Balmont carried her body back from the perfidious rock. If she was crying "a-oo" as she leapt, Balmont was there to answer. While she recovered in a hotel, Balmont visited her daily (*Prokofiev 2008*, 220). Richard Taruskin, in his two-volume study of Stravinsky's Russian years, writes that "a-oo" occurs in two of Rimsky-Korsakov's operas, in Nápravník's opera *Dubrovsky*, and Stravinsky's song "Pastorale," a vocalise on the "a-oo" text. It was "a kind of password among the Russian Symbolist poets" (*Taruskin 1996*, vol. 1, 364).

The song portrays the eager, urgent anticipation of the poet's quest in the "fluttering semi-quavers" of the piano, showing impatience; on the cry of "A-oo" there is an octave leap. The tension slacks in the postlude, emphasizing the lover's diminishing hopes; a "quiet, unresolved final cadence leaves a question mark" (*Martyn*, 267).

Of all the songs in Rachmaninoff's songbook, the Opus 38 songs are the most contemporary in feeling, and unlike the others in their compositional patterns. They fit together as a cycle, and as such are often performed as a cycle. Outside Russia, singers who have mastered the sounds of the Russian language have in recent years recorded the entire cycle: Heidi Grant Murphy, Dawn Upshaw, Joan Rodgers, Teresa Cahill, and, of course, Elisabeth Söderström. These performances are all very good, and more will come. The mezzo-soprano Magdalena Kožená sang the entire cycle in her recital at Carnegie Hall in February 2013. Of male singers, only the fine Soviet tenor Aleksei Maslennikov has recorded them all.

Твой нежный смех был сказкою изменчивою,
Он звал, как в сон зовёт свирельный звон.
И вот венком, стихом тебя увенчиваю,
Уйдём, бежим вдвоём на горный склон.

Но где же ты? Лишь звон вершин позванивает.
Цветку цветок средь дня зажёг свечу.
И чей-то смех всё вглубь меня заманивает.
Пою, ищу. "Ау! Ау!" кричу.

Tvój nézhnyj smékh byl skáskaju izménchivaju,	Your gentle laughter was a fairy tale of changing mood,
On zvál, kak f són zavjót svirél'nyj zvón.	Calling like a flute that summons me to dream.
I vót venkóm, stikhóm tebjá uvénchivaju,	And so with a wreath of verse I crown you,
Ujdjóm, bezhým vdvajóm na górnyj sklón.	Let's go, let's run together to the mountain slope.
No gdé zhe tý? Lizh zvón vershýn pazvánivajet.	But where are you? I only hear the ringing sound of the heights.
Tsvetkú tsvetók sred' dnjá zazhók svechú.	A flower for a flower in daylight lit a candle.
I chéj-ta smékh fsjó vglúp' menjá zamánivajet.	And someone's laughter deep inside allures me.
Pajú, ishchú. Aú! Aú! krichú.	I sing, I search. "A-oo! A-oo!" I shout.

Text. **Konstantín Dmítriyevich Balmónt**, 1909. From *Хоровод времени* (Circle dance of time), St. Petersburg, 1909. Set only by Rachmaninoff.

Meter. Binary. Iambic pentameter:

And with a wreath of verse I crown you now,
Let's run together to the mountain slope.

Music. Op. 38, no. 6. D-flat Major. 3/4, Andante. For High Voice: c^1–b^2 flat. The finished manuscript is dated 14 September 1916. First published with Opus 38 by Russian Music Publishers in Moscow and Petrograd in 1916. Dedicated to **N. P. Kóshetz**.

Recordings. Borele, Bryleva, Cahill, Del Grande, Dodoka, Evtodieva, Gerasimova, Kharitonov, Kudriavchenko, Kurenko, D. Kuznetsova, Lee, Maslennikov, I. Maslennikova, H. Murphy, Rodgers, Söderström, Suchkova, Tear, Upshaw.

After Russia (1917–1943)

When the Romanov dynasty fell in February 1917, Rachmaninoff finished the spring concert season in various Russian cities, donating part of his earnings to the soldiers of "my now liberated country" (*B/L*, 204). In April he went to his estate in Ivanovka to oversee the spring sowing. He found chaos there, as a fanatical group of SRs (members of the Social Revolutionary Party) from a neighboring district had been urging the villagers at Ivanovka to take over the estate—buildings, livestock, vehicles and equipment—claiming it as their own communal property. Life in a household near Russian fields, streams, and forests was a sacred value for Rachmaninoff. He had put everything he earned since 1909 into Ivanovka, but now realized it was all in jeopardy. He would have simply given his people everything, but could not, owing to large outstanding debts (*LN* 2, 103). Within five years, nothing remained. (For reminiscences by descendants from Ivanovka, with photographs of the Rachmaninoff and Satin families as well as the restored property and museum today, see *Ermakov*.)

Rachmaninoff spent the summer in the Caucasus and the Crimea; in Yalta on 5 September he gave what turned out to be his last performance in Russia. When he returned to Moscow, he took up an old task long put off, the revision of his First Concerto, working on it so intensively that he failed to realize that the sounds of gunshots on the night of 25 October meant another change in government. Now his work was constantly being interrupted by obligatory meetings of the "soviet" of his apartment building to discuss such matters as the reallocation of apartment space and duty rosters for snow removal by the residents. Concert life was halted temporarily, and he now had no way to earn the money he needed to support his family; he could borrow, and he did, but he hated to do so. In late November, out of the blue and "by the grace of God," came a telegram from a Swedish concert manager offering him an invitation to perform abroad, his first offer since the beginning of the war. It was a solution to his immediate problem, but "his acceptance created far more serious problems that remained with him till his dying day as an émigré" (*B/L*, 205-6). He was given passports and exit visas for himself and his family to make a two-month concert tour of Norway and Sweden (*LN* 2, 414). On 23 December, at the Finland Station in Petrograd, they boarded a train to Finland and traveled from Finland by open sledge and train to Stockholm. Chaliapin could not see them off, but sent a jar of caviar and a loaf of home-made white bread to the station for the journey (*VOR 1*, 48).

Rachmaninoff soon understood that he could earn a steady income only by becoming a concert pianist. He would have to learn new repertoire, regain his technique, and practice intensively. From February to July 1918 he played twelve engagements in Scandinavian cities, including one in Stockholm in May, where he accompanied the brilliant Russian soprano Adelaida Andreyeva-Skilondz in a recital of his songs. (Elisabeth Söderström, who made splendid recordings of all of Rachmaninoff's songs, studied singing with Andreyeva-Skilondz from an early age [see *Söderström* 1992].) With several invitations to America, including one to become conductor of the Boston Symphony (which Rachmaninoff turned down), he got an American visa and sailed with his family from Oslo to New York through still dangerous waters, arriving 10 November 1918, the day before the war ended. Sergey Prokofiev, already in New York via Japan, heard of his arrival and went to see him. They talked for an hour. Rachmaninoff complained about getting old and losing all his money to the Bolsheviks, and patiently showed Prokofiev how to bandage the tip of his wounded finger so he could still feel the keys: "Rachmasha is truly a marvelous person!" exclaimed Prokofiev in his diary (*Prokofiev 2008*, 353). Prokofiev soon learned to his dismay, however, that as long as Rachmaninoff was in America, no other Russian had any chance of making a major career as a pianist there, so popular was Rachmaninoff already with the American audience.

As someone had said to him when he was leaving Russia, his true fortune was in his hands, those large, soft paws which he knew how to take care of. Starting in January 1919 Rachmaninoff played up to seventy concerts every year, mostly in North America but with many appearances in Europe; he played with symphony orchestras in most years, especially the Philadelphia Orchestra, which became his favorite; he gave dozens of solo recitals every year, not only in Boston and New York, but in Altoona, Davenport, Asheville, Corpus Christi, Fresno, Syracuse, and dozens of other American cities which had a suitable hall where Steinway & Sons could deliver and tune a piano for him (a service they provided all his life). He set a standard no one ever surpassed. He liked recording, and left a legacy on piano rolls and discs, though the Victor company never saw fit to record more of his extensive repertoire, including works by Beethoven, Schubert, Chopin, and Liszt.

When he lived on Riverside Drive in New York in the twenties, to his great joy he hosted Stanislavsky and his traveling players. He built a fine new house on the shore of Lake Lucerne, but when the Second World War began, he and Natalia lived in their house in Beverly Hills, where he could tend his garden. He sent money to his old friend Bunin and other émigrés in need, and donated generously to Russian war relief. Eventually, he came back to composition, writing major works like the "Rhapsody on a Theme of Paganini." He felt songs needed a Russian audience, and thus he wrote no more of them once he had left Russia. After his last recital in Knoxville on 17 February 1943, he did not feel well and returned to California, where he died a few weeks later on 28 March 1943, just short of his seventieth birthday.

Two Sacred Songs (1916)

1.

After drafting the Opus 38 songs, Rachmaninoff evidently gave to Nina Koshetz the pencil sketches to two "sacred" songs. After Koshetz died in 1965, her daughter Marina Koshetz (1912–2001) donated them to the Rachmaninoff collection in the Library of Congress in 1970. She published them in 1973, indicating that they were "originally intended to form part" of the opus (*T/N*, 173). Such an intention is dubious, however, because the texts below, especially the first one, a prayer, are not suited for the Opus 38 cycle. Except for the recording made by Joan Rodgers in 1994 or 1995 on Chandos, I have not found any performance history for these two songs.

The text of the first song is by "K. R.," pseudonym of Konstantin Romanov (1858–1915), Grand Duke and uncle to Nicholas II (see *TCS*, 237-250). He was an amateur musician and poet. Rachmaninoff had set one of his poems in 1895 in his Opus 15 choruses for women's or children's voices. The text here, called "A Prayer," was written in 1886 in the palace at Pavlovsk outside St. Petersburg, where the Grand Duke lived, and where he died before the events of 1917 that brought down the Romanov dynasty. It is a pious poem, and the song begins as a slow chant. It culminates in the penultimate line on the phrase "deep love."

Научи меня, Боже, любить Всем умом Тебя, всем помышленьем, Чтоб и душу Тебе посвятить И всю жизнь с каждым сердца биеньем.	Teach me, o God, to love Thee with all my mind, all my thoughts, To consecrate to Thee my soul And all my life with each beat of my heart.
Научи Ты меня соблюдать Лишь Твою милосердную волю, Научи никогда не роптать На свою многотрудную долю.	Teach me to obey Only Thy gracious will. Teach all of us here Not to complain of our difficult lot.
Всех, кого Ты пришел искупить Ты Своею Пречистою Кровью, Бескорыстной, глубокой любовью Научи меня, Боже, любить!	All whom Thou came to redeem With Thy Precious Blood With Thy deep, pure love, Teach me, o God, to love.

Text. **K. R.**, written 4 September 1886 in Pavlovsk.

Meter. Ternary. Three-foot anapest:

Teach me love for Thee, Lord, with my mind,
With each thought and each beat of my heart.

Music. 1916. Without opus. D major. 3/4, Slowly, with deep feeling. For High Voice: c^1—a^2 flat. Published in 1973, Belwin-Mills Publishing Corp., Melville, N. Y., as "Two Sacred Songs." Dedicated to **N. P. Koshetz**.

Recordings. Rodgers.

2.

The second song is by Feodor Sologub, the poet we encountered in Song 82. The song is in two parts that correspond to the two stanzas in Sologub's poem: the first stanza with its characteristic images of the Russian natural world (the steppe grass, the forest and field, the dusty road), and the second with images of man, the word, the song of praise, and time in endless renewal.

In the first half of the song, the piano supports the vigorous opening shout of glory in the voice part with repeated chords that indicate rapidly pealing bells, as the voice culminates in a double line of rising vocalise. The second half begins slowly and quietly, in keeping with a hushed summoning of new words of praise one after the other. Then the vigor of the opening resumes, with a vocalise in rising intonation repeated multiple times.

Всё хочет петь	All things want to sing
и славить Бога, —	and glorify God, —
Роса, и ландыш,	The dew, the lily-of-the-valley,
и ковыль,	the tall steppe grass,
И лес, и поле, и дорога,	And forest, and field, and road,
И ветром зыблемая пыль.	And the dust blown by the wind.
Ah, (vocalise, repeated).	Ah, Ah…
Они зовут за словом слово,	They summon word upon word,
И песню их из века в век	And their song from age to age
В иных созвучьях слышит снова	In other harmonies is heard again
И повторяет человек.	And sung anew by man.
Ah… (vocalise, multiple repeats).	Ah, Ah…

Text. **Feódor Sologúb (Feódor Kuzmích Tetérnikov)**, written 8 October 1898. First published in *Русский вестник* (Russian Herald), 1902, No. 10, p. 461. Sourced 31 March 2013 at http://www.fsologub.ru/lib/poetry/poetry_369.html.

Meter. Binary. Iambic tetrameter:

All Glory sung to God again
In other harmonies is heard.

Music. 1916. Without opus. E major. 4/4, [With animation] (*T/N*, 173). For High Voice: c^1—a^2 flat. Published in 1973, Belwin-Mills Publishing Corp., Melville, N. Y., as "Two Sacred Songs." This publication erroneously identifies the poet as "G. Sologub." Dedicated to **N. P. Koshetz**.

Recordings. Rodgers.

Bibliography

Abraham, Gerald. *Essays on Russian and East European Music.* Oxford and New York: Oxford University Press, 1985.

________. "Russia." In *A History of Song,* ed. Denis Stevens. Westport: Greeenwood Press, 1982.

________. *Slavonic and Romantic Music.* New York: St. Martin's Press, 1968.

Agin, M. S. *Vokal'no-èntsiklopedicheskii slovar'. Biobibliografiia* [Vocal encyclopedia. Bio-bibliography]. Five vols. Moscow: Gnesin Music Academy, 1991-1994.

Aikhenval'd, Iulii I. *Siluèty russkikh pisatelei* [Silhouettes of Russian writers]. Moscow: Respublika, 1994.

Apukhtin, A. N. *Polnoe sobranie stikhotvorenii* [Complete poems]. Edited by R. A. Shatseva. Biblioteka poèta, Bolshaiia seriia. Leningrad: Sovetskii pisatel', 1991.

Asaf'ev, Boris Vl. *Russkaia muzyka XIX i nachalo XX veka* [Russian music of the 19th and Early 20th Century]. Leningrad: Muzyka, 1979.

Baedeker, Karl. *Baedeker's Russia 1914.* London: George Allen & Unwin, 1971.

Balakirev, M. *Romansy i pesni dlia golosa s fortepiano* [Romances and songs for voice and piano]. Two vols. Moscow: Muzyka, 1978, 1979.

Bal'mont, Konstantin. *V bezbrezhnosti* [In boundlessness]. Moscow: T-vo skoropechatni A. A. Levenson, 1895.

________. *Polnoe sobranie stikhov* [Complete poems]. Moscow: Skorpion, 1909.

Barr, Steven C. *The Almost Complete 78 rpm Record Dating Guide.* Huntington Beach CA: Yesterday Once Again, 1992.

Beketova, Ekaterina Andreevna. *Stikhotvoreniia.* Posmertnoe izdanie. [Poems. Posthumous edition]. SPb: Tipografiia brat'ev Panteleevykh,1895. [Seen at Library of Congress].

Benedetti, Jean. *The Moscow Art Theatre Letters.* New York: Routledge, 1991.

Bennett, John R. *Melodiya: A Soviet Russian L. P. Discography.* Westport and London: Greenwood Press, 1981.

Bertensson, Sergei and Jay Leyda with the assistance of Sophia Satina. *Sergei Rachmaninoff A Lifetime in Music.* Bloomington and Indianapolis: Indiana University Press, 2001.

Bialik, B. A., ed. *Russkaia literatura kontsa XIX-nachala XX v.*[Russian literature of the late 19th-early 20th centuries]. Moscow: Nauka, 1972.

Bialyi, G. A., ed. *Poety 1880–1890-kh godov* [Poets of the 1880–1890s]. Second ed, Biblioteka poeta, Bol'shaia seriia. Leningrad: Sovetskii pisatel', 1972.

Birkbeck, William John, ed. *Russia and the English Church during the last fifty years, containing a correspondence between Mr. William Palmer, fellow of Magdalen College, Oxford, and M. Khomiakoff, in the years 1844-1854.* London: Rivington, Percival & Co., 1895. Republished in 1969 by Gregg International Publishers in Farnborough, England.

Blackmore, E. H. and A. M. *Selected Poems of Victor Hugo.* Chicago and London: University of Chicago Press, 2001.

Blagoi, D. D. "Tiutchev v muzyke" [Tiutchev in music]. In *Literaturnoe nasledstvo,* "Fedor Ivanovich Tiutchev." Vol. 97, Book 2. Moscow: Nauka, 1989.

Blok, Aleksandr. *Sobranie sochinenii* [Collected works]. Edited by V. N. Orlov et al. Vol. 5 (1962). Moscow-Leningrad: Gosudarstevennoe izdatel'stvo khudozhestvennoi literatury, 1960–63.

Bogdanov-Berezovskii, V. M., ed. *Molodye gody S. V. Rakhmaninova* [Young years of S. V. Rachmaninoff]. Moscow-Leningrad: Gos Muz Izd, 1949.

Borovsky, Victor. *Chaliapin: A Critical Biography.* New York: Alfred A. Knopf, 1988.

________. *A Triptych from the Russian Theatre: An Artistic Biography of the Komissarzhevskys.* Iowa City: University of Iowa Press, 2001.

Boyd, Malcolm. "Medtner and the Muse." *The Musical Times* 121, no. 1643 (January 1980): 22-25.

Briantseva, Vera Nik. *S. V. Rakhmaninov.* Moscow: Vsesoiuznoe izdatel'stvo "Sovetskii kompozitor", 1976.

Briusov, Valerii. *Sobranie sochinenii v semi tomakh* [Collected works in seven volumes]. ed. P. G. Antokol'skii et al. Seven vols. Moscow: Khudozhestvennaia literatura, 1973-5.

Broude, Inna. *Ot Khodasevicha do Nabokova: nostal'gicheskaia tema v poezii pervoi russkoi emigratsii* [From Khodasevich to Nabokov: the theme of nostalgia in the poetry of the first Russian emigration]. Tenafly: Hermitage, 1990.

Brown, Clarence. *Mandelstam*. Cambridge, England: Cambridge University Press, 1973.

Brown, Malcolm Hamrick. "Native Song and National Consciousness in Nineteenth-Century Russian Music." In *Art and Culture in Nineteenth-Century Russia*, edited by Theofanis George Stavrou, 57-84. Bloomington: Indiana University Press, 1983.

Buckler, Julie A. *The Literary Lorgnette. Attending Opera in Imperial Russia*. Stanford, California: Stanford University Press, 2000.

Bullock, Philip Ross. "Ambiguous Speech and Eloquent Silence: The Queerness of Tchaikovsky's Songs." *19th-Century Music* 32, no. 1 (2008): 94–128.

Bunin, Ivan. "Ia opiat odinok (Kak svetla, kak nariadna vesna)." *Zhurnal dlia vsekh* No. 12, December (1900).

_________. *Vospominaniia* [Memoirs]. Moscow: Zakharov, 2003.

Calvocoressi, M. D. and Abraham, Gerald. *Masters of Russian Music*. New York: Knopf, 1936.

Campbell, Stuart, ed. *Russians on Russian music, 1880–1917*. Cambridge: Cambridge University Press, 2003.

Cannata, David Butler. "Rachmaninoff's Concept of Genre." *Studies in Music from the University of Western Ontario* 15 (1995): 59-73.

_________. *Rachmaninoff and the Symphony*. Bibliotheca Musicologica, Innsbruck-Wien. Lucca: LIM Editrice, 2000.

Challis, Natalia. *The Singer's Rachmaninoff*. New York: Pelion Press, 1989.

Chambers, Helen. *Humor and Irony in Nineteenth-Century German Women's Writing: Studies in Prose Fiction, 1840–1900*. Rochester, New York: Camden House, 2007.

Chekhov, Anton. *Letters of Anton Chekhov*, translated by Michael Henry Heim, in collaboration with Simon Karlinsky. Selection, Commentary and Introduction by Simon Karlinsky. New York: Harper & Row, 1973.

_________. *Sobranie sochinenii v dvenadtsati tomakh* [Collected works in twelve volumes], ed. V. V. Ermilov et al. Moscow: Gosudarstvennoe izdatel'stvo khudozhestvennoi literatury, 1960-64.

_________. *The Complete Plays*, translated, edited, and annotated by Laurence Senelick. New York and London: W. W. Norton & Company, 2006.

Cooke, Brett. *Pushkin and the Creative Process*. Gainesville, Florida: University Press of Florida, 1998.

Copland, Aaron and Vivian Perlis. *Copland: 1900 through 1942*. New York: St. Martin's/Marek, 1984.

Creighton, James. *Discopaedia of the Violin*. Toronto and Buffalo: University of Toronto Press, 1974.

Cunningham, Robert. *Sergei Rachmaninoff: a bio-bibliography*. Westport, Conn: Greenwood Press, 2001.

Danilova, Alexandra. *Choura: The Memoirs of Alexandra Danilova*. New York: Alfred A. Knopf, 1986.

Day, Timothy. *A Century of Recorded Music: Listening to Musical History*. New Haven: Yale University Press, 2000.

Draper, Hal. *The Complete Poems of Heinrich Heine*. Boston: Suhrkamp/Insel and Oxford University Press, 1982.

Dubrovskaia, E. "Vse romansy Rakhmaninova" [All Rachmaninoff's romances]. *Muzykal'naia zhizn'*, no. 13 (1975).

Duke, Vernon. *Passport to Paris*. Boston, Toronto: Little, Brown and Company, 1955.

Elliott, Martha. *Singing in Style: A Guide to Vocal Performance Practices*. New Haven and London: Yale University Press, 2006.

Emelianova, Nina Nik. *Ivanovka v zhizni i tvorchestve Rakhmaninova* [Ivanovka in the life and work of Rachmaninoff]. Voronezh, 1984.

Èrenburg, Il'ia. *Liudi, Gody, Zhizn'* [People, years, life]. 3 vols. Moscow: Sovetskii pisatel', 1990.

Ermakov, Aleksandr Ivanovich. *Ivanovka. Vremena. Sobytiia. Sud'by.* [Ivanovka. Times. Events. Fates.] Moscow: Izdatel'stvo fonda Iriny Arkhipovoi, 2003.

Ewen, David. *Musicians Since 1900.* New York: The H. W. Wilson Company, 1978.

Fanning, David. Notes to CD Hyperion A67700 "Rachmaninov: 24 Preludes" (Steven Osborne, piano). 2008.

Fay, Laurel E. *Shostakovich: A Life.* New York: Oxford University Press, 2000.

Fedorov, Boris, ed. *Pamiatnik Otechestvennykh muz, izdannykh na 1827 god Borisom Fedorovym* [Souvenir of the muses of the fatherland, issued for 1827 by Boris Fedorov]. Sanktpeterburg: Tipografiia Aleksandra Smirdina, 1827.

Fet, A. A. *Stikhotvoreniia i poèmy* [Poems and long poems]. Edited by B. Bukhshtab. Biblioteka poèta, Bolshaiia seriia. Leningrad: Sovetskii pisatel', 1986.

_________. *Vechernye ogni* [Evening lights]. Edited by D. D. Blagoi and M. A. Sokolova. Moscow: Nauka, 1971.

Finck, Henry T., ed. *One Hundred Songs by Ten Masters in Two Volumes.* For Low Voice. Two vols. The Musicians Library. Boston: Oliver Ditson Company. New York: Chas. H. Ditson & Co. Chicago: Lyon & Healy., 1917.

Frame, Murray. *The St. Petersburg Imperial Theaters: Stage and State in Revolutionary Russia, 1900–1920.* Jefferson, North Carolina and London: McFarland and Company, Inc., 2000.

Friedrich, Paul. *Music in Russian Poetry.* Middlebury Studies in Russian Language and Literature, Vol. 10. New York, etc.: Peter Lang, 1998.

Frolova-Walker, Marina. "The Miserly Knight: A Betrayal of the Sacred?" Glyndebourne Festival Opera Program, 20 May – 29 August 2004.

Furst, Lilian R. "Lighting Up Night." In *A Companion to European Romanticism*, edited by Michael Ferber. Oxford: Blackwell Publishing, 2005.

Galina, G. *Stikhotvoreniia* [Poems]. St. Petersburg: M. I. Troianskogo, 1902.

_________. *Stikhotvoreniia G. Galinoi* [Poems of G. Galina]. St Petersburg: Pirozhkov, 1906.

Garden, Edward. "Russia (Solo Song)." In *Romanticism 1830-1890*, edited by Gerald Abraham, 704-725. Oxford, New York: Oxford University Press, 1990.

Gasparov, Boris. "Pushkin in Music." In *The Cambridge Companion to Pushkin*, edited by Andrew Kahn. Cambridge: Cambridge University Press, 2006.

Glass, Beaumont. *Hugo Wolf's Complete Song Texts.* Geneseo, New York: Leyerle Publications, 2000.

Glinka, Mikhail Ivanovich. *Polnoe sobranie romansov i pesen* [Complete romances and songs]. Edited by N. N. Zagornyi. Leningrad: Gosudarstvennoe muzykal'noe izdatel'stvo, 1955.

_________. *Memoirs.* Translated by Richard B. Mudge. Westport, Connecticut: Greenwood Press, 1980.

Glinsky, Albert. *Theremin: Ether Music and Espionage.* Urbana and Chicago: University of Illinois Press, 2000.

Golenishchev-Kutuzov, A. A. *Sochineniia grafa A. Golenishcheva-Kutuzova* [Works of Count A. Golenishchev-Kutuzov]. 3 vols. Vol. 1. SPb: R. Golike and A. Vil'borg, 1904–1905.

_________. *Zatish'e i buria* [Calm and storm] (1868–1878). S.-Peterburg: Tipografiia R. Golike, Ligovka No. 22, 1878.

Gorky, Maxim. *Chaliapin. An Autobiography as told to Maxim Gorky.* Translated and edited by Nina Froud and James Hanley. New York: Stein and Day, 1967.

Grainger, Percy [1882-1961]. *Grainger on Music*, ed. Malcolm Gillies and Bruce Clunies Ross. New York and Oxford: Oxford University Press, 1999.

Grekov, Nikolai Porfirevich. *Stikhotvoreniia N. P. Grekova* [Poems of N. P. Grekov]. Moscow, 1860.

Grigorian, K. N. "Isaakian v perevodakh Bloka (k probleme poeticheskogo perevoda)" [Isahakian in translations of Blok (on the problem of poetic translation)]. In *Aleksandr Blok. Issledovaniia i materialy* [Alexander Blok. Studies and materials]. Leningrad: AN SSSR-IRLI (PD), 1987.

Guyau, M. *Vers d'un Philosophe*. Paris: Librairie Germer Baillière et Cie., 1881.

________. (Giuio). *Stikhi filosofa* [Poems of a philosopher]. Translated by Ivan Ivanovich Tkhorzhevskii. St. Petersburg, 1901.

Hacken, Richard. *Into the Sunset: Anthology of Nineteenth-Century Austrian Prose*. Riverside, California: Ariadne Press, 1999.

Hall, James Husst. *The Art Song*. Norman: University of Oklahoma Press, 1953.

Harrison, Max. *Rachmaninoff. Life, Works, Recordings*. London and New York: Continuum, 2005.

Harvith, John and Susan Edwards Harvith. *Edison, Musicians, and the Phonograph. A Century in Retrospect*. New York, Westport, London: Greenwood Press, 1987.

Haylock, Julian. *Sergei Rachmaninoff: An Essential Guide To His Life and Works*. London: Pavilion, 1996.

Henrysson, Harald. *A Jussi Björling Phonography*, second edition. Stockholm: Svenskt Musikhistoriskt Arkiv, 1993.

Hodge, Thomas P. *A Double Garland. Poetry and Art-Song in Early-Nineteenth-Century Russia, Studies in Russian Literature and Theory*. Evanston, Illinois: Northwestern University Press, 2000.

Holden, Amanda, ed. *The Viking Opera Guide*. London: Viking, 1993.

Hugo, Victor. *Selected Poems of Victor Hugo*. Translated by E. H. and A. M. Blackmore. Chicago and London: The University of Chicago Press, 2001.

Iakovenko, Sergei Borisovich. *Pavel Gerasimovich Lisitsian: Uroki odnoi zhizni* [Pavel Gerasimovich Lisitsian: Lessons of a life]. Moscow: Muzyka, 1989.

________. *Volshebnaia Zara Dolukhanova* [The enchanting Zara Dolukhanova]. Moscow: SOBA, 1996.

________. *Pavel Gerasimovich Lisitsian v iskusstve i zhizni: Fakty, dialogi, razmyshleniia*. [Pavel Gerasimovich Lisitsian in art and life: facts, dialogues, reflections]. Moscow: Realii, 2001.

________. *Nadezhda Kazantseva v iskusstve i zhizni* [Nadezhda Kazantseva in art and life]. Moscow: Izdatel'stvo Fonda Iriny Arkhipovoi, 2004.

Ianin, V. A. and Griunberg, P. N. *Katalog vokal'nykh zapisei Rossiiskogo otdeleniia kompanii "Grammofon"* [A catalogue of vocal recordings of the Russian branch of the "Grammophone" Company]. Moscow: Iazyki slavianskoi kul'tury, 2002.

Ippolitov-Ivanov, M. M. *50 let russkoi muzyki v moikh vospominaniiakh* [50 years of Russian music in my recollections]. Moscow: Gos Muz Izd, 1934.

Iuzefovich, V. A. *Sergei Kusevitskii. Tom pervyi. Russkie gody* [Serge Koussevitzky. First volume. Russian years]. Moscow: Iazyki Slavianskoi Kul'tury, 2004.

Ivanov, Georgii Konstantinovich. *Russkaia poeziia v otechestvennoi muzyke (do 1917 goda)* [Russian poetry in music of the fatherland (to 1917)]. Two vols. Moscow: Muzyka (vol. 1, 1966); Sovetskii kompozitor (vol. 2, 1969).

Ivanov, Georgii Vladimirovich. *Sobranie sochinenii v trekh tomakh. Tom tretii: Memuary, Literaturnaia kritika* [Collected works in three volumes. Volume three: Memoirs, Literary criticism]. Moscow: Soglasie, 1994.

Jackson, David M. "Rachmaninov: Ten Songs." In *Song on Record 2*, edited by Alan Blyth, 169-179. Cambridge: Cambridge University Press, 1988.

Johnson, Graham. *Gabriel Fauré: The Songs and their Poets*. Burlington, VT & London: Ashgate Publishing; Guildhall School of Music & Drama, 2009.

Joseph, Charles M. *Stravinsky Inside Out*. New Haven and London: Yale University Press, 2001.

Kahn, Andrew, ed. *The Cambridge Companion to Pushkin*. Cambridge and New York: Cambridge University Press, 2006.

________. *Pushkin's Lyric Intelligence*. Oxford and New York: Oxford University Press, 2008.

Kandinskii, A. "Literaturnoe nasledie Rakhmaninova" [Literary heritage of Rachmaninoff, a review of *LN*]. *Sovetskaia muzyka*, 1982, no. 6, 91-102.

Kandinskii-Rybnikov, A. "Problema Sud'by i avtobiografichnost' v iskusstve S. V. Rakhmaninova" [The problem of Fate and the autobiographical in the art of S. V. Rachmaninoff]. Paper presented at the conference *S. V. Rakhmaninov: k 120-letiiu so dnia rozhdeniia* [S. V. Rachmaninoff: on the 120th anniversary of his birth]. Moscow, Nauchnye trudy Moskovskoi gosudarstvennoi konservatorii im. P. I. Chaikovskogo. Sbornik 7 [Scientific works of the Moscow State Conservatory named for P. I. Tchaikovsky. Vol. 7], 1995.

Kashkin, N. "Kruzhok liubitelei russkoi muzyki" [Circle of lovers of Russian music], *Russkoe slovo*, 20 Feb. 1907. (A review of Rachmaninoff's Op. 26.)
Katz, Martin. *The Complete Collaborator*. Oxford: Oxford University Press, 2009.
Kazack, Wolfgang. *A Dictionary of Russian Literature Since 1917*. London: Overseas Publications Interchange Ltd, 1988.
Keldysh, Iurii Vsevolodovich. *Rakhmaninov i ego vremia* [Rachmaninoff and his times]. Moscow: Muzyka, 1973.
Kelly, Catriona. *Russian Literature: A Very Short Introduction*. Oxford: Oxford University Press, 2001.
Kenneson, Claude. *Musical Prodigies*. Portland, Oregon: Amadeus Press, 1998.
Khodasevich, V. F. *Vladislav Khodasevich. Sobranie sochinenii v chetyrekh tomakh* [Vladislav Khodasevich. Collected works in four volumes]. Edited by I. P. Andreeva and S. G. Bocharov, and others. Vol. 4. Moscow: Soglasie 1996–1997.
Khomiakov, A. S. *A. S. Khomiakov, Polnoe sobranie sochinenii* [A. S. Khomiakov, Complete collected works]. 4 vols. Moscow: Universitetskaia tipografiia na Strastnom bul'vare, 1900.
________. *Sochineniia bogoslovskie* [Theological works]. Sankt-Peterburg: Nauka, 1995.
________. *Stikhotvoreniia i dramy* [Poems and plays]. Edited by B. F. Egorov. Biblioteka poeta, Bol'shaia seriia, Second ed. Leningrad: Sovetskii pisatel', 1969.
Kol'tsov, A. V. *Polnoe sobranie stikhotvorenii i pisem A. V. Kol'tsova* [Complete collected poems and letters of A. V. Koltsov]. Edited by Arsenii Ivanovich Vvedensky. Sanktpeterburg: Prosveschchenie, 1896.
________. *Polnoe sobranie sochinenii A. V. Kol'tsova*. [Complete collected poems of A. V. Koltsov]. Ed. A. I. Lianshchenko. S-Peterburg: Akademiia nauk, 1911.
Korabelnikova, L. Z., et al. *Istoriia russkoi muzyki* [History of Russian music]. Vol. 10 B, 1890–1917. Moscow: Muzyka, 2004.
Korinfskii, Apollon. *Gimn krasote i drugie novye stikhotvoreniia* [Hymn to beauty and other new poems]. S.–Peterburg: Parovaia skoropechatnia Ia. I. Libermana, 1899.
Kotliarov, Iu. and V. Garmash. *Letopis' zhizni i tvorchestva F. I. Shaliapina* [Chronicle of the life and work of F. I. Chaliapin], 2 vols. Leningrad: Muzyka, 1984, 1989.
Kravitt, Edward F. *The Lied. Mirror of Late Romanticism*. New Haven and London: Yale University Press, 1996.
Kupferberg, Herbert. *Those fabulous Philadelphians; the life and times of a great orchestra*. New York: Charles Scribner's Sons, 1969.
Kuprin, Aleksandr. "Stikhotvoreniia G. Galinoi" ["Poems of G. Galina"]. *Zhurnal dlia vsekh* VII, no. 7 (1902): 633.
Kutsch, K. J. and Leo Riemens. *Grosses Sängerlexikon*. 7 vols. München: K.G. Saur, 2003.
L'vov, M. *L. V. Sobinov*. Moscow-Leningrad: Gosudarstvennoe muzykal'noe izdatel'stvo, 1951.
Lamm, Pavel Aleksandrovich, ed. *S. V. Rakhmaninov. Vokal'nye proizvedeniia, neopublikovannye avtorom* [S. V. Rakhmaninov. Vocal works not published by the author]. Moscow and Leningrad: Muzgiz, 1947.
Langley, Robin. "Field, John, §2: Piano playing and teaching." *Grove Music Online*, (Accessed 26 Nov. 2012).
Lawrence, D. H. *Sex, Literature and Censorship*. Edited by Harry T. Moore. New York: Twayne Publishers, 1953.
Ledkovsky, Marina, and Charlotte Rosenthal, Mary Zirin, ed. *Dictionary of Russian Women Writers* (*DRWW*). Westport, Connecticut and London: Greenwood Press, 1994.
Lehmann, Lotte. *More Than Singing: The Interpretation of Songs*. New York: Boosey & Hawkes, Inc., 1945.
Leonard, Maurice. *Slobodskaya: A Biography of Oda Slobodskaya*. London: Victor Gollancz Ltd, 1979.
Lermontov, Mikhail. *A Hero of Our Time*. Translated by Vladimir Nabokov. Garden City, New York: Doubleday, 1958.
________. *Polnoe sobranie sochinenii v desiati tomakh* [Complete works in ten volumes]. Vol. 1. Moscow: Voskresen'e, 1999.
Levik, Sergei. *Zapiski opernogo pevtsa* [Notes of an opera singer]. Moscow: Iskusstvo, 1962.
________. *The Levik Memoirs: An Opera Singer's Notes*. London: Symposium Records, 1995.

Liberman, Anatoly. *On the Heights of Creation: The Lyrics of Fedor Tyutchev.* Greenwich, CT and London: JAI Press Ltd, 1992.

Lieberman, Richard K. *Steinway & Sons.* New Haven & London: Yale University Press, 1995.

Logvinov, A. S. "Pamiati T. G. Shevchenko." In *Literaturnoe nasledstvo: Ivan Alekseevich Bunin,* [Literary heritage: Ivan Alekseevich Bunin], Book 1, edited by O. I. Mikhailov. Moscow: Nauka, 1973.

Lotman, Iu. M. *Kommentarii, A. S. Pushkin, Evgenii Onegin* [Commentaries, A. S. Pushkin, *Eugene Onegin*]. Moscow: Atrium, 1991.

L'vov, M. *L. V. Sobinov,* "Mastera Bol'shogo teatra" [L. V. Sobinov, "Masters of the Bolshoi Theater"]. Moscow-Leningrad: Gosudarstvennoe muzykal'noe izdatel'stvo, 1951.

Maes, Francis. *A History of Russian Music: from Kamarinskaya to Babi Yar.* Translated by Arnold J. Pomerans and Erica Pomerans. Berkeley, Los Angeles, London: University of California Press, 2002.

Maikov, A. N. *Polnoe sobranie sochinenii A. N. Maikova* [Complete collected works of A. N. Maikov]. Vols 1-3. St. Petersburg: Marx, 1884.

Martyn, Barrie. *Rachmaninoff. Composer, Pianist, Conductor.* Aldershot: Scolar Press, 1990.

_________. *Nicolas Medtner: His Life and Music.* Aldershot, England: Scolar Press (Ashgate Publishing in USA), 1995.

McMillin, Arnold. "Gilding the Lily: Pushkin's Lyrics in the Hands of Russian Composers." In *Two Hundred Years of Pushkin,* edited by Robert and Joe Andrew Reid. Amsterdam and New York: Rodopi, 2004-1.

_________. "Russian Music in and around Chekhov." *Australian Slavonic and East European Studies* 18, no. 1-2, 2004-2: 1-16.

Mei, Lev Aleksandrovich. *Polnoe Sobranie Sochinenii* [Complete collected works]. Five vols. S-Peterburg: Izdanie N. G. Martynova, 1887.

Merezhkovskii, Dmitrii M. *Stikhotvoreniia (1883-1887)* [Poems 1883-1887]. S-Peterburg: Tip. Trenke i Fiusno, 1888.

_________. *Stikhotvoreniia i poèmy* [Poems and long poems]. Novaia biblioteka poèta. Sankt-Peterburg: Gumanitarnoe agentstvo "Akademicheskii Proekt," 2000.

Miller, Philip L., ed. *The Ring of Words.* New York and London: Norton, 1973.

Milstein, Nathan and Solomon Volkov. *From Russia to the West: The Musical Memoirs and Reminiscences of Nathan Milstein.* Translated by Antonina W. Bouis. New York: Limelight Editions, 1991.

Minskii, N. M. *Stikhotvoreniia* [Poems]. S.–Peterburg: Tipografiia V. S. Balasheva, 1887.

Mintzer, Charles. *Rosa Raisa : a biography of a diva with selections from her memoirs.* Boston: Northeastern University Press, 2001.

Mirsky, D. S., Prince. *Russkaia lirika: malen'kaia antologiia ot Lomonosova do Pasternaka* [Russian lyrics: a little anthology from Lomonosov to Pasternak, reprint of 1924 Paris edition]. New York: Russica, 1979.

_________. *A History of Russian Literature. From its Beginnings to 1900.* Ed. Francis J. Whitfield. New York: Vintage Books, 1958.

Moiseiwitsch, Maurice. *Moiseiwitsch. A Biography of a Concert Pianist.* London: Frederick Muller Limited, 1965.

Moore, Gerald. *Am I Too Loud?* Memoirs of an Accompanist. London: Penguin Books, 1966.

_________. *Furthermoore, Interludes in an Accompanist's Life.* London: Hamish Hamilton, 1983.

Morozova, L. I. and B. M. Rozenfel'd. *Lermontov v muzyke* [Lermontov in music]. Moscow: Sovetskii kompozitor, 1983.

Morris, Manuel. *The Recorded Performances of Gérard Souzay.* A Discography. Westport, CT and London: Greenwood Press, 1991.

Muratova, K. D. *Istoriia russkoi literatury XIX veka* [History of Russian literature of the 19th century, a bibliography]. Moscow-Leningrad: AN SSSR, 1962.

_________. (Muratova 2). *Istoriia russkoi literatury kontsa XIX-nachala XX vv.* [History of Russian literature of the late 19th - early 20th centuries, a bibliography]. Moscow-Leningrad: AN SSSR, 1963.

Musset, A. de. *Poésies complètes*. Edited by Maurice Allem, Bibliothèque de la Pléiade. Paris: Librairie Gallimard, 1951.

Nezhdanova, A. V. *Antonina Vasil'evna Nezhdanova. Materialy i issledovaniia* [Materials and studies]. Ed. V. A. Vasina-Grossman et al. Moscow: Iskusstvo: 1967.

Nikitin, Boris S. *Sergei Rakhmaninov. Dve zhizni*. [Two lives]. Moscow: Izdatel'stvo "Znanie", 1993.

_________. *Sergei Rakhmaninov. Fedor Shaliapin*. Moscow: OT i SS, 1998.

Nordlinger, Jay. "Salzburg Chronicle." *The New Criterion*. Vol. 22, no. 2 (October 2003): 53-4.

Norris, Geoffrey. "Rachmaninoff's Student Opera." *The Musical Quarterly*. Vol. 59, no. 3 (1973): 441-8.

_________."Rachmaninov in London [Rachmaninov's London Debut]." *The Musical Times*. Vol. 134, no. 1802 (1993): 186-188.

_________. "Rachmaninoff's Reception in England 1899–1938." *Studies in Music from the University of Western Ontario* 15 (1995).

_________. *Rachmaninoff*. The Master Musicians. Oxford: Oxford University Press, 2001.

_________. "Rachmaninoff, Serge" in online resource *Oxford Music*. Oxford University Press, 2007—2013 [cited 3 April 2013].

Obolensky, Dimitri, ed. *The Penguin Book of Russian Verse*. Baltimore: Penguin Books, 1962 and later printings.

_________. ed. *The Heritage of Russian Verse*. Bloomington and London: Indiana University Press, 1976.

Orlov, Vladimir Nikolaevich, ed. *K. D. Bal'mont. Stikhotvoreniia* [K. D. Balmont. Poems], Biblioteka poèta, Bol'shaia seriia. Leningrad: Sovetskii pisatel', 1969.

_________. ed. *Aleksandr Blok v vospominaniiakh sovremennikov* [Alexander Blok in recollections of contemporaries]. Moscow: Khudozhestennaia literatura, 1980.

Osborne, Charles. *The Concert Song Companion*. New York: Da Capo Press, 1985.

Pailleron, Édouard. *Amours et haines*. Paris: Calmann Lévy, Éditeur, 1889.

Palmieri, Robert. *Sergei Vasil'evich Rachmaninoff*. A Guide to Research. New York & London: Garland Publishing, Inc., 1985.

Parrott, Jasper and Vladimir Ashkenazy. *Beyond Frontiers*. New York: Atheneum, 1985.

Pasternak, Boris. *I remember: sketch for an autobiography*. Translated by David Magarshack. New York: Pantheon, 1959 and subsequent editions.

_________. *Proza* [Prose]: *1915-1958*. Ann Arbor: The University of Michigan Press, 1961.

Pearson, Edward Hagelin. "Nina Pavlovna Koshetz." *The Record Collector*. Vol. 39, no. 1: 1-41.

Petrovskii, Miron. "'Ezda v ostrov liubvi', ili chto est' russkii romans" [A journey to the isle of love, or what the Russian romance is]. *Voprosy literatury*, no. 5 (1984): 55-90.

_________ and Valentina Morderer, eds. *Russkii romans na rubezhe vekov*. Kiev, 1997.

_________. *Akh romans. Èkh romans. Okh romans. Russkii romans na rubezhe vekov* [Ach romance, etc. The Russian romance at the turn of the {19th and 20th} centuries.] Sankt-Peterburg: Geran', 2005.

Pettifor, Tom. "Rachmaninov proves Tolstoy wrong by topping poll of favourite." *The Independent*, March 2005, 30.

Philip, Robert. *Performing Music in the Age of Recording*. New Haven and London: Yale University Press, 2004.

Phillips-Matz, Mary Jane. *Leonard Warren, American Baritone*. Portland, Oregon: Amadeus Press, 2000.

Pleshcheev, A. N. *Stikhotvoreniia A. N. Pleshcheeva* [Poems of A. N. Pleshcheyev]. Fourth edition. St Petersburg: Ed Bykov, 1905.

_________. *Polnoe sobranie stikhotvorenii* [Complete poems], ed. M. Poliakov. Biblioteka poèta, Bol'shaia seriia. Moscow-Leningrad: Sovetskii pisatel', 1964.

Pollin, Burton R. *Music for Shelley's Poetry*. An Annotated Bibliography of Musical Settings of Shelley's Poetry. New York: Da Capo Press, 1974.

Polonskii, Ia. P. *Ozimi. Chast' 1. Novyi sbornik stikhov Ia. P. Polonskogo* [Winter wheat. Part 1. New book of poems of Ia. A. Polonsky]. Sanktpeterburg: tip. V. S. Balasheva, 1876.

_________. *Polnoe sobranie stikhotvorenii Ia. P. Polonskogo v piati tomakh* [Complete poems of Ia. A. Polonsky in five volumes]. S.–Peterburg: A. F. Marks, 1896.

Prokhorov, Vadim. *Russian Folk Songs. Musical Genres and History*. Lanham, Maryland, and London: The Scarecrow Press, Inc, 2002.

Prokof'ev, Grigorii Petrovich. "Pevets intimnykh nastroenii (S. V. Rakhmaninov)" [Poet of intimate moods (S. V. Rachmaninoff)]. *Russkaia muzykal'naia gazeta*, no. 7, 14 Feb. 1910.

________ . "Kontserty v Moskve" [Concerts in Moscow], *Russkaia muyzykal'nogo gazeta*, 1914, no. 1, 27-9.

Prokofiev, Sergey. *Diaries: 1915–1923*. Translated by Anthony Phillips. Ithaca, New York: Cornell University Press, 2008.

Propp, V. Ia., ed. *Narodnye liricheskie pesni* [Lyric folk songs], Biblioteka poèta, Bol'shaia seriia. Leningrad: Sovetskii pisatel', 1961.

Pushkin, A. S. *Polnoe sobranie sochinenii. Stikhotvoreniia 1826-36. Skazki* [Complete works. Poems 1826-36. Fairy tales]. Edited by M. A. Tsiavlovskii. Vol. 3, Books 1 and 2. Moscow-Leningrad: Izdatel'stvo Akademii Nauk SSSR, 1948-49.

________ . *Polnoe sobranie sochinenii v desiati tomakh* [Collected works in ten volumes]. Edited by B. V. Tomashevskii. Moscow: Izdatel'stvo Akademii Nauk SSSR, 1962–1965.

________ . *The Little Tragedies*. Translated, with Critical Essays, by Nancy K. Anderson. New Haven and London: Yale University Press, 2000.

Rachmaninoff, Sergei. "Some Critical Moments in My Career." *The Musical Times*, 1 June 1930, 557-8.

________ . Letters and articles. (***LN***). See "Short Titles," p. 263.

________ . *Pis'ma* [Letters]. Edited by Z. Apetiants. Moscow: Gosudarstvennoe Muzykal'noe Izdatel'stvo, 1955.

________ . *Romansy. Polnoe sobranie* [Romances. Complete collection]. Moscow: Gosudarstvennoe Muzykal'noe Izdatel'stvo, 1957, 1963. (Short Title: PSR.)

Randel, Don M., ed. *The Harvard Dictionary of Music*. Cambridge, Mass. and London, England: The Belknap Press of Harvard University Press, 2003.

Ratgauz, Daniil. *Stikhotvoreniia* [Poems]. Kiev, 1893.

________ . *Pesni liubvi i pechali* [Songs of love and sadness]. Sanktpeterburg and Moscow: M. O. Vol'f, 1902.

Rayfield, Donald. *Anton Chekhov: A Life*. New York: Henry Holt and Company, 1998.

Rayno, Don. *Paul Whiteman. Pioneer in American Music*. Volume I: 1890-1930. Lanham, Maryland and Oxford: The Scarecrow Press, 2003.

Reed, John. *The Schubert Song Companion*. Manchester and New York: Mandolin (St. Martin's Press), 1993.

Restout, Denise. *Landowska on Music*. New York: Stein and Day, 1964.

Richter, Laurence R. *Rachmaninov's Complete Song Texts*. Russian Texts of the Complete Songs of Sergei Rachmaninoff with phonetic transcriptions, literal and idiomatic English translations. Geneseo, New York: Leyerle Publications, 2000.

Riesemann, O. von. *Rachmaninoff's Recollections told to Oskar von Riesemann*. London and New York: Macmillan, 1934.

Rimsky-Korsakov, Nikolay Andreyevich. *My Musical Life*. Translated by Judah A. Joffe. Edited by Carl Van Vechten. Third ed. New York: Alfred A. Knopf, 1947.

Romanov, Konstantin Konstantinovich. Stikhotvoreniia K. R. [Poems of K. R.].Third ed. 1879–1885 ed. SPb, 1899.

Rosen, Charles. *The Romantic Generation*. Cambridge, MA: Harvard University Press, 1995.

Ross, Alex. "The Chosen," *The New Yorker*, March 29, 1999, 113.

Russell, Peter. *The Themes of the German Lied From Mozart to Strauss. Studies in the History and Interpretation of Music*, vol. 84. Lewiston, New York; Queenston, Ontario; Lampeter, Wales: The Edwin Mellen Press, 2002.

Rytsareva, M. G., ed. *Avtografy S. V. Rakhmaninova v fondakh Gosudarstvennogo tsentral'nogo muzeia muzykal'noi kul'tury imeni M. I. Glinki. Katalog-spravochnik. 2-e izdanie, rasshirennoe i dopolnennoe* [Autographs of S. V. Rakhmaninov in archives of the M. I. Glinka State Central Museum of Musical Culture. Catalogue-Reference. Second edition, expanded and supplemented.]. Edited by E. E. Bortnikova and F. A. Krasinskaia. Moscow: Sovetskii Kompozitor, 1980.

Sabaneev, L. L. *Vospominaniia o Taneeve* [Memories of Taneyev]. Moscow: Klassika-XXI, 2003.

Sadie, Stanley and Tyrrell, John, ed. *The New Grove Dictionary of Music and Musicians*, 2nd ed. London, 2001.

Salys, Rimgaila. *Leonid Pasternak. The Russian Years, 1875–1921*. Oxford: Oxford University Press, 1999. The frontispiece of this book is No. 966, charcoal on paper.

Senelick, Laurence. *The Chekhov Theatre: A century of the plays in performance*. Cambridge: Cambridge University Press, 1997.

Seroff, Victor I. *Rachmaninoff*. New York: Simon and Schuster, 1950.

Severianin, Igor. *Tost bezotvetnyi. Stikhotvoreniia. Poèmy. Proza* [Unanswered toast. Poems. Long poems. Prose]. Moscow: Respublika, 1999.

Shaginian, Marietta. *Sobranie sochinenii v deviati tomakh* [Collected works in nine volumes]. Vol. 9. Moscow: Khudozhestvennaia literatura, 1975.

Shaliapin, Fedor Ivanovich. *Literaturnoe nasledstvo. Pis'ma* [Literary heritage. Letters]. Two volumes. Ed. E. A. Grosheva. Moscow: Iskusstvo, 1960.

Shaman, William, and others. *EJS, discography of the Edward J. Smith Recordings: the Golden Age of Opera, 1956–1971*. Westport: Greenwood Press, 1994, and a second volume with short title *More EJS*. Westport: Greenwood Press, 1999.

Shelley, Percy Bysshe. *Shelli. Polnoe sobranie sochinenii v perevode K. D. Bal'monta* [Shelley: Complete works translated by K. D. Balmont]. Novoe 3-xtomnoe pererabotannoe izdanie [New 3-volume revised edition]. Vol. 1. S-Pb: "Znanie", 1903.

Shelokhaev, V. V. et al., ed. *Russkoe zarubezh'e* [the Russian emigration]. Moscow: ROSSPEN, 1997.

Shenderovich, Evgenii. *V kontsertmeisterskom klasse: Razmyshleniia pedagoga* [In the concert master's class: thoughts of a pedagogue]. Moscow: Muzyka, 1996.

Shevchenko, Taras. *The Poetical Works of Taras Shevchenko*. Translated from the Ukrainian by C. H. Andrusyshen and Watson Kirkconnell. Toronto and Buffalo: University of Toronto Press, 1964.

_________ . *Sobranie sochinenii v chetyrekh tomakh* [Collected works in four volumes]. Moscow: Pravda, 1977.

Simpson, Anne. "Dear Re: A Glimpse Into the Six Songs of Rachmaninoff's Opus 38." *College Music Symposium*, Vol. 24, no. 1 (1984): 97-106.

Slonimsky, Nicolas, ed. *50 Russian Art Songs From Glinka to Shostakovich* (In 3 Volumes). Introduction and Translations by Nicolas Slonimsky. For Voice and Piano. English and Russian Texts. 3 vols, Am-Rus Vocal Series. Radio City, New York: Leeds Music Corporation, 1949 (vol 1), 1950 (vol 2), 1951 (vol 3).

_________ , ed. *Baker's Biographical Dictionary of Musicians*. Seventh Edition. New York: Schirmer Books, 1984.

_________ . *Perfect Pitch: A Life Story*. Oxford, New York: Oxford University Press, 1988.

_________ . *Lectionary of Music*. New York: McGraw-Hill, 1989.

Slonimsky, Nicolas and Kuhn, Laura, ed. *Baker's Biographical Dictionary of Musicians*. 6 vols. New York: Schirmer, 2001.

Smith, Russell and Peter Burgis. *Peter Dawson: The World's Most Popular Baritone*. With complete song title discography. Sydney: Currency Press, 2001.

Soboleva, A. A. *Sergei Vasil'evich Rakhmaninov: Biobibliograficheskii ukazatel'* [Biobibliographial index]. Tambov, 1993.

Sobolevskii, Aleksei Ivanovich, ed. *Velikorusskie narodnye pesni*. Seven vols. Sankt-Peterburg: Gos. tip., 1895–1902.

Söderström, Elisabeth. *In My Own Key*. Translated by Joan Tate. London: Hamish Hamilton, 1979.

_________ . "A life of Mozart singing." *Early Music*, vol. 20, no. 1 (1992).

Sokolova, Olga Iv. *Sergei Vasil'evich Rakhmaninov*. Moscow: Muzyka, 1987.

Sologub, Fedor. *Sobranie sochinenii* [Collected works]. Peterburg: Shipovnik, 1909.

Stanislavsky, Konstantin. *My Life in Art*. Translated by J. J. Robbins. New York: Theatre Arts Books, 1952.

Steane, John B. *Singers of the Century*. Vol. 1. Portland, Oregon: Amadeus Press, 1996.

_________ . *Singers of the Century*. Vol. 2. Portland, Oregon: Amadeus Press, 1998.

_________ . *Singers of the Century*. Vol. 3. Portland, Oregon: Amadeus Press, 2000.

Stein, Deborah and Robert Spillman. *Poetry into Song: Performance and Analysis of Lieder.* New York, Oxford: Oxford University Press, 1996.

Stevens, Denis, ed. *A History of Song.* Westport: Greenwood Press, 1982.

Sushkova, Ekaterina (E. A. Khvostova). *Zapiski* [Notes], 1812-1841. Edited by Iu. G. Oksman. Leningrad: Academia, 1928.

Swan, A. J. and Katherine. "Rachmaninoff: Personal Reminiscences." *The Musical Quarterly* vol. 30, no. 1 and 2 (1944): 1-19, 174-191.

Sylvester, Richard D. *Tchaikovsky's Complete Songs: A Companion with Texts and Translations.* Russian Music Series. Bloomington and Indianapolis: Indiana University Press, 2002; 2004 (reprint).

Taruskin, Richard. "Aleko." *The New Grove Dictionary of Opera*, 1992.

_________. *Stravinsky and the Russian Traditions: A Biography of the Works through Mavra.* Two vols. Berkeley, Los Angeles: University of California Press, 1996.

_________. *Defining Russia Musically.* Princeton: Princeton University Press, 1997.

Taylor, Philip S. *Anton Rubinstein: A Life in Music.* Edited by Malcolm Hamrick Brown. Russian Music Series. Bloomington and Indianapolis: Indiana University Press, 2007.

Teliakovskii, Vladimir Arkad'evich. *Dnevniki Direktora Imperatorskikh teatrov: 1901–1903* [Diaries of the director of the imperial theaters: 1901–1903]. Sankt-Peterburg/V. A. Teliakovskii. Edited by M. G. Svetaeva. Moscow: Izd-vo "Artist–Rezhisser–Teatr", 2002.

_________. *Imperatorskie teatry i 1905 god* [The imperial theaters and the year 1905]. Edited by E. M. Kuznetsov. Leningrad: Academia, 1926.

Terras, Victor. *Poetry of the Silver Age.* Dresden–München: Dresden University Press, 1998.

Threlfall, Robert. *Sergei Rachmaninoff. His Life and Music.* London: Boosey and Hawkes, 1973.

Threlfall, Robert and Geoffrey Norris. *A Catalogue of the Compositions of S. Rachmaninoff.* London: Scolar Press, 1982.

Tiutchev, F. I. *Lirika* [Lyrics]. Edited by K. V. Pigarev. Moscow: Nauka, 1965.

_________. *Polnoe sobranie stikhotvorenii* [Complete poems]. Edited by A. A. Nikolaev, Biblioteka poèta. Bol'shaia seriia. Leningrad: Sovetskii pisatel', 1987.

_________. *Polnoe sobranie sochinenii i pisem v 6 tt* [Complete poems and letters in 6 vols.]. Edited by V. N. Kasatkina. Moscow: Klassika, 2002.

Tsuker, A. M. "Rakhmaninov i Bunin." [Rachmaninoff and Bunin]. Paper presented at the international conference "The Epoch of Sergei Rachmaninoff" (Theses). Tambov, Ivanovka: 1998.

Tsvetaeva, Marina. *Izbrannaia proza v dvukh tomakh* [Selected prose in two volumes]. New York: Russica, 1979.

Unbegaun, Boris O. *Russian Versification.* Oxford: Clarendon Press, 1963.

Uvarova, E. D., ed. *Estrada Rossii. Dvadtsatyi vek. Leksikon* [The Russian musical stage. Twentieth century. Lexicon]. Moscow: ROSSPEN, 2000.

Valkenier, Elizabeth K. *Ilya Repin and the World of Russian Art.* New York: Columbia University Press. 1990.

Vasina-Grossman, Vera. *Russkii klassicheskii romans XIX veka* [The Russian classical romance of the 19th century]. Moscow: Izdatel'stvo Akademii nauk SSSR, 1956.

Viardot, Pauline. *Muzykal'nyi portret Poliny Viardo* [Musical portrait of Pauline Viardot], ed. G. Preobrazhenskaia. Moscow: Muzyka, 1994.

Vinokur, N. G. and P. A. Kagan. *Pushkin v muzyke* [Pushkin in music]. Moscow: Sovetskii kompozitor, 1974.

Wilson, Elizabeth. *Jacqueline du Pré. Her life, her music, her legend.* New York: Arcade, 1999.

_________. *Rostropovich. The Musical Life of the Great Cellist, Teacher, and Legend.* Chicago: Ivan R. Dee, 2008.

Worth, Paul W. and Jim Cartwright. *John McCormack: A Comprehensive Discography.* New York, Westport, London: Greenwood Press, 1986.

Zhukovsky, Vasili. *Stikhotvoreniia V. A. Zhukovskogo* [Poems of V. A. Zhukovsky], Ninth edition, ed. P. A. Efremova. Sankt-Peterburg: Izd. Glazunova, 1894-5.

Ziegler, Garry. "Rachmaninoff's Early Voice." *Studies in Music from The University of Western Ontario*, vol. 15 (1995): 39-47.

Index of Singers

The following is an index to the singers listed in the preceding pages. Only the singers of Rachmaninoff's songs are listed, not those of other composers who set the same lyrics, nor of intrumentalists who have recorded transcriptions of Rachmaninoff's songs. The information given for each singer—nationality, voice type, and dates—will identify the singer; more information can be found in *Baker's*, Wikipedia, and other reference sources. In some entries, the accompanist and year of performance are provided.

For various reasons, a decision was made to provide only an index of singers in this volume, rather than an annotated discography of the recordings, as one finds in my book *Tchaikovsky's Complete Songs*. Much has changed in the intervening years. Older records that were once very rare are being remastered and reissued on CD. Newer recordings are often repackaged and reissued with new record numbers. Above all, however, the availability of recordings, both individual songs and complete albums, has grown to include downloads from Web sites such as iTunes or Amazon. Many live performances can also be heard (and often seen) on YouTube. This abundance of material, readily accessible on the Web, should satisfy the needs of all the readers of this book, singers, scholars, and music-lovers, except for those passionate discophiles whose interests take them to rare LPs and 78-rpm recordings that exist only in libraries and archives. Information about these historical materials, including libraries where they can be found, is available in the Library of Congress Catalog, WorldCat, and other library catalogs on the Web. Information about Russian singers and recordings before 1917 can be found in *Ianin* and *OP*.

For the beginner there is fortunately a splendid recording of the complete songs of Rachmaninoff sung by the Swedish soprano Elisabeth Söderström, with Vladimir Ashkenazy at the piano. (This set, originally released on LPs by Decca throughout the 1970s, is available on three CDs and also as individual downloads.) The obvious disadvantage of the Söderström-Ashkenazy set is that, all songs being sung by a single singer, many of them have been transposed from the original keys. Another excellent set, which maintains the original keys by distributing the songs among the appropriate voice types, features Joan Rodgers (soprano), Maria Popescu (mezzo-soprano), Alexandre Naoumenko (tenor), and Sergei Leiferkus (baritone), all with Howard Shelley at the piano. This set, recorded and originally released on the Chandos label in the 1990s, is available on three CDs and as individual downloads. Either of these compilations can be used as a reference set or starting point from which to explore the many other great and even greater performances of individual songs by other artists.

Among the finest individual recordings of Rachmaninoff's songs, which no one should neglect, are some by the older generation, including Alexander Kipnis, Jennie Tourel, Sergei Lemeshev (especially the 1947-1950 recordings with Abram Makarov on the Aquarius label), and selected recordings made late in professional life by Nina Koshetz, Maria Kurenko, and Oda Slobodskaya. Exemplary Rachmaninoff interpreters of the near past and present include Zara Dolukhanova, Pavel Lisitsian, Boris Christoff, Irina Arkhipova, Nicolai Gedda, Valentina Levko, Elisabeth Söderström, Sergei Leiferkus, Ewa Podleś, Joan Rodgers, and Dmitri Hvorostovsky. The significance of these and other outstanding performances is in many cases mentioned with the discussion of individual songs

Abdrazakov, Askar. Russian bass, born 1969.
• Song 34.

Aleksandrovich, Aleksandr. Russian tenor, 1881–after 1955.
• Song 45.

Amaize, Odekhiren. American bass-baritone, born 1953.
• Songs 1, 10, 13, 30, 33, 39, 48, 59, 73.

Ameling, Elly. Dutch soprano, born 1934.
• Song 32.

Anderson, Marian. American contralto, 1897–1993.
• Songs 12, 14 (in English). Franz Rupp, piano, William Primrose, viola, 1941.

Andreyeva-Delmas, Lyubov. Russian mezzo-soprano, 1886–1954 (see *OP* 1, 26).
• Song 19.

Ariè, Raffaele. Bulgarian bass, 1922–1988.
• Song 34. Wilfred Parry, piano, 1954.

Arkhipova, Irina. Russian mezzo-soprano, 1925–2010.
• Songs 12, 13, 17, 20, 22, 38, 39. John Wustman, piano, 1970.
• Songs 10, 11, 15, 16, 19, 23, 26, 29, 37, 42, 45, 56, 58, 66. Ivari Ilja, piano, 1981.

Asawa, Brian. American countertenor, born 1966.
• Songs 12, 22, 30, 76, 79 (with orchestra).

Atlantov, Vladimir. Russian tenor, born 1939.
• Songs 10, 12, 25, 28, 32, 37, 45, 55, 61.

Baillie, Isobel. Scottish soprano, 1895–1983.
• Song 38, 56 (in English).

Bandrowska-Turska, Ewa. Polish soprano, 1894–1979.
• Songs 38, 40.

Barber, Terry. American countertenor. Recorded 1998.
• Song 76.

Battle, Kathleen. American soprano, born 1948.
• Songs 12, 13, 40, 76.

Baturkin, Andrei. Russian baritone, born 1966.
• Songs 25, 49, 58.

Björling, Jussi. Swedish tenor, 1911–1960 (see *Henrysson*).
• Songs 12, 38 (in English). Stockholm Concert Orchestra, Nils Grevillius, cond., 1947.

Bock, Albert. German baritone, born 1905. Leico Records, recorded 1962 in Vienna.
• Songs 18, 73 (in German). Hans Weber, piano.

Bolotin, Isidor. Russian tenor, 1907–1961.
• Songs 14, 19, 29. Aleksandr Goldenweiser, piano, 1945.

Bolshakov, Aleksei Alekseyevich. Russian baritone, 1914–1979.
• Songs 10, 59.

Bolshakov, Nikolai Arkadiyevich. Russian tenor, 1874–1958.
• Song 45. 1906/1907 (*OP* 1, 64).

Boons, Claudine. Belgian soprano, 1894–1945.
• Song 14 (in French). Orch. of the Théâtre Royal de la Monnaie, cond. Florian Weiss, 1929.

Borele, Yelena. Latvian soprano. Recorded 2004.
• Songs 20, 21, 22, 23, 38, 40, 56, 75, 78, 80, 82, 83.

Borg, Kim. Finnish bass, 1919–2000.
• Songs 23, 38.

Borisenko, Vera (Veronika). Belorussian mezzo-soprano, 1918–1995.
• Songs 7, 10, 11, 13, 15, 19, 24, 29, 38, 45.

Borodina, Olga. Russian mezzo-soprano, born 1963.
• Songs 12, 17, 19, 20, 22, 29, 38, 40, 45.

Braslau, Sophie. American contralto, 1892–1935.
• Song 19.

Bryleva, Elena. Russian soprano, born 1961.
• Songs 13, 40, 78, 79, 80, 81, 82, 83.

Burchuladze, Paata. Georgian bass, born 1951.
• Songs 1, 9, 11, 12, 31, 34, 35, 39, 44, 48, 52, 61.

Cahill, Teresa. English soprano, born 1944.
• Songs 78, 79, 80, 81, 82, 83.

Cebotari, Maria. Russian-Austrian soprano, 1910–1949.
• Song 13 (in German). Berlin Staatskapelle Orch., Robert Heger, cond., 1935.

Cehanovsky, George. Russian-American baritone. 1892–1986.
• Songs 12, 52, 61.

Celine, Annette. Brazilian soprano. Recorded 1999.
• Songs 13, 32, 38, 76.

Cernay, Germaine. French mezzo-soprano, 1900–1943.
• Song 38 (in French). Gustave Cloëz, piano, 1930.

Chaiter, Yoram. Ukrainian bass, born 1964.
• Songs 12, 13, 17, 20, 24, 28, 30, 39, 40, 48, 59, 61.

Chaliapin, Feodor. Russian bass, 1873–1938.
• Song 59 (1914).

Christoff, Boris. Bulgarian bass, 1914–1993.
• Songs 10, 11, 13, 14, 19, 20, 27, 34, 39, 40, 48, 52, 54, 58, 59, 61.
Alexandre Labinsky, piano, 1958.

Christova, Maria. Bulgarian soprano. Recorded 1966.
• Songs 13, 38.

Crona, Nils. Swedish bass. Recorded 1995.
• Songs 9, 11, 31, 35, 48.

Crooks, Richard. American tenor, 1900–1972.
• Song 53 (in English).

Danto, Louis. Polish-Canadian tenor, 1929–2010.
• Songs 12, 13.

Dawson, Peter. Australian bass-baritone, 1882–1961 (see *Smith*).
• Song 52 (in English).

Davrath, Netania. Israeli soprano, 1931–1987.
• Songs 13, 14, 32.

Davtian, Araks. Armenian soprano, 1949–2010.
• Songs 13, 32, 38, 39, 80, 81.

Davydova, Vera. Russian mezzo-soprano, 1906–1993.
• Song 41.

DeGaetani, Jan. American mezzo-soprano, 1933–1989.
• Songs 5, 14, 24, 29, 37, 38, 52, 53, 66.

Del Grande, Peter. American baritone, c1945–1995.
• Songs 2, 6, 7, 9, 10, 11, 12, 13, 14, 15, 16, 17, 18, 20, 24, 25, 26, 27, 31, 32, 33, 46, 48, 53, 56, 57, 58, 59, 62, 63, 64, 65, 66, 67, 68, 69, 70, 71, 72, 73, 74, 78, 79, 80, 81, 82, 83.

Delunsch, Mireille. French soprano, born 1962.
• Songs 32, 40.

Demianov, Daniil. Russian bass. Recorded 1949.
• Song 62.

Dessay, Natalie. French soprano, born 1965.
• Song 76.

Dickson, Donald. American baritone, 1911–1972.
• Songs 32, 45 (in English, with orchestra).

Diciute-Treciokiene, Alodia. Lithuanian mezzo-soprano, 1905–1997.
• Songs 22, 29.

Dilbèr (Dilber Yunus). Chinese soprano, born 1958.
• Songs 13, 40, 76.

Dimitrieff, Nina. Russian-American soprano. Sang in New York, 1910–1916.
• Songs 1, 12.

Dionne, Chantal. Canadian soprano, born 1972.
• Songs 13, 15, 20, 22, 23, 32, 38, 44, 56, 63, 75, 80, 81, 82.

Di Tullio, Eileen. American soprano. Recorded 1961.
• Song 40 (in English).

Dnishev, Alibek. Kazakh tenor, born 1951.
• Songs 13, 20, 32, 37, 40, 45.

Dodoka, Viktoriya. Russian soprano. Studied at Moscow Conservatory 1988–1995.
• Songs 13, 14, 16, 20, 21, 22, 23, 32, 36, 38, 39, 40, 45, 56, 58, 66, 78, 79, 80, 81, 82, 83.

Dolukhanova, Zara. Russian-Armenian mezzo-soprano, later soprano, 1918–2007.
• Songs 11, 16, 21, 26, 37, 38, 82. Berta Kozel', piano, 1948-53.
• Songs 12, 82. Aleksandr Yerokhin, piano. Leningrad, live, 1958.
• Songs 11, 16, 26, 29, 37, 63. Nina Svetlanova, piano, 1966-68.
• Song 12. Nina Svetlanova, piano. Electrecord (Romania).
• Songs 38, 41, 51, 58, 81, 82. Vladimir Khvostin, piano, 1981.

Domingo, Placido. Spanish tenor, born 1941.
• Songs 12, 13.

Domnich, Ilona. Russian soprano. Recorded 2009.
• Songs 45, 56, 81.

Dorliak, Nina. Russian soprano, 1908–1998.
• Songs 39, 40.

Eizen, Artur. Russian bass, 1927–2008.
• Song 13.

El-Tour, Anna. Russian soprano, 1886–c1954 (see *OP* 2, 92-3).
• Song 19.

Evtodieva, Viktoria. Russian soprano. Sang in Tchaikovsky Competition 1998.
• Songs 79, 83.

Fagan, Leslie. Canadian soprano. Concerts since 2001 in Toronto and New York.
• Songs 13, 26, 40.

Farrar, Geraldine. American soprano, 1882–1967.
• Songs 38, 40, 57 (all in English).

Farrell, Eileen. American soprano, 1920–2002.
• Song 53 (in English).

Firsova, Vera. Russian soprano, 1918–1993.
• Songs 38, 40, 56, 58.

Fiset, Marianne. Canadian soprano. Recorded 2009.
• Songs 13, 19, 20, 32, 40.

Fleming, Renée. American soprano, born 1959.
• Songs 12, 13, 16, 26, 40, 76, 82.

Fomina, Nina. Russian soprano, born 1937.
• Song 50.

Furdui, Svetlana. Russian mezzo-soprano. Sang with Opera Orchestra of New York 1995.
• Songs 12, 16, 17, 19, 20, 22, 25, 26, 27, 29, 30, 37, 38, 39, 44, 45, 48, 58, 78, 80.

Furlanetto, Ferruccio. Italian bass, born 1949.
• Songs 10, 12, 20, 25, 32, 33, 34, 38.

Galante, Inessa. Latvian soprano, born 1954.
• Songs 13, 32, 37, 40, 56, 76, 78.

Gedda, Nicolai. Swedish tenor, born 1925.
• Songs 14, 40. Erik Werba, piano. Salzburg, live, 1959.
• Songs 40, 52. Erik Werba, piano. Salzburg, live, 1961.
• Songs 13, 32, 40. Gerald Moore, piano, 1965.
• Songs 12, 13, 14, 29, 32, 37, 38, 39, 52, 53, 56, 65, 66, 67, 72, 76. Alexis Weissenberg, piano, 1967, 1969.
• Song 40. Geoffrey Parsons, piano. London, live, 1971.
• Songs 13, 20, 23, 38, 56. Liya Mogilevskaia, piano, 1980.
• Songs 4, 32, 55. Erik Werba, piano. Leningrad, live, 1980.
• Songs 13, 63. Eva Pataki, piano, 1987.

Gerasimova, Natalia. Russian soprano, born 1950.
• Songs 78, 79, 80, 81, 82, 83.

Gerzmava, Hilba. Russian soprano, born 1970.
• Songs 17, 20, 36, 37, 38, 40, 56, 66.

Ghiaurov, Nicolai. Bulgarian bass, 1929–2004.
• Songs 20, 55.

Ghiuselev, Nicola. Bulgarian bass, born 1936.
• Song 73.

Gigli, Beniamino. Italian tenor, 1890–1957.
• Song 12 (in English). Enrico Sivieri, piano. Concert in Helsinki, 31.10.1954.

Gilchrist, Jane. English soprano. Recorded 2006.
• Song 76.

Gmyria, Boris. Ukrainian bass, 1903–1969.
• Songs 10, 13, 22, 30, 55, 61.

Golovin, Dmitry. Russian baritone, 1894–1966.
• Song 55.

Gontsov, Vadim. Russian baritone, 1915–1997.
• Song 50 (with Maria Kurenko).

Gorchakova, Galina. Russian soprano, born 1963.
• Songs 19, 20, 21, 28, 38.

Gorin, Igor. Austrian-American baritone, 1904–1982.
• Songs 12, 13.

Gorokhovskaya, Evgenia. Russian mezzo-soprano, born 1940.
• Songs 17, 22, 24, 29.

Gruberova, Edita. Slovak soprano, born 1946.
• Songs 13, 32, 40.

Grishko, Mikhail. Ukraininan baritone, 1901–1973.
• Songs 45, 59.

Gruszczynski, Stanislaw. Polish tenor, 1891–1959.
• Song 32.

Gryzunov, Ivan. Russian baritone, 1879–1919.
• Song 52.

Guleghina, Maria. Ukrainian-Russian soprano, born 1959.
• Songs 10, 13, 15, 19, 21, 22, 23, 28, 29, 32, 33, 38, 39, 40, 42, 44, 45, 52, 56, 58, 76.

Guliayev, Yury. Russian baritone, 1930–1986.
• Songs 13, 28, 44, 48, 55, 59, 61, 62.

Guryakova, Olga. Russian soprano, born 1971.
• Songs 15, 32, 36, 38.

Hendricks, Barbara. American soprano, born 1948.
• Songs 12, 13, 32, 40, 81.

Hislop, Joseph. Scottish tenor, 1884–1977.
• Song 53 (in English).

Hvorostovsky, Dmitri. Russian baritone, born 1962.
• Songs 10, 12, 13, 20, 30, 39, 48, 52, 59. Oleg Boshniakovich, piano, 1990.
• Songs 11, 17, 32, 45. Mikhail Arkadiev, piano, 1993.
• Songs 14, 22, 28, 37, 40, 46, 55, 58, 61. Mikhail Arkadiev, piano, 1994.
• Song 13. Ivari Ilja, piano, 2010.
• Songs 1, 8, 10, 11, 12, 14, 17, 20, 22, 25, 28, 30, 31, 32, 33, 37, 39, 40, 45, 48, 49, 52, 55, 58, 59, 61. Ivari Ilja, piano, 2011.

Isachenko, Konstantin. Russian tenor, 1882–1959.
• Song 52.

Isakova, Nina. Russian mezzo-soprano, born 1928.
• Songs 15, 24, 28, 36, 58.

Ivanov, Aleksei. Russian baritone, 1904–1982.
• Songs 15, 55.

Ivanov, Andrei. Russian baritone, 1900–1970.
• Songs 10, 17, 53, 70, 71.

Izotova, Kira. Russian soprano, born 1931.
• Songs 13, 22, 37, 38, 41, 58, 66, 78, 81.

Kabaivanska, Raina. Bulgarian soprano, born 1934.
• Songs 19, 20, 32, 39.

Karnobatlova-Dobreva, Blagovesta. Bulgarian soprano, born 1936.
• Songs 19, 20, 38, 40.

Karolik, Maxim. Bessarabian-American tenor, c1900–1963.
• Songs 49, 52.

Kasimova, Fidan. Azeri soprano, born 1948.
• Songs 38, 78, 80.

Katulskaya, Yelena. Russian soprano, 1888–1966.
• Songs 36, 40.

Kullman, Charles. American tenor, 1903–1983.
• Song 12 (in English).

Kurenko, Maria. Russian-American soprano, 1890–1980.
• Songs 12, 13, 19, 26, 38, 39. 40, 41, 42, 45, 48, 49, 50, 54, 55, 56, 57, 58, 59, 60, 63, 66, 67, 70, 72, 74, 75, 76, 78, 79, 80, 81, 82, 83, 1950–1951.

Kushpler, Zoryana. Ukrainian mezzo-soprano. Opera debut in Prague 2001.
• Songs 12, 22, 45, 48.

Kuuzik, Tiit (Dietrich) Janovich. Estonian baritone, 1911–1990.
• Songs 12, 13, 57.

Kuznetsova, Dina. Russian-American soprano. Sang at Glyndebourne Festival 2009.
• Songs 79, 80, 83.

Kuznetsova, Maria. Russian soprano, 1880–1966.
• Song 19.

Labinsky, Andrei. Russian tenor, 1871–1941.
• Songs 12, 22, 52.

Lapina, Marina. Russian soprano. Recorded 1995. Soloist, Bolshoi Opera.
• Songs 13, 14, 19, 23, 32, 38, 40, 50, 74, 78, 82.

Laptev, Konstantin. Ukrainian baritone, 1904–1990.
• Song 61.

Larin, Sergej. Russian tenor, 1956–2008.
• Songs 4 (in French), 10, 12, 13, 20, 23, 25, 28, 32, 37, 38, 39, 40, 44, 45, 48, 51, 52, 55, 56, 58, 59, 61, 67, 69, 74, 78, 80.

Lawrence, Helen. English soprano. Sang in opera and recitals; debut Wigmore Hall 1968.
• Song 13 (1999).

Lawrence, Marjorie. Australian soprano, 1907–1979.
• Song 32 (in English).

Lear, Evelyn. American soprano, 1926–2012.
• Songs 13, 17, 19, 20, 28, 32, 38, 55, 56, 76.

Lee, Nelly. Russian soprano, born 1942.
• Songs 12, 13, 16, 19, 20, 22, 23, 26, 37, 39, 40, 42, 45, 56, 58, 63, 66, 75, 76, 78, 79, 80, 81, 82, 83.

Leiferkus, Sergei. Russian baritone, born 1946.
• Songs 1, 2, 6, 8, 9, 10, 11, 12, 13, 17, 18, 25, 27, 30, 32, 33, 34, 35, 38, 43, 44, 48, 49, 50, 52, 59, 61, 62, 64, 68, 71, 73, 77.

Lemeshev, Sergei. Russian tenor, 1902–1977.
• Songs 12, 13, 14, 20, 23, 24, 25, 32, 37, 38, 39, 40, 41, 45, 55, 58, 59, 66, 81.

Levko, Valentina. Russian contralto, born 1926.
• Songs 10, 12, 16, 18, 21, 23, 24, 28, 30, 36, 43, 46, 58, 60, 66. Grigorii Zinger, piano.
• Songs 11, 16, 19, 29, 31, 48, 58. Yulia Selivokhina, piano, 1987.

Lisitsian, Pavel. Russian baritone of Armenian heritage, 1911–2004.
• Songs 4, 10, 12, 20, 25, 30, 31, 39, 45, 47, 55, 59, 61.

Lisovsky, Konstantin. Russian tenor, born 1932.
• Songs 8, 14, 46, 63, 65.

Lloyd, Robert. English bass, born 1940.
• Songs 12 (in English), 53 (in English).

Ludwig, Christa. German mezzo-soprano, born 1928.
• Songs 13, 14.

Lyon, Ed. British tenor. Recorded 2004.
• Song 32.

Magomayev, Muslim. Russian-Azeri baritone, 1942–2008.
• Songs 10, 12, 13, 20, 32, 45, 48, 55, 61.

Makarina, Olga. Russian soprano. Sang at New York City Opera 1995.
• Songs 12, 13, 19, 20, 22, 23, 37, 38, 40, 76, 82.

Makarova, Natasha. Russian soprano. Recorded 1997.
• Songs 13, 19, 20, 22, 32, 38, 39, 45.

Maksakova, Maria. Russian mezzo-soprano, 1902–1974.
• Song 19.

Maslennikov, Aleksei. Russian tenor, born 1929.
• Songs 59, 74, 78, 79, 80, 81, 82, 83.

Maslennikova, Irina. Russian soprano, 1918–2013.
• Songs 45, 80, 83.

Maslennikova, Leokadiya. Russian soprano, 1918–1995.
• Songs 22, 26, 40, 45, 58, 69.

Mattila, Karita. Finnish soprano, born 1960.
• Songs 13, 36, 39, 63, 74.

Maynor, Kevin. American bass, born 1954.
• Song 11.

Mazurkevich, E. Soviet soprano.
• Song 5.

McCormack, John. Irish tenor, 1884–1945 (see *Worth).*
• Songs 12, 13, 40, 53, 56 (all in English).

McFerrin, Bobby. American vocalist, born 1950.
• Song 76.

McNair, Sylvia. American soprano, born 1956.
• Song 76.

Melton, James. American tenor, 1904–1961.
• Songs 12, 13, 53, 56 (all in English).

Mera, Yoshikazu. Japanese countertenor, born 1971.
• Song 76.

Merrill, Robert. American baritone, 1917–2004.
• Song 12 (in English).

Michaels Bedi, Patrice. American soprano. Recorded 1996.
• Song 63.

Mikhailova, Maria. Russian soprano, 1864–1943 (see *OP 1*, 331-2).
• Song 19.

Milashkina, Tamara. Russian soprano, born 1934.
• Songs 11, 32, 42.

Milcheva, Alexandrina. Bulgarian mezzo-soprano, born 1936.
• Songs 12, 13, 14, 17, 19, 22, 25, 26, 27, 33, 37, 40, 43, 48, 52, 55, 58, 59, 61.

Milina, E. Ya.. Russian soprano. Recorded 1908 (*Ianin*, 520).
• Song 19.

Mirakian, Vahan. Armenian tenor. Sang in Tchaikovsky competition 1966.
• Songs 15, 28, 40, 45.

Mishura, Irina. Russian mezzo-soprano. Recorded 1996.
• Songs 10, 12, 32, 38, 39, 41, 55.

Mkrtchyan, Lina. Armenian contralto, born in Odessa. Recorded 1994.
• Songs 10, 11, 12, 13, 19, 22, 29, 32, 38, 48.

Moffo, Anna. American soprano, 1932–2006.
• Song 76.

Mok, Judith. Dutch soprano, born 1958.
• Songs 13, 14, 76, 78.

Morozov, Aleksei. Russian baritone, born 1946.
• Songs 12, 20, 44, 48.

Mróz, Leonard. Polish bass, born c1947.
• Songs 11, 34.

Murphy, Heidi Grant. American soprano, born 1966.
• Songs 40, 44, 78, 79, 80, 81, 82, 83.

Murphy, Suzanne. Irish soprano. Recorded 2005.
• Song 76.

Murzayev, Sergei. Russian baritone. Recorded 1995. Soloist, Mariinsky Opera.
• Songs 18, 24, 25, 30, 48, 50, 52, 58, 61, 68.

Naoumenko, Alexandre. Russian tenor. Recorded 1996.
• Songs 4, 5, 13, 14, 20, 26, 36, 37, 42, 54, 57, 63, 65, 67, 72, 74.

Nelepp, Georgy. Russian tenor, 1904–1957.
• Songs 54, 55.

Nesterenko, Yevgeny. Russian bass, born 1938.
• Songs 9, 13, 20, 25, 40, 48, 50, 52, 68, 73, 77.

Netrebko, Anna. Russian Soprano, born 1971.
• Songs 13, 40 (with orchestra).

Nezhdanova, Antonina. Russian soprano, 1873–1950.
• Songs 13, 38, 40.

Nikitina, Galina. Ukrainian mezzo-soprano, 1877–? (*OP 1*, 358).
• Songs 33, 45.

Nortsov, Panteleimon. Russian baritone, 1900–1993.
• Songs 12, 17, 20, 44, 47, 55, 61, 80.

Obraztsova, Yelena. Russian mezzo-soprano, born 1939.
• Songs 13, 19, 29, 30, 39, 51, 74.

Obukhova, Nadezhda. Russian mezzo-soprano, 1886–1961.
• Songs 14, 19, 20, 29, 30.

Ognivtsev, Aleksandr. Russian bass, 1920–1981.
• Songs 10, 12, 13, 18, 20, 24, 25, 28, 33, 34, 35, 39, 40, 48, 55, 56, 58, 59, 61, 69.

Oja, Iris. Estonian mezzo-soprano, born 1977.
• Songs 10, 11, 12, 18, 20, 22, 29, 31, 45, 46, 49, 52, 60, 61.

Oleinichenko, Galina. Russian soprano, born 1928.
• Songs 40, 56, 76.

Olli, Kalevi. Finnish baritone, born 1951.
• Songs 10, 11, 12, 13, 14, 15, 16, 17, 18, 19, 20, 21, 22, 23, 24, 25, 26, 27, 28, 29, 30, 31, 32, 33, 34, 35, 36, 37, 38, 39, 40, 41, 42, 43, 44, 45.

Orda, Alfred. Polish-English baritone. 1915–2004.
• Songs 10, 11, 12, 14, 32, 38, 45, 48, 52, 56, 61.

Orfenov, Anatoly. Russian tenor, 1908–1987.
• Song 78.

Otdelenov, Vladimir. Russian baritone, 1924–1993.
• Song 17.

Pelle, Nadia. Canadian soprano. Recorded 1994.
• Song 53.

Petrenko, Mikhail. Russian bass, born 1976.
• Song 12.

Petrov, Ivan. Russian bass, born 1920.
• Songs 13, 39.

Piavko, Vladislav. Russian tenor, born 1941.
• Songs 3, 13, 20, 39, 44, 45, 48, 51, 52, 55, 58, 61.

Pirogov, Aleksandr. Russian bass, 1899–1964.
• Songs 1, 6, 11, 12, 18, 48, 49, 58.

Pishchayev, Gennady. Russian tenor, born 1927.
• Song 13.

Plishka, Paul. Ukrainian-American bass, born 1941.
• Songs 14, 32.

Podleś, Ewa. Polish contralto, born 1952.
• Songs 11, 12, 22, 24, 29, 30, 32, 52, 61.

Pogossov, Rodion. Russian baritone, born 1978.
• Songs 10, 12, 25, 61.

Politkovsky, Vladimir. Russian bass-baritone, 1892–1984.
• Song 59.

Pons, Lily. French-American soprano, 1898–1976.
• Songs 13 (in French), 40 (in French and English, see *Shaman*, vol. 2), 76.

Popescu, Maria. Canadian mezzo-soprano, born 1961.
• Songs 7, 8, 11, 16, 19, 24, 29, 31, 41, 43, 46, 47, 48, 52, 53, 59, 60, 69, 70.

Popp, Lucia. Slovak soprano, 1939–1993.
• Song 38.

Preobrazhenskaya, Sofia. Russian mezzo-soprano, 1904–66.
• Songs 10, 12, 22.

Price, Leontyne. American soprano, born 1927.
• Songs 19, 28, 37, 45, 80.

Pusar, Ana. Slovenian soprano, born 1954.
• Songs 13, 14, 15, 19, 20, 21, 22, 23, 28, 31, 36, 37, 38, 39, 40, 42, 44, 45, 53, 56, 66, 69, 72, 78, 80.

Radina-Figner, Renée. Russian soprano, 1872–1944.
• Song 19.

Raitscheff, Peter. Bulgarian tenor, born 1935.
• Song 13.

Rautio, Nina. Russian soprano, born 1957.
• Songs 10, 12, 13, 15, 16, 17, 19, 20, 21, 22, 28, 29, 32, 37, 38, 39, 40, 45, 48, 49, 52, 58, 61, 78.

Reizen, Mark. Ukrainian-Russian bass, 1895–1992.
• Songs 1, 10, 12, 34, 61.

Reshetin, Mark. Russian bass, born 1931.
• Songs 11, 28, 31.

Rodgers, Joan. English soprano, born 1956.
• Songs 3, 13, 15, 21, 22, 23, 28, 32, 38, 39, 40, 44, 45, 50, 51, 55, 56, 58, 63, 66, 75, 76, 78, 79, 80, 81, 82, 83; two unpublished songs.

Rosing, Vladimir. Russian tenor, 1890–1963.
• Songs 10 (in English), 12, 13, 23, 32, 61.

Rouzaud, Gabrielle. French soprano. Recorded 1934.
• Song 13 (in French).

Rozhdestvenskaya, Natalia. Russian soprano, 1900–1997.
• Songs 58, 75.

Rozum, Aleksandr. Russian baritone, 1923–1987.
• Songs 10, 17, 28, 39, 45, 55, 59, 61.

Rudenko, Bella. Ukrainian soprano, born 1933.
• Songs 22, 38, 40, 56.

Sari, Ada. Polish soprano, 1886–1968.
• Songs 19, 32.

Savenko, Vasily. Russian bass-baritone, born 1949.
• Songs 13, 23, 30, 33, 63, 67.

Schwarzkopf, Elisabeth. German soprano, 1915–2006.
• Song 53 (in English).

Seleznev, Georgy. Russian bass, born 1938.
• Songs 10, 30, 33, 45, 48, 59.

Semenchuk, Ekaterina. Russian mezzo-soprano, born 1976.
• Songs 7, 17, 20, 24, 38, 58.

Serkebayev, Yermek. Kazakh baritone, born 1926.
• Songs 10, 12, 20, 22, 25, 45, 59, 61.

Sharubina, Nina. Belorussian soprano. Recorded 1994.
• Song 19.

Shaposhnikov, Sergei. Russian baritone, 1911–1973.
• Songs 2, 12, 18, 27, 31, 48.

Sheremet, Sergei. Russian baritone. Recorded 1998.
• Song 59.

Shevelev, Nikolai. Russian baritone, 1874–1929.
• Songs 32, 44, 52, 55, 61.

Shirley-Quirk, John. English bass-baritone, born 1931.
• Song 50 (with Elisabeth Söderström).

Shpiller, Natalia. Russian soprano, 1909–1995.
• Songs 11, 22, 38, 42, 79, 80, 81, 82.

Shtoda, Daniil. Russian tenor, born 1977.
• Songs 8, 13, 37, 38, 39, 56.

Shumskaya, Yelizaveta. Russian soprano, 1905–88.
• Songs 12, 13, 23, 32, 38, 57.

Silja, Anja. German soprano, born 1940.
• Songs 12, 13, 20, 22, 38, 39, 40, 49, 58, 76.

Simonova, Liudmila. Russian mezzo-soprano. Recorded 1974.
• Songs 12, 22, 29.

Siniavskaya, Tamara. Russian mezzo-soprano, born 1943.
• Songs 11, 12, 22, 26, 29, 37, 38, 40, 58, 61.

Siparis, Rimantis. Lithuanian bass-baritone, 1927–1990.
• Song 40.

Slivinsky, Vladimir. Russian baritone, 1894–1949.
• Song 32.

Slobodskaya, Oda. Russian-English soprano, 1888–1970 (see *Leonard*).
• Songs 19, 23, 38, 40, 53.

Slovtsov, Piotr. Russian tenor, 1886–1934.
• Song 55, 1913.

Smirnov, Dmitri. Russian tenor, 1882–1944.
• Songs 13, 38, 56.

Söderström, Elisabeth. Swedish soprano, 1927–2009.
• Songs 1–83. Vladimir Ashkenazy, piano, 1975–1979.

Sotkilava, Zurab. Georgian tenor, born 1937.
• Songs 13, 20, 32.

Souzay, Gerard. French baritone, 1918–2004 (see *Morris*).
• Songs 10, 40, 59.

Stepanovich, Dmitri. Russian bass, born 1974.
• Song 1.

Stevens, Risë. American mezzo-soprano, 1913–2013.
• Song 12 (in English), 53 (video, in English).

Storozhev, Nikita. Russian bass, born 1950.
• Songs 12, 20, 25, 32, 33, 44, 45, 48, 52, 61.

Suchkova, Natalia. Russian soprano. Recorded 1999.
• Songs 1–83.

Sumatchova, Svetlana. Russian soprano. Recorded 1994.
• Songs 7, 13, 19, 22, 23, 36, 38, 51, 56, 58.

Sutey, Rudolf Alexander. German bass. Recorded 1977.
• Songs 33, 34, 64, 68, 71, 73.

Swenson, Ruth Ann. American soprano, born 1959.
• Song 76.

Talvela, Martti. Finnish bass, 1935–1989.
• Songs 10, 13, 14, 20, 40, 52, 58, 59.

Tcheresky, Luba. Russian-American soprano. Recorded 1950s.
• Song 37.

Tear, Robert. English tenor, 1939–2011.
• Songs 13, 23, 28, 35, 37, 44, 51, 53, 54, 55, 57, 58, 63, 72, 79, 81, 83.

Te Kanawa, Kiri. New Zealand soprano, born 1944.
• Song 76.

Tikhonov, Pavel. Russian bass, 1877–1944.
• Song 10.

Timokhin, Vladimir. Ukrainian tenor, 1929–1999.
• Song 3.

Tkachenko, Ninel. Ukrainian soprano, born 1928.
• Song 14.

Tourel, Jennie. Russian-American mezzo-soprano, c1900–1973.
• Songs 12, 13, 14, 19, 32, 37, 38, 45, 56, 61, 81.

Troyanos, Tatiana. American mezzo-soprano, 1938–1993.
• Songs 12, 23, 32, 38.

Upshaw, Dawn. American soprano, born 1960.
• Songs 78, 79, 80, 81, 82, 83.

Urmana, Violetta. Lithuanian soprano, born 1959.
• Songs 12, 32, 40, 45, 75.

Valletti, Cesare. Italian tenor, 1922–2000.
• Songs 12, 23 (in English). Town Hall Recital, Leo Taubmann, piano, 1960.

Vallin, Ninon. French soprano, 1886–1961.
• Song 38 (in French).

Vassilieff, Alexis. Russian countertenor. Recorded 1998.
• Songs 25, 39, 48, 59.

Vayne, Kyra. Russian-English soprano, 1916–2001.
• Songs 13, 32, 38.

Verbitskaya, Evgenia. Russian mezzo-soprano, 1904–1965.
• Songs 1, 11, 28, 29.

Verrett, Shirley. American mezzo-soprano, 1931–2010.
• Songs 14, 32.

Viktorova, Valentina. Russian mezzo-soprano. Recorded 1945.
• Songs 28, 29.

Vinogradov, Georgi. Russian tenor, 1908–1980.
• Songs 51, 58, 66.

Vishnevskaya, Galina. Russian soprano, 1926–2012.
• Songs 13, 22, 32, 37, 58, 70, 76.

Viting, Yevgeny. Russian dramatic tenor, 1884–1959.
• Song 38.

Vladimirov, Evgeny. Russian bass. Recorded 1978.
• Songs 1, 48.

Weiler, Sherri. American mezzo-soprano. Recorded 1998.
• Songs 12, 13, 19, 32, 38, 48.

Welitsch, Alexander. Macedonian baritone, 1906–1991.
• Songs 68, 71.

Westman, James. Canadian baritone, born 1972.
• Song 10.

Woytowicz, Stefania. Polish soprano, 1922–2005.
• Songs 13, 56, 61, 76, 79, 80 (all in Polish except 76, "Vocalise").

Yakovenko, Sergei. Russian baritone, born 1937.
• Song 62.

Yeend, Frances. American soprano, 1913–2008.
• Songs 12, 14.

Yourenev, Georgi. Russian baritone, 1891–after 1948 (see *OP* 2, 166).
• Song 52.

Zakharov, Vladimir Petrovich. Russian baritone. Artist with Moscow Philharmonic and All-Union Radio; in 1958 he sang the Baron in a film of *The Miserly Knight*.
• Song 64.

Zamiatina, Julia. Russian soprano. Recorded 1998.
• Songs 78, 80, 81.

Zbruyeva, Eugenia. Russian contralto, 1868–1936.
• Song 19.

Zelenina, Maria. Russian soprano. Recorded 2000.
• Songs 13, 37, 40, 76.

Zhadan, Ivan. Ukrainian-Russian-American tenor, 1902–1995.
• Songs 13, 38, 56, 69, 74.

Zhurina, Irina. Russian soprano, born 1946.
• Song 13.

Zimmermann, Margherita. Argentine mezzo-soprano, born 1942.
• Songs 8, 13, 14, 19, 20, 22, 31, 38, 53, 59.

Zlatogorova, Bronislava. Russian contralto, 1905–1995.
• Song 55.

Zvetkova, Mariana. Bulgarian soprano. Recorded 1996.
• Song 32.

Index of Song Titles in Russian

Index of Song Titles in English

Note: Many of Rachmaninoff's songs have been listed in recordings and concert programs by titles other than those used in this book. Some of these alternative translations are included in the list below.

Index of Names

Singers are not included here unless mentioned in the text. A complete list of singers can be found in the Index of Singers.

Richard D. Sylvester graduated from West Point in 1956. He studied English Language and Literature as a Rhodes Scholar at Worcester College, Oxford. After service in the U.S. Army, he received a PhD in Slavic Languages and Literatures at Harvard University. He is the author of *Tchaikovsky's Complete Songs* (IUP, 2002) and articles about and translations of Russian poets. With Marian Schwartz, he translated Nina Berberova's *Moura: The Dangerous Life of the Baroness Budberg* (2005). He is currently Professor of Russian Emeritus at Colgate University.

Lightning Source UK Ltd.
Milton Keynes UK
UKOW03n2202020514

231004UK00011B/226/P

9 780253 353399